AUSTRALIAN SOCIETY

AUSTRALIAN SOCIETY

A SOCIOLOGICAL INTRODUCTION

edited by

A. F. DAVIES AND S. ENCEL

F. W. CHESHIRE

Melbourne Canberra Sydney

Library of Congress Catalog
Card Number 65-21217
Copyright
First published 1965
Reprinted 1966, 1967, 1968
F. W. Cheshire Publishing Pty Ltd.,
380 Bourke Street, Melbourne
Garema Place, Canberra
142 Victoria Road, Marrickville, N.S.W.
Set and designed in Australia
Printed in Hong Kong

Contents

The Contributors

DR. DAN L. ADLER is Professor of Psychology, San Francisco State College, California.

R. T. APPLEYARD is Professor of Economic History, University of Western Australia. Author of *British Emigration to Australia* 1947-1960.

T. BRENNAN is Associate Professor of Social Studies and Director, Department of Social Work, the University of Sydney, and editor of *The Australian Journal of Social Issues*. Author of *Midland City, A Study of Social Change in Western South Wales, Reshaping a City*, and joint author of *Country Town*.

W. J. CAMPBELL is Professor of Education, University of Queensland. Author of *Television and the Adolescent* and *Growing Up in Karribee*.

A. F. DAVIES is Reader in Political Science, University of Melbourne. Author of *Local Government in Victoria, Australian Democracy* and *Private Politics*.

LINCOLN H. DAY is Associate Professor, Department of Sociology, Yale University; formerly visiting Fellow, Department of Demography, Australian National University. Co-author (with his wife, Alice Day) of *Too Many Americans*.

S. ENCEL is Professor of Sociology, University of New South Wales. Author of *Cabinet Government in Australia*.

F. H. GRUEN is Professor of Agricultural Economics, Monash University.

L. R. HIATT is lecturer in Anthropology, University of Sydney.

K. S. INGLIS is Professor of History, University of Papua-New Guinea. Author of *Hospital and Community, The Stuart Case*, and *Churches and the Working Classes in Victorian England*.

H. G. KIPPAX is a leader writer and critic for the *Sydney Morning Herald*. Editor of *Three Australian Plays*.

ALEX KONDOS is a market research executive with a large food manufacturing company.

J. R. LAWRY is lecturer in Education, University of Queensland.

D. W. McELWAIN is Professor of Psychology, University of Queensland.

J. M. MAIN is senior lecturer in History, Flinders University.

MAXWELL NEWTON is an economist and journalist, formerly managing editor of *The Australian* and *The Australian Financial Review*.

LEONARD TIERNEY is Reader-in-charge, Department of Social Studies, University of Melbourne. Author of *Children Who Need Help*.

Acknowledgments

MANY people helped to make this book possible. To Dr. Andrew Fabinyi, of Cheshires, we owe special thanks for his support and encouragement of the project from its inception. We were materially assisted by a grant given jointly by the University of Melbourne and the Australian National University, for which we have to thank the good offices of Professor W. Macmahon Ball and Professor L. F. Crisp. Valuable help with editorial work was given by Mrs. Maida Stern and Mrs. Netta Burns. The burden of typing and retyping manuscripts was shared by Mrs. Burns and Mrs. Patricia Coulthard. Mr. Peter Daniell drew the charts contained in chapters 14 and 18. The material on which the appendix to chapter 6 is based was kindly made available by Mr. Roy Morgan of the Australian Gallup Poll. For the cover picture, we are indebted to the News and Information Bureau, Canberra. Mr. David New was responsible for the technical details of publication.

A book which attempts to cover a wide range of social phenomena in any depth is likely to require the collaboration of a number of writers with special interests in a variety of fields. In planning this book, we endeavoured from the beginning to make the collaboration as real as possible by keeping authors informed of one another's intentions, by circulating drafts, and by an active interchange of views between contributors and editors. Further opportunities for discussion were provided by a weekly seminar held at the Australian National University during 1963, which enabled most authors to try out early drafts of their chapters on a critical but sympathetic audience. We owe special thanks to our contributors for responding so cheerfully to editorial suggestions. The individual chapters speak for themselves; the shape of the book as a whole is our joint responsibility, including its deficiencies.

A.F.D.
S.E.

PART I

A. F. DAVIES and S. ENCEL

Introduction

THIS study sets out to do two comparatively new things: to describe present-day social relationships in this country fairly thoroughly, and to set a frame for future sociological inquiries. Sociology, as an academic discipline seeking to illuminate the results of social surveys (including the census) by systematic thinking about social groups and institutions, is the Cinderella of Australian (as of English) universities—historians and economists in both countries having willingly cast themselves as the ugly sisters. Readers may therefore be agreeably surprised at the quantity of descriptive material that contributors have been able to marshal—much of it, in line with this below-stairs status, unpublished or unlisted. The typical art form of the writer on Australian social affairs is the one-volume study which aspires to sum up a complex community in an array of subjective assessments of varying quality. The brilliant generalizations of Hancock's *Australia* (which settles the hash of sociology with a reference to "the dismal paraphernalia of sociological research") have become jaded by frequent repetition in its numerous *epigoni* Without the basic knowledge which we try to present, these assessments—whether our own or those of talented publicists—are bound to be somewhat eccentric.

The quality, however, of much of this unconsidered hoard—the product in the main of isolated work at the fringes of other disciplines—is not high. Few studies have come close enough to the inter-face of the personal and the collective, to the "individual operations which go to make up the social structure" (Simmel) to be quite free-standing. For the most part, too, they have drawn as little on the reforming zeal of the early poverty surveys as on the theoretical rigour of contemporary American work. Yet for all their simplicity and disconnectedness, their air of innocent first soundings, they can teach us new—and firm—things. And our contributors have often found striking ways to exhibit their latent connections one with another and with abiding concerns in each field. Inescapably then, this volume marks a kind of staging camp, where the air of disorder reflects the need to check and sort possessions against the next forward move.

Mannheim once noted that sociological thought inherently inclined towards debunking and demystification. More than one contributor has chosen to approach his subject through an attack on the myths prevalent about it—myths which seem "articulate vehicles of a people's wishful thinking"

1

(Benedict) as well as spuriously plausible explanations of the problematical.

The notion of a community dominated by egalitarianism and uniformity is perhaps the chief of these. Our text repeatedly suggests that the force of egalitarian sentiment is both narrower and weaker than traditionally believed, and that it is cut across by powerful pressures towards stratification and hierarchy. In fact, there is a well-developed system of social differentiation and class consciousness—and a certain indifference to important forms of inequality (Ch. 3). The social inferiority of the Roman Catholic community —itself by no means undifferentiated (Ch. 10)—is taken up in several places, not least in connection with the rise in the last decade of a Church-based political party. Large inequalities of opportunity persist in the schools (Ch. 5), while the egalitarian demands marking early welfare legislation have now faded into complacency and administrative rigidity (Ch. 7).

Again, the notion of Australia as a man's country—one in which women and women's values are subordinate, and "mateship" among men the most highly valued relationship—seems to need re-examination in the light of studies of family life (Chs. 8, 9). If. indeed, husbands have come largely to resign the conduct of family relations to their wives, a more complex picture of sex roles is required. Much self-conscious masculinity (*e.g.* that of the public bar) appears less as arrogant choice than as compensation for the small sphere of competence accorded in the home. The Australian mother's monopolization of the upbringing of the children may also encourage a strain of latent homosexuality in sons, further confirming the cultural stress on male companionship.

A land of opportunity? Myths about unusual chances for individual achievement also come up for review. The cruder fantasies of "free enterprise" and *laissez faire,* so dear to the business community, are laid in Ch. 15, and limitations on individual opportunity are exposed by the studies of social mobility and social origin reported in various chapters. Lack of intellectual curiosity, the willingness to accept secondhand notions and a derivative cultural life, resentment of criticism and intolerance of nonconformity, may be seen at work as a damper on creativity in several fields of intellectual and cultural life. The general sense in which the growth of impersonal, mass bureaucratic organizations works to reduce the significance of individual discretion in public life and fixes on it, indeed, a set of external forms emptied of most of their personal meaning, is attested at several points in the text. The rise of "organization men", of social conformism, of the "normal personality", rigid and controlled, all energy bent on socially approved constructiveness, lies at the edge of several discussions, though like the playwrights castigated in Ch. 13, we may be fairly blamed for not having closed frontally with suburbia.

In planning this volume, we were concerned that the society should be seen as a whole, and that the separate essays—breaking down, wherever necessary, conventional academic divisions—should emphasize common links. Contributors have drawn carefully on the data of the latest (1961) census. Most, too, have worked to establish some historical perspective, a task often made easier by Australian historians' own feeling for sociological questions. A sense, we hope, emerges of a society very much the product of its own history, with institutions, attitudes and norms (as described in various chapters) evolved over more than a century; now an on-going whole, with continuities which make it recognizably the same from one generation to the next, despite sharp economic or political change. Its sturdy resistance, indeed, to alteration by the affluence of recent years is the key to many present strains.

Essays on major areas of social life and their distinguishing institutions will inevitably differ in mode of analysis. We do not ask the same questions of business corporations, or schools, or newspapers, as of churches; and contributors have freely chosen their approach within each field. But the common aim of synthesizing, in each institutional order, recent concepts and fresh findings has lent them an agreeably common tone, despite a diversity of intellectual influences even within the sociological tradition. The more general chapters on social class, the family, the urban and rural communities are so many modest attempts to sum up at different levels the relationships between these institutional orders and individual "life-spheres", and to assess what opportunities and difficulties they may have in store for us. We could wish that national character studies were further advanced; our society has in its formative years of hardship and isolation clearly laid down a distinctive stamp. Australians, unlike Americans, have never had to ask who they were. Or Canadians: a recent volume which performs for Canada a task similar to the one we have attempted here (Blishen *et al, Canadian Society: Sociological Perspectives*), opens with an endeavour to isolate the uniqueness of a community sandwiched between Britain and the United States. The analysis peters out in a list of deliberate attempts, at the political level, to create a national consciousness. In Australia, however, the comparatively unforced growth of such a consciousness goes side by side with a comfortable acceptance of cultural dependence on the same countries.

Large gaps remain, reflecting both the difficulties of planning such an enterprise and the blank spaces in our knowledge. The role of science and technology has yet to be explored. We can say little about "deviance"—crime, delinquency, mental disorder, suicide, alcoholism; or the assimilation of immigrants and the life of minority groups; or the role of the innumerable voluntary associations which absorb the interests and energies of so many people. Sport remains untouched. Apart from our two studies of the arts in relation to society, we cannot speak about "culture"; nor have we discussed the nature of work, with its special discontents, conflicts, and satisfactions. An examination of these and other questions awaits the further growth of the study of Australian society.

R. T. APPLEYARD

2   The Population

POPULATION is the raw material of the social scientist, and until an inventory
is made of its numbers and structure, studies of the rural and urban communities, the economy, politics or the underprivileged cannot easily be set in
perspective. I shall treat the subject in two parts: first, an outline of the determinants of population growth, then an analysis of the present population
structure. As this will show that immigration has played a major part in
determining both past rates of growth and present structure, I will then consider in more detail the demographic implications of immigration and some
aspects of the immigrants' absorption in Australia. But the reader is fore-
warned that the surprising dearth of data on the absorption of immigrants
brings the "results" of the discussion dangerously close to the boundary of
conjecture.

What are the special characteristics of the Australian population today?[1]
Like many other non-European Western countries, Australia has a "young"
demographic structure—in 1961 72% of its population was under 44 years
of age—which engendered high annual birth rates (over 2% of the population between 1956 and 1960) and a low and almost stationary death rate
of eight persons per thousand of the population. Together with a sustained
intake of immigrants, these rates have produced an annual average increase
in population of over 2% since the war which, if maintained, will double
the Australian population by about 1995.

White settlement in Australia began with the arrival of the first fleet in
1788, and population at first grew only spasmodically and mainly by the
addition of more convicts, military and some free settlers. When Macquarie
left the colony in 1821 only 30,000 persons were settled around Sydney, over
one-half of whom had served or were serving sentences; only 1,300 persons
had entered the colony as free settlers.[2] Other colonies were established and
grew slowly with the arrival of convicts and settlers. Natural increase was of
marginal importance in the growth of colonies. The main reason was the large
excess of males in the population. Because the majority of births occur within

---

[1] When this paper was written the published results of the 1961 census were confined
largely to "counts" on each census question. The absence of two-way tabulations
seriously restricts the interpretation of census data and it has been necessary to use
annual statistics in parts of the paper.

[2] W. D. Borrie, *Population Trends and Policies*, p. 33.

4

marriage, an important condition for natural increase is that there shall be a fairly equal number of males and females of marriageable age. The serious shortage of females in the colonies led to experiments in shipping whole cargoes of single women from England.[3]

The first major intake of free settlers into the Australian colonies came as a result of the gold rushes. Over one million people entered Australia between 1852 and 1861, a movement which not only exacerbated the high masculinity ratio, but emphasized the major role of immigration as the determinant of population growth. In fact, between first settlement and 1861, net immigration supplied approximately 871,000 persons representing three-quarters of the total growth in colonial populations. The year 1861 was nonetheless the turning point in the dominance of immigration and during the following forty years, *i.e.* until Federation, it provided only 28% of the increase in population. As Borrie has observed, from the aspect of population growth, the gold-rush period ended the pioneer phase of Australia's development.[4] After 1860, the relatively higher proportion of women amongst the immigrant arrivals lowered the masculinity ratio which had previously impeded natural increase. By 1900 there were 105 males to 100 females and a high percentage of the females were in the reproductive age groups, crude marriage rates were high and the average age of women at marriage was low. The composition of the population was thus more favourable to fertility than at any previous period.[5]

This relatively normal demographic structure was seriously affected by the economic depression of the 1890s. Marriage rates declined, immigration was reduced to a trickle, and the birth rate, which had been 35 per thousand in 1890, fell to 27 in 1900. Even so, the depression only intensified a decline in the birth rate which had begun several decades before and was to continue until the beginning of the second world war. The decline was not peculiar to Australia; France, the United States and Great Britain also experienced a similar trend which was largely the result of couples having fewer children than in the early Victorian period.

The first sixteen years of the twentieth century was a period of relative demographic stability in Australia. The birth rate remained around 25 to 28 per thousand of the population and immigration (which dried up between 1902 and 1906) was revived and sustained until the outbreak of the war when the population stood at nearly five millions. Hostilities not only took their toll of dead and wounded, but by separating husbands and wives reduced the birth rate. Marriage rates also declined and immigration ceased. After the war the birth rate failed to recover to pre-war levels; it appears that couples were voluntarily restricting their family size and thus maintaining the declining trend in the birth rate which had begun during the nineteenth century. The birth rate was reduced even further during the depression of the 1930s and reached the lowest recorded level in 1933. Immigration fell right away, in fact there was a net loss by migration, so that the actual increase in population was only 0.8% per annum between 1931 and 1935. Both the birth rate and immigration picked up during the late 1930s but were once again adversely affected by the resumption of hostilities in 1939.

[3] Margaret Kiddle, *Caroline Chisholm.*
[4] *Op. cit.,* p. 35.
[5] *Ibid.,* pp. 38-9.

Australia's Population since the War

The major demographic events outlined above, especially those of the twentieth century, left their mark on the structure of the population at 1945. This can be most clearly depicted by the "population pyramid", a device used by demographers to show changes in the structure of the population. Where the numbers of births and deaths have been constant, but the former exceeding the latter, the numbers at each age will be smaller than those alive at the age immediately below so that if the ages are arranged one above the other, from the youngest to the oldest, the result will be a pyramid. In other words, none of us is immortal and under the conditions given there will always be more five year olds than ninety-five year olds. Diagram I is the population pyramid

Diagram I

AUSTRALIA : AGE PYRAMID (1947)

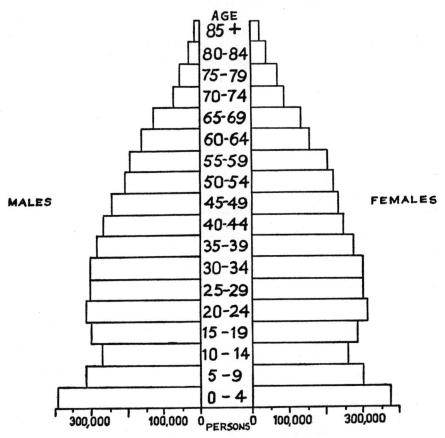

of the Australian population at 1947. The effect of the 'thirties depression is clearly shown in this pyramid which has "squared" below the 30–34 years age group and is noticeably indented in the 10–14 years age group, *i.e.* it reflects the reduced number of births during the period 1933–1937.

This, then, was the base upon which Australia's post-war population has been built, a base which, on then current rates of growth, was insufficient to replace the population. In 1944 the National Health and Medical Research Council declared that:

> . . . natural increase in population will dwindle rapidly after 1950, and by about 1980 deaths will exceed births. . . . In about twenty years the population will reach 8,000,000, remain temporarily stationary and then decline, returning to the present level about the end of the century.

Indeed, this evidence was used by the first Minister for Immigration, Mr. Arthur Calwell, to justify a large-scale immigration programme.[6] But by 1946 the birth rate, which between 1931–5 had averaged only 16.9 per thousand, rose to 23.6. To some extent, this was the result of renewed family-building which had been delayed during the war years. It also began a long-run revival of the birth rate which had been gradually falling since the 1870s; after 1946 it has remained steady at around 22 per thousand of the population.

What factors were responsible for the recovery of the birth rate? In the first place, marriage rates have been high: at the 1947 census 49% of young women aged 20–24 years qualified as "ever married"; by 1954 the proportion had risen to 59%, and in 1961 it was 60%. The marriage rate has an important bearing on the birth rate simply because the younger a woman marries the longer she is exposed to the chance of bearing children. High marriage rates have also been facilitated by an excess of males in the reproductive age groups: in 1958 there were 6% more males than females. Second, the immigration programme, which during the war Mr Calwell had been appointed to launch, got under way during the late 1940s despite considerable difficulties over shipping. The inflow of immigrants between 1947 and 1961 has been the largest of any fifteen-year period in our history: 1,480,000 immigrants and their Australian-born children have been added to the population. This represented 54% of the growth of males and 47% of the growth of females in the total population. The importance of immigrants has been underscored by Borrie who estimated that in the total gain of 402,200 families between 1947 and 1954, 174,300 were the result of immigration. Together with the high proportions marrying at younger ages, Borrie estimates that the numerical increases in the age-groups 25–39 as a result of immigration has been the main factor responsible for high post-war birth rates.[7]

Favourable marriage rates, masculinity ratios and the immigration of persons in the fertile age groups have been mainly responsible for increases in fertility, especially amongst the 20–24 and 25–29 year old females who are usually the most fertile groups in a population. In 1947 there were 166 births per thousand married females aged 20–24 years but by 1959 the rate had risen to 219. The rate for 25-29 year old married females in 1947 was 186, and for 1959, 214 per thousand. Death rates have barely changed since 1947 and the resultant actual increase in population has varied from 3.2% in 1949 and 1950 to 1.5% in 1947 and 1.8% in 1953. The reason for the variations, when natural increase has remained fairly steady, lies with changes in net immigration and these will be discussed later in the chapter.

---

[6] A. A. Calwell, *How Many Australians Tomorrow?*, p. 2.

[7] W. D. Borrie, *The Next Fifteen Years*, unpublished manuscript, Department of Demography, Australian National University, pp. 6–8.

7

The effects of all these changes on the structure of the Australian population are depicted in Diagram II, the age pyramid of the population in 1961. The major difference between this pyramid and the 1947 pyramid (Diagram I) is that the square shape of the latter (below the 30–34 years group) has been replaced by a fairly normal pyramid shape. The contribution of immigration to this reshaping process is depicted by the shaded area of each age

Diagram II

AUSTRALIA : AGE PYRAMID (1961)

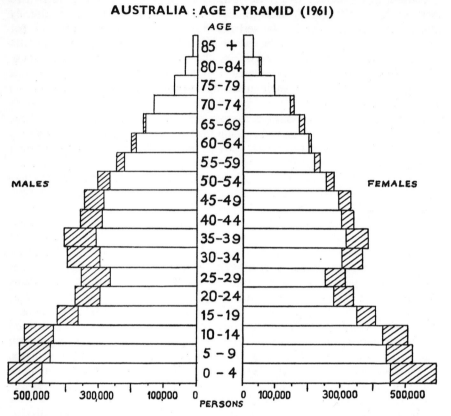

AGE

| 85 + |
| 80-84 |
| 75-79 |
| 70-74 |
| 65-69 |
| 60-64 |
| 55-59 |
| 50-54 |
| 45-49 |
| 40-44 |
| 35-39 |
| 30-34 |
| 25-29 |
| 20-24 |
| 15-19 |
| 10-14 |
| 5 - 9 |
| 0 - 4 |

MALES

FEMALES

500,000   300,000   100,000   0   0   100,000   300,000   500,000

PERSONS

IMMIGRANTS (NET), 1947-61 AND THEIR CHILDREN BORN IN AUSTRALIA

group. It has been especially important in the 0-14 years age group. Even so, a large proportion of the reshaping process has been the result of natural increase although, as already indicated, it includes the Australian-born children of post-war immigrants.[8] Despite the large intake of immigrants since the war, there have been too few of the appropriate ages to "fill" the indents caused by the low birth rates of the 1930s. Part of the reason appears to be that the countries from which our immigrants have been drawn were similarly affected by low birth rates during the immediate pre-war years.

[8] Between 1946 and 1961 there were 289,300 births to overseas-born couples and another 319,500 births to couples one spouse of which had been born overseas. See Department of Immigration, *Australian Immigration Quarterly Statistical Bulletin*, vol. 2, no. 4, 1962, p. 23.

What have been some of the consequences, and what will be some of the expected consequences, of such a population structure? Already we have experienced unprecedented demands on primary and secondary schools as a result of the post-war "baby boom" and immigration programmes. A large number of young people (represented by the 10–14 years age group in Diagram II) have already graduated to the 15–19 years age group and are causing "pressures" on the work force and on universities. Several universities have attempted to solve the problem by restricting enrolments but all have had to increase their facilities and resort to larger classes. School leavers have already found difficulty in getting jobs, and the problem will probably continue for several more years. Possibly the most important aspect is that the numbers seeking jobs and university education will not diminish over the next few years. Indeed, if the *proportions* of 17–19 year olds entering universities increases—and there are socio-economic pressures in this direction—the actual numbers seeking entry will be even greater than expected. The dimensions of the problem are revealed, first, by the number of persons in the 0–4, 5–9 and 10–14 years age groups (Diagram II) and, second, by the projected growth of 13–15 and 16–19 year olds compared with the expected growth of the total population (Diagram III).

The 1961 census indicated that the drift of people to the capital cities has not yet been stemmed. The 5.9 million persons in Australia's metropolitan areas represented an increase of 21% over the population in the cities in 1954 (adjusted to 1961 boundaries) whereas the 1.9 million persons in rural areas represented an increase of only 3%. Sydney and its suburbs contained just over 2 million and Melbourne just under 2 million of the 10.5 million Australians. Together with the four other state metropolitan areas, 56% of the population were "suburbanites"—and this excludes medium sized towns like Wollongong, Newcastle and Geelong.

The Impact of Immigrants

The chapter so far has been largely an inventory of Australia's population growth and structure. Other contributors to the volume will elucidate some of the economic and social consequences of these demographic trends and patterns. The remainder of this chapter deals with several socio-economic aspects of the absorption of Australia's post-war immigrants. We saw that about half the growth in population between 1947 and 1961 was due to immigrants and their Australian-born children. Where did these immigrants come from?—and why? C. A. Price has calculated the regional gains of net immigrants during the period as follows:[9]

United Kingdom and Dominions	-	32%
Northern Europeans	-	-	-	18%
Eastern Europeans -	-	-	-	20%
Southern Europeans	-	-	-	27%
Rest of world	-	-	-	-	3%

It is noteworthy that the proportion of immigrants from British countries, which between 1901 and 1921 was 89%, has dropped to a post-war average of 32%. By long tradition the overwhelming majority of Australia's immi-

[9] C. A. Price, "Overseas Migration to and from Australia, 1947-1961", *Australian Outlook*, vol. 16, no. 2, 1962.

9

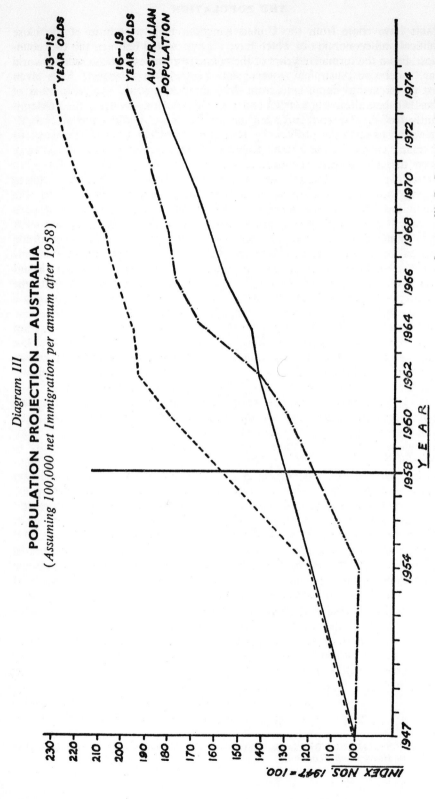

Diagram III

POPULATION PROJECTION — AUSTRALIA

(Assuming 100,000 net Immigration per annum after 1958)

13–15 YEAR OLDS

16–19 YEAR OLDS

AUSTRALIAN POPULATION

Y E A R

1947 1954 1958 1960 1962 1964 1966 1968 1970 1972 1974

INDEX NOS. 1947 = 100.

230 220 210 200 190 180 170 160 150 140 130 120 110 100

Source: W. D. Borrie and R. Rodgers, A.N.U.

grants have come from the United Kingdom mainly because of the close political and economic ties which have always existed between the two countries. From the formative years of the colonies to the end of the second world war, successive Australian governments (colonial and federal) have given first preference to immigrants from the United Kingdom. Even the influx of non-Britishers during the 1850s and 1860s did nothing to affect the predominantly British character and allegiance of the Australian population. F. K. Crowley has shown that between 1860 and 1919, 45% of the total intake of immigrants from the United Kingdom were actually assisted in one way or another by Australian governments.[10]

By the end of the second world war the United Kingdom was in no demographic condition to maintain the role of provider of immigrants for the Dominions. A long-run decline in its birth rate had set in and by 1950 it not only had one of the lowest rates of natural increase in the world, but 39% of its population was aged 45 years or older. This demographic condition also created a fairly sustained labour shortage, so there was no real economic incentive (i.e. the "push" of unemployment) to emigrate. The United Kingdom government nonetheless renewed its assisted passage agreement with the Australian governments and this has brought out 440,000 Britons for only a fraction of the cost of ordinary passages. Indeed, the intake of settlers from the United Kingdom has been larger than the intake from other countries not only because of Australia's economic and ethnic attraction to Britishers, but because about 75% of British settlers have been assisted. The conditions of assistance for non-Britishers have been neither so generous nor so comprehensive.

By 1948 the Australian government conceded that if its avowed annual "target" of immigrants equal to 1% of the population was to be achieved, it would have to encourage a large number of non-British immigrants. A major reason for setting such a high target was that the country's vulnerability to invasion had been exposed during the second world war. A large-scale immigration programme, it was argued, together with policies designed to increase the Australian birth rate, would increase the population more rapidly to the point where it would be possible to defend the country against an aggressor. The government accepted the proposition that 2% per annum was the maximum effective rate of total population growth, and as the rate of natural increase had been about 1% then immigration should contribute an equal percentage. The fascinating story of events which led to the break in the traditional policy that Australia's immigrants should be of British stock is yet to be told. But it seems fairly certain that had the United Kingdom been demographically able to supply the numbers, and had the ships been available to bring them to Australia, the break may never have been made. As it was, there existed in continental Europe almost a million displaced persons who, for one reason or another, were unable or unwilling to return to their European homelands. During his visit to Europe in 1947 Mr A. A. Calwell, the first Minister for Immigration, made contact with representatives of the International Refugee Organization and signed an agreement to accept 12,000 Baltic refugees, "on humanitarian grounds". This act was the first major

[10] F. K. Crowley, "The British Contribution to the Australian Population", *University Studies in History and Economics*, University of W.A., July 1954, p. 87.

break in the tradition that assisted migrants should come only from the United Kingdom. Between 1948 and 1951, 167,000 displaced persons entered Australia, but the grounds on which they were admitted soon changed from humanitarian ones to migrants' ability to contribute to the economy. A major clause in the agreement with the I.R.O. was that the Australian government could allocate refugees to jobs at which they were required to remain for two years. This was a godsend to the Australian economy simply because it was experiencing a severe labour shortage, especially for unskilled workers in country areas. Irrespective of their skills, the majority of refugees were allocated to jobs on farms, mines and public works projects—jobs which Australian workers avoided. There can be no doubt that the contributions which refugees made to output of these basic industries went a long way towards subduing inflation which, by 1951, had reached serious proportions. In addition, many displaced persons were housed in temporary huts, former army camps and some even in tents, so they did not exacerbate what was at that time a very acute housing shortage.

A small study which the writer conducted in Western Australia during 1953 showed that 36% of male displaced person workers were allocated to the building and construction industry compared with only 9% of Western Australian workers in this industry.[11] Some 15% of the displaced persons were allocated to jobs in the "Public Authority" group compared with 8% of native workers, but only 2% of displaced persons were allocated to the "Finance and Property" and "Commerce" groups compared with 14% of the work force there.

When the Displaced Person Scheme petered out in 1951 the Australian government signed bilateral agreements with the governments of the Netherlands, West Germany and Italy in order to maintain the non-British assisted proportion of immigrants. Under these new agreements, and unlike the Displaced Person Scheme, immigrants have been selected on the basis of vacancies for their skills in Australia. Between 1951–2 (when these agreements were negotiated) and March 1963, 69,000 German, 65,000 Dutch and 45,000 Italian immigrants had been assisted to Australia. Together with arrivals under the later agreements with Austria, Belgium, Greece, Malta and Spain they have comprised the backbone of non-British assisted migration. In addition, some 400,000 *non-assisted* immigrants have been drawn from Europe; mainly Southern Europeans who have been sponsored by relatives already in Australia. The diversity of origin of Australia's post-war settlers suggests that post-war Australian governments, unlike pre-war governments, have been " . . . less concerned with grading Europeans in terms of assimilability than with preserving what they consider to be a reasonable balance between the nationalities".[12]

The second salient feature of the estimates on p. 9 is that there have been only minor changes in the *racial*, as distinct from the ethnic, composition of net immigration. Post-war Labour governments imposed tight restrictions on the entry of non-Europeans. Subsequent Liberal-Country Party governments

---

[11] The percentage of native work-force distribution relates to the 1947 census. R. T. Appleyard, "Displaced Persons in Western Australia—Their Industrial Location and Geographical Distribution: 1948-1954", *University Studies in History and Economics,* University of W.A., vol. 2, no. 3, 1955, p. 74.

[12] C. A. Price, *op. cit.,* pp. 169–70.

have been slightly more flexible in their execution of the Immigration Act: over 2,000 non-European spouses of Australian citizens, and non-Europeans who had been in Australia for fifteen years or longer (*e.g.* business men, market gardeners, teachers), have been naturalized since 1956. At present there are over 10,000 Asian students in Australia. Despite these timely changes, however, "White Australia" still remains the cornerstone of immigration policy.

It has already been noted that one of the most important "contributions" of displaced persons related to their employment—they were allocated to jobs for which Australian labour could not be found. Data on the occupations of immigrants at the 1961 census are not available and the 1954 census included questions only on the industrial classification of workers. By then all displaced persons would have completed their two-years employment contracts with the government and, presumably, many would have returned to the occupations for which they were trained, as far as this was possible.[13] The 1954 census showed that 15.8% of all Australasian-born males were employed in manufacturing industry (as defined by the census) compared with 23% of north-western Europeans, 37% of central and eastern Europeans and 31% of southern Europeans. Comparable figures for the building and construction industry were Australasian-born 6%, north-western Europeans 15%, central and eastern Europeans 12% and southern Europeans 12%. Each of these ethnic groups was under-represented in commerce (compared with Australasian-born) and, with the exception of southern Europeans, under-represented in primary industry.[14] Clearly, the major contributions of immigrants have been in the manufacturing, building and construction industries. Unlike the inter-war years when immigrants were required for land settlement, post-war immigrants have been sought to meet the needs of a relatively diversified and rapidly expanding economy.

Finally, what effect have immigrants had on the religious structure of post-war Australia? Once again it is necessary to fall back on the results of the 1954 census. It should be noted that the census tables of religion by birthplace relate only to the religious affiliation of the population at 1954. They do not indicate whether and to what extent immigrants changed their pre-migration religious affiliation after they reached Australia. Assuming that this is not a major problem, it appears that 38% of post-war settlers (1947–54) have been Roman Catholics, compared with 21% of the total population in 1947, and 40% have been Protestants compared with 67% of the total 1947 population.[15]

Of the *effect* of these estimates on the religious affiliations of the total population, Dr Price makes two comments. First, new settlement has been

---

[13] Ex-lawyers and professional soldiers were unable to return to their occupations and many professional workers (medical men, engineers and teachers) experienced difficulty in meeting the "requirements" of the new society.

[14] W. D. Borrie, *The Needs of Tomorrow: The Population Factor*, a paper prepared for section K, Agriculture & Forestry, ANZAAS, 1962. Many of the southern Europeans in primary industry were pre-war immigrants who established themselves on small farms. Since the war these immigrants have sponsored relatives and friends in their former homeland.

[15] C. A. Price, "The Effects of Post-War Immigration on the Growth of the Population, Ethnic Composition and Religious Structure of Australia", *Australian Quarterly*, vol. 29, no. 4, 1957.

responsible for over one-half of the increase in the number of Roman Catholics, Orthodox and Lutherans (this does not take account of the effects of children born to new settlers after their arrival). In other words, immigration has been a considerably more potent force in the expansion of these three denominations than natural increase or conversion. Second, when the *rates* of gain or loss, in terms of the proportionate strengths of the various religions, are examined it appears that new settlement alone was responsible for the Roman Catholics, Orthodox and Lutherans gaining 1.3%, 0.4% and 0.3% respectively in seven years, primarily at the expense of British Protestants.

The Adjustment of Immigrants

The second major task is to try and assess some patterns of adjustment required by the large post-war immigration, *i.e.* the adjustment of newcomers to Australian society as well as the adjustment of Australians to the newcomers. There is, unfortunately, an incredible lack of research findings on these questions, especially when one considers that immigrants and their children have been responsible for about half the post-war increase in Australia's population. Apart from one or two demographic and socio-economic studies at the Australian National University and others by psychologists in Western Australia and Victoria, there is virtually nothing upon which one can draw. No community study of the two-way adjustment process has been conducted (or even contemplated) as far as this writer knows. Here and there interested observers have made comments on the probable impact of post-war immigrants on Australian society, but these have not been based on systematic research.

Writers who, in the past, have attempted to define Australian culture and attitudes have generally agreed on one point: our great distance from other countries and the fact that very few people came here merely as visitors, has had an important bearing on our attitudes towards foreigners. During the formative years of the Australian colonies nearly all the "immigrants" came from the British Isles. Later, there were periods when Continental and even Asian immigrants were admitted, but, as Crowley observes, "the Australian people have remained predominantly British by descent as well as by allegiance".[16] In addition, the bulk of British "migrants" were drawn from the middle and lower working classes, many having been transported as convicts. While the forces working towards the establishment of a colonial society were powerful, other forces were working against the transplanting of English, Welsh, Scottish and Irish societies. These groups mingled together and, to the extent possible in a society where men greatly outnumbered women, married and raised children in a physical and human environment which was vastly different from the motherland. Emancipists in particular, while not exactly seeking to establish a New Jerusalem, were usually flexible enough to remodel their attitudes according to the demands of the new situation. While the heritage was without doubt British in character, by the 1880s generations of Australian-born had moulded an *Australian* social and culture pattern which, according to Borrie, they identified as their own.[17] Once the pattern was established, the influx of non-British immigrants appeared to exert very little

[16] F. K. Crowley, *op. cit.,* p. 55.
[17] W. D. Borrie, "Australia", in *The Positive Contribution by Immigrants,* U.N.E.S.C.O. series, Population and Culture, p. 113.

influence on it. The two main non-British groups—Italians and Germans—have been more successful in retaining many of their social and cultural traits than in exerting influence on Australia's social and cultural patterns.

There is the danger that this sort of "explanation" can be taken too far—that once established Australian social and cultural patterns remained the same and were impervious to outside influence. It does appear, however, that while fairly considerable changes were exerted from *within,* they do not appear to have been significantly affected by immigrants. Borrie suggests that Australians have not always been willing to understand and learn from their minorities. Cultural uniformity, he writes, is to some extent the product of isolation and in their zealous protection of material standards of living Australians have been prone to detect "undesirable" cultural traits among migrants when they have offered economic competition, or have threatened to undercut existing standards. This fear not only aroused opposition to the Italians during the 'thirties but led to the insistence that even immigrants from the British Isles during the inter-war years should be settled on the land so that they would not compete for the few available jobs.

We have noted that Displaced Persons were the first major group of assisted non-Britishers to reach Australia. If Australians were not willing to learn from minorities and tended to mistrust them, what was their reaction to this major change in the immigration programme? Public opinion polls are our only guide. A poll taken in September 1947 revealed that 45% of respondents did not know what was meant by "Displaced Person" and another 9% thought they did, but didn't. Only 23% were in favour of the initial agreement to admit 12,000 Displaced Persons per year, 19% were against and 4% had no opinion. Most opposition to the scheme came from farm workers (67% of those in the sample opposed the agreement) and unskilled workers (53%). Least opposition came from farm owners. Most of the opposition to the scheme, according to the pollsters, was the result of the acute housing shortage. Others "reasons", less frequently mentioned, were "Bring British first" and "There are enough foreigners here already". Fifteen months later another poll showed that the proportion who didn't know what a Displaced Person was had fallen from 54% to 36%. This was exactly the increase in the percentage who favoured admitting Displaced Persons (23% to 41%). It appears that once Australians "discovered" the Displaced Persons (and possibly made personal contact with them), they favoured the scheme to bring more of them to Australia. The percentage of respondents opposing the scheme at the second poll (19%) was unchanged.

While these figures suggest a change in attitudes by Australians towards refugee immigrants, they do not necessarily represent a different attitude towards all foreign-born persons. It must be emphasized that the Displaced Person scheme took place during economic conditions highly favourable to their absorption. During their two-year contracts with the government, many refugees just did *not* compete with Australians for jobs or houses. In Western Australia, for example, the dependants of refugees were housed in former army huts, often outside the metropolitan area; and the workers were accommodated in tents or huts near their places of employment. Refugees allocated to basic extractive industries (*e.g.* mining and timber getting), sometimes obtained housing with the job and could thus live with their families.

15

For Displaced Persons, the adjustment to Australian society was not easy. A large majority of them arrived here penniless and even though they were allocated jobs within a few days and provided with accommodation of a sort, they faced tremendous problems of personal adjustment to the new language, institutions and culture. In many ways they bore the brunt of Australia's experiment with non-British immigrants. Without doubt many Australians were suspicious of the newcomers and the newcomers were aware of it. But they were obliged to try and take root in what they believed was an unfriendly host society. In a rare study on the problems of immigrant adjustment, Murphy reports that of 30 or 40 Displaced Persons whom he interviewed after they had been in Australia for longer than one year, only three had "satisfactory private contacts, as evidenced by having an Australian home where they felt confident of welcome and a friendly reception".[18] The first two years in Australia demanded an exhaustive process of adjustment to its economic, social and cultural patterns. There is considerable evidence that the process took its toll: kinfolk solidarity was weakened when the children of refugees became attracted to the behaviour patterns of the host society. Murphy observed that, as a group, the Displaced Persons tended to have a higher incidence of neurosis than other immigrants simply because of their unfortunate history of displacement in Europe associated with the exacting process of re-settlement.

When the pool of Displaced Persons dried up, the bilateral agreements which followed were much less favourable to Australia than those made with the I.R.O., and immigrants were selected on occupational grounds. Unlike Displaced Persons, they were not "forced" to emigrate. Their decisions were quite "free" in the sense that they voluntarily decided to migrate probably because they believed Australia offered them better economic opportunities. While there is no evidence to verify it, immigrants under the bilateral agreements probably had an easier row to hoe during their first years in Australia than did Displaced Persons. Even so, language difficulties, housing shortages and adaptation to a new physical and human environment are not easily handled. Research which the writer has done on British immigrants in postwar Australia suggests that even when immigrants are *not* confronted with language difficulties and are provided with temporary housing on arrival, they find the adjustment to Australian society difficult to make. British immigrants seem to find the problems more difficult to identify than do non-Britishers. Perhaps they tend to expect a "Britain of the South Seas" where everything will be the same except the weather and the pay-packet, but instead find that the problems of adjustment are more subtle and consequently more difficult to cope with than those faced by non-Britishers.

Very little is known about changes, if any, in Australian attitudes towards immigrants. It does appear, however, that after many years of aloofness we now seem to be prepared to listen to immigrants, and immigrants believe that they will be heard. Whether these changes have occurred at all class levels cannot be answered without a good deal of investigation, but it does appear that working-class Australians now mix a little more readily with foreigners then they did during the early post-war years. To what extent this is the result

18 H. B. M. Murphy, "The Assimilation of Refugee Immigrants in Australia", *Population Studies*, vol. 5, no. 3, 1953.

of familiarity, or the fact that immigrants have now been here long enough for prejudices to mellow and for some immigrants to have reached responsible positions in employment is unclear. Whatever the changes, if any, Australians do have their ethnic preferences. In a public opinion poll in 1951, respondents were handed a card listing seven nationalities and asked to check whether they wanted each as immigrants. Some 77% of respondents wanted Dutch immigrants, 73% Swedes, 57% French, 51% Germans, 41% Greeks, 31% Yugoslavs and 26% Italians. Seven per cent did not want any of them. There is clearly a high correlation between preference and latitude of the country; it would be fascinating to have procured the preferences of Australians at various intervals over the last thirty or forty years.

PART II

A. F. DAVIES and S. ENCEL

---

3   Class and Status

WHAT is happening to the Australian class structure today? Are the familiar marks and embattled interests of class difference being washed away in the flood of affluence? Or, as technology and bureaucracy ramify, are we fastening upon ourselves a social hierarchy as fine and detailed as that of the English? Is class losing its political importance in the face of the more pointed and specific demands of interest groups? Are we developing, in terms of income and standard (and possibly also style) of living, an enormous middle class with relatively little above or below it? Or are there large groups who are missing out on this social escalation, so that behind the veneer of consumer comforts there is a new structure of inequality helping to consolidate what Robin Boyd calls our "split-level culture"?

These questions, and others like them, are hard to answer. The study of class and status in Australia is in an intolerably neglected state. Even to ask such questions goes a little against the grain of the egalitarian tradition. In this discussion we have tried to approach the subject in a fairly systematic fashion, both through structure and through opinion. But first, we must look at the strong local presuppositions which make such an examination specially difficult.

Discussion of class and social stratification has been dominated for a century by the "dead level" interpretation[1] of Australian history—the notion of an egalitarian paradise (or purgatory), fed alike by travellers' tales and by much historical writing. Sir Keith Hancock's *Australia* (1930) did for Australia something of what de Tocqueville did for America. Hancock traced the egalitarian theme through economics, government, culture, and manners. The crucial assumption of Australian society, he argued, was that of "fair and reasonable" standards for everyone, as expressed in the judgment of Henry Bournes Higgins in the Harvester case before the Arbitration Court in 1907, which fixed a national basic wage according to the needs of Walt Whitman's "divine average". Thus was expressed "the decision of a people to seek general well-being rather than special excellence".[2]

The rise of the Labour movement in the generation before the first world war was marked by insistence upon the reality of a specifically Australian social and political pattern. The passions of class and nationalism, Hancock

[1] R. M. Crawford, *An Australian Perspective.*
[2] *Cambridge History of the British Empire*, vol. 7, p. 510.

18

observes, were inextricably intertwined; Australia was to be a new and different country where the class divisions of the old world had no place. An early trade union leader had already contrasted the working class with their docile counterparts in England who were "content to labour on and permit the upper classes to think and act for them".[3] Henry Lawson's poem "For'ard" (1893) saw a time when "the curse of class distinctions from our shoulders shall be hurled". Human equality, wrote Joseph Furphy in *Such is Life* (1903) was "self-evident . . . and impregnable as any mathematical axiom". D. H. Lawrence, in 1922, noted the absence of that "distinction in the very being" between the proletariat and the ruling classes to be found in England. An early sociological study by an Australian saw the community as "intolerant of special privileges . . . with no aristocracy of birth, of talent or of skill".[4] A generation later, C. Hartley Grattan introduced Australia to Americans as a country where the middle classes had been a minor social and political force.[5]

A critical examination of this received wisdom soon exposes its ambiguities. As far back as 1908, a special correspondent of the London *Times* noted that the coin of egalitarian sentiment was two-faced:

> Australians often claim with pride that they are free from class distinctions and class prejudice. They are so in a sense. Feudal notions of graded rank are almost extinct, and every man is as good as any other man in his own conceit. In another sense, however, class distinctions are real enough in Australia. An Australian working man may not touch his cap to his employer, who, like himself, can only eat one dinner, wear one hat, and vote one vote, and who, in other important respects, is a social and political unit of no greater weight than any of the workmen he employs; but that working man is, I think, far more conscious than an English one of separate class notions and incompatible class interests. He divides the world into two portions, working men and capitalists. There is, he thinks, a more or less definite amount of wealth which the two have to divide, and he is quite convinced that the proportions in which that division is now made are indefensible and iniquitous.[6]

Ambiguity about class runs through the most important recent account of the evolution of the Labour movement, Robin Gollan's *Radical and Working-Class Politics* (1960). Social stratification, he observes, "had never been accepted by more than a tiny minority", yet he interprets the industrial struggles of the 1890s as meaning that "a large proportion of the population was now confirmed in the status of wage earners with little prospect of ever changing that status".[7] The author, like his trade-union protagonists, is evidently convinced of the importance of "class" although he wavers on the question of stratification. At the Intercolonial Trades Union Congress of 1884, a speaker declared that "class questions require class knowledge to state them, and class sympathies to fight for them", and then went on to

---

[3] Chairman of the Trades Hall Committee, Melbourne, in 1859 (quoted by Gollan, *Radical and Working Class Politics*, p. 69).

[4] C. H. Northcott, *Australian Social Development*, 1918, p. 17.

[5] *Introducing Australia*, esp. ch. 2, and essay in Grattan (ed.), *Australia*.

[6] *The Times*, London, 26 September, 1908.

[7] Gollan, *op. cit.*, pp. 111–4.

identify the classes as "Land, Commerce, Capital, and Labour".[8] The industrial conflicts of the 1890s, Gollan claims, were "open class war" with governments "openly taking the side of the employing class".[9]

D. W. Rawson, in a sharply-worded criticism of Dr Gollan's book, sees it as a prime example of the "pseudo-Marxist" approach which permeates much of Australian historical writing.[10] This leads to a tendentious use of the concept of class, which forms the basis of a theory of political struggle while the reality of social differences due to class and status is ignored, or described in a muddled and contradictory fashion. Many political scientists have tried to escape from this confusion by insisting that political struggles should be described not in terms of class, but of conflicts between interest groups. This is by no means a novel view. The French socialist Albert Métin warned his readers in 1901 not to be misled by class-conscious postures within the Labour movement. "In appearance, they [the Labour parties] are what we should call a *class party*, carrying on a struggle against the bourgeoisie. In reality, they include employers and salaried workers and are concerned simply with obtaining good working conditions in the world as it is."[11]

The rejection of class explanations of Australian history and politics may be justified; what is unjustified is the related assumption that Australia is a society virtually free of social differentiation. Such a view is part of the "Australian legend" recounted by the historian Russel Ward, but although *a priori* incompatible with the characteristics of a complex industrial society, it remains influential not only in popular attitudes but in more sophisticated statements by people who should know better. Thus, Connell wrote some years ago that the education system was moving towards the elimination of distinctions between schools and the disappearance of special "knowledge, attitude or skills" derived from school instruction.[12] Taft and Walker assert that "Australians are indifferent to the fact that some can be educated privately and some simply acquire a state education, that some go to a university and others have neither the money nor inclination to do so".[13] As shown in chapter 5, education has always been a factor in social advancement and has become increasingly important in the past 20 years.

Taft and Walker also contend that middle-class Australians share with the working-class a "militant equalitarianism against authority or prestige figures . . . [the middle class] supports the welfare state, maintains the right of workers to strike and to look after their own interests, and eschews the servility associated with certain necessary occupational roles".[14] Studies of opinions about class, or of the relation between class and voting, do not bear this out.[15] Walker has also stated that in commerce or industry the salary

8 Quoted, *ibid.*, p. 85.

9 *Ibid.*, p. 109.

10 *Quadrant*, vol. 5, no. 1, 1960.

11 *Le socialisme sans doctrines*, p. 74.

12 W. F. Connell, "Education and Social Mobility in Australia", *Transactions of the Third World Congress of Sociology*, p. 76.

13 R. Taft & K. F. Walker, in A. M. Rose (ed.), *The Institutions of Advanced Societies*, p. 141.

14 *Ibid.*, p. 144.

15 Cf. Creighton Burns, *Parties and People*; A. F. Davies, "Politics in the New Suburb", *Australian Journal of Politics and History*, vol. 8, no. 2, 1962; D. W. Rawson, *Australia Votes*, chs. 10–12.

of the "second-highest level executives is usually not more than three times that of the lowest-paid adult male employee".[16] This is not borne out by surveys of professional and managerial salaries, or by evidence in industrial cases, which suggests that the salaries mentioned by Walker range from four to seven times the basic wage.[17] Influenced by such assertions, Lipset comes to the whimsical conclusion that the lower wage differentials in Australia as compared with the U.S.A. may be due to the influence of "mateship". He is on firmer ground when he concludes that a strong emphasis on social equality and on "achievement" rather than "ascription" as a basis for social position tends to "maximize the legitimacy of the existing distribution of privilege and thus minimize the conditions for left-wing extremist protest".[18]

Many of the arguments about the importance of class derive from confusion, ignorant or wilful, about the meaning of the concept and kindred terms like status, prestige, and power. European and English visitors, noting the absence (or apparent absence) of the particular social distinctions to which they are accustomed, have helped to perpetuate the myth of Australian classlessness. Nevertheless, a perceptive visitor who lives in the country long enough may do a "double-take", shifting from the impression that distinctions of class and status are unimportant to a realization that they are both important *and* different. "Behind the egalitarian façade," observes one such visitor, "there is hidden in private relations a fairly well defined social scale . . . the fundamental difference between Australia and Britain is that status which can be acquired is more significant than the social position which is inherited."[19]

The existence of such a well-defined scale is suggested by studies of occupational prestige. Taft, using the 20 occupations of the British (Hall-Jones) scale, found that schoolchildren and students in Perth ranked occupations in much the same way as English respondents.[20] Taft's results are confirmed in much greater detail by Congalton, who tested a scale of 134 items, first on a random sample of 303 persons in Sydney and then on 1,189 university students in all states,[21] with very high agreement between the two groups. Subjects were asked to rank the occupations on a 7-point scale. Those most highly regarded were, in the following order: doctor, university professor, solicitor, architect, professional engineer, director of large enterprise, owner of business worth more than £50,000, dentist, veterinary surgeon, clergyman, university lecturer, school principal.

At the bottom of the list were truck driver, railway shunter, porter, nightwatchman, waitress, packer, barman, cane cutter, seasonal labourer, wharf labourer, charwoman and roadsweeper. Jobs in the middle ranges, where such studies often encounter wide disagreements, were also placed fairly securely.

[16] K. F. Walker, *Industrial Relations in Australia*, p. 329.

[17] See, *e.g.*, P. C. Molhuysen in *Australian Economic Papers*, no. 1, 1962; K. Gravell, *Professional Incomes in Victoria*.

[18] S. M. Lipset, "The Value Patterns of Democracy", *American Sociological Review*, vol. 28, no. 4, 1963.

[19] Jeanne MacKenzie, *Australian Paradox*, pp. 130–1.

[20] R. Taft, "Social Grading of Occupations in Australia", *British Journal of Sociology*, vol. 4, no. 2, 1953.

[21] A. A. Congalton, *Social Standing of Occupations in Sydney*, 1962; *Occupational Status in Australia*, 1963. A later study using a different list is reported in "Uncertainties in Community Stratification", unpublished paper read to Section F, ANZAAS, 1964.

Though Congalton's studies confirm the wide acceptance of stratification as a fact of social life, they are not designed to investigate the dilemmas and contradictions of status, and they may leave the misleading impression that people see class in terms of a continuous series of gradations. Studies of occupational prestige are of little help in showing how people would assign occupations among social strata.[22] Awareness of the latter can readily be demonstrated by other methods, such as those discussed below.

Confusion over the meaning and significance of class in Australia parallels a similar confusion in the U.S.A. In a notorious Gallup Poll of 1939, most of the respondents said there were no social classes in the United States. When pressed, 88% identified themselves with the "middle class". Both responses, observes Reissman, are related to an underlying belief in social equality: "the psychological emphasis is upon the word 'middle' and not the word 'class'."[23] The concept of class derived from Europe is identified with class-consciousness, inherited social position, and political power; in America, with occupation, income, and education.[24]

These controversies reflect the impossibility of isolating a single Platonic abstraction which can be shown to underlie, override, or incorporate all the numerous usages found in real life. Any valid theory of social stratification must recognize the existence of at least three distinct dimensions—class, status, and power.[25] This threefold scheme is largely derived from Weber, whose analysis in its turn owes a great deal to Marx. Like Marx, Weber saw class as a result of the relationship of individuals to the means of production, or the "market situation"; status, on the other hand, was based on the existence of differing styles of life which depended on the "work situation"; both were related to the power and authority accruing to various social groups. In addition, Weber argued that "domination" (*Herrschaft*) constituted a separate basis for stratification, especially in the form of the bureaucratic organization characteristic of industrial capitalism.[26] In a prosperous society the importance of the latter dimension has become increasingly marked.[27]

But even this three-dimensional scheme is traversed by conflicting notions as to where lines of class division should be drawn, and of the advantages in classifying social groups in one pattern rather than another. An agreed set of terms and measures is hardly in sight.[28]

In the meantime, the study of occupations promises some escape from these intractable problems. Durkheim, in *The Division of Labour in Society*, noted many years ago that individuals form social groupings "according to the par-

[22] On this point see, *e.g.*, Leonard Reissman, *Class in American Society*, pp. 144–64; Albert J. Reiss, *Occupations and Social Status*; A. F. Davies, "Prestige of Occupations", *British Journal of Sociology*, vol. 3, no. 2, 1952.

[23] Reissman, *op. cit.*, p. 12. The psychological meaning of the terms "middle class", "working class", and "lower class" is discussed at length by Richard Centers, *The Psychology of Social Classes*, esp. pp. 27–9, 76–8.

[24] Arnold M. Rose, "The Concept of Class and American Sociology", *Social Research*, vol. 25, no. 1, 1958.

[25] W. G. Runciman, *Social Science and Political Theory*, ch. 8.

[26] See the essays on "Class, Status, Party" and "Bureaucracy" in Gerth & Mills (eds.), *From Max Weber: Essays in Sociology*; and the discussion by Bendix in *Max Weber: An Intellectual Portrait*, pp. 290-301, 412-49.

[27] Runciman, *loc. cit.*

[28] This problem is discussed by A. F. Davies, "Concepts of Social Class", *Australian Journal of Politics and History*, no. 2, 1956.

ticular nature of the social activity to which they consecrate themselves. Their natural milieu is no longer the natal milieu, but the occupational milieu. . . . In a general way, classes and castes probably have no other origin nor any other nature; they arise from the multitude of occupational organizations." The study of occupations provides a measure of class which is comparatively solid and reliable, which even the unsophisticated can recognize with some precision, which seems to establish a straightforward consciousness of common identity, susceptible to statistical analysis, and capable of experimental replication. All analyses of class, from Marx onwards, have relied to some extent on occupation, especially as "occupation can also be a summary indicator for other class characteristics, especially income and education, which in turn also reflect upon other class characteristics such as life styles and attitude patterns".[29] In Australia, it is particularly tempting to see the study of occupations as a guide to the class structure because it provides at least one solid possibility of extending our scanty knowledge of class differences. In view of this temptation, it is all the more important to recognize that occupation is an *index* and not a *synonym* of class. The next section, which deals with some facets of occupational change in Australia during the past 25 years, does more to raise questions about class differentiation than to answer them.

CLASS STRUCTURE AND OCCUPATIONAL CHANGE

The study of occupational stratification is greatly hampered by poor official statistics. Until the census of 1947, no direct question on occupation had been included in the census form; questions were restricted to industry and to employment status. In 1947, for the first time, an occupational scale was used following the lines of the well-known Edwards classification used in the U.S. census of 1940.[30] This scale had a number of unsatisfactory features. (The wide and confusing category of "commercial and clerical" included postmen, butchers, accountants, typists, messengers and "public servants"—all of them to be distinguished on such grounds as education, income, style of life, and social prestige; "domestic and protective service occupations" heaped together domestic servants, receptionists, hairdressers, undertakers, jockeys, policemen and firemen, and soldiers. The category "administrative" included not only government officials but proprietors, directors and managers in private business, and officers of ships and aircraft.) But it did give a fairly complete and consistent ordering of occupations by level of skill.

How far this profile has changed in the course of the century is impossible to compute accurately. On the basis of such figures as do exist, Hughes and Rawson recently estimated that, until 1947 at least, most of the changes had been fairly small. Omitting primary industry, the proportion of manual workers remained practically constant from 1921 to 1947, and the growth in the proportion of white-collar workers was relatively small and slow, no more than enough to compensate for the falling proportion of employers and self-employed which was noticeable during the same period, and amounting

---

[29] Reissman, *op. cit.*, p. 158.
[30] A. E. Edwards, *A Socio-Economic Grouping of the Gainful Employed Workers of the U.S., 1930*; Theodore Caplow, *The Sociology of Work*, pp. 32-48.

to perhaps 5%.[31] The scale of these changes may be compared with occupational movements in the United States.

TABLE 1

Occupations in 1947 (%)

Occupational Group	Males	Females	Persons
1. Rural, Fishing and Hunting..	17·9	3·1	14·6
2. Professional and semi-professional ..	3·5	11·3	5·1
3. Administrative	5·6	4·7	5·4
4. Commercial and clerical	16·4	38·1	21·4
5. Domestic and protective	6·4	16·5	8·4
6. Craftsmen	20·0	2·3	16·1
7. Operatives	20·7	20·3	20·6
8. Labourers	6·5	—	5·0
9. Indefinite or unstated	3·0	3·7	3·4
	100·0	100·0	100·0

Note.—The percentages relate not to total population but to total number in the work force. Out of 3·8 m. males enumerated in the population, 2·5 m. (65%) were in the work force; and out of 3·8m. females, only ·7m. (18·7%).

Although the general picture is similar, white-collar occupations clearly grew more rapidly in America, as did the professions. In 1910, 4.5% of the American work force were classified as professionals; by 1950 the proportion was 8.9%. The 1947 figure for Australians was only 5.1%.

TABLE 2

Occupational Trends in Australia and U.S.A. (%)

		Rural	Self-Employed	Employers	Commercial and Clerical
	1921	26	17	7	(?16-17)
	1933	21	17	9	—
Australia	1947	16	13	7	21·4
	1954	13	11	6	—
	1910	25·4	9·4	—	8·6
U.S.A.	1950	12·0	7·5	—	18·9
	1954	11·0	7·4	—	19·5

Sources: Hughes & Rawson, *loc. cit.*; Reissman, *op.cit.*, pp. 307-8.

The above table shows the similarity of occupational trends, though white-collar and professional employment have continued more slowly in Australia.[32] The impact of post-war industrial development can, however, be seen from the next table, which is adapted from the 1961 census. Again, the failure of the Commonwealth Bureau of Census and Statistics to provide

[31] Helen Hughes and D. W. Rawson, "Collective Bargaining and the White-Collar Pay Structure", *Journal of Industrial Relations*, vol. 2, no. 2, 1960.
[32] In the 1960 U.S. census, "professional, technical and kindred workers" had risen to 12%; "clerks and salesmen" to 23%; "managers, officials and proprietors" to 9%.

detailed and readily comparable data over a period makes it difficult to establish trends. No occupational data came from the 1954 census. For the 1961 census, instead of improving and developing the 1947 classification, the Bureau decided to adopt the International Standard Classification issued by the International Labour Organization in 1958, largely in the interests of international comparability. This classification is itself subject to criticism, representing as it does a compromise between the conflicting views of various national statistical authorities, the result of which is a failure to distinguish clearly between grade of occupation on the one hand and sphere of employment on the other.

TABLE 3

Occupations in 1961 (%)

	Occupational Group	Males	Females	Persons
0.	Professional, Technical and Related Workers	6·6	13·8	8·4
1.	Administrative, Executive and Managerial	8.0	4·0	7·0
2.	Clerical Workers	7·6	28·9	13·0
3.	Sales Workers	5·9	12·7	7·6
4.	Farmers, Fishermen, etc.	13·7	3·5	11·1
5.	Miners, Quarrymen, etc.	1·1	—	0·8
6.	Workers in Transport and Communications	7·7	2·5	6·4
7/8.	Craftsmen, Production-Process Workers and Labourers, n.e.c.	42·9	16·7	36·4
9.	Service, Sport and Recreation	4·1	15·8	7·0
10.	Armed Services, Enlisted Personnel ..	1·3	0·1	1·0
11.	Inadequately Described or Unstated ..	1·1	2·0	1·3
		100·0	100·0	100·0

In a total work force of 4.2m persons, 3.1m. were males. The *total* increase in the number of females employed was 47.7% over 1947, corresponding to a rise in the female component of the work force from 22.1% to 25.6%, and an increase in the proportion of females employed from 18.7% to 20.4% of the total female population. The proportion of the female work force who were married has also risen spectacularly; it was 11% in 1933, 20% in 1947, 34% in 1954, and 42% in 1961. Because of the difference in the classifications, comparisons between particular occupational groups are more difficult to make. Nevertheless, we can see a notable rise in the proportion of female white-collar and professional workers. If we compare the "commercial and clerical" group of 1947 with groups 2 and 3 (clerical and sales) of 1961, there is a rise from 273,051 to 441,480, *i.e.* 61.5% In 1961, clerical workers were by far the largest single component of the female work force (28.9%), and 59% of all clerical workers were females; in 1947, by contrast, clerical workers only slightly outnumbered "operatives" in the female work force (160,000 against 145,000). Category O (professional, technical and related workers) in the 1961 census is comparable with "professional and semi-professional" occupations in 1947. Here, there was an increase of 81.1% over the 1947 figure, corresponding to a rise from 11.3%

to 13.8% of the female work force. In medicine, 11.1% of doctors were women, compared with 8.7% in 1947; in dentistry, 5.1% against 2.7%; in architecture, 4.1% against 2.7%. In the case of draftsmen, the proportion almost trebled, from 3.6% to 10.3%.

These data provide comprehensive evidence of the rise in women's employment noted by MacKenzie.[33] They also underline the discrepancy between the importance of women in particular occupations, the shortages in certain key fields which are unlikely to be met without greater employment of women, and the persistence of deeply-rooted prejudices against female employment. As MacKenzie notes, this is a class problem, especially where it touches the matter of equal pay.[34] The very phrase "status of women" is an acknowledgment of this fact, and the obvious inequality of women's status, at least in public and professional life, is an important reflection on the accepted myth of an egalitarian society. The preponderance of women in clerical occupations, which appears likely to continue, may well be encouraged by resistance to equal pay or even to the removal of the marriage bar which is almost universal in the public services. The displacement of higher-paid male clerks by women is an instance of class-consciousness operating against objective economic interest, and it is noteworthy that the new militancy of white-collar organizations (discussed below) includes pressure for equal pay. The women's vote has been invoked as a partial explanation for the failure of the Labour Party to win the 1963 Federal election, and Labour leaders are showing a new readiness to concede that changes in the economic status of women demand a new approach to women voters.

Turning to the work force as a whole, the two most spectacular increases took place in Groups 0 and 1. In Group 0 (professional and technical), the increase was 117% over 1947, corresponding to a rise from 5.1% of the work force to 8.4%; in Group 1 (administrative, executive, and managerial), the increase was 70%, corresponding to a rise from 5.4% of the work force to 7%. Professional and technical groups which have exhibited an outstanding rate of growth are draftsmen (111%), artists (106%), architects (92%), and medical practitioners (79%).

Other sources also testify to the growth of professional groups. Membership of the Institution of Engineers (Australia), which now covers 75% of all professionally qualified engineers, rose from 4,259 in 1939 to 7,612 in 1951 and 16,722 in 1963.[35] Teachers in primary and secondary schools numbered 42,700 in 1939, 45,000 in 1947, and 87,500 in 1963. Academic staffs of universities grew from 1,300 in 1939 to 2,050 in 1947, and 5,000 in 1964.[36]

An outstanding factor in the growth of professional and administrative employment is the expansion of government activities since 1939, which has been most spectacular in the case of the Commonwealth. The Commonwealth Public Service grew from 47,000 in 1939 to 176,000 in 1964. In 1938 the number of *permanent* positions in the Third (clerical and professional)

[33] Norman MacKenzie, *Women in Australia*, part 3.
[34] *Ibid.*, pp. 180–2.
[35] B. E. Lloyd and W. J. Wilkin, *The Education of Professional Engineers in Australia*, pp. 59–60.
[36] *Commonwealth Year Books*, 1939 and 1947; Commonwealth Statistician, *Social Statistics*, 19, 21 and 22, 1964.

Division was 8,300; by 1961 it had grown to 36,300. In 1938, the number of professional positions in the Third Division was 719 (9% of the total); in 1961 it was 6,065 (17% of the total). That is, the number of professional positions rose almost twice as fast as that of all positions, and their range also increased greatly. To these figures should be added the growth of other Federal agencies which are not part of the Commonwealth Public Service. CSIRO, for example, grew from a small and limited body with 500 employees in 1939 to a widely diversified organization of 5,000 people in 1964, including 1,500 scientific and experimental officers.

The expansion of professional and managerial occupations is linked with the educational "explosion", which has affected Australia as it is affecting all other advanced industrial societies. In 1939 there were 1,178,000 pupils enrolled at primary and secondary schools; in 1964 there were 2,360,000, an increase of 100% in a period when the total population rose by 60%. Enrolments at technical schools and colleges rose from 90,000 in 1939 to 261,000 in 1962. University students numbered 14,200 in 1939, and 75,000 in 1964.[37] Higher education is now seen as occupying "a strategic place as a central determinant of the economic, political, social and cultural character of a society".[38] Another writer has observed, not without considerable distaste, that education is becoming "a route to increased status, with its consequences for social mobility, and its requirement of diversity in terms of professional stratification."[39]

These influences may be expected to bring about a considerable degree of social mobility within the Australian community. However, overseas studies suggest that the degree of mobility is habitually exaggerated in countries with a strong egalitarian tradition like the English-speaking democracies, especially by comparison with more class-bound communities like those of Western Europe. After an exhaustive review, Lipset and Bendix conclude that "the overall pattern of social mobility appears to be much the same in the industrial societies of various Western countries."[40] Industrial societies appear to reach a fairly stable level of mobility once their economic development has passed a certain point. The actual rates may be accounted for on the basis of five factors: (1) the number of available vacancies, (2) different fertility rates as between classes, (3) the relative prestige of occupations, (4) the number of inheritable status-positions, (5) legal restrictions on potential opportunities. Actual and imagined degrees of mobility often differ significantly. Mobility rates seem to be effectively determined by the occupational structure, and are influenced only marginally by differing social values.[41]

So far, there is little reliable evidence on actual rates of inter-generational social mobility in Australia. What there is, supports Lipset and Bendix's conclusions. One piece of evidence comes from surveys of government officials and businessmen carried out by Encel in 1956 and 1957. Replies were received from 325 directors and managers drawn from 180 large and

[37] For a detailed discussion of the expansion of education at the secondary and tertiary levels see the articles by W. D. Borrie and A. R. Hall in *Vestes*, vol. 5, no. 3, 1962.
[38] Jean Floud and A. H. Halsey, introduction to Halsey, Floud, Anderson (eds.) *Education, Economy, and Society*, p. 3.
[39] G. H. Bantock, *Education in an Industrial Society*, p. 87.
[40] S. M. Lipset and Reinhard Bendix, *Social Mobility in Industrial Society*, p. 13.
[41] *Ibid.*, pp. 71–4.

27

medium-sized commercial and industrial firms; 327 senior Commonwealth officials drawn from all departments and large statutory authorities; and 217 senior state officials from N.S.W. and Victoria. Results are given in the accompanying table.

TABLE 4

Social Origins of Businessmen and Officials (%)

Father's Occupation	1947 census (Males)	Fathers of Businessmen	Fathers of Commonwealth Officials	Fathers of State Govt. Officials
1. Rural	17·9	7	10	10
2. Professional and semi-professional	3·5	17·5	16	20
3. Administrative and business ..	5·6	33	11	10
4. Commercial	7·4	19	20	11
5. Clerical	9·0	8	15	20
6. Skilled workers	20·0	9·5	16	14
7. Unskilled and semi-skilled workers	27·2	2	6	7
8. Other	9·4	4	6	8
	100·0	100·0	100·0	100·0

Despite the appreciable differences between businessmen and officials, the preponderance of fathers in professional, administrative and commercial occupations is clear. Almost 70% of businessmen were drawn from these groups, compared with 47% of Commonwealth officials and 41% of state officials, whereas in the census they accounted for 16.5%. There is appreciable

TABLE 5

Occupational Level of N.S.W. Males, 1960

	Sons (n=4,526) %	Fathers (n=4,459) %
Professional	4·5	2·8
Semi-Professional	4·2	1·1
Administrative, Managerial	1·9	3·4
Proprietary	2·4	5·1
Clerical and Sales	15·5	8·8
TOTAL "White Collar"	28·5	21·2
Skilled-Unskilled Labour	57·3	57·2
Service	5·8	4·9
TOTAL "Blue Collar"	63·1	62·1
Rural	8·4	16·7
	100·0	100·0

mobility out of the commercial into the business group, which reflects changes in the scale and scope of industry under the impact of postwar industrialization. The Commonwealth service has provided a notable avenue for mobility out of the commercial group, and the state services for mobility out of the clerical group. But the total picture is very far from the folk legends of "office boy to managing director" or "telegraph messenger to Director-General".

A similar pattern of relative stability appears from Allingham's comparison of the occupations of fathers and sons in New South Wales in 1960. His data were derived from the Registrar-General's marriage records.[42]

Although these figures confirm the general picture of an increase in white-collar and professional occupations, they suggest that this has not come about through mobility out of manual occupations. A picture of the slow structural changes emerges from Allingham's comparison of the occupations of bridegrooms in N.S.W. in 1947 and 1960.[43]

TABLE 6

Occupations of N.S.W. Bridegrooms, 1947 and 1960

	1947 (n=30,172) %	1960 (n=29,328) %
Professional and semi-Professional	3·5	6·4
Other White Collar	20·9	22·9
TOTAL "White Collar"	24·4	29·3
Domestic and Protective Service	5·8	5·9
Craftsmen	23·9	27·6
Operatives	22·2	17·3
Labourers	10·1	9·9
TOTAL "Blue Collar"	62·0	60·7
Rural	10·4	7·8
Indefinite, Not Stated	2·0	1·3
Not in Labour Force	1·1	0·9
	100·0	100·0

Sources: Demography Bulletins, 1947 and 1960.

The table suggests that despite increased mobility since the war, it has had little effect in "blue collar" occupations.

The occupational background of schoolteachers has been studied by Bassett and Pike. Bassett made two studies, one of entrants to Armidale Teachers' College, N.S.W., from 1929 to 1957, and one of all married male teachers

[42] J. Allingham, "Occupational Mobility in Australia" (unpublished MS, Australian National University, 1964).

[43] Comparable results are reported using a similar technique in Natalie Rogoff, *Recent Trends in Occupational Mobility*, which compares marriage licence data in Indianapolis in 1910 and 1950.

29

with children, also in N.S.W., who had more than 20 years' service.[44] In both cases the great majority of entrants (69.5% and 78.5% respectively) were children of manual workers, small shopkeepers, etc. Bassett found no obvious differences in his Armidale study for those in training before and during the war, and those in training after the war. He found too that 6.8% of the Armidale recruits had fathers who were teachers, and in his second study of teachers' families, that 3.7% of the families had followed teaching for three generations and 41.3% for two generations. The proportion of the sons of teachers who became teachers was 25% and daughters 38.4%, though of those actually qualified to enter, 39.4% of the sons and 64.1% of the daughters did so.

Pike[45] made a study of entrants to Sydney Teachers' College in 1926, 1927, 1931–2, and 1936. Like Bassett, he found a remarkable stability in the social pattern of recruitment. In each of the four years the bulk of the trainees (52–61%) came from the homes of manual, sales and clerical workers, shopkeepers and farmers. Approximately 10%, in each year, were the children of teachers.

OCCUPATIONAL CHANGE AND CLASS INTERESTS

The expansion of professional and managerial occupations has been accompanied by attempts by members of these groups to assert claims to a distinctive status in the Australian community. The multiplication of professional groups is a major feature of social history in the past 150 years. The chief distinguishing characteristic of a profession has been described as "the application of an intellectual technique to the ordinary business of life acquired as the result of long and specialized training". The progressive differentiation of such techniques, and of those who practise them, is likely to continue indefinitely. "Science advances and techniques multiply. In the long run, technical advance implies an increase in the numbers of those doing more or less specialized intellectual work relative to the number of those who are engaged in manual labour or in an unspecialized intellectual region." As a by-product, the business of management and administration is also becoming professionalized. With the growth of large scale organization, "all those who occupy the important positions will gradually come within professional associations, or at least under professional influence".[46]

Professional status carries with it the legal recognition of belonging to a select group, social prestige, the ability to press for higher salaries and fees, and great influence over the content of professional education. This status is buttressed by the formation of qualifying associations, the introduction of examinations and recognized training courses, and the establishment of codes of professional conduct. In recent years, professional groups have also used publicity to advance or safeguard their status. In Australia, the importance of industrial arbitration as a method of determining salaries and working conditions has led professional groups to resort to industrial tribunals in an attempt to achieve the desired recognition. The decisions of the Common-

[44] G. W. Bassett, "The Occupational Background of Teachers", *Australian Journal of Education*, vol. 2, no. 2, 1958; "Teachers and their children", *idem.*, vol. 5, no. 1, 1961.
[45] R. M. Pike, unpublished paper presented to Section F, ANZAAS, 1964.
[46] A. M. Carr-Saunders and P. A. Wilson, *The Professions*, pp. 491-3.

wealth Arbitration Commission in the professional engineers' cases of 1961 and 1962 provide an instructive case history.[47]

The engineers' cases represent the climax of a long struggle by the organized engineers to gain recognition as a fully professional group through the use of the arbitration machinery. The official objective of the Association of Professional Engineers of Australia is to obtain salaries which "will enable all Professional Engineers to maintain a standard of living and a status in keeping with the reasonable needs of a professional man". During the hearing of the first case, one of the engineers' spokesmen used the hallowed words "fair and reasonable" to describe this standard of living in terms of a car, a house and a couple of decent suits. This is a far cry from the Harvester case of 1907. The use of the traditional rhetoric of wage justice in a claim such as this underlines the extraordinary role of arbitration in our society, and the subtle expansion of its functions beyond the older conceptions of a living wage or the capacity of industry to pay. In effect, the Arbitration Commission accepted the claim made in the A.P.E.A.'s manifesto that "the salaries and conditions under which professional engineers work have for the most part been determined on a basis appropriate for non-professional employees . . . it is necessary, in the interests of the profession and of the community as well as of individual engineers, that professional engineering employees should have their salaries determined on the basis of their common needs and interests as members of a learned profession".

The A.P.E.A. was joined in its claim by the Professional Officers' Association (P.O.A.) of Commonwealth government employees, and by the Association of Architects, Engineers, Surveyors and Draftsmen of Australia (A.A.E.S.D.A.). The P.O.A. has existed since the early years of Commonwealth administration. The A.A.E.S.D.A., perhaps the most "militant" of the three, was formed on a national basis in 1944, and spans both "professional" and "sub-professional" occupations. The A.P.E.A. was established in 1946, to represent professional engineers in salary negotiations, and after a modest start it now embraces perhaps half of the profession.

In the earlier Scientific Officers' Case before the Public Service Arbitrator in 1954, in which the P.O.A. was involved, the tribunal accepted the contention that the higher education required to train a research worker gave his occupation a special "work value" which should be recognized in terms of salary.[48] The engineers' cases went a step further, as it was also argued that the prestige and social importance of the engineering profession should be reflected in its renumeration. The judgment acknowledges that "this is a technological age in which the needs of mankind continue to become more comprehensive and more complex", that the satisfaction of these needs depends greatly on the skill of the engineer, and that low salaries prevent the professional engineer from occupying "the honoured place in the community which was his right and entitlement".

Since 1939 there has been a world-wide tendency for wage and salary differences to contract. In Australia this takes the form of a shrinking of the "margin" for skill according to which wages and salaries above the basic wage

[47] S. Encel, "Social Implications of the Engineers' Cases", *Journal of Industrial Relations*, vol. 6, no. 1, 1964.
[48] *C.P.S. Arbitration Reports*, 1954, determinations 51 and 52. See also J. R. Kerr, "Work Value", *Journal of Industrial Relations*, vol. 6, no. 1, 1964.

are traditionally fixed.[49] Professional groups have striven to counteract this by using the arguments already described, and the success of the engineers has prompted emulation. In 1961 an Association of Professional Scientists was formed, and in 1963 it joined with the A.P.E.A. and the A.A.E.S.D.A. in the Council of Professional Associations, originally established in 1956.[50] The shrinkage of margins has also provoked a new sense of militancy among white-collar workers, who are increasingly looking to trade-union methods to restore their former status.[51] The advance of office mechanization, with its rapid transition in one generation from the desk calculator to electronic data processing, is bringing about a revolution in the status of the clerical worker, who is being pushed more and more into the position of a machine-minder —deformed into a detail worker, as Marx predicted.[52] This is nowhere more evident than in banking, once one of the most gentlemanly of all occupations.[53] The average bank manager nowadays is paid about £2,000 a year, which puts him a long way behind men with comparable responsibilities in the public services, in manufacturing industry, and in schoolteaching. Many bank managers, when they retire, are forced to look for work to supplement their superannuation, and many young bank officials, trying to raise a family in middle-class style, do extra work in their spare time.[54]

White-collar unionism received a boost with the formation in 1956 of the Australian Council of Salaried and Professional Associations (A.C.S.P.A.), into which several earlier associations are merged. A.C.S.P.A.'s activities have included publicity campaigns to increase union-consciousness among white-collar workers. From the beginning, it has been concerned with the problem of restoring margins to something like their pre-war level, the rationale of which was expressed in the so-called "A.C.S.P.A. formula".[55] The margins case of 1959, in which A.C.S.P.A. conducted a combined claim on behalf of a number of its constituent associations, was argued along these lines. On this and subsequent occasions, A.C.S.P.A. was joined by the Australian Council of Trade Unions and by the High Council of Commonwealth Public Service Associations, the largest federation of government employees in Australia. The long-term interests of these bodies may draw closer together, and further from those of the professional bodies, with all the social and political implications that may flow from this. Until 1954, claims for professional salaries followed the basic-wage-cum-margin approach which is characteristic of most claims before industrial tribunals. The engineers' cases suggest that professional groups may now be able to use quite different arguments, and that their interest in arbitration will be sharply distinct from that of the traditional white-collar occupations. As the Arbitration Commission declared in its judgment, the professional engineer "should stand on his own feet and have his salary determined in the light of the nature of his employ-

---

[49] P. C. Molhuysen, *loc. cit.*; Hughes & Rawson, *loc. cit.*; K. Gravell, *loc. cit.*

[50] *Nation*, 7 March 1964.

[51] R. J. O'Dea, "The White-Collar Worker", *Quadrant*, vol. 3, no. 4, 1959.

[52] *Capital*, vol. 1, ch. 12, *passim*.

[53] R. N. McMurry, "Recruitment, Dependency, and Morale in Banking", *Administrative Science Quarterly*, vol. 3, no. 1, 1958.

[54] Melbourne *Herald*, 21 September 1962, interview with the federal president of the Australian Bank Officers' Association.

[55] A.C.S.P.A., *The Australian National Income and Its Distribution*, Sydney, 1959.

ment . . . there has in the past been too much attention to salary patterns, the appropriate position in wage structure relations with other employees, and possible repercussive effects". Moreover, following upon a decision by the High Court that the Commission had complete jurisdiction in the case, the Commission's judgment made it clear that claims could be brought under the relevant section of the Conciliation and Arbitration Act by "professional, semi-professional or craft organizations". In other words, the Arbitration Commission, and other tribunals following its lead, are prepared to recognize the right of professional groups *as such* to a special economic and social status as compared with the majority of the organizations affiliated with A.C.S.PA. The growth of professionalism is, in itself, an important reason why margins cannot be "restored".

IMAGES OF CLASS

What can we learn by survey methods of people's ideas and feelings about social class? Some historians have answered: not very much.

As a historical relationship, class is a fluency which evades analysis if we attempt to stop it dead at any given moment to anatomize its structure. The finest-meshed sociological net cannot give us a pure specimen . . . the relationship must always be embodied in real people and in a historical context.[56]

But the immediate problem has been lack of survey data.

For many years the 1949 Melbourne survey stood alone.[57] A national opinion poll at the time of the 1961 Federal election,[58] and an electorate survey with a tangential bearing,[59] have since joined it. A small pilot survey was undertaken for this volume in Melbourne in 1962.[60] We have grouped the findings of these studies under the headings: acceptance of class, class signs and class maps, class attributes and views, and social mobility.

Identification with class

The A.P.O.P. 1961 national poll (fixed choice) gave:

(n = 1,605)

Upper middle class	5.5%
Middle class	44.0%
Lower middle class	12.0%
Working class	38.5%

And it showed that, when called on, every respondent can identify with some class. Given a very open choice (*"If you had to say which group or section of the community you belonged to . . . ?"*),[61] in the La Trobe survey, four out

---

[56] E. P. Thompson, *The Making of the English Working Class,* preface.

[57] O. A. Oeser and S. B. Hammond (eds.), *Social Structure and Personality in a City,* pt. 5.

[58] A.P.O.P., November 1961. The class breakdowns are published here for the first time. We are indebted to Mr. Roy Morgan for making his questionnaire and duplicate punched cards available.

[59] Creighton Burns, *Parties and People,* pt. 2.

[60] Interviews were carried out by Nation's Opinion Service, Melbourne. The sample consisted of 150 adults, one-third randomly selected in the suburbs of Hawthorn ("Old Middle"), Footscray ("Old Industrial") and Ringwood ("New Outer"). The Ringwood group were the articulate core of a previous random sample of 267 (see "Politics in the New Suburb", *loc. cit.*).

[61] Cf. 1949 Melbourne survey, *loc. cit.,* 265–6.

of five respondents called in the help of some notion of class, however vague, to fix their position in society for the interviewer:

Middle class	44%
Working class	37%
Other class	2%
Evasive/Anti-class	9%
Non-class groups	8%

In the 1962 survey, where people were given a *maximum* chance to decline, three out of five nevertheless felt that "(*they*) *personally belonged to a social class*".

In short, most people readily accept a class label from the familiar stock; a further one in four accepts it only reluctantly, with a sense that it sits on him awkwardly, or might mislead; only one in ten rejects the idea of being classed with some asperity, and sometimes the whole notion of there being classes.

Though the surveys have not turned up enough of these "Anti-class" people to say anything useful about them, just a little is known about the "Evasives". One might expect them to be those with shaky or guilty status claims. But this did not seem to have been the case in the La Trobe sample, where many of the evasive people—especially young people, or housewives—were simply too snugly embedded in their surroundings either to discriminate or to feel themselves tagged.

"Don't know. Never thought of it really. Just the normal section."

"Can't think of anything to say to that at all. We're all much of a muchness around here."

Others—the lost and isolated—reached out wanly to "the community as a whole", or mumbled, "Don't belong to anything" (migrants, invalids). Others —often old residents in the district—clutched at a precarious "lone-wolf" individuality which company might extinguish ("Independent", "Free thinker", "Individualist"). Others again had scruples against classing—at least in public. A final batch—nearly all frequent church attenders—gave the answer, "Just an ordinary person" with a certain steely humility.

The 1962 survey found people more likely to be evasive if they lived in a mixed district, or were middle-aged, Roman Catholics, or middle children. They were much readier to identify with a class in a homogeneous district, and to see those round about as belonging to the same class (thus *all* Old Industrial "working class" respondents saw theirs as a working class suburb, while two-thirds of district "middle class" people saw it as middle class; *no* "middle class" New Outer people saw theirs as a working class district, but over half the "working class" New Outers did).

Class signs and class maps

That most people accept a class tag—in fact, almost always one of two main ones—does not prevent their having varied and personal concepts of class. The 1962 survey explored this by asking if people thought there were class differences in Australia, and, if they assented (as they usually did), what they rested on. They were then asked to name and describe each of the classes they saw.

Ideas on the basis of class differences can be summarized in a simple table.

34

Adding Education-and-money and Snobbishness-and-money to Scale of Expenditure, near majority opinion is that class is primarily a matter of money.[62] It is almost the prerogative of "working class" respondents to say that class differences depend on Power-and-privilege and Snobbishness (and of the middle-aged within the "working class" group). Only "middle class" people are disposed to see Education, Restricted intercourse, Manners-and-cultivation, or Low behaviour as the decisive marks of class.

TABLE 7

Basis of Australian Class System

(n = 146 — 16 "no class differences")

	%
Scale of expenditure	32
Snobbishness	9
Snobbishness and money	9
Education	4
Education and money	8
Power and privileges ("Haves"/"Bosses")	10
Restricted intercourse	12
Manners, cultivation	5
Low behaviour	5
Other	6
	100

Respondents' class schemes varied a good deal in complexity and definiteness, and in the amount and type of feeling with which they were invested. As Hammond predicted, "These views will not be just another set of attitudes towards social objects, but will be in part the individual's description and evaluation of himself in comparative social terms."[63] With somewhat ruthless sorting, however, he managed to encompass those in the 1949 survey in four principal "standpoints" as follows:

		% of sample
1.	"Middle class" in an Upper-Middle-Lower scheme ..	26
2.	"Middle class" in an Upper-Middle-Working scheme ..	29
3.	"Working class" in an Upper-Middle-Working scheme ..	26
4.	"Working class" in a Capitalist-Worker scheme ..	11
	No scheme	8

Each could be shown to take a fairly consistent view of politics and social order, and to have a fairly homogeneous membership (the first, of people in danger on family or economic grounds of being considered "working class" by others; the fourth, of those in revolt against middle class families).

[62] The fixed choice question of the 1949 survey gave a rather different result; *loc. cit.*, p. 284.
[63] *Loc. cit.*, p. 263.

The class schemes of the 1962 sample will be presented in a somewhat more complicated form, distinguishing "ordinary/average" from "middle" class, and taking some account of the size of classes seen.

Hammond's "standpoints 1-3" can, with a little ingenuity, be resurrected from these data.[64] They account for 32%, 22% and 11% of the sample, respectively. But we have *no* cases for his "Capitalist-Worker" scheme.

TABLE 8

Class Schemes, Melbourne, 1962

	Old Industrial	Old Middle	New Outer	Total
1. Large MIDDLE CLASS*–LOWER CLASS–UPPER CLASS ..	4	12	11	23
Large MIDDLE CLASS (subdivided)–Large LOWER CLASS	—	2	1	3
Large ORDINARY–Small LOWER	—	3	1	4
2. Large MIDDLE CLASS (may be subdivided)–Large WORKING CLASS–Small Top	4	5	5	14
Large WORKING CLASS–Large MIDDLE CLASS (may be subdivided)–Small Top..	3	—	—	3
Large MIDDLE CLASS–Large WORKING CLASS	—	2	—	2
3. Large WORKING CLASS–Smaller MIDDLE CLASS–Small Top	6	1	3	10
Smaller MIDDLE CLASS–Large WORKING CLASS–Small Top	4	9	3	16
Large WORKING CLASS–Large WEALTHIER	3	—	—	3
4. Large WORKING CLASS–Small Top	12	—	8	20
Small Top–Large WORKING CLASS	—	2	—	2
5. Large ORDINARY–Small Top/WEALTHIER	2	2	5	9
Small WEALTHY–Large ORDINARY	—	1	—	1
Large ORDINARY–Small Top–Small Low	7	1	4	16
Miscellaneous–Functional, occupational	—	3	5	8
No scheme	5	7	—	12
	50	50	46	146

* First-named class respondent identifies with.

"Upper classes" of three sorts cropped up in the descriptions—a "wealthy" distinguished by consumption style, an "upper" marked by snobbery and social exclusiveness, and a "bosses" wielding social power. It happened, however, that no respondents with a WORKING-Another CLASS scheme used this "boss" sense. Hammond concluded his discussion:

> A surprising degree of uniformity in the naming of social strata has been demonstrated and also a very high degree of consistency with relatively few frames of reference. This commonness of responses must be due to common influences such as political propaganda, education and interests. It seems likely that such overall uniformity could emerge only if many cases had been given these frames of reference almost ready made by one or another source.

[64] By ignoring the differences between our Groups 2 and 3, and treating ORDINARY-TOP-LOW as UPPER-MIDDLE-LOWER.

One need only observe that a class-war climate of opinion is now well behind us. And the greater complexity of the 1962 responses is itself prime evidence of that.

"Working class" in these schemes also had several uses: as the decent ones, backbone of society; as the strugglers—to be pitied; as the "labourer class . . . no hopers . . . drifters" (approaching LOWER). A decent "middle class" saving remnant—or steadying keel—jostled a *"wealthier* only", and a group seen as snobbish and grasping.

Class attributes and views

Those who claimed to be "working class" usually had a good deal in common with others making the same claim. We look first at common features of their background, and then at typical opinions.

In the 1962 survey, over half of those identifying as "working class" had primary or junior secondary education only; two-thirds of those identifying as "middle class", senior secondary or tertiary. "Working class" respondents are two-thirds in manual occupations—only one-fifth of "middle class" subjects are. They are a little older. Men over 55 are as likely to be "working class" as "middle class"; men under 35 break 2:7.

In the A.P.O.P. 1961 poll the age relation did not hold. However, the occupational and educational findings were even more dramatic. In this national sample three-quarters of the "working class" were in manual occupations, while less than one-third of the "middle class" were. Some 80% of the "working class" had primary or some secondary education only; some 60% of the "middle class" had higher secondary or tertiary education.

"Working class" respondents also lived in worse houses, as assessed by interviewers using standard grades based on their outside appearance. In the La Trobe survey, for example, Class 5 houses accommodated 78% of "working class" people, and 48% of "middle class"; Class 4 houses 14% of "working class" people, and 43% of "middle class". ("Class 5" is defined as "a good working class house—the average type—representing some 60% of Melbourne houses". "Class 4" is a distinct cut above that.) This finding may be put another way: of the third of the sample living in "superior" (by local standards) housing, only one in five sticks to the working class. Style of life considerations evidently play a vital part in many people's class identification.

"Class" views differed most on voting. Indeed, the match between "class" and party vote in sample surveys is commonly so close as to suggest that they may be largely alternative measures of the same thing—general social stance.

In the A.P.O.P. poll (and the La Trobe survey) two-thirds of those calling themselves "working class" voted A.L.P.; and two-thirds of the "middle class" Liberal. In the 1962 sample, four-fifths of the "working class" voted A.L.P. and just over half the "middle class" Liberal. Asked whether they were strong, moderate, or weak, supporters of their chosen party, over half the A.L.P. "workers", and three-quarters of the Liberal "middle class", wished to be thought moderate only. "Cross-class" voters were more tepid still in their support.

37

Cross-class voters take on more flesh when occupation, too, is taken into account, so we may have:

The A.P.O.P. poll allows an estimate of their actual numbers. "Middle-class" manual workers were most numerous (312; no. 4 in the diagram), voting A.L.P. 50%, Liberal 35%, Don't Know/Other 15%. Their claim to middle class status is thus, in most cases, separate from their political stance, which remains in line with their job.[65] A solid third, however, pursued their status aspiration to its political conclusion. Next came non-manual people claiming to be "working class" (158; no. 1 in the diagram). They voted A.L.P. 53%, Liberal 32%, D.K./Other 15%. A good half ran "class" and vote together, but one-third kept them distinct. The groups with congruent class and occupation but idiosyncratic vote were smaller. Manual, "working-class" Liberals numbered 59 (no. 2 in the diagram), i.e. 13% of the manual-"working class" group as a whole, compared with 99 Non-manual-"middle class"-Labour voters (15% of the whole group; no. 3 in the diagram).

In the La Trobe survey "working class" Liberals had more skilled jobs, more concern with religion, and more political competence and interest than the "working class" group as a whole. The move to the new suburb had snapped a Labour link in a third of these cases; few had a record of consistent Liberal voting. A group of wives who had "married down" and preferred their father's to their husband's politics stood out[66] (and several recently converted husbands, who had been unable to carry "loyal" wives with them). They gave, as the main reason for their vote, satisfaction with the government's record.

"Middle class" Labour voters (twice as numerous) also tended to be more politically alert and competent than the "middle class" average. Belonging usually to white-collar unions, they showed a cheerful class dualism; "middle class" in consumption style and social status, they clung to a *political* "working class" loyalty, often with some spirit. Family loyalty was important, especially in wives and young men.[67]

---

[65] Cf F. Zweig, *The Worker in an Affluent Society*, who found a large group considering themselves working class only inside the factory and middle class outside.

[66] Cf. Hammond's comment that with women "class of origin is more important than present class in determining standpoint", *loc. cit.*, p. 276.

[67] As well as these habitual "middle class" Labourites, the survey found a substantial group of by-election "swingers" (one-third of the whole). These were people who had been shaken out of their normal Liberal allegiance by accumulated grievances ("time for a change", inflation, trade policy, pensions, South Africa, defence expenditure . . .) and saw a chance to "give Bob a jolt". They tended to be older people well up the white collar hierarchy.

Party support in Australian conditions has of course relatively little to do with conservatism-radicalism. A follow-up to the La Trobe survey disclosed a rock-like complacency about social inequality. Asked their opinion of the statement: *People in certain jobs get paid too much, and in others not enough,* Labour voters turned out every bit as socially complacent as Liberal voters.[68]

One part of the 1962 survey was designed to test the present strength of radical attitudes. Although only one "working class" respondent in nine found the press acceptable (cf. one "middle class" person in three), criticisms tended to be mild and unacute ("large headlines", "fuss about nothing"). Outer suburban subjects were more critical than those from the industrial district.

Asked how they would dispose of the profits of a large company if it were entirely up to them,[69] subjects chose the following possibilities first out of a list of suggestions:

	"Working class" %	"Middle class" %
To the present shareholders	24	50
Light compromise scheme	29	34
Schemes showing some hostility to shareholders	47	16

The "light compromise scheme" read: "a small limited return to shareholders, the rest as a bonus to employees". The other schemes divided all the profits among employees in various ways.

While four-fifths of "middle class" subjects disapproved of hypothetical strikes by wharf labourers and schoolteachers in circumstances detailed in one question, nearly one-third of "working class" subjects approved of the teachers' strike and nearly one-half of the wharfies'. Old Industrial and New Outer were equally approving (or disapproving) of union militancy.

The 1961 A.P.O.P. figures show an interesting difference on expectations of the danger of war. Replies to the question, "Is there bound to be a major war sooner or later?" were as follows:

	No	Yes	Don't Know	
"Working class"—manual occupation	34%	43%	23%	100%
"Middle class"—non-manual occupation	49%	35%	16%	100%

A great deal of useful information on basic attitudes lies unexamined in the occupational breakdowns of public opinion polls.

Social mobility

Objectively, social mobility in the 1962 sample was not great, which confirms other studies quoted earlier in the chapter.

	Father manual	Father non-manual	
"Working class" respondents	60%	40%	100%
"Middle class" respondents	37%	63%	100%

In Old Industrial, 68% of those in manual occupations had fathers in manual occupations; in Old Middle, 78% of the non-manual had non-manual fathers.

Residential immobility is striking: three-quarters of the sample reported no move in the last five years, and even fewer expected to move within the next five years. Roughly half had *exactly* the same job five years ago, but

---

[68] "Politics in the New Suburb", *loc. cit.*; J. Collins, "A Note on Social Attitudes and Political Differences"; *Australian Journal of Politics and History*, vol. 9, no. 1, 1963.
[69] Taken from A. W. Jones, *Life, Liberty and Property*, pp. 362, 383-8.

57% expected to *move up* occupationally in the next five years. Over two-thirds feel better off financially than their fathers at the same time of life. Most hesitated, however, to claim a higher social position than their parents. (Some 37% said their status was better; 54% the same; 9% worse). This hesitation was strongest in "working class" responses: only one "working class" subject in five (cf. one "middle class" person in three) said their status was superior to their parents'.

Satisfaction with jobs seems high. Only one Old Industrial respondent in three said he had ever considered another occupation; and only one Old Middle subject in two. But two-thirds of the New Outer subjects had considered changes; presumably they are the mobile ones, and know it. By the same token, they feel themselves most "stuck" in their present positions.

One respondent in five actually called his present job his dream occupation. If given a free choice, however, almost four-fifths would be doing something quite different as follows:

TABLE 9

Preferred Occupation

	Old Industrial	New Outer	Old Middle	Total
Professions (implying a degree)	3	10	14	27
Semi-professions (teaching, nursing, pharmacy, social work, journalism)	4	2	3	9
Farmer	4	9	3	16
Manager, business executive	3	3	2	8
Skilled trade	10	—	2	12
Clerk, salesman, shopkeeper	4	—	3	7
Artistic/humanitarian	2	6	3	11
Previous	3	4	2	9
Other (inc. None)	1	2	1	4
	34	36	33	103

Asked to say what stopped them taking up the work they would have liked most, subjects said enough about personal shortcomings to prevent its being a bitter story, but "working class" answers were decidedly sourer than "middle class" ones, which were mostly blandly environmental. "Working class" subjects blamed "personal shortcomings" a quarter as often as "middle class" subjects, and "parents' poverty or non-support" twice as often—and perhaps they are right.

CONCLUSION

As T. H. Marshall has observed, "it is both remarkable and slightly ludicrous that we need to carry out the most elaborate research to discover the shape of stratification in modern societies".[70] It is less remarkable if we contrast the relative informality, complexity and nebulousness of the present social order with the apparently strict simplicity of earlier systems.

The economic order continues to define large groups with common interests in industrial relations, trade unionism and income distribution, but these

[70] "Changes in Social Stratification in the 20th Century" *Transactions of the Third World Congress of Sociology*, vol. 3, pp. 1-17.

carry over into politics only weakly, or not at all. As class loyalties, in the 19th-century sense, cease to be the compelling political bonds, religious, ethnic, and sheerly psychological ties come more clearly into prominence in the political audience. The processes of collective decision-making have spread to involve a wide range of functionally autonomous groups.

Parallel to the diffusion of power in the environs of the "easy-going State" goes a relaxation of stereotyped status judgments. In anonymous city and sleepy town alike, individual prestige becomes increasingly local, personal and manipulable. The reference groups which sustain the individual's sense of achievement are more and more self-chosen.

That these are trends should not, however, blind us to other contradictory movements which are full of interest, nor lead us to conclude that we are already some unimaginable distance from the class system of the 'thirties, or even that described by Bryce in 1911.[71] Working class attitudes continue to reflect a basically collectivist view of society, and middle-class attitudes a basically individualist one.[72] R. H. Tawney long ago noted as crucial the working man's realization that "if he is to attain well-being at all he must attain it not by personal advancement but as the result of a collective effort".[73] The great modern change is that within an increasingly bureaucratic environment of large public and private organizations, the traditional outlooks are being modified. The collectivism of the manual workers becomes diluted by greater "family-centredness";[74] the individualism of the white-collar worker is influenced by "instrumental collectivism" which makes him aware of the value of unionism. But this does not mean that the white-collar worker, still less the salaried professional man, is aligning himself with the interests and attitudes of the manual worker. Mills remarked that white-collar workers accept unions as "something to be used, rather than as something in which to believe. They are . . . valued for their help on the job. . . . Acceptance of them does not seem to lead to new identifications in other areas of living."[75]

Nor should we lazily assume that affluence automatically snuffs out radicalism. Rising prosperity may even sharpen consciousness of class if status differences lengthen or harden at the same time. Working-class affluence

> may turn out to have political consequences the reverse of those usually attributed to it . . . the development of marked discrepancies between income and status hierarchies tends to be productive of radical attitudes on the part of those who are unable to secure a degree of social recognition commensurate with their economic standing.[76]

Radical currents in the Labour movement arise from just such discrepancies, as in the case of skilled workers in Germany.[77] Bell and others have described

[71] James Bryce, *Modern Democracies*, vol. 2, pp. 197–8.

[72] J. H. Goldthorpe and D. Lockwood, "Affluence and the British Class Structure", *Sociological Review*, vol. 11, no. 2, 1963.

[73] R. H. Tawney, *Equality*, p. 151.

[74] See, *e.g.*, Zweig, *op. cit.*

[75] C. Wright Mills, *White Collar*, p. 308. A similar picture is given by Lockwood in *The Blackcoated Worker*.

[76] Goldthorpe and Lockwood, *loc. cit.*

[77] Lipset and Bendix, *op. cit.*, ch. 2; Mattei Dogan, "Le vote ouvrier", *Revue Française de Sociologie*, no. 1, 1960.

the emergence of the "Radical right" in America as the result of status politics arising from the divergence between rapid economic change and the position of old-established status hierarchies.[78]

The educational system is now more than ever the mainspring of social differentiation. As we can see from chapter 5, it is some way yet from providing equal opportunities in Australia, or from preventing serious waste of talent. The powerful modern influences working to keep the educational (and occupational) order "open", though clearly in the ascendant, will run repeatedly against vested interests in professional, religious, and ethnic preferment, and cannot be expected to have it all their own way. With the growth of education as a factor in stratification, public decisions about the allocation of resources to education, and the relative importance of various sectors of the educational system, may assume as much significance in politics as did full employment and the redistribution of income a generation ago.

A prime instance of the operation of these factors is the changing character of the Catholic community in Australia. Economic prosperity, occupational mobility, the exodus from the inner suburbs, and the educational explosion are combining to bring about a revolution in the status of the Irish-Catholic minority. One effect of this revolution is to expose the religious dimension of the Australian status structure, and thus to underline the long-standing existence of an elaborate system of social stratification. Because class in Australia has no history, many people are becoming aware of status distinctions as though they were a new phenomenon which marked the fading of the old egalitarian society. The relations between class, status, prestige and power have always been complex, and as study of them progresses it is likely to underline the continuity between the divisions appearing on the contemporary scene and those inherited from previous generations.

[78] Daniel Bell (ed.), *The Radical Right* (new edition, 1963).

4 Religious Behaviour*

Affiliation, Belief and Behaviour

At each census Australians are requested, but not compelled, to state their religion. In 1961 they responded as follows:

		Percentage of population
Church of England	3,668,931	34·8
Catholic (including Roman Catholic)	2,620,011	24·6
Methodist	1,076,395	10·2
Presbyterian	976,518	9·3
Lutheran	160,181	1·5
Greek Orthodox	154,924	1·5
Baptist	149,819	1·5
Protestant (undefined)	98,551	·9
Churches of Christ	95,641	·9
Congregational	73,526	·7
Salvation Army	51,084	·5
Seventh-day Adventist	31,626	·3
Other Christian	116,919	1·1
Total Christian	9,274,126	88·2
Hebrew	59,343	·6
Other non-Christian	9,475	·1
Indefinite	24,762	·2
No religion	37,550	·4
No reply	1,102,930	10·5
	10,508,186	100

The pattern of affiliations revealed in this table can be explained almost wholly in terms of migration: a very large majority of Australians identify themselves, at census time, with whatever was the faith of their ancestors in Europe. The only denominations on the list not brought out from Europe by immigrants are the Churches of Christ and the Seventh Day Adventists, two sects of mid-nineteenth century American origin. The only substantial changes in the pattern since 1947—rises in the proportions of Catholic, Lutheran and Greek Orthodox adherents—have been caused by migration.

* The writer is grateful for a grant from the Social Science Research Council towards a study of which this essay forms part.

43

The persistence through generation after generation of adherence to a particular denomination suggests that religion in Australia is, among other things, a habit.[1] The Victorian footballer, Lou Richards, explaining why he came to play for Collingwood rather than one of eleven other teams, has said that he was born into a Collingwood family. The Australian believer asked why he adheres to one denomination rather than another could normally give a similar answer.

The census does not tell us what effect religious affiliation has on people beyond disposing them to cast a kind of vote on census day. The editor of a recent volume called *The Pattern of Australian Culture* declares that religion "cannot be regarded as a cultural force in Australia" and leaves it out of the book.[2] Can that be right? Does the custom of religious affiliation impinge on no other aspect of our corporate life? It could hardly seem so to any observer of, say, our labour movement, our drinking laws, our Sundays, or our schools. At many points the attachment of Australians to religion affects their public and private lives; and at the same time other aspects of those lives affect their apprehension and practice of religion. To study this encounter of faith and society is the task of sociology.

Many of the relevant questions have been asked already of other countries, and especially of America. "Does a man's religious commitment *really* influence his everyday actions, especially a man who lives in the highly secularized environment of the modern . . . metropolis? Is there *really* a difference between the believer and the unbeliever in the market place or in the voting booth? Does the *type* of religious commitment make a difference: do the actions of Protestants differ from those of Catholics and Jews in the fields of politics, economics, and family life? If so, are these differences due to the influence of their religion, or to something else?"[3] What is it like for Protestants and Catholics to struggle for moral authority and political power in a community?[4] How are parishioners of a particular church distributed along a scale from indifference to utter devotion?[5] How far have the doctrine, polity and *mores* of a church been changed by infiltration or assault from the society in which it lives?[6] What kinds of people join heterodox sects?[7] Can "secularization" be measured and mapped over the century or so of industrial

[1] The evidence for continuity is to be found in the six Commonwealth censuses (1911–61), in the census of 1901 taken in co-operation by all states, and in numerous censuses of individual colonies before 1900. There is no comparable information about Great Britain or the United States, where the census contains no question on religion. Students of the sociology of religion in Australia thus have a rich source not available for the other countries. So far this source has been barely tapped. The basic information gathered in each Commonwealth census is reported in *Commonwealth Year Books*, which are the source for any figures cited in this essay for which no other source is indicated.

[2] A. L. McLeod (ed.), *The Pattern of Australian Culture*, p. vi.

[3] G. Lenski, *The Religious Factor*, p. 1.

[4] K. Underwood, *Protestant and Catholic*.

[5] J. H. Fichter, S.J., *Social Relations in the Urban Parish*.

[6] H. R. Niebuhr, *The Social Sources of Denominationalism*; W. Herberg, *Protestant-Catholic-Jew*; P. L. Berger, *The Noise of Solemn Assemblies*. This last work refers to other recent studies.

[7] Most work on this matter is American; but for the study of Australia, the one investigation made so far of English sects is perhaps more relevant: B. R. Wilson, *Sects and Society*. Wilson's bibliography refers to much of the American literature.

urban society?[8] So little work has been done towards answering such questions in their Australian setting that any review of it must be both cursory and patchy.

Some Australians are readier than others to let their behaviour be affected by the churches for which they vote at the census. Many who profess affiliation are not counted as members by their putative denominations; but criteria for membership vary so much from church to church that it is fruitless to compare numbers. Attendance at worship is a more illuminating index of religious activity. According to the Gallup Poll in 1961, 27% of Australians said that they went to church every week, 48% said that they went occasionally, and 25% said that they never went. The poll showed substantial differences from denomination to denomination between profession and reported behaviour. Among professed Catholics, 54% said that they went to church every week; for Methodists the figure was 31%; for Presbyterians, 14%; for Anglicans, 13%. Although the figure for Baptists was not given on this occasion, earlier polls had shown that they were the only Protestant group in which more than half the professed adherents said that they attended worship every week. In terms of attendance, Catholics appear to be the largest denomination: of every 100 Australians claiming to attend church every week, about 45 are Catholics, 21 Anglicans, 10 Methodists, 7 Presbyterians and 4 Baptists. Among those who say that they attend worship occasionally or never, some 45 in every 100 are Anglicans, 14 Methodists, 12 Catholics, 12 Presbyterians and 1.5 Baptists. When these figures are read alongside the census figures, it appears that the practice of adhering nominally to a church without participating actively in its worship is most common among Anglicans and Presbyterians, less common among Methodists, and strikingly less common among both Baptists and Catholics.

The Church of England has the lowest proportion of attendance to census adherence mainly because it is informally regarded by people of English origin as the residual church. As an Anglican journal has said, the Church of England in Australia has many "sleeping partners . . . alienated in their sympathies from the Church of England even though they are not religious enough to join any other Church or irreligious enough to become agnostics or atheists. . . . This makes the statistics look bad. . . ."[9] People of a similar disposition and a Scottish origin help to make the Presbyterian statistics look bad; it is the kirk of their ancestors, not some other church, that they are staying away from.

It is probably these two denominations whose statistics are affected most by the reluctance of people to be candid, on the census form, about their indifference or hostility to religion. According to the census, adherents of "no religion" amount to only 0.4% of the population. Yet in a survey of the Melbourne suburb of Ringwood, 43% of those respondents who called themselves "working class", and 24% of "middle class" respondents, said that they had no church affiliation.[10] In another outer suburb of Melbourne, studied by

---

[8] The work of French pioneers on this subject is sketched in F. Boulard, *An Introduction to Religious Sociology* (translated and introduced by M. J. Jackson). On England see K. S. Inglis, *Churches and the Working Classes in Victorian England;* E. R. Wickham, *Church and People in an Industrial City.*

[9] *Australian Church Record,* Sydney, 1 March 1962.

[10] A. F. Davies, "Social Class in the New Suburb", *Westerly,* no. 3, 1961, p. 17.

Scott and U'Ren, 23% said that they had no religious affiliation, or did not specify one.[11] The churchless, it appears, are more inclined to reveal themselves in an informal private interview than on a census form, and certainly outnumber the 10.5% who decline to answer the census question. The private surveys, however, report only on adults, while the census figures include what parents say about the religion of children. It may be that some parents who describe themselves as having no religion, or who make no reply, allot their children to a religious denomination and do so fairly arbitrarily, on the basis of a class in religious instruction at school or a Sunday School picnic.

Why are Catholics such active worshippers? An answer occurs readily to anti-Catholics: that the priests, who dominate their flock, make the sheep go to Mass. It is indeed true that presence at Mass is spiritually necessary to Catholics in a sense more precise than is attendance at a religious service for Protestants. But as this is true of Catholics everywhere, it cannot explain why the proportion of Catholics attending worship in some European countries is so far below the proportion in Australia. There must, it seems, be social as well as spiritual reasons for the Australian pattern. What are they? A short answer is that the ancestors of most Catholics came from Ireland, where a solidarity between the priest and the plain man had grown up under alien Protestant rule; that a sense of community persisted among the descendants of Irish immigrants; and that the Catholic Church set up a system of schools which became both popular and efficient.[12] Why, finally, are Baptists so much likelier than other Protestants to attend worship? Gallup Polls tell us that in attitudes as well as behaviour, Baptists are more inclined than other Protestants to let their religion, rather than some other aspect of their social identity, be decisive. Why? How far is their following a stable one, protected by kinship and other sources of fellowship against the corrosion of secularity? How far is membership fluid, and how far, if at all, does the movement act as a staging-camp for seekers moving between the larger, more worldly Protestant groups and the warmer heterodox sects? Do Baptist congregations draw more nourishment than other Protestants from revivalist campaigns such as that of Billy Graham (himself a Baptist)? Why is it that old-fashioned anti-Popery burns so brightly among them?

Since most Australians approve of religion, it is likely that some exaggerate their propensity to attend worship when they are asked about it. Scott and U'Ren asked people not merely to say whether they went to church but to describe what happened there. "Overall, less than 50% could give any details at all of what takes place at church. It appeared in many cases that what knowledge was possessed was based on church participation in childhood."[13] Some of those who answer "occasionally" to Gallup interviewers may mean that they went when they were children. Attendance figures are not, of course, a direct index of piety. They include not only the devout, but the lady who goes to show a new hat rather than to hear the sermon.[14] On the other hand,

---

[11] D. Scott and R. U'Ren, *Leisure*, p. 22.

[12] See H. Mayer (ed.), *Catholics and the Free Society*, chapters 1, 2 and 5.

[13] *Op. cit.*, p. 40.

[14] A clergyman may recognize this fact without being depressed by it. "What if Mother does treat churchgoing as a hat parade, and Dad analyses the congregation during the Communion? Their children may yet catch a spark of the Divine flame. . . ." (Rev. J. G. Steele in *Anglican*, Sydney, 15 April 1960.)

many people who do not attend worship are not wholly indifferent. In England, the Gallup Poll reports, 79% believe that one can be a Christian without going to church. Scott and U'Ren found that the proportion of people regarding the church as important was much higher than the proportion who ever went to worship.

It is theoretically possible that many people who profess adherence to a church but do not attend its worship perform religious acts at home. "In any community," wrote Alan Walker in 1945, "in addition to organized religion, certain religious practices are usually carried on within the homes of the people." He was writing of Cessnock, where, he found, "little home-religion remains". Family prayers had stopped, Protestant ministers agreed; grace before meals was said in only 15% of homes; some Catholic families said the rosary, but a priest reported that the practice was declining.[15] The Gallup Poll reported in 1951 that over the whole nation, grace before meals was said by 34% of families—which suggests either that "home-religion" was abnormally low in Cessnock or that some people in the national survey crossed their fingers and answered in terms of what they felt they ought to do. In 11% of homes, it was claimed, a child said grace; in 10%, father; in 8%, mother; in 1%, another person; and in 4%, everyone. Among professing Baptists, 52% reported grace; Methodists, 46%; Presbyterians, 33%; Anglicans, 26%. These bodies of Protestants, it will be noted, rank themselves in the same order both as sayers of grace and as public worshippers. Catholics, according to this survey, were much less active as sayers of grace than as churchgoers: only 32%—a proportion just below the average for all Australians—reported the practice. Until an enterprising sociologist conceals microphones under dining-tables, there is no way of deciding whether these figures are accurate. It is likewise difficult to test what the Gallup interviewers have been told about bible-reading. In 1954 the Bible was reported to be in 86% of Australian homes: only cookery books (90%) and dictionaries (88%) were more common, 70% reported an atlas, 66% a gardening book, 53% an encyclopedia, and 45% a street directory. Bibles were thus almost twice as numerous as street directories. How long is it, people were asked, since you read the Bible for ten minutes or more? 18% said that they had done so within the last week, and a further 21% said that they had done so within the last six months. The 63% who said that they had spent ten minutes at the Bible within the last nine years included 80% of Baptists, 71% of Presbyterians, 67% of Methodists, 63% of Anglicans and 50% of Catholics. As in the case of church attendance and grace before meals, Baptists professed to be the most active among Protestants. Presbyterians, who lagged behind Methodists in the other cases, were here ahead. Half the Catholic population reported not having spent ten minutes at the Bible within the last ten years. A similar question in 1960 showed differences not only between denominations but between age-groups: people who said that they had looked at the Bible within the last week included 34% of those over 40, 24% of those in their thirties, and only 19% of those in their twenties.

"Home-religion" does not appear to flourish among those Australians who adhere nominally to a church but do not attend its worship. A Methodist

---

[15] A. Walker , *Coaltown: a Social Survey of Cessnock*, p. 65. As often when religiosity is said to have declined, the facts about present apathy are far more precise than the facts about past fervour.

minister has argued that it may be a mistake to consider such people as adherents at all. "Is it the proud boast of the Christian Church that about 90% of the Australian population claims Christian allegiance (or adherence) . . . when . . . a large proportion of these people are only further perjuring their souls by so doing? When on his census form a person says . . . that he was born in Ceylon, probably he was; but when he says he is a Methodist, there is at least an even chance that his grandmother's sister's husband knew a man who lived near a church, or something nearly as remote. . . . There may be some value in the census figures for 'Methodists' or any other category of religion, but only if they are handled with care by a qualified researcher. . . . "[16] But few church leaders can distinguish clearly the spiritual perjurer from the decent suburban man just out of their reach. An Anglican clergyman testifies:

> You will find, as you chat to your non-church-going neighbour, that he will blithely tell you that he frequently watches the Epilogue on television, he occasionally hears a religious talk, that he always gives a donation to the Salvation Army annual Self-Denial appeal, and that he would never dream of passing the church by when his daughter wants to get married. So there is a combination of friendliness with indifference.[17]

A Methodist paper gives this portrait of the nominal Christian who is "not a pagan or a moron" but is "right there on the fringe of the Church's life":

> As an infant he was baptized in the Church; as a child attended Sunday School; as a youth held membership in the youth organizations; there was a time when his life was vitally linked with the life of the local Church. But then marriage came, and with the arrival of a family together with the strong demands and pressures of modern life, the drift from the Church took place. . . . Father now takes the children to Sunday School and more often than not calls for them an hour later; but the habit of worship of former years has been lost, and so it's home to mow the lawn, wash the car, catch up with the odd jobs . . . , and, if the weather is good, take the family for a picnic drive on Sunday afternoon.
> We meet him at Lodge, Rotary, Apex or Lions Club, we fraternize with him on the bowling green, the cricket field, the tennis club, the golf links. We rub shoulders with him in the office, the factory, the workshop. . . . He is a good fellow and we value his friendship. He is always ready to give a pound or, if he can afford it a fiver, to the special appeals that the Church makes from time to time. . . . [18]

How is such a man, asks the paper, to be moved "from the fringe into the warmer circle of the Church's fellowship"?[19] To some church leaders this now seems the central question in a country such as Australia. The Methodist journal offers no easy answer. Its solution is to call for a recognition that evangelism is the only reason for the Church's existence, to exhort "everyone, even unto the least in the smallest congregation", to be an agent of Christ's

[16] *Spectator*, Melbourne, 9 January 1963.
[17] A. V. Maddick in *Anglican*, 13 December 1962.
[18] *Methodist*, Sydney, 16 July 1960.
[19] *Ibid.*, 23 July 1960.

mission. "When this vision and sense of vocation comes upon the Church in the setting of its local congregation the problem of Christian nominality will have largely disappeared." No doubt; but how many of the Australians, Catholic or Protestant, who do attend church regularly, can be fired in the 1960s with apostolic zeal to reach the friend on the fringe? For more than a century Protestant and Catholic leaders in Australia, as in other urban nations, have been deploring the corrosion of church life by the worldly world. The menace of the secular society has had two aspects, which may be labelled pleasure and commerce; and by 1960 the most popular pastime of Australians, including churchgoers, was to sit in front of an electronic device which purveyed both. Fifty years ago the president of the Methodist Conference in New South Wales said: "the difficulties that we find it hardest to cope with arise from the large mass of inertia within our own churches and from the growing absorption in material things of those that are without and even to a large extent of those that are within."[20] And that was even before the moving pictures talked and hire purchase became part of the Australian way of life. By 1958, so it seemed to a Catholic paper, "the traditional conception of the place of religion in personal as well as public life has become completely alien to the thought of the Australian 'man in the street'. The assumption upon which our whole social order of today is built is that the chief business of men is to organize their earthly life efficiently in terms of material well-being and happiness. . . . "[21] If the marginal Christian cannot be reached except by the spiritual heroism of a rank and file which has itself been so affected by the ideology of pleasure and commerce, he seems likely to stay on the edge.

A study of what religion means to Australians might begin by asking what adherents know about the doctrines of their church. The authors of one sociological investigation argue that Methodist farmers have done better than their Catholic neighbours because "their religious ideology . . . gives meaning to work as a means of achieving salvation" whereas

> the resolution of tension for the Catholics has tended to be a cathartic, rather than a creative, process, and the dispensation of grace is directly related to the diligence with which one performs his tasks towards the Church as an institution. These tasks do not require an economic means for their realization, for grace is disbursed by external means rather than directly realized in personal experience.[22]

Even if this were an accurate account of the relevant theology, which it is not, we should want evidence that the farmers in question *knew* what their Church's doctrine of grace was; and no such evidence appears to have been sought.[23] What evidence there is suggests that even among church-goers, knowledge of doctrine is slender. In Perth a newspaper reporter asked forty people in a busy street what they knew of Easter. "Fewer than half of those

---

[20] J. E. Carruthers, Retiring Address to Methodist Conference of N.S.W., 1914, in J. E. Carruthers, Addresses, etc. (Mitchell Library).

[21] *Tribune*, Melbourne, 23 October 1958.

[22] O. A. Oeser and F. E. Emery, *Social Structure and Personality in a Rural Community*, p. 39.

[23] A Methodist minister has said to the writer: "There is not a scrap of evidence in my experience of rural communities to suggest that farmers (or any one else) worked hard or less hard according to their religion."

interviewed knew that Our Lord was crucified on Good Friday and rose again on Easter Day. . . . A housewife laden with shopping thought that Easter celebrated the first full moon of the year. . . . An oil company representative . . . said that Easter celebrated the birth of Christ. . . . For an elderly pensioner, Easter had no special significance. A bus inspector said he 'would not have a clue'. A G.P.O. messenger said: 'I do not take much notice of Easter.' "[24] A more systematic exploration of religious knowledge was undertaken in 1960 and 1961 on behalf of a programme of Church of England Character Guidance Courses for recruits and apprentices in the Australian Regular Army.[25] There were two groups of subjects, 770 regular army recruits and 143 apprentices. The recruits, whose average age was twenty, came from every state and from many occupations. They answered a questionnaire a month or so after they entered the army. The apprentices, who had been selected for technical training and entered from secondary school, had been at the army school in some cases for one or two years, attending church services as part of their training, when they answered the questionnaire; and they gave better informed answers than the other group. Most could name the two Testaments of the Bible (78% of recruits, 85% of apprentices). Not many could say in which book the story of the Creation is told (22%, 33%). Most could say where Jesus was born (62%, 70%); not quite as many knew where he was crucified (49%, 65%). More could identify Pontius Pilate (32%, 55%) than could name the three Persons of the Trinity (21%, 41%). A higher proportion could say who Jesus Christ was (84%, 92%) than could answer any other question except: What does Christmas Day celebrate? (91%, 96%). Not quite as many knew what Good Friday celebrated (63%, 75%), and fewer knew what Easter Day celebrated (49%, 70%). Hardly any knew what Whitsunday celebrated (0.9%, 2%). Few knew how many days there are in Lent (21%, 39%). Most could say what the word "crucified" meant (65%, 80%), but not what the word "gospel" meant (9%, 13%). Not many could say what a creed was (6%, 22%), and fewer still could say what the word "Catholic" meant in the phrase "I believe in the Holy Ghost, the Holy Catholic Church" (4%, 12%). Only 19% of the recruits could write out the Lord's Prayer. (In the case of the apprentices, the ability to do so was not tested.) "The Church of England," both groups were told, "has two main Sacraments. One is Holy Communion. What is the other?" The answer as set out in the Thirty-nine Articles is Baptism; and 80% of the recruits and 90% of the apprentices had been baptized. Not many knew the answer (9%, 17%). The greatest difference between the recruits and the better-instructed apprentices appeared when both groups were asked: What is Confirmation? 28% of recruits had been confirmed, but only 8% answered accurately; 58% of apprentices had been confirmed, and 42% knew what had happened to them. "The analysis", wrote the chaplain who compiled it, "indicates that the average young Australian man knows very little of the simple facts of the Christian Faith, of the Bible and of Church practice."

Ignorance may, however, go with loyalty and even with ardour; solid fidelity does not depend on a nice understanding of doctrine. Liston Pope

---

[24] *Anglican*, 14 April 1961.
[25] *Ibid.*, 6 September 1962; *Australian Church Record*, 13 September 1962.

found that mill workers in North Carolina showed "no interest in theological questions; they simply accept notions coming from a wide variety of sources and weld them together without regard for consistency".[26] Kenneth Underwood says of a lower middle-class Protestant family in Massachusetts: "To ask the Bakers the meaning for them of the doctrine of 'justification by faith alone' produces only an embarrassed admission of ignorance."[27] Yet these people are, by some tests, keen Protestants. Ronald Frankenberg reports that in the divided chapels of Wales, "while the theological reasons for schism are no longer remembered by chapel-goers, the social rift between the chapels remains and invades every sphere of social activity".[28] A mild form of identification with the church as a community is reported in Alan Dougan's study of Bathurst. Although only a quarter of the population are active members of churches, "on special occasions most members of the community relate themselves in some way to their church and in argument would defend it. It would be an almost unheard of thing for the clergyman not to be welcome in a house occupied by members of his denomination, whether active or nominal."[29] If examined about doctrine, the people of Bathurst might fail; when attendance at worship is counted, they score low; but their lives are affected by religion in ways that are visible only if a denomination is seen as a sort of large family. The sense of family may not only lead people to welcome the minister; it may affect their public behaviour—by moving them, for example, to vote against an outsider at elections. It is said to be a law of political behaviour in South Australia that only a Methodist can win the seat of Wallaroo. This does not mean that the successful candidate must assent to, or even follow, the theology of John Wesley, or prefer certain forms of church government to others. It means simply that the Methodists who are so numerous on the Yorke Peninsula must think of their man as one of them.

A sense of identification with a religious denomination, or more broadly with a religious tradition (especially, in Australia, the Protestant tradition) may thus affect the sentiment and conduct of somebody who does not go to church and performs no private worship. The examples given above are rural; and for several reasons, among them the greater tendency for religious denominations in the country to be endogamous, the rural nominal adherent is more likely than the urban one to be aware that he belongs to a religious family. It may, indeed, be more illuminating to see the urban denominational community as a club than as a family. Whatever analogy the observer uses, he must look at other evidence than figures of adherence and attendance if he is to survey adequately the place of religion in the lives of Australians. Private and public attitudes to alcohol, betting, Sunday observance and censorship are all affected by religious affiliation. So, in Australia as elsewhere, are the rites of passage—those ceremonies which mark a person's journey through the stages of life. The rest of this essay, which omits many important

[26] L. Pope, *Millhands and Preachers*, p. 87.

[27] K. Underwood, *Protestant and Catholic*, p. 89. "The Bakers" are a composite picture.

[28] R. Frankenberg, *Village on the Border: a Social Study of Religion, Politics and Football in North Wales*, p. 58.

[29] A. Dougan, "Social Factors in Denominationalism: an investigation of some of these factors in the city of Bathurst, N.S.W." M.A. thesis, University of Sydney, 1960, p. 147. This is the only Australian investigation comparable in sophistication and depth to good American studies.

matters, will be made up of exploratory remarks about religion and the lives of Australians from marriage to death.

Marriage

A wedding is the one event in the lives of most Australians in which they submit, however nominally, to the authority of a Christian minister. The proportion of Australians who said in 1961 that they were Christians (88.2%) was almost exactly the same as the proportion married that year who went to a church rather than a registry office (88.4%). Fifty years ago the proportion of church marriages was higher (in 1911, 96%). It would be risky to interpret the difference as revealing a simple decline in spirituality, if only because the higher percentage of the old days included customers of the entrepreneur in Sydney who advertised: "Marriages legally solemnized by clergymen any denomination. No notice required. Any hour. Witnesses free. Fee, 15s."[30] It included, too, the clients of certain religious denominations which no longer exist, and which used to be described by the Commonwealth Statistician with a candour that has also disappeared:

> The extraordinary number of marriages credited to some denominations, the number of whose adherents, according to the Census returns, was very small indeed, is not inconsistent with the supposition that some of these denominations have been created for the purpose of obtaining the registration necessary to conduct marriages, or to be connected with a so-called "Matrimonial Agency".[31]

Whatever the reasons, the proportion of brides and grooms willing to be married without any religious auspices has trebled in the last fifty years. One writer has hinted that the 11%–12% who marry at a civil ceremony may tend to be the same people as the 11% who decline to identify themselves at the census with any religious denomination.[32] If that were so, we should expect a close correlation state by state between the two rates; and there is not. The variations from state to state in rates of civil marriage are so great, indeed, as to discourage any simple generalization about the phenomenon. In 1961 the proportion of marriages not celebrated in a church was 15.4% in New South Wales, 14.8% in Western Australia, 13.5% in Tasmania, 11.3% in South Australia, 9.1% in Victoria, and 3.8% in Queensland. (In the Northern Territory it was 19.8%, and in the Australian Capital Territory 19.6%). Even when allowance is made for differences state by state in religious affiliation and in the distribution of population between rural and urban areas, large differences remain.

The propensity to have ministers of religion celebrate marriage declined most sharply in the 1920s: the civil marriage rate more than doubled between 1921 and 1931, and rose by only 1% in the next twenty years. The rise in civil marriage is doubtless not unrelated to the rise in divorce. Superficially the correlation is striking; both the divorce rate and the proportion of civil marriage have moved from about 4% fifty years ago to about 12% now.

---

[30] *Sydney Morning Herald,* 11 April 1900.

[31] *Commonwealth Year Book,* 1, 1901-7, p. 198.

[32] B. Fitzpatrick, *The Australian Commonwealth,* p. 13: "Although only a handful specifically stated they had no religion, the percentage not answering at all is roughly equivalent to the percentage of marriages celebrated by civil registrars."

But the two proportions have moved differently decade by decade; and even if all re-marriages of divorced people were now performed in registry offices (which they are not), that would still leave many civil marriages unaccounted for.

Australians are still much more attached to church marriages than other English-speaking peoples. In New Zealand civil marriages are half as common again as in Australia, and in England and the United States they are more than twice as common as here.[33] Australian couples who describe themselves as adherents of the Church of England appear more likely than those of any other church to marry in a registry office. If, however, an Anglican marries an adherent of another denomination, and does so at a religious ceremony, the wedding is likelier to be in the church of the non-Anglican partner than in the Church of England.[34] Affiliation to the Presbyterian, Methodist or Baptist denomination pulls more strongly on a person approaching marriage than does affiliation to the Church of England. It is likely that transfer of adherence at marriage accounts for certain slight long-term changes in denominational affiliation within Protestantism, and especially for the declining adherence to Congregationalism.[35] In some marriages of mixed denominations, neither partner's church gains or loses at the altar. Even after marriage today, Dougan found in Bathurst, two Protestants might continue to belong to their respective denominations. The "mixed marriage" of partners from two non-Catholic denominations is a source of possible tension, which may be serious if, for example, one partner adheres to the Church of England in a "high" diocese, or if both live in a country town where each denomination tends to live a separate communal life. But the mixture is mild, compared with the mixture of Catholic and Protestant.

When a Catholic marries a Protestant, romance has proved stronger than religion. The mixture is deplored by the clergy on both sides. The Australian Catholic Truth Society has even addressed to Protestants a pamphlet called *Don't marry a Catholic* (1958). The canon law of the Catholic Church forbids mixed marriages unless the bishop grants a dispensation, which he will normally do if he believes that the alternative will be a greater evil. If the parties, instead of seeking a dispensation from the Catholic bishop, marry in a Protestant church—as the late Prime Minister, J. B. Chifley, a Catholic, did in 1914—the Catholic is excommunicated and the marriage is regarded by his church as an adulterous union. Protestant ministers resent the undertakings required from the non-Catholic partner. As the Anglican bishops put

---

[33] *New Zealand Official Year Book*, 1962, p. 128; *Facts and Figures about the Church of England*, 1962, p. 57; P. H. Jacobson, *American Marriage and Divorce*, pp. 55-9. In New Zealand the rate was 18% in 1960; in England it was 28% in 1957. For the United States there are no official figures and wide variations between states; Jacobson estimates that from 1939 to 1948 the national rate was about 25%.

[34] This statement is based on a comparison of annual marriage statistics for 1960 with figures of religious affiliation as shown at the census of 1961. The writer is grateful to certain demographers who helped him read these and other statistics relating to marriage, who pointed out hazards in the way of interpreting them, and whom he will not name lest some other demographer, finding the interpretation reckless, should judge them guilty by association.

[35] Traffic between non-Catholic denominations may be more common than is indicated by figures which report only net gains or losses. Dougan found that in Bathurst a quarter of the active Presbyterians had come from other denominations, especially the Church of England. Change of denomination was usually associated with a marriage of mixed denominations.

it at Lambeth in 1948: "The Conference earnestly warns members of our communion against contracting marriages with Roman Catholics under the conditions imposed by modern Roman Canon law, especially as these conditions involve, among other things, a promise to have their children brought up in a religious system which they cannot themselves accept." An Anglican clergyman in Australia warns an enquirer that

> heartache follows in the life of most of those who sign this promise. Your children may consider you as one who is completely unwilling to share in their religious life; and so the bonds of confidence and security will be sundered. On the other hand, they may, through loyalty to you, withdraw from the spiritual life of the Roman Catholic Church. Either way, their religious development will be impeded.[36]

The Catholic priest who wishes Protestants well, and the Protestant who is friendly towards Catholics, are just as hostile to mixed marriages as those less amiably disposed. Mixed marriages, said a Catholic student of them in 1902, "are not only dangerous to the Catholic religion, but destructive of every form of religion".[37] Three years later the Catholic bishops described mixed marriages as "those unions, unfortunately frequent amongst us in Australia, where the interests of the Faith are set aside for sordid interests or worldly advantage . . . "[38]—implying that the will to marry out of the church is a sign of social ambition. "Unhappily", said another Catholic observer early in this century, "Catholic wives sometimes forsake the acquaintance and friendship of earlier years, especially if their marriage elevates them, even imperceptibly, in the scale of wealth or in social recognition."[39] Whether or not the Catholic partner moves up in the eyes of the world, he or she is likely to move out of a Catholic milieu. This is especially true in country towns; but even in the cities, husband and wife are unlikely to have mutual friends with a strong church affiliation. The partners will tend either to move in separate groups (and this is likely to be a source of strain) or to find friends who are not themselves identified closely with any church; and if each of the partners had a strong affiliation before marriage, the latter alternative represents a loss to both churches. Meanwhile each partner has a mother-in-law alert to see where, if anywhere, the children are baptized, and where they go to school.[40]

But it is easy, in interpreting the religious implications of mixed marriages, to confuse cause and effect. Someone contemplating such a marriage is, in a sense, already part of the way out of his church. The marriage of Joseph Benedict Chifley and Elizabeth McKenzie in 1914 illustrates this and other aspects of the practice.[41] In Bathurst, where Catholics tend even today to form a separate community, it was no light decision for a Catholic and a Protestant to marry each other, as these two people decided in 1914. The bride was the daughter of a Scottish immigrant who was a seatholder, and

[36] A. V. Maddick in *Anglican*, 27 January 1961.
[37] M. MacNamara in *Australasian Catholic Record*, VIII, 1902, p. 306.
[38] Pastoral letter of plenary council, *ibid.*, XI, 1905, p. 573.
[39] T. A. Fitzgerald in *ibid.*, VIII, 1902, p. 228.
[40] For American evidence that mixed marriages are more hazardous than others, see J. T. Landis in *American Sociological Review*, vol. 14, 1949, pp. 401–7; and for testimony from American clergy that both partners' churches lose by mixed marriages, see K. Underwood, *Protestant and Catholic*, pp. 168–9.
[41] All that follows about the marriage is taken from L. F. Crisp, *Ben Chifley*.

later an elder, at St. Stephen's Presbyterian Church. The groom's mother and his father's father were immigrants from Ireland, and he took his second name from a suggestion by the Mother Superior of a Benedictine convent where his mother once worked. In leisure activities their paths would not have crossed. They met because the groom and the bride's father both worked on the railways. By reading the works of infidels—Bellamy, Jack London, Shaw and Gibbon—Chifley had perhaps loosened his mental loyalty to the church of his fathers before he met Miss McKenzie. To court her, Chifley had to enter her milieu. "Not a partygoer or dancer, Chifley would nevertheless escort Elizabeth and accompany her home whenever she wished to attend social gatherings of friends or her Presbyterian church community." The marriage was for Chifley "a crisis in his life", for it meant that the sacraments of his church were withdrawn from him.

> It meant a breach of family solidarity, a breach of solidarity with friends in and out of Bathurst and with a strongly Roman Catholic neighbourhood. Elizabeth McKenzie, with an equally strong and proud Presbyterian connection, was firm for marriage according to the rites in which she had been brought up. Chifley's most intimate Roman Catholic friends sought to make clear to him how painful they and his family would find any weakening of religious discipline on his part. Feeling as he did about Elizabeth, he decided that the issue reduced itself to this. He was an engine driver, often away from home at night. He could not ask the wife who would be staying in Bathurst by herself to break with family (if it should come to that) and be altogether alone during his absences. "One of us", as he said to a friend at the time, "has to take the knock. It'd better be me."

They were married at a Presbyterian Church in Sydney, "primarily to spare embarrassment or awkwardness which his family and friends might have felt had he married in the Presbyterian Church in Bathurst. There was no account of the wedding in the columns of either of the Bathurst newspapers." Chifley's parents received the bride as their own (a Catholic friend recalled) "as we all did, and life went on as usual, except for this shadow always in the background". Chifley drove his wife to and from her church every Sunday, and attended Mass every week himself. For him, says his biographer, "the marriage had severed no traditional Church loyalties. Moreover, his maintenance of attendance no doubt softened the situation for the Chifley family." His church-going "remained anything but casual and irregular down the years, suggesting something deeper than a desire to remain on good terms with his old associates. It may, of course, have stemmed from his compelling urge to belong, to maintain solidarity and continuity." But in the eyes of the church he was living in adultery. "I do go to Church regularly", he wrote late in his life, "but I am afraid the Church does not regard me as one of its model children." On another occasion, to a Protestant, he said: "I was brought up a Catholic but I'm not one now." When Chifley moved to Sydney and later to Canberra, his wife did not go with him. As he was dying, a priest was called. The bishop permitted him to have a church burial. His story is a vivid reminder of the pathos that can lie behind the statistics about mixed marriages.

The one sure way of reducing the figure is to arrange social segregation of Catholics from Protestants. An American priest has said that "if parents insisted that their sons and daughters date only Catholics, the number of mixed marriages could be decreased by 50%".[42] In their efforts to provide a Catholic social environment for young people, the church and parents in Australia are given a great deal more help than in the United States by the dual school system. Half the Catholic children of the United States are educated in the company of non-Catholic children in the public schools. In Australia the proportion was similar seventy years ago; but the challenge of the liberals and sectarians who imposed the trinity of freedom, compulsion and secularity evoked from Australian Catholics such a prodigious response that by 1950 four-fifths of their children were in church schools. In 1902 a priest reflected that "friendship formed in school days may ripen into friendship of another kind in after years".[43] It has since become abnormal for Catholic and non-Catholic children to meet each other at school; and that appears to be the main reason why mixed marriages have become less common. They might be more frequent if Catholic parents were to become less satisfied with church schools, or if the pressures from a society that is largely Protestant and secular were to erode, in many Catholic minds, the belief that marriage is a sacrament.

To André Siegfried, a Frenchman visiting the United States, it seemed that in Catholic countries marriage has been considered as a sacrament, and hence the family, as an institution, is regarded as more important than the individuals who form it; but in a Protestant nation, marriage has been not a sacrament but "a contract, carried out under the auspices of the Church, between two human beings who pledge their faith, and thus the individuals are more important than the institution".[44] There is bound to be confusion, so Siegfried argues, "in a country where the two essentially different conceptions of marriage, that of Catholics and that of Protestants, exist side by side". In Australia, too, this is one source of confusion, or complexity, in thinking about marriage. "What is marriage?" asks an Anglican. "Isn't it a Sacrament of the Church, doesn't the Prayer Book urge the partners to take the Holy Communion as soon as possible after it? Or is it a lawful means of letting two people live together in social righteousness?"[45] Anglicans are well placed to see the dilemma, belonging as they do to a church which regards itself as both Catholic and Protestant. If the celebrant takes the "Protestant" view of marriage, has he any right to investigate the spiritual fitness of bride or groom for the ceremony? Outside the Catholic Church, clergymen in Australia will normally marry anybody who asks. Most of the exceptions are Anglicans who try to pay at least lip-service to the stringent conditions laid down in the Prayer Book. Many Anglican clergy who ignore these conditions think that they are wrong to do so. When incumbents throughout Australia were asked, with reference to marriage: "Is our pastoral reluctance to press such 1662 Prayer Book requirements as are relevant today, a significant factor in perpetuating the spiritual slackness of Anglicans?" nearly four-fifths answered Yes.[46] One Anglican clergyman has said that his church "ought to have

---

[42] Quoted in J. H. Fichter, S.J., *Dynamics of a City Church*, vol. I of *Southern Parish*, p. 98.
[43] M. MacNamara, *loc. cit.*
[44] A. Siegfried, *America at Mid-Century*, p. 221.
[45] *Anglican*, 24 July 1959.
[46] *Ibid.*, 28 February 1963.

56

enough moral courage to refuse a large percentage of the marriages she now solemnizes. To the statement that we would lose many people by doing this, I can only reply that you cannot lose something you haven't got in the first place, and I don't suppose that more than about ten per cent. of those who come to be married are churchgoers."[47]

The "Protestant" wedding tends to be the fulfilment of a secular romance, on which the minister confers ecclesiastical and public blessing. Many who relish the church service, and are moved by it, nevertheless include in it elements that are not Christian. To most Protestant participants, indeed, a wedding would be incomplete if it lacked two secular tunes composed by Germans in the 1840s. The bridal chorus from Wagner's *Lohengrin*, which is normally played on the organ as the bride enters the church, can hardly seem appropriate to a Christian who knows his Wagner: it is sung in the bridal chamber after the wedding of Lohengrin and Elsa, whose marriage, as one church paper has pointed out, "is soon to end unconsummated because of the nagging curiosity of the bride and the enchanted state of the groom".[48] Mendelssohn's incidental music to Shakespeare's *A Midsummer Night's Dream*, which is usually heard as the bride and groom walk out of the church, was intended to be played, as this church paper puts it, "between Act IV, in which Bottom, transformed into an ass, courts a temporarily bewitched Titania, and Act V, in which Bottom and Flute and their clowning cronies act out a hilarious performance of the story of Pyramus and Thisbe". Most brides and grooms may well be unaware of the theatrical contexts of these two marches; but when the bride chooses a secular song to be sung by a soloist, she can hardly be ignorant of its words. The most popular songs are said to be "something like 'O Promise Me' or 'Because' ".[49] When God appears in these songs, it is to bless secular romance ("Because God made thee mine"); and one of the most popular of the genre, "I Love You Truly", can be read fairly as anti-Christian in implication, since its burden is that the beloved alone is enough to banish sorrow, doubt and fear. Few brides who request this song would think it proper to have the same sentiments sung at a wedding in twentieth-century rather than nineteenth-century idiom. Yet the theology of "Because" is exactly that of, say, "You Were Meant For Me" ("I'm content the angels must have sent you"); and "I Love You Truly" is identical in doctrine with most of today's Top Thousand. The music at Protestant weddings in Australia, like the hostility of hard-core Protestants to alcohol, is a legacy of nineteenth-century culture-religion. Both the romantic movement in music and the temperance movement were novelties embraced by a generation of Protestants who wanted, as H. R. Niebuhr has put it, to "accommodate Christ to culture while selecting from culture what conforms most readily to Christ".[50] Both have been assumed by later generations to be a permanent part of their spiritual heritage. A few Protestant ministers, in revolt against culture-religion, sip alcoholic drinks on principle. Some, disturbed at the secularity of weddings, discourage the use of Victorian love-

---

[47] *Ibid.*, 25 December 1959.

[48] *Presbyterian Life*, Melbourne, 14 November 1958, paraphrasing an American college organist.

[49] *Ibid.*

[50] H. R. Niebuhr, *Christ and Culture*, p. 103.

songs. But these are difficult matters to explain to the laity. One minister in Melbourne has banned "I Love You Truly" from his church; but such boldness is rare.

Divorce

More than one in ten of present Australian marriages are likely to end in divorce.[51] The incidence of divorce has trebled since 1900. There is no way of knowing whether it will continue to rise, no system of measurement which will show whether a rising divorce rate represents a gain or a loss of human happiness, and no reason why somebody who regards marriage as a sacrament should agree with somebody who regards it as a contract when the two discuss whether a rising divorce rate is evidence of a decline in morality. If a divorce rate is an index of social morality, then Australia is much less moral than Italy, rather less moral than Canada, Belgium, Norway and the Netherlands, about as moral as the United Kingdom, France and Finland, and almost three times as moral as the United States.

In 1959 Australians were given an opportunity to discuss the relation of divorce to Christianity and morality when the Federal government introduced a Matrimonial Causes Bill designed to replace existing state laws. The bill recognized one ground for divorce which had been recognized previously only in Western Australia: separation for five years, without either party having committed any of the traditional "matrimonial offences" such as adultery or cruelty or even desertion. The measure provoked vehement Catholic criticism, in which it was not always easy to distinguish opposition to this particular provision from opposition to divorce as such. Most fire was nevertheless directed against the provision for separation after five years. The Commonwealth Attorney-General and architect of the bill, Sir Garfield Barwick, recognized that this provision might be invoked against a spouse whose religion made him unable to tolerate divorce. "He may say: 'I have some religious or sentimental reason for not wanting to be divorced.'". The reply, said Barwick, was "that the interests of the community in ensuring that the other party to the marriage did not form an illicit union and was able to form a sound union would overbear those sentimental or religious scruples on the part of the respondent".[52] Neither the suggestion that the laws of the church are on a par with sentimentality nor the implication that adultery (or illegitimacy) is worse than divorce could be expected to reconcile Catholic critics. Catholic laymen formed an Association for the Defence of the Family to oppose the bill. It was said to have collected 150,000 signatures for a petition begging the Queen to disallow the legislation. The Association claimed to have some support from non-Catholics; and it certainly had as an ally the Anglican Archbishop of Melbourne, who said that the bill reflected the disintegration of family life.

The bill passed both houses and became law. It was not regarded as a party measure, and a number of Catholic politicians voted for it. They may well have suspected that on this issue the leaders of their church were not being followed by most of the laity. There was evidence already to suggest

---

[51] Lincoln Day calculates in chapter 11 that if the divorce rate by duration of marriage remains what it was in the mid-1950s, 10%–12% of present marriages will end in divorce.

[52] *Commonwealth Parliamentary Debates*, 8 Eliz. II, H of R 25, p. 2858.

that on divorce, Australian Catholics tended to be more heterodox, or disloyal, than on any other matter (except possibly contraception). One church journal, noting the proportion of professing Catholics registered as divorcees at the 1947 census, found it "alarming".[53] The alarm was perhaps excessive, since a Catholic defies his church only if he obtains a civil divorce and then re-marries; and the census report is silent on how often that happens. In 1957, however, the Gallup Poll revealed evidence of serious discord between the mind of the Church and the minds of Australian Catholics: 50% of Catholics were in favour of having divorce laws; at least 50% of them thought that desertion and adultery should be grounds for divorce; and 38% even thought that *mental cruelty*—not a ground in any part of Australia—should be a ground. Interpretations of this poll have differed. It would certainly have displeased any Pope; but an Australian Catholic who is himself among the 50% in favour of having divorce laws suggests that the figure "might only mean that a good section of these have no intention of using the divorce courts, but have been merely 'corrupted' by living in a free (and religiously plural) society: they will not forbid those practices which seem licit to others".[54]

A Gallup Poll on the Matrimonial Causes Act of 1959 suggested that the "corruption" goes deep. Not only were large majorities of adherents to every Protestant denomination in favour of the provision for divorce after five years' separation: even among Catholics, almost as many approved as disapproved; 45% were against it, 42% were for it, and 13% were undecided. The *Jesuit Year Book* has said that Gallup Polls are "particularly useful to those who are interested in seeing where there is a greater need for instruction of the people as a whole and especially among Catholics".[55] A diocesan weekly put the matter more sternly.

> Catholics, unless very poorly instructed, are not in favour of divorce, whatever the grounds, because they regard divorce as contrary to Christ's explicit teaching. One can only conclude that half the number of Catholics questioned in this poll, if they were Catholics, were not entitled to be regarded as representative Catholics and quoted as such because of a gross ignorance of their faith. In short, an opinion in favour of divorce is not a Catholic opinion.[56]

On this view any survey would show that the percentage of "representative" Catholics in favour of what their church teaches is 100; or, as the Rev. Dr. Leslie Rumble has said, "in the Catholic Church, priests and people alike are committed to the authoritative teachings of their Church; and so long as Catholics retain their faith, they accept those authoritative teachings".[57] Such assertions are either circular or untrue. In the case of divorce, it appears that the "secular" or "Protestant" view of marriage is tending to replace, or at least to dilute, the "Catholic" view in the minds of about half the Catholics of Australia, including many thousands who attend Mass regularly and receive

[53] *Australian Messenger of the Sacred Heart,* 1 July 1958.
[54] S. M. Ingham in *Journal of Religious History,* December 1961, p. 261. See also letter from Peter Kelly in *Nation,* 8 April 1961.
[55] *Jesuit Year Book,* 1962, p. 23.
[56] *Advocate,* Melbourne, 12 January 1961.
[57] *Catholic Weekly,* Sydney, 21 August 1958.

the sacraments. Catholic sociologists in the United States have discussed the problem in terms which seem broadly applicable to this country. "The marriage problem of our modern urban society", writes an American priest, "has infiltrated into and become a part of the Catholic parochial system."[58] It may be that the secular approach to marriage has made deeper inroads into American than into Australian Catholicism; but if so the difference is not vast. When sociology has infiltrated as far into Catholicism in Australia as in America, we shall know. So long as a Catholic does not want actually to use facilities offered by his society but condemned by his church, a mixture of attitudes to marriage may co-exist in his mind without pain; but if he should decide to divorce and remarry, he and his church collide publicly. No priest will perform or recognize the second marriage ceremony.

Non-Catholic clergy in Australia, as elsewhere, are not agreed about the propriety of re-marriage after divorce. In the Church of England, policy varies from diocese to diocese. "Fairly early in our ministry", an Anglican testifies,

> clergy are compelled to satisfy their conscience about remarriage of divorcees. In this Diocese [of Sydney], permission must be granted to clergy by the Archbishop to perform a remarriage, and this is generally given only for the innocent person in a divorce for adultery. But can I salve my conscience by passing the buck to a Diocesan rule, which I feel to be contradictory to Scripture?[59]

Other Anglicans reply variously that the Bible does not forbid divorce, that Christians have not the right to impose their views on others, that divorce is not sin but rather the appointed remedy for sin, and that "people do not obey God's laws and cannot, except the Holy Spirit works in them".[60] One interpreter of the Anglican position has said both that "the Church cannot remarry a divorced Church member while the former partner is still alive" and that "inasmuch as any is innocent the Church may advise a second marriage rather than condemning a person to a life of virtual celibacy".[61] Protestant ministers outside the Church of England find themselves pulled in different directions by church tradition (which may or may not be expressed in formal documents) and criteria of compassion and justice which they share with the nominal adherent and the unbeliever.

Among ecclesiastical responses to the problem of divorce, "marriage guidance" has lately become prominent. Since 1945 a number of marriage guidance councils have been established in Australia under religious auspices. When clergymen said that the Commonwealth law of 1959 would weaken the institution of marriage, the Attorney-General insisted that the bill was designed to strengthen it, especially by encouraging the work of marriage guidance. Indeed, the Act requires a solicitor to tell a client interested in divorce about the organizations which offer counselling; and a judge, if he sees any chance of reconciliation, is supposed to withhold a decree of divorce

---

[58] J. H. Fichter, S.J., *Dynamics of a City Church*, p. 96. See also J. H. Thomas, S.J., "The urban impact on the American Catholic family", *American Catholic Sociological Review*, vol. 10, 1949, p. 260.

[59] *Australian Church Record*, 18 January 1962.

[60] *Ibid.*, 15 February, 1 March, 15 March 1962.

[61] A. V. Maddick in *Anglican*, 9 August 1962.

until the case has been referred to a counsellor. Subsidies from the Federal government have encouraged marriage guidance bodies to expand. As most of hem are run by clergymen, this represents a substantial, if informal, association of church and state.

There are Catholic as well as Protestant marriage counsellors; but the origin of the movement is Protestant and the ideology of its pace-makers tends to be Protestant and secular-progressive. The leading practitioner in Australia, an Anglican clergyman, speaks of "marriages which, though not legally dissolved, have broken down in every sense that matters".[62] Those last five words are incompatible with the sacramental view of marriage; and so is his opinion that the churches should "realize that the old patriarchal family is on the way out" and place less emphasis on the indissolubility of marriage. The Catholic marriage counsellor is less likely than the Protestant to advise clients to use the divorce law which pays part of his salary. Nor, presumably, would he ever recommend the use of contraceptives.

Contraception

Six out of ten Australians approve of birth control as a means of limiting population. If ever the foolishness of basing decisions on majority opinions was aptly illustrated, said a Catholic commentator, it was by this figure.[63] No Protestant observer deplored it. Yet fifty years ago it would have shocked clergymen in all denominations. Protestants, Catholics and many secular moralists agreed with a Royal Commission in New South Wales which said in 1904 that the use of contraception, which had begun lately to affect the birth rate, was evidence that "the people" were "led astray by false and pernicious doctrine into the belief that personal interests and ambitions, a high standard of ease, comfort, and luxury, are the essential aims of life, and that these aims are best attained by refusing to accept the consequences which nature has ordained shall follow from marriage. . . ."[64] Catholic and Protestant denunciations differed only in tone. Catholics, drawing on the "natural law", tended to see the contraceptive as denying life to an individual human being. Protestants, proud and anxious imperialists, tended to see it as weakening the British race. Protestant opinion, in Australia as elsewhere, has altered so profoundly since 1920 that many Protestants now do not know that their fathers were hostile to the practice. "The Protestant Church", writes a Methodist editor, "has constantly advocated planned parenthood".[65] Yet in 1912 an eminent Presbyterian minister could call contraception "race-murder", and appeal for a united front of Protestants and Catholics against it. "We are indeed glad", he said, "for the support of any Church —Protestant or Catholic—or any public body that will take part in banishing this diabolic mode of crime. . . ."[66] A year later a bishop addressing an Anglican Church Congress deplored "that dark blot of race suicide that has infected Christian nations like the plague" over the past thirty years; and quoted an English bishop who asked: "Are we witnessing the decline of the West and the rise of the East? Are the nations that have been entrusted

---

[62] W. G. Coughlan, in A. P. Elkin (ed.) *Marriage and the Family in Australia*, p. 118.
[63] *Catholic Weekly*, 18 February 1960.
[64] C. M. H. Clark, *Select Documents in Australian History* 1851–1900, p. 670.
[65] *Methodist*, 20 September 1958.
[66] J. L. Rentoul, *The Church's Word to Australia in a "Century of Unrest"*, 1912, p. 12.

with the guardianship of the Christian faith, refusing their inheritance, and by a wanton race suicide surrendering the sceptre of the East?"[67] To a similar congress as late as 1925, the Bishop of Adelaide invoked the authority of "common sense, the best medical opinion, and the great majority of bishops in our Church" for the conclusion that "birth-control is right and possible; artificial birth-control is wrong".[68] The practice of a large proportion of church-going Australians was thus condemned unambiguously; but the non-Catholics among them had not long to wait before their behaviour would be approved. The resolutions of Anglican bishops at Lambeth Conferences are a fairly accurate index of the change in non-Catholic ecclesiastical opinion. In 1920 they issued a solemn warning against "the use of unnatural means for the avoidance of conception". In 1930 they concluded (by a majority of about three to one) that sometimes contraception might not be immoral, but they condemned "motives of selfishness, luxury, or mere convenience". In 1958 they passed unanimously a resolution about "responsible parenthood" which registered their toleration of contraception.[69]

Insofar as Protestant hostility had cultural and patriotic sources, it was more vulnerable than the Catholic position to changes in the world. The recovery in Australia's birth rate after 1945, which showed (as did the similar rise in America) that people equipped with contraceptives might nevertheless choose to have more children than their parents had, probably came too late to affect Protestant attitudes, though it may have provided reassurance. Population movements elsewhere were more decisive. "It is surely not the will of God that children should be brought into the world to die of starvation", says a leading Methodist minister, Dr. A. H. Wood.[70] The criticism of the Catholic position which is implied in that remark is expressed more warmly by other Protestant ministers. In an age when the traditional causes of discord between Protestant and Catholic have lost much of their force, contraception has helped to keep sectarian conflict alive. To the Protestant as to the secular moralist, the Catholic position can appear recklessly inhumane. To many Catholics, Protestant tolerance is one sign of a general abandonment to the wicked world. The official spokesman for the Catholic Church in Sydney, Dr Rumble, described the Lambeth resolution of 1958 as a blind betrayal of Christian principles; the proposition, adopted by the Anglican bishops, that one may use contraceptives provided one does so in accordance with one's Christian conscience, appeared to him self-contradictory; and he noted with satisfaction that not all Anglicans agreed with the resolution.[71] He quoted one clergyman who observed: "The supreme attraction of Rome is to be found in its ethical rigorism. . . . It represents the last loyalty of the human race to its own highest moral standards. It is the iron bulwark of Christianity against the overwhelming invasion of the corrupting neo-paganism of our times."[72] In Australia, said a Catholic archbishop who commented on the decision taken at Lambeth, "Catholics are thus forced to

[67] *Church Congress Report,* Brisbane, 1913, p. 233.
[68] *Church Congress Report,* Melbourne, 1925, p. 173.
[69] N. St. John Stevas, *Life, Death and the Law,* pp. 72-3.
[70] *Bulletin,* 5 August 1961.
[71] *Catholic Weekly,* 30 October 1958.
[72] *Tribune,* Melbourne, 11 December 1958.

stand almost alone in upholding the traditional Christian ideals of chastity and family life. I trust that the new ethnic groups that are coming among us will help the Church to reinforce the thoroughly Christian moral standards in Australia."[73]

Australian Catholics do, indeed, now stand almost alone on the matter. How united do they stand? Not all Catholics can give cogent expositions of their Church's position to puzzled or hostile outsiders. "The 'population explosion' ", says a diocesan paper in Melbourne, "has caused a lot of questioning about the Christian attitude towards contraception. . . . Generally speaking, a well-read Catholic—especially if he reads the Catholic Press steadily—need not resort to a priest to get his answers."[74] But most Australian Catholics do not read a church paper; and for some the difficulty of expounding their church's teaching is enhanced by their own disobedience of it.

When contraception first became common in Australia, some said that Catholics would not take to it; the confessional would confer "special immunity from this hideous mode of child murder, or rather, the power to prevent it".[75] At this time Catholics wanting to limit their families could do so only by continence or disobedience. After 1930 priests were able to recommend a third alternative: use of the newly discovered "safe period". The fertility of Australian Catholics has since declined considerably, as shown in chapter 10. How far has the decline been achieved by methods which the Catholic church forbids? As in the United States, fertility began to fall before the use of the "safe period" was widely known; and as in America the fall has been more apparent in urban than in rural areas. If Australian Catholics behave as American Catholics do, then only a little over half of them are in clear agreement with their church about contraception; three in ten couples use forbidden methods of contraception; and the proportion rises to half among couples who have been married for ten years· and are still fecund.[76] In America, documentation of the phenomenon and candid Catholic discussion of it are more common than in Australia. The main causes of the decline in the Catholic birth-rate, an American nun argued in 1944, were "urban culture, the weakening of the moral and religious fiber of our people, and the economic structure of present day society".[77] If the causes are as formidable as that, what on earth can the cure be? A Jesuit answers that anybody wishing to solve the problem must devise "a means of lessening the socio-economic pressures of secular society which push towards the use of contraceptives. At the same time he will have to strengthen the motivation force of the Catholic value system within the cultural environment of American Catholics".[78]

[73] Rev. Dr J. D. Simonds, quoted in *Advocate*, 11 September 1958.

[74] *Tribune*, 8 December 1960.

[75] J. L. Rentoul, *op. cit.*, p. 12. He was reporting an opinion held by others.

[76] R. Freedman, P. K. Whelpton and A. A. Campbell, *Family Planning, Sterility and Population Growth;* T. J. Casey, S.J., "Catholics and Family Planning", *American Catholic Sociological Review*, vol. 21, 1960, p. 125; G. Lenski, *The Religious Factor*, esp. p. 151. "Birth control" is of course a vague term, and even "contraception" may be ambiguous. All the authors cited in this note are careful to distinguish between permitted and forbidden practices.

[77] Sister Leo Marie, O.P., "Is the Catholic birth rate declining?", *American Catholic Sociological Review*, vol. 3, 1944, p. 183.

[78] T. J. Casey, *loc. cit.*, p. 135.

How? One method is to deny offenders the sacraments. "If a person uses contraceptive methods of birth prevention", a troubled Australian Catholic asks, "is it a mortal sin endangering one's eternal salvation?" Yes, replies Dr Rumble; for the ordinarily well-instructed Catholic, it is.[79] Yet there are Catholics who use contraceptives and go on receiving the sacraments. "I have some married friends", a Catholic in Victoria testifies,

> who believe that the "safe period" is a myth, and who admit making a regular practice of avoiding children by use of artificial preventives. They point out that the sin of artificial birth-prevention is not nearly as grave as the sin of having unwanted children who cannot be properly fed, clothed and educated. As these friends attend Mass and Confession regularly they have started me wondering.

"Well, really", observes Rev. Ambrose Ryan, O.F.M.,

> I am not in a position to comment fully on this matter. All I know is that a priest . . . who is aware that Catholic parents openly disobey the law of God and of the Church and are not prepared to amend their conduct . . . is bound to put them off from absolution until they promise seriously to amend. I am a priest. I did not make God's laws concerning married life; I only administer them. And I am forbidden to give absolution in such cases, except the partners agree to amend their conduct.[80]

It would appear from this exchange that there may be priests who are unwilling to treat disobedient couples as severely as they are expected to.[81]

For many women, and perhaps for their priests, it would be a relief if the Catholic church decided to tolerate the contraceptive use of anovulant pills. "Now, thanks to the uncovering of one of Nature's benign provisions . . . " an Australian priest said of the "safe period" in 1934, "there seems at least to be every reason for hope that there is a natural and lawful way out of the difficulty."[82] Some Catholics have spoken similarly of the new pills; but there is no evidence yet that the Church will approve of them.

Australian churches were in their positions before the pills were marketed here. Protestant ministers held out a tentative welcome, and Dr Rumble, following a statement by Pope Pius XII in 1958, declared that the pill was no different in principle from any other contraceptive: as a positive interference with the vital natural functions it was forbidden and opposed to the moral law.[83] A Catholic sociologist predicted that oral contraception and restrictive immigration policies would together "weaken our population potential and endanger the security of Australia".[84] Others spelt out according to taste this new vision of race suicide. A correspondent in the *Sydney Morning Herald* said:

> We will lose our Australian characteristics to an unnecessary degree, as it will be necessary to attract more migrants in order to fill the unnatural void.

[79] *Catholic Weekly*, 20 December 1962.
[80] *Advocate*, 25 August 1960.
[81] K. Underwood, *Protestant and Catholic*, pp. 92–3, appears to have found a similar leniency in the United States.
[82] *Australasian Catholic Record*, new series, XI, 1934, p. 102.
[83] *Daily Telegraph*, 9 September 1959.
[84] J. Zubrzycki in *Catholic Weekly*, 11 May 1961.

We will become a nation of old people; our social services will be strained to the limit, to the detriment of the economic growth of the country, and hardships will result on the people themselves.[85]

Doctors who believed in contraception were pronouncing the pills safe, and doctors who did not were saying, as had been said a generation ago of contraceptive appliances: "Never let us forget that if we strike against Nature, she always hits back."[86]

The Catholic chemist is never allowed by his church to sell appliances intended wholly for contraception—a prohibition which, if he obeys it, loses him money and goodwill. The pills are in a different category, since contraception is not their only possible use; and the chemist has been encouraged by priests to believe that if a customer wants the pills primarily to treat an irregularity, he may dispense them to her. There is another difference: unlike contraceptive appliances, pills can be obtained in Australia only if a doctor prescribes them. The pill is rapidly replacing the appliance; and since the Catholic chemist may well regard it as not his business to ask the customer about her motives, contraception may not be much longer a source of discomfort and loss to him. The Catholic doctor, however, may face now a dilemma which he was spared when most contraceptives were bought without a prescription; for he must know, even if the chemist does not, why his patient wants the pills. It remains to be seen whether, in the event of the pills being declared free of any danger to the user, the law will continue to require a doctor's prescription. If that requirement is removed, then the only deterrent to taking the pills, apart from moral or theological scruple, will be financial.

The pill may or may not differ theologically from previous forms of contraception. Technically, it differs from them all: it appears to remove *entirely* the risk of pregnancy. In 1960 an English physician remarked in Sydney that parents would soon have to guide their children in the best use of oral contraceptives. Clergymen invited by the press to comment spoke variously. An official spokesman for the Church of England said that the pills would do more good than harm because they would reduce the likelihood of illegitimate children. The president of the Methodist conference declared, untruly, that chastity was the only means to prevent illegitimacy. An official Catholic spokesman said that parents who did as the doctor suggested would be teaching their children how to violate the moral law.[87]

It has often been remarked that in modern industrial society the doctor tends to do things done formerly and elsewhere by priests. Doctors who are approached by unmarried women for advice about contraceptive appliances have to make a moral judgment before deciding whether to give it; some do, some do not. Since Australian women have to approach a doctor if they want anovulant pills, and since the proportion of unmarried women intending to have sexual intercourse seems to be rising, the Australian doctor, whether he likes it or not, will have to decide more often than in the past whether to abet extra-marital intercourse. His decision is likely to be affected by the character and intensity of his religious convictions.

[85] *Sydney Morning Herald,* 22 June 1962.
[86] "Family Doctor" in *ibid.,* 16 June 1962.
[87] *Bulletin,* 8 March 1961.

Death

Although the roles of doctor and clergyman have been converging, the fact of death keeps them separate. Once a patient is pronounced dead, the doctor's work is done and the clergyman performs the least congenial of his professional tasks. The relation between Australians and the clergy is nowhere more uneasy than at the grave. This is especially true of the millions who profess adherence to Protestant churches but who seldom or never approach a clergyman except to ask him to celebrate a rite of passage. The Catholic may be less uneasy than the Protestant. A dying person and his loved ones are likelier if Catholic to know a clergyman personally. If called to the death-bed, the priest has a specific physical and spiritual task to perform: he has to administer the sacrament of extreme unction. The Protestant minister, if called, must depend on his own verbal resources: he does not purport to be the bearer of a sacrament. The priest is likelier, morever, to be on harmonious terms with the funeral director. Except in country towns too small to support more than one undertaker, Catholics normally engage a funeral director who is himself a Catholic and whose trade is exclusively or principally Catholic. One such firm, tutoring Catholics in "How to arrange for a funeral", begins: "1. Inform your parish priest immediately."[88] No such advice is offered in advertisements directed at Protestants. "It is not uncommon", reports an Anglican clergyman in Perth,

> for the [Anglican] priest to be the last consulted about the time of the burial. In the Diocese of Perth most undertakers, when dealing with Anglicans, normally ask the relatives whom they would like to officiate and if necessary suggest a suitable person, who may or may not be the duly appointed pastor of the parish. The chosen person is then advised: "There will be a funeral at such and such a time: could you take it?" He could add "take it or leave it", and the more easily since at the main cemetery a rostered priest is at hand for left-overs. . . . Perhaps the depths were plumbed in a letter once received from a respected retired priest in which he referred to "the undertaker for whom I work".[89]

However tactful or unrapacious the undertaker may be, his relationship with a clergyman begins awkwardly if it is he, not a relative of the dead person, who asks the minister to perform the funeral service. The clergyman has misgivings similar to those about officiating at baptisms and weddings for possibly faithless strangers; and to these qualms is added a distaste at being employed by an interloping tradesman.

In the case of baptism and marriage, nominal Christians feel the church to be an appropriate setting: brides like to walk down the aisle; parents like water to be sprinkled from the font. In the case of funerals, most Australians want the service of a clergyman but not the setting of a church. They prefer to hire from the undertaker his "funeral parlour", whether the minister likes it or not. A Methodist minister has noted wryly that the image of a "four-wheeled Christian", who comes to church only when conveyed there for baptism, marriage and funeral, exaggerates the religiosity of nominal adherents, since "surprisingly few funeral services in the metropolitan area are

[88] Advertisement in *Catholic Weekly*, 5 May 1960.
[89] *Anglican*, 16 January 1959.

held in a church". A survey of one week's notices in Melbourne newspapers, he found, showed that 67% of funerals left funeral parlours, 16% left Catholic churches, 10% left Protestant churches, and 7% left private homes. "We set aside our buildings for worship and fellowship", he wrote,

and unless there are exceptional circumstances we should use them. We should be especially concerned that our loyal people be encouraged to think that at their death the praise of God should sound within the very walls where in life they delighted to seek Him and find Him. In most country districts, the rightful place of the church has not been usurped. Let us keep it that way, and at the same time try to rectify the rush for cold efficiency in the city.[90]

Other clergymen speak less mildly. "Perhaps the worst form of paganization in our Church," says an Anglican in Sydney,

has been the gradual acceptance by both clergy and laity alike of the funeral parlour burial service. In these thickly carpeted "sanctuaries" some of the nastiest excesses of vulgarity and bad taste are committed. It is usual for the coffin to be open before the service begins to allow the relatives and friends of the departed to have their last look and orange coloured lights are switched on to take away something of the pallor of death. Sentimental, sickly, recorded songs are then played, such as "Beyond the Sunset". Under such circumstances the minister has to battle to present the Christian teaching of the Resurrection. No undertakers, or crematorium authorities for that matter, find it necessary to provide copies of the burial service and the congregations in such places become mere spectators. There is simply no reason why in the city and suburbs Church of England funeral services should not take place in the parish churches. While we continue to allow the Church to be dictated to by undertakers we are throwing away that ministry of reconciliation which can only properly be given in the parish church.[91]

Critics of the "funeral parlour" have noted that it can yield profit to the proprietor only because ministers of religion collaborate with him. Why then do the ministers co-operate? "A number of clergy to whom I have spoken . . . " answers an Anglican,

have deplored the manner in which the parlour has taken the place of the church; but, they say, what can be done when a certain section of the clergy just won't play ball and prefer to regard themselves as under the jurisdiction of the undertaker at funerals?[92]

If a minister refuses, he knows that the task and the fee will be accepted by somebody else. And how can he tell somebody whose spouse or parent or child has just died that what he proposes is in poor taste and bad theology? How can the bereaved, even if he himself has aesthetic or doctrinal qualms, resist the bland suggestions of the parlour's proprietor? For as ministers know, "some undertakers exert pressure on relatives, at a time when they are least likely to want to argue or resist, to use the funeral chapel instead of the

[90] *Spectator*, 10 September 1958.
[91] J. F. S. Campbell, "The paganization of the urban church", *Anglican*, 3 February 1961.
[92] *Anglican*, 20 February 1959.

church. . . . [93] An American professional manual, *Psychology of Funeral Service,* observes that the grief-stricken "are less capable of reasoning than under normal conditions. . . . They want to do the accepted thing. . . . "[94] Leaders of the profession go so far as to look severely on certain cheap operators in their ranks who advise customers to use a church. "This saves them from having a chapel," says the chairman of the Australian funeral directors' conference. A columnist in the *Anglican,* noting this remark, suggested coolly that "there is nothing improper about suggesting that a funeral service should be held in a church".[95] The columnist deplored the parlours but admitted that they are popular. Why? Because "a large proportion of our population has no active church membership—and so maybe there is a reluctance to seek the use of a church for a funeral". Undertakers could well defend their operations as commercial television entrepreneurs defend theirs, by saying that the public choose freely and the fastidious are few.

The rites devised by undertakers, as clergymen note, reflect and perhaps encourage doubts about the Christian doctrine of the Resurrection. Advertisements for a new "Australian Memorial Park" in Sydney assume a readier response among Catholics than among Anglicans to Christian orthodoxy: in the *Catholic Weekly* a picture of the proposed "lawn cemetery" has superimposed on it a statue of Jesus whose plinth bears the words: "I am the Resurrection and the Life."[96] For readers of the *Anglican,* however, the picture has on it, instead of the statue, a rose, and the words "180 acres of peace".[97] The burial rites for members of the Returned Servicemen's League, like the Act of Remembrance and Dedication at its sub-branch meetings, appear to be designed to accommodate people who cannot find comfort in the traditional message of Christianity about life after death. From this and other evidence, we may infer that although the churches to which most Australians adhere profess the doctrine of the resurrection of the body, many adherents are not sustained, when they contemplate death, by a serene belief in the doctrine. *How* many, it is impossible to say. The Gallup Poll has not asked people about heaven. It has, however, asked them about hell. Nearly 50% of people interviewed in 1959 expressed a belief that on the other side of death lies some kind of hell, and nearly 25% see it as a place of everlasting fiery torment. Hell burns more vividly in Catholic than in Protestant imaginations; 62% of Catholics, but only 17% of non-Catholics, foresee eternal fire for the damned. Another 13% of Catholics and 29% of non-Catholics see a milder, or vaguer, hell; 11% of Catholics and 28% of non-Catholics believe in no hell, while 14% of Catholics and 26% of others are undecided. Most Protestants, and two out of five Catholics, thus reject or have doubts about a doctrine which the authors of the New Testament plainly believed to be terribly important. All in all, there is considerable evidence for the view, expressed by a Catholic paper, that Australians exhibit a "fading

---

[93] *Ibid.*

[94] *Time,* 14 November 1960. A survey of the U.S. clergy, cited by *Time,* has shown that 51% of Protestants and 41% of Catholics believe that undertakers exploit bereaved families.

[95] *Anglican,* 3 November 1961.

[96] *Catholic Weekly,* 11 April 1963.

[97] *Anglican,* 18 April 1963.

sense of immortality".[98] The paper observes that the words "Death is so permanent", used by the Australian Road Safety Council, seem

> to imply, as a recognized fact beyond all challenge, that death is equivalent to human annihilation. The typical modern, like the ancient pagan, buries or cremates the body of his loved one, weeps a little, and then turns his back and goes on with the business of life. In this atmosphere it is all too easy for the Christian believer, living in the world, to lose his vivid sense of the actuality and imminence of "the life of the world to come".

To the most utopian of secular reformers, it has not seemed impossibly bold to hope that once injustice and poverty have been overcome, death itself might be, if not conquered, at any rate postponed indefinitely. In the ideology of the Enlightenment, the hope of life beyond death was replaced by something daringly close to the abolition of death.[99] In the richest parts of the world, including Australia, the hope expressed by secular utopians has been nurtured by a steadily lengthening span of human life since 1880, and especially since 1900. An Australian born in the 1880s could be expected at birth to live less than fifty years. By the 1950s a full twenty years had been added to the expectation. "Why is it," asks a reader of the *Anglican,* "that our society seems almost impervious to our presentation of the Christian Faith?" A clergyman replies that "suffering and death have always dominated Christian thinking. Now they are pushed to the hem of life. The spiritual challenge which goes with these two phenomena of life has been fobbed off."[100] As the span of life has increased, candid public speech about death has diminished; what to earlier generations seemed solemn mourning has been defined as morbid gloom; and a physical acquaintance with the facts of death has tended to be confined to the eyes and hands of professional specialists. Public mourning has declined steady ever since 1875, when a Funeral Reform Association founded by T. S. Mort and others urged people to abandon ornament, pall and mutes. By the end of the century a black armband was becoming a popular substitute for the vestments of mourning. Soon even that was uncommon, and for the first time in history mourning was regarded as an almost wholly private activity.[101]

In the past forty years Australians have been as readily persuaded to have dead bodies burned as to abandon traditional mourning. " 'Progress' is the watchword of the times in everything," declared the Cremation Society of Australia in 1924, "including the manner of disposing of the dead."[102] When these words were written there was only one crematorium in the continent (at Adelaide); by 1960 there were sixteen, and about one in every three bodies was going to them. The proportion is all the more striking because until 1964 cremation was forbidden to Catholics. This prohibition was imposed during conflict between the church and European anti-clericals in the nineteenth

---

[98] *Advocate,* 2 November 1961.

[99] There are strikingly similar expressions of this hope in Condorcet, *Outline of the Progress of the Human Mind,* 1794; and J. Strachey, *The Coming Struggle for Power,* 1935.

[100] *Anglican,* 13 December 1962.

[101] The change was not of course confined to Australia. Compare how the living cope with a corpse in D. H. Lawrence, *Sons and Lovers,* 1913, and Mary McCarthy, *The Group,* 1963.

[102] *Official Handbook of the Cremation Society of Australia,* 1924, p. 18.

century. The church could place no *practical* obstacle in the way of such a sinful act as using contraceptives; but cremation, like re-marriage after divorce, could not occur in the Catholic community so long as it was prohibited because it required the participation of a priest. A Catholic undertaker could nevertheless take a body to a crematorium; and it has even been held permissible for a Catholic to advertise: "Cremations arranged."[103] The Catholic undertaker who has non-Catholic customers would otherwise be turning away a great deal of business. The auspices of the cremation movement have been largely hygienic and medical. Since the movement was launched, in the 1870s, it has flourished in non-Catholic countries, though there were, at first, Protestant misgivings. The pioneer of cremation in Australia, Dr J. M. Creed, observed in 1887: "Many worthy persons object to the burning of the dead from a dread that it might tend to weaken belief in the doctrine of the resurrection; though it needs but little thought to realize that the beneficent Being, the Author and Ruler of the universe, must be as able to recreate the body whether it has been resolved into its original elements by the ordinary process of decay or by the quicker and more cleanly method of burning."[104] After the first shock there was no solid opposition to cremation from non-Catholic churchmen in Australia. "The Church which I serve", said an Anglican bishop in the 1930s, "certainly utters no caveat against this growing custom and its practice would seem to be growing daily among the faithful of our Church."[105] It was indeed growing. In England a bishop was cremated in 1935, and in 1944 a primate, William Temple, was cremated. In Australia it took a full generation for the reformers to raise the capital, find the land, and persuade legislators to permit the practice and people to want it. Their arguments have been so diverse, and the movement has been so little discussed, that it is difficult to know which of the reasons they offered have proved the most persuasive. They have assumed that people do not want to mourn as they used to; indeed, "mournful" is a pejorative word in cremationist literature.[106] They have assumed, too, that people now want to remove themselves as far as possible from dead bodies. They have argued not only that cremation is more sanitary, humane, reverent and economical than earth burial, but that it is also more egalitarian. It provides "for all classes, without distinction, a commodious and beautiful building . . . where all meet upon the same level, rich and poor alike, and where the remains of the humblest person receive the same respectful care and attention as bestowed upon the most wealthy and renowned."[107] Perhaps this part of the ideology has appealed especially to Australians. At any rate, by 1960 the proportion of cremations to deaths was higher in Australia than anywhere except Britain, where the modern movement had its effective beginnings: 32.3% of bodies were cremated in Britain, 30% in Australia, 29.5% in

103 *Australasian Catholic Record*, new series, XX, 1943, pp. 263–4.

104 J. M. Creed, "Cremation", *Transactions of the Intercolonial Medical Congress of Australasia*, Adelaide, 1888, p. 291.

105 Rev. Dr H. Crotty, late of Bathurst, quoted in *A Sanctuary of Remembrance*, Cremation Society of Australia, p. 2 (n.d.).

106 Cremation, it is said, will "readily take the place of the dreary and mournful funeral usually associated with earth burial. . . . " *Official Handbook of the Cremation Society*, p. 18.

107 *Ibid.*, p. 23.

New Zealand, 29% in Denmark and 25% in Sweden.[108] As Australia has a substantially higher proportion of Catholics than the other countries, it is clear that her non-Catholics have taken to cremation more readily than people in any other country. The proportion of cremations to deaths in Australia rose from 22% in 1950 to 30% in 1960, and the rise continues. How is it to be explained? And why should Australian habits have come to differ so strikingly from those of the United States? For although the proportions of non-Catholics are similar, cremation is now five times as common in this country. The greater urban concentration in Australia has perhaps been relevant, both in making the argument from civil hygiene seem more cogent and in placing a higher proportion of the population within easy reach of a crematorium. Undertakers, moreover, have opposed cremation in America but not in Australia. Why the profession has responded so diversely would itself require explaining; and so would the greater preference among Americans for preserving the remains of dead people in a condition imitating life.

Advance agents of the American way of death have not, so far, tried to sell cosmetic embalming to Australians. They have begun, however, to market here the "memorial park" or "lawn cemetery" and the accompanying gospel of buying graves "before need". Like the cremators, the salesmen of lawn cemeteries insist that their procedure is, among other things, more democratic than traditional burial. They discourage stratification in death; every grave in the lawn cemetery is to be surmounted by the same kind of brass plaque. The promoters declare also that their product is more Christian, because more cheerful, than the traditional cemetery, with its "gloom, hopelessness and despair. As Christians", says James Kenger, an American apostle of lawn, "we believe in eternity, yet these places are symbols of a gruesome end."[109]

In the new cemeteries as in the old ones, bodies are disposed according to denominational divisions. "Why do the various denominations have separate portions of cemeteries?" asks a Catholic. "Because cemeteries are religious places," replies Dr Rumble, "and the various denominations are different and separate religions". Dr Rumble sees not only separation, but a pleasing pluralism, in the practice. "To my mind, the different sections in a cemetery, sacred to people according to their different religious beliefs, reflect the same tolerance, quite devoid of bigotry, which enables us to live peaceably together despite differences of religion. . . . "[110] Not everybody is convinced; certainly not those on whom denominational loyalties sit lightly. "I have contemplated the purpose behind this segregation in death," writes a newspaper reader. "Surely, once we have passed from this life we are then in the hands of the One Shepherd and all join in the one fold, or do we think that there may be certain preferences?"[111] This questioner appears to believe that in life as in death, it would be best for all Christians to live in one house. There are critics of burial arrangements who accept the division of Christians into different houses but who wish that the gates between at any rate the non-Catholic houses could be left open. "I conducted a funeral service," a Methodist

[108] *Pharos, Official Journal of the Cremation Movement*, London, August 1960, p. 12.
[109] *Sun-Herald*, Sydney, 7 August 1960.
[110] *Southern Cross*, Adelaide, 8 May 1959.
[111] *Canberra Times*, 25 September 1963.

71

minister complains, "but I was not allowed to enter the Church of England cemetery. I have never forbidden any Anglican to enter our burial grounds."[112] In some parts of Australia, cemeteries are divided not thoroughly into denominational sections but into Catholic and Protestant. To some Anglican clergy, jealous of their denominational identity, this seems too promiscuous. For Catholics, as Dr Rumble implies, united burial is no more feasible than united worship. A Catholic may attend the funeral of a non-Catholic; but he is not normally permitted to attend a religious service whether in the church or the funeral parlour or at the cemetery; and at the graveside of a non-Catholic, he is supposed to draw apart until the service is over. Catholic or Protestant, the Australian is usually buried with other members of the ecclesiastical family to which, ardently or nominally, he adheres. In death as in life, the religious divisions which Europeans brought with them to Australia are still apparent.[113]

The Persistence of Religious Practice

There is much evidence for thinking that Australian Christianity is becoming more secular in character. We rest not only on Sunday, the day which Christians have long devoted to worship, but also on Saturday, the day which modern industry sets aside for play. The piety of worshippers is no doubt diluted by their enjoyment of secular leisure as well as by possession of the material abundance which they produce from Monday to Friday. As in the week, so in the year: the holy days of Christianity have been joined by secular holidays (festivals of nation or empire or class), and invaded by such symbols of worldliness as the Easter Bunny and Father Christmas. The average churchgoer, and even the average clergyman, is less likely than the medieval European or the twentieth-century tribal aborigine to see the light or shadow of the sacred falling on the round of his daily life, to believe (as Voltaire put it) that a particular Providence changes the economy of the world for your sparrow or your cat.

But to say that secularity has seeped into the churches is not to say that people are drifting away from them. In the United States, it has been remarked, both secularism and piety are flourishing. There, in the most technologically advanced of countries, religious practice is more widespread than in any other literate society: about 95% of the people claim affiliation to a religious body, about 60% are counted as members of churches, and about 40% report weekly attendance at worship. In Australia the proportions are uniformly lower, though higher than in Britain. In the twenty years since the Gallup Poll began to provide information about our religious behaviour, no decline in habits of worship is apparent. Indeed, more than one student of the Gallup Poll figures has read them as showing an increase in churchgoing since 1950. This may be attributing to the figures a finer accuracy than the Poll's methods warrant. On the other hand, there may have been such an increase: the proportion of Catholics, who tend to worship more frequently than most other people, has been rising a little; and there may be a propensity

---

112 *Methodist,* 6 August 1960.

113 In 1962 the Gallup Poll asked: "Do you think the day will come when all Christians of the world—Catholics, Protestants and all other Christian groups—will be united into one Church?" 31% said Yes, 55% said No, and 14% were uncertain. In no denomination was there a majority for Yes.

to more active church affiliation among mildly prosperous families in new suburbs. How habits of worship compare with those of other generations is hard to say. The only thorough study of religious practice in the early days concludes that Australian churches have never been able to claim the active allegiance of more than a minority of the people.[114]

If the story of decline misrepresents both past and present behaviour, why has it been so widely believed? It has been told by two small but articulate groups, secular liberals and preachers. Many secular liberals readily agree with Marx that religion is the opium of the people, or with Freud that "The more the fruits of knowledge become accessible to men, the more widespread is the decline of religious belief, at first only of the obsolete and objectionable expressions of the same, then of its fundamental assumptions also."[115] Their conviction that in a technically advanced, literate, urban society such as ours, religion must be tending to disappear, is nourished every week by clergymen who thunder, as a thousand generations have thundered, that the world has lately begun to abandon the paths of righteousness. "Few will deny that, speaking generally, church attendance is declining; that the sons and daughters of our people in the past generation have slipped with amazing ease into habits of indifference, and that Australians are becoming a non-churchgoing people."[116] Thus an Anglican clergyman in Australia on the eve of the first World War—a moment which, in the pulpit rhetoric of the 1960s, is often made to sound idyllic. "The Gorgon presence of atheism, the Arctic chill of religious indifferentism, the growing passion to make amusement the chief business of life, the hard and cruel competition in business, and the utter weariness of life which all these things together generate, are certainly telling against the attendance on public worship, and thinning the congregations in many a large city church once regularly filled, and even overflowing, every Sabbath Day."[117] That was an Australian Methodist in 1888. Half a century earlier, Judge Burton wrote the first serious essay on the religious behaviour of Australians. In New South Wales in 1839, he estimated, average weekly attendance at Protestant worship was no more than 11,000 in a population of 102,000; and in 1836, he reported from official statistics, Catholic attendances amounted to 2,450 out of some 22,000 who could be counted as Catholics. The figures did not surprise him.

> Those indeed who should (had they been so disposed) have set about laying the foundation of their city in righteousness, were far otherwise engaged; deeply immersed in selfish pursuits, they were seeking their own future wealth. . . . [118]

A generation earlier, in 1812, a select committee told the House of Commons that "the religious feelings of the Colony appear to have been weak . . . "[119]

---

[114] J. Barrett, "Church, State and People in Eastern Australia, 1835–1850", Ph.D. thesis, Australian National University, 1963, p. 399. For a pioneering essay on the social range of one denomination, see A. Dougan, "The Kirk and Social Problems of the 1830s in N.S.W.", *Royal Australian Historical Society, Journal and Proceedings*, March 1963, p. 457.

[115] S. Freud, *The Future of an Illusion*, p. 69.

[116] L. V. Biggs in *Church Congress Report*, 1913, p. 247.

[117] J. H. Fletcher, *The Second Century of Australian History*, 1888, p. 12.

[118] W. W. Burton, *The State of Religion and Education in New South Wales*, 1840, p. 7.

[119] C. M. H. Clark, *Sources of Australian History*, p. 113.

Then as now, people who lamented the moral and spiritual state of the country mentioned local and contemporary conditions for it: as sun and surf are invoked today, the peculiarities of a raw penal colony were named by the earliest observers. Perhaps they thought that in contemporary England or America, as in good old days everywhere, people were more godly. Yet in the England from which the first white Australians came, Wilberforce and his evangelical friends were saying that Satan had never had it so good; and in the young United States, the Methodist Church was denouncing

> our manifold sins and iniquities—our growing idolatry, which is covetous and the prevailing love of the world . . . the profanation of the Sabbath, . . . disobedience to parents, various debaucheries, drunkenness and such like,

while the Presbyterian General Assembly observed "a general dereliction of religious principles and practice among our fellow-citizens. . . . "[120] Jehovah, it is recorded, had similar complaints about the people of Israel. The farther back we go, the sparser is the information about religious practice; and we may never know enough to plot long-term trends precisely. Yet even when figures are available, prophetic gloom can lead a preacher to ignore or forget them: the attendance of Australians at religious worship is often understated in Protestant sermons.

It has been suggested earlier in this essay that a sense of identification with a religious body affects Australian lives in ways not visible if we look only at attendance. The identification is mild, but it persists from generation to generation; and what is done temperately and intermittently in an acquiescent environment might be done more ardently if part or all of Australian Christianity were seriously menaced by an enemy. In the Soviet Union, nearly fifty years after a revolution whose founders meant to abolish superstition, a Communist organ warns party members that religious beliefs formed over the centuries have permeated the people's existence and have attained the status of irrational habit.[121] For many Australians, it is said, religious behaviour is only a habit. Perhaps; but it does not follow that they or their descendants will sooner or later give it up; and it is possible that a foreign or domestic threat could attach them to their religion with unforeseen tenacity.

Failing such a threat, no "revival" within any of the main streams of Australian Christianity appears likely. Revivalism, on American lines and often conducted by American visitors, has been a normal part of Protestant evangelism here for more than a century; but there has never been any solid evidence that it shifted for long the boundary between the church and the world. At most it has helped to keep warm those people who are already inside the house of God. The place of revivalism in the Protestant churches is one aspect of Australian religion awaiting study; and so is a closely related matter: the appeal of small heterodox sects which recruit people who find the larger churches too cold. One turns to Dougan for the only insight so far offered: wondering why the Catholic church and the Seventh Day Adventists

---

[120] Quoted by P. Miller in *The Shaping of American Religion,* vol. I in J. W. Smith and A. L. Jamison (eds.), *Religion in American Life,* pp. 351–2. The Methodist statement was made in 1795, the Presbyterian in 1798.

[121] For evidence of the survival of religious practice, see W. Kolarz, *Religion in the Soviet Union.*

elicit more vigorous activity from their adherents than any other denomination in Bathurst, he observes that "the Catholic type and sect type churches both provide something closer to a total social environment for their members" than do the larger Protestant denominations.[122] Who joins the Pentecostalists, Jehovah's Witnesses, Christadelphians, Mormons and other dissident bodies? How successful, in their turn, are these sects in preventing members from returning to a larger fold, lapsing into indifference, or moving to another heterodox flock? How many Australians are simultaneously orthodox and heterodox, adhering to a traditional church but attracted also by beliefs which their clergy regard as false? In particular, are editors judging shrewdly or wrongly when they print columns of astrology? Who reads them, and with what effects on their behaviour?[123] Among other small groups not investigated adequately are two overlapping minorities, atheists and Jews.[124] And there are large questions still to be answered thoroughly about majority behaviour. How do religious affiliation and political preference affect each other?[125] Why do more women than men participate in Church activities? How far is this difference explicable in terms of the clubs, lodges and other associations open only to men?[126] How did it happen that for Protestants, but not for Catholics, the hotel and the church came in Australia to be antithetical institutions?[127] A student who addressed himself seriously to such questions could add much to our knowledge of Australian society.

[122] A. Dougan, op. cit., p. 162.

[123] In England, so Geoffrey Gorer reports, more people believe that " there is something in horoscopes" than believe in hell or the devil. One in four say that occasionally or regularly they follow the advice of astrologers. They tend also to be "the most fervent in the practice of their religion; and those groups who are most sceptical about fortune-telling and horoscopes are also the least religious in belief or practice". G. Gorer, Exploring English Character, pp. 269-70. In July 1964 a new daily newspaper, The Australian, aiming at a national circulation among "influential people", included a section "for those who trust the stars".

[124] On Jews see P. Y. Medding, "The Melbourne Jewish Community since 1945", M.A. thesis, University of Melbourne, 1962; C. A. Price, Jewish Settlers in Australia.

[125] On this huge subject, two leads worth following are: R. N. Spann, "The Catholic Vote in Australia", in H. Mayer (ed.), Catholics and the Free Society; J. D. Bollen, "The Temperance Movement and the Liberal Party in New South Wales Politics, 1900-1904", Journal of Religious History, June 1961, pp. 160–82.

[126] "These clubs provide fellowship for men. Women still find a social group within the Church. . . ." A. Dougan, op. cit., p. 160. " 'The club is my church' is the attitude of quite a few men . . . four-fifths of the members of the licensed clubs are not church supporters." A. J. McIntyre, Sunraysia: a Social Survey of a Dried Fruits Area, p. 137.

[127] A correspondent writing to the Canberra Times (2 December 1960) has suggested a device to connect the two cultures symbolized in these two buildings: " 'Halfway Houses' possibly entitled 'Chubs'—halfway in atmosphere between the churches and the pubs and clubs."

5   Education

EDUCATION is commonly but incorrectly regarded as what goes on in the school—the formal learning of subjects which introduce children to their cultural environment and prepare them for citizenship and employment. But the education of children is largely informal, and is shared by all the social groups with which the child has contact—indeed, he may reject the values implicit in school life. Teachers and parents do not always recognize the lack of continuity between the formal and informal aspects of education. The structure of school courses seems often to assume the existence of a homogeneous school population, differing perhaps in ability but sharing common experiences and values. Study of the sociological factors involved in education examines the problems arising from these discontinuities and seeks to contribute to the solution of the problems they set. More sociology in teacher-training courses, special programmes in schools to compensate for culturally impoverished homes, grants to children from poor families and efforts to raise the understanding—and status—of education in the community would clearly all be helpful.

A pluralist and highly diversified society now belies the old comfortable myth of egalitarianism and lack of class or cultural distinction in Australia. If a uniform system of education helped to create this egalitarian tradition, the split into denominational, independent and state schools encouraged divisiveness. The whole subject of the influence of education on Australian social development is in fact obscured by myths, whose removal demands the breaking of prejudices and stereotypes and the substitution of objective facts. Historical and sociological study of the nature of Australian educational institutions, the role of education in social change and control, the teacher's place in school and society, the process of socialization, group dynamics and the transmission of values is urgent.

Meanwhile, education is administered without much reference to sociological theory or data. The myth of Australian education will be illustrated by reference, first, to the historical tradition of education; second, to commonly held contemporary views; and thirdly, an assessment based on general sociological theory and recent research in Australia.

The history of education in Australia is now being seriously studied, but there is no comprehensive and reliable standard history, and the few significant monographs so far produced hardly disturb the traditional image of Australian education based largely on the development of public systems of primary education.

THE RECEIVED TRADITION

The myth can be stated briefly. Between 1872 and 1893 state systems, financed by public funds and administered by a Minister of the Crown and a government department of education or public instruction, were established. Each was centrally administered and rigidly controlled by a thorough system of inspection; each was free, secular, compulsory, efficient and utilitarian.

These initial characteristics of public education remain important components of the myth. Few other indications of purpose have been provided since the passing of the various Education Acts, which remain the basic legislation in all states. The minor amendments passed from time to time arouse small comment.

The Education Acts did not in fact make education free, secular, and compulsory in all cases and at once. Efficiency was measured by attendance and strict observance of prescribed courses of study. Attainment was measured by public examinations and rigorous inspection by departmental officials. Efficiency thus became indistinguishable from conformity to the supposed whim of head-teacher or inspector or public examiner or all of these invigilator stereotypes. (Indeed, for a time in most states the vicious system of payment by results was used as a basis of the teacher's salary.) This system provided a measurable test of efficiency in spite of being an inferior system for evaluating understanding, personal development or teaching skill. Apparently satisfactory results were obtained because of the ability of the pupils and teachers to prepare for the type of test used; administrators and the public, if interested, were satisfied with the standard achieved. Education in Australia has not met the high promise of the 1870s when state departments were established amid enthusiasm. Australians have come too easily to accept as adequate the system to which they have become accustomed. Whether or not the education offered to young Australians in the last ninety years has been as useful to them as individuals or to the nation in developing the national resources of ability and lifting the level of culture as some other type of education is problematic. Assessing its effectiveness runs against the problem of the lack of discussion of aims in the Education Acts, official reports and regulations.

Non-government schools—numerous and in many cases, important—fit uneasily into the pattern of myths about society and education. In fact the large, exclusive, old-established, fee-charging schools, found in the capital cities and some of the provincial centres, form the feet of clay of the egalitarian image of Australian education. Catholic schools have become increasingly important, as they have developed into what amounts to a second school system providing primary and secondary education for a minority group—a visible sign of a pluralism which must be recognized. Prompted in part by the abolition of state aid to church schools, this second system sprang from the intransigence of the church over the question of control of education which it was not prepared to share with the secular state in any compromise proposed from about 1870 onwards. Its position threatened the concept of the liberal secular state and set Catholics apart as a separate group within society. The Catholic community, largely working and lower-middle class in its social composition towards the end of last century, strengthened the popular non-Catholic view that the separate system contributed to social stratification and maintained the division between the Catholic minority and the rest of the population. On the other hand, the Catholic working class, which supported the Labour movement, and the Catholic schools, which catered mainly for the primary education of the lower classes, fitted into the popular image of the egalitarian society. But this was not sufficient to break down the opposition to state aid to denominational schools, based on the argument that aid would tend to increase the gap between the two school systems and the majority and minority groups in society. The nature of the differences between the two school systems and the Catholic and non-Catholic groups needs to be examined in the light of present conditions and not in terms of the myth. It seems at least likely that socio-economic factors contributed as much as religious differences to the creation of the myth that there are two irreconcilable groups and school systems.

The changing status of Catholics in the community is related to the extension of the Catholic secondary schools and the increase in Catholic students attending universities. The rapid development of secondary education has imposed heavy burdens on Catholic resources for building schools and staffing specialist subjects. Many Catholic children already attend state primary and secondary schools. Various solutions have been suggested. Lay catechists are trained in Brisbane to provide religious instruction to Catholic children in state schools. Lay teachers are employed in increasing numbers. Archbishop Young of Hobart suggested in 1963 that parish schools should be closed so that the secondary schools could be given more support. If the church continues its system of schools, and shortages of trained staff and overcrowded classes remain, Catholic children will encounter educational and occupational disadvantages, and divisions arising from religious differences will be sharpened. On the other hand, the church seems unlikely to give up the view that education is fully effective for a Christian only when sustained within the framework of Christian values, and permeated by Catholic religious beliefs.

The tradition of Australian education as presented ignores aspects of its development inimical to the egalitarian myth. The rise of the schools and the spread of educational opportunities is usually linked with the growth of democracy and the extension of the franchise. There *was* a connection—some support came from politicians who believed that their masters must be educated—but other factors stand out. That educational development was regulated by a decision-making *élite,* with very varied motives, is still not widely recognized. In the first years of settlement in New South Wales, these included the moral responsibility of caring for the children of convicts, of rescuing them from the evil influences of their surroundings, and later of developing "habits of industry and regularity and . . . the principles of the Established Church".[1] Religious indoctrination, moral regeneration, and social control—to keep the lower orders in their place or to educate them for employment as clerks and mechanics, that is, sufficiently to be useful but not a danger to the upper classes—are clearly identifiable motives. Further research seems certain to revise the received tradition drastically, as it brings

[1] Bathurst to Macquarie, 13 May 1820, *H.R.A.*, I, x, 304.

forward evidence that conformity to social class standards has been and remains a significant feature in educational planning. Limited educational opportunity, depending to a large extent on the changing needs of the community, has been mistaken for equal opportunity for all.

EDUCATIONAL PLANNING

The methods of educational policy-making and planning are more significant for the future than the myth of Australian education. In most cases, discussion and analysis proceed in purely quantitative terms. Problems of finance, population, and staff all need qualitative assessment as well. A review of contemporary statements about education will illustrate some of the contradictions and weaknesses inherent in policy and planning based on unexamined assumptions.

The federal White Paper of 1962, *The Commonwealth and Education*, acknowledges new trends in education and increased enrolments which demand new courses, and changes in the structure of secondary and tertiary education to cater for a higher proportion of continuing students and for more overseas students. Although "it is recognized that education is a matter of great social importance and that there can be no richer investment than the intellectual and social development of our future citizens", and that expenditure must continue to grow with the growth of population and the increased demand for trained staff, the Government appeared reluctant to take positive action because of the responsibility of the states for education.

The White Paper does not go below the surface of educational needs and problems to consider the effectiveness of expenditure, or the relation between the education provided and the balanced professional, personal, and social development advocated by the Prime Minister on another occasion.[2]

The *Report of the Committee on State Education in Victoria*[3] surveys the state system, but ignores the educational implications of changing social and industrial conditions except to note in passing "the changing pattern of employment" and "the doubling of the total horse-power of industrial engines". Quantitative growth of schools, holding power, the number of pupils and public examination candidates are considered systematically. The Report recommends spending £48 million over five years, but sets no qualitative standards for the assessment of progress and future needs. Recommendations are based on administrative convenience, or the availability of money, buildings, and teaching staff. The Committee showed no interest in whether the proposals it accepted or rejected were educationally sound. Problems of loss of talent and the realization of educational opportunities are passed over lightly, although both are crucial problems in most countries and were currently being examined elsewhere in Australia. School cleaning was one of the few questions discussed on the basis of experimental findings.

Education in Australia—Students' Report[4] is limited on the whole to obvious propositions about formal education. It is unsatisfactory when dealing with the objectives of education or the problems of social change. It

[2] Address to the Australian College of Education, *The Challenge to Australian Education*, 1961.
[3] Government Printer, Melbourne, 1960.
[4] Students' Representative Council, University of Melbourne, 1963.

assumes that equality of opportunity operates satisfactorily at present, and in particular that there is "not much wastage amongst the top two or three per cent of (talented) students".

The *Wyndham Report*[5] is an exception to the dull uniformity of official statements and reports. It discusses aims and thoroughly assesses all aspects of secondary education in New South Wales. Its conclusions are not popular amongst supporters of selective high schools, who see comprehensive schools as a threat to academic standards. The greatest strength of the Report is the stress placed on the cultivation of talent in its proposed new syllabus for secondary education. The problem is how to meet "the needs of all adolescents without impairment to the potentialities of any",[6] at a time when there are too few well-qualified teachers to provide the intellectual stimulation required to make the comprehensive schools and the core curriculum work.

Ultimately, decisions about education are made at the political level, and this is an area of compromise rather than creativity. The departments of education are by nature self-perpetuating; some administrators are out of touch with society and educational theory and practice. Authoritarianism, which permeates the organization of state departments, state and independent schools and classrooms, and inhibits creativity, freedom and responsibility in education, is not merely the result of rigid centralized control of schools and examinations. It stems largely from the unquestioning acceptance of authority by the community. It is strengthened in the case of state departments by ministerial control and responsibility to parliament. It exists in all but a few experimental private schools.

During the last ten years there has been an unprecedented volume of discussion about the place of education in Australian society. Much of the criticism has been directed at the traditions of imitating successful overseas reforms or of extending existing systems with a minimum of disturbance to the status quo. The critics have directed their fire at conventional features of education like the excessively utilitarian character of the universities, the uncritical acceptance of "equality of opportunity" without any realization of some of the uncomfortable implications of this concept, and the failure of secondary education to adapt itself to new demands. Unfortunately, these criticisms rarely lead to positive suggestions for the reshaping of education so that it can perform a different social role.[7]

Various left-wing critiques of education published in recent years[8] have concentrated on governments, officials, and Labour politicians who have accepted a quantitative approach to questions of finance and the content of courses, and utilitarian standards regarding the value of education as a means of vocational training and preparation for citizenship. Labour, in its desire to spread the benefits of education, accepts the values enshrined in middle

---

[5] *Report of the Committee Appointed to Survey Secondary Education in New South Wales*, 1956.

[6] *Ibid.*, p. 63.

[7] See, *e.g.*, P. H. Partridge, in *Melbourne Studies in Education* 1960–61; H. P. Schoenheimer, in *Primary Education Today*, Victorian Institute of Educational Research, 1960; J. R. Darling, *Educational Values in a Democracy*; C. D. Hardie, in the *Australian Quarterly*, June 1955; Alice Hoy, in *Australian Journal of Education*, no. 1, April 1957; W. D. Neal, in *Australian Journal of Education*, vol. 6, no. 3, 1962.

[8] See, *e.g.*, Davies and Serle (eds.) *Policies for Progress*, ch. 8; *Outlook*, special number, August 1962.

class educational institutions and transforms the principles of equality of opportunity into the belief that all men could and should benefit from this particular education—a belief which is "neither socialist nor sensible". In a system dominated by middle class values, society required of the school two things: to provide a standard of literacy sufficient for social and administrative communication; and to prepare children for employment in categories of work where the proportion of skilled to unskilled labour is determined by economic requirements. The level of education was lifted, but at the same time restricted to technological skills, useful to society and not a threat to it. The school assumes a sameness about children whatever their environmental background; the same skills, the same rate of learning. But it is in the acquisition of skills and the rate of learning that class differences function at all levels of education. The lower class child is at a disadvantage. As yet the educational system does little about the differences, for example, by designing measures for "strengthening and enriching the literary background of intellectually under-privileged children", and it is only the fittest who survive the primary school programme, concerned largely with mechanical skills, language skills and vocabulary, all of which favours the middle class child. Any recent liberalization of educational opportunity has resulted from economic necessity. A concern for educational justice demands that "the individual child, in the totality of his setting—family, school, society—must be taken as the unit of education". The findings of empirical research carried out recently in Australia tend to support the case presented by the socialist groups in the public discussion of Australian education.

At its 1963 federal conference, the A.L.P. became the first Australian political party to adopt a constructive education policy, which went beyond the usual election promises of more schools and more funds to basic social issues such as equality of education. Equality involves "not only the removal of social obstacles for talented individuals, but the provision of social conditions which will give all individuals positive inducements to achieve the realization of their own capabilities".[9] The A.L.P. advocated increased expenditure, expansion of facilities, improvement of the quantity and the quality of education, long-range planning and the establishment of a Commonwealth department of education. Both parties in the 1963 election showed an awareness of public interest in education, and undertook to provide more funds immediately to relieve the crisis.

There are disturbing features about the public record regarding finance, student population and staffing.

The Commonwealth government, although it has no constitutional power over education, directly finances it in the A.C.T. and other territories, in the Services, and through the departments of Repatriation, Immigration, Health and Social Services. The State governments, besides their Education departments, spend through the departments of Public Works (school buildings), Health (school medical services and pre-school centres) and Agriculture (agricultural colleges and extension services). Funds for education come from revenue, loan funds, and parents' contributions for extra equipment. Direct financial assistance was not given, until 1964, to independent, non-state schools, with the exception of a subsidy to grammar schools in Queens-

---

[9] A.L.P. Federal Conference, 1963, policy statement on education.

land, grants-in-aid to mission schools in Papua and New Guinea, and subsidies to mission schools in the Northern Territory. Since the 1963 election the Commonwealth, Victorian and Queensland governments have announced plans for an additional 25,000 scholarships for secondary education. In 1964 the Commonwealth government honoured an election promise by providing £5 millions annually for expenditure on school science laboratories and equipment, payable both to state and non-government schools—a small but significant break in the traditions of a century.

In recent years education has taken a larger share of public expenditure. In particular, spending on school buildings, teachers' salaries and teacher training has risen since 1945. The need for this higher spending rests on increases in the school population which are due to a higher birth rate and large-scale immigration. Neglect during the depression and the war had to be made good. Children are also tending to stay longer at school. However, educational finance is in a crisis, with demands for further increases.

Professor P. H. Karmel,[10] who has examined the economics of Australian education, claims that education affects productivity through the skill of the work force, the ingenuity and inventiveness of technologists and scientists and the knowledge and understanding of administration, and that there is a high correlation between the educational effort of different countries and their annual rates of production as well as a correlation between enrolment ratios for children and young people in the relevant age groups and the gross national product per head. The present expenditure is low by comparison with other countries, and the right of individuals to education is a powerful argument for greater effort to make education available to all without discrimination as to class, colour, creed or income.

Karmel attempted to measure Australia's educational effort by using the school enrolment ratios of certain age groups, the proportions of population in certain age groups, and the proportion of the work force engaged in education. In spite of the limitations of the statistics, Karmel illustrates the substantial rise in the relative importance of education in the community. Over fifty years the enrolment ratios, in the age group 15–19 years, trebled for boys and doubled for girls; the proportion of the work force engaged in education increased by 50%. Nevertheless, the enrolment ratios of the age groups 15–19 and 20–24 years in Australia compare "very unfavourably with those of many countries. . . . Australia ranks 12th for the age group 15–19 years and last but one for the age group 20–24 years."[11]

The proportion of national resources which should be devoted to education is difficult to determine. A rise in the proportion of the gross national product devoted to education may be due to many factors. If the school population is large, the proportion of the gross national product expended will be relatively high, and the recent increase in relative expenditure on education is due to this factor. However, an apparent increase of expenditure may conceal a fall, difficult to demonstrate, in the quality of education.

Karmel points out that by comparison with other countries, "Australia spends a relatively low proportion of gross national production on education. In current expenditure Australian ranks fifteenth in the list and in total

[10] P. H. Karmel, *Some Economic Aspects of Education*, p. 3.
[11] *Ibid.*, p. 13.

expenditure equal eleventh".[12] In terms of current expenditure all the countries ranked above Australia, except four, had smaller proportions of their population who were of school and college age, and for all countries with a total expenditure above Australia, only one had a larger proportion of school and college age and a higher rate of population growth. There was a rise in the proportion of gross national product expended on education from about 2.2% in 1953–4 to 2.9% in 1958–9 and 3.3% in 1960–1. At the same time there was a 25% increase in the ratio between school age members (6–16 years) of the community, and males between the ages of 15 and 64 years. Since the proportion of gross national product devoted to education in other countries has also risen, the Australian figure can only be taken as relatively low. By 1970 most other countries will be spending relatively more than Australia is now spending on current educational services and two-thirds of them will be spending relatively more on current and capital educational programmes combined".[13]

TABLE 1

Net Expenditure on Education—Australia (£1,000)

	1949–50	1954–5	1959–60	1960–1
1. Total, Education Department and schools	25,816	60,018	101,703	115,371
	=100	232·4	397·8	448
c ..	100	149·45	220·75	
2. Administration	938	2,088	3,920	4,413
	=100	222·6	417·9	470·4
3. Transportation	b	4,865	6,493	7,225
		=100		148·5
4. Training of teachers	1,243	3,741	7,901	8,777
	=100	300·9	635·6	706·1
5. Primary	18,631	37,586	57,338	63,659
	=100	201·7	307·7	341·6
6. Secondary..	5,004	11,738	26,051	31,596
	=100	234·5	520·6	631
7. University..	1,351	4,363	8,504	10,352
	=100	322·9	663·8	766
8. Technical	3,708	7,291	13,266	14,514
	=100	196·6	257·7	391
9. Agricultural	488	963	1,073	1,181
	=100	197·3	219·8	242
10. Libraries	740	1,644	2,662	3,032
	=100	222·1	359·7	409·7
11. Deaf, Dumb, Blind	133	309	515	600
	=100	232·3	387·2	451
12. Total expenditure by a	32,236	74,588	127,783	145,350
six states only	=100	231·3	396·3	450·8
c	100	148·7	219·9	

    a. Six states only.
    b. Included in other items.
    c. Allowance is made for inflation.
Source: Annual Reports of Commonwealth Grants Commission.

[12] *Ibid.*, p. 17.
[13] *Ibid.*, p. 18.

Total expenditure on education, which includes private schools' buildings and costs, is hard to estimate. Table 1 shows state governments' net expenditure on education.

From 1949–50 to 1960–1 spending increased 450% without allowing for inflation. The increase has not been spread evenly over all areas: the most pressing problems, administration, teacher training, secondary, university, and deaf dumb and blind education exceeded the rate of general increase; primary, technical and agricultural education, and libraries fell below. Increased expenditure is not a guarantee of the quality of education, although parents and politicians alike seem satisfied when it means new classrooms, scholarships and bus allowances. Allowances and tax concessions help all sections of the community, including children from low income families to remain longer at school.

The number of children in schools, and the growing proportion staying on at school, keeps education costs rising. Table 2, compiled from the Australian Council for Educational Research tables, shows the number of children aged 14 and 17 at school as percentages of the number of the same generation at school when 13 years of age. The marked differences between states, which require further study before they can be fully explained, suggest considerable inequality of opportunity between states.

TABLE 2

Children at school as % of their age group

Year	N.S.W.		Vic.		Qld.		S.A.		W.A.	
	14	17	14	17	14	17	14	17	14	17
	%	%	%	%	%	%	%	%	%	%

The percentages shown below are based on number of 13 year old children attending school in this year.

Year	N.S.W. 14	N.S.W. 17	Vic. 14	Vic. 17	Qld. 14	Qld. 17	S.A. 14	S.A. 17	W.A. 14	W.A. 17
1951 ..	95		65		71		62		68	
1956 ..	97	7	77	11	72	10	75	5	75	8
1961 ..	99	9	87	17	83	18	85	9	87	12
1962 ..	99·5	10	90	18	85	20	88	10	90	13
1963 ..	100	10	92	19	87	21	90	11	92	14
1964 ..	100	10·5	94	20	89	22		12	97	15
1965 ..	100	11		20		24		13	97	15

Note.—Percentages of 14-year-olds are estimates after 1956; percentages of 17-year-olds are estimates after 1962. The New South Wales figures prior to 1958 are estimates based on actual figures for government schools, and a proportion of those aged 17·0 and above in non-government schools. There are differences in methods of compilation in the various states.

The number of students attending schools has risen (see Table 3) as a result of the post-1945 birthrate increase and the increased proportion staying on beyond the age of fifteen.[14] It has been argued[15] that "the existing overpopulation in Australian universities . . . has arisen almost wholly from the increasing ratio of young people attending our universities". Further expansion of university population is inevitable, even if the population of each age entering universities is held constant, because of the bulge in the birth-rate

[14] W. D. Borrie, "Schools and Universities and the Future", *Vestes*, vol. 5, no. 3, 1962.
[15] W. D. Borrie and R. M. Dedman, *University Enrolments in Australia 1955–70*, p. 3.

after 1945. It is possible that demands for highly qualified graduates could be met from the enlarged group of students without drawing on the untapped resources of groups not at present undertaking advanced studies.

The immediate problem is to provide school and university places, or suitable and acceptable alternatives, for young people seeking further education. Staffing is a crucial problem, because of the size of the age group from which staff can be drawn and the time required for training. In the case of government schools, Table 3 indicates the lag between increased enrolments and the provision of the extra staff required to maintain the status quo. Not until 1961 was there a slight improvement in the teacher/pupil ratio.

TABLE 3

Staffing and Enrolment in Government Schools

	1950	1955	1960	1961
1. Enrolments in government schools	1,027,459 =100	1,336,742 130·1	1,612,046 156·8	1,662,678 161·6
2. Teachers in government schools	36,085 =100	45,104 124·9	57,032 155·8	60,029 166·3
3. Ratio Enrolment Teachers × 100	(a) =100	104·1	100·6	(b) 97·1

Source: Commonwealth Bureau of Census & Statistics, Social Statistics, No. 10, Schools 1961; No. 1, 1960; plus various Commonwealth Yearbooks.

(a) Teacher-pupil ratio 1:28·4 in 1950.
(b) Teacher-pupil ratio 1:27·6 in 1961.

In spite of increased expenditure the situation, in some vital aspects, is worse now than it was in the early 1950s. Overcrowding of classrooms is still prevalent, and many emergency classes still exist. In 1959 more than half the pupils in large Victorian primary schools were in classes of more than 40, and 10% were in classes of 50 or more. The number of emergency classes doubled between 1955 and 1959. State departments claim that the present staff-student ratio is the "best balance that can be anticipated at present between what is educationally desirable and what is practicable with the resources of accommodation and staff either available or in prospect".[16] State ministers released a critical review of the position late in 1963[17] which notes that in addition to what is needed to cope with new enrolments, 1,000 extra classrooms are needed to eliminate makeshift accommodation, and 3,600 classrooms and 5,200 teachers to remove unreasonably large classes. Efforts to reduce class size have not been very successful. More than half of primary and secondary classes are too large, and it has not been possible to increase the teaching force sufficiently to meet the needs. Assuming that it was desirable to reduce the staff-student ratio from the present 1:27.6 to 1:20, an additional 23,105 teachers would be required for government schools alone. Just over 6,000 teachers a year are produced from the training courses in the

[16] *A Statement of Some Needs of Australian Education,* Australian Education Council, 1963, p. 25.
[17] *Ibid.*

states to fill the gaps caused by retirements and resignations without alleviating the backlog of large classes, shortages of qualified teachers and the use of many temporary teachers, especially in secondary schools.

Absolute numbers of teachers do not indicate the grave shortage of qualified staff. Many teachers are teaching subjects in the secondary schools for which they possess inadequate qualifications. Primary teacher training in itself is no qualification for secondary teaching, but education departments are using primary teachers without good academic qualifications as a means of meeting the shortage of qualified secondary teachers. The shortage of qualified teachers is recognized in science and mathematics, but it is also acute in modern languages, history, geography and even English, which is too commonly regarded as a subject anyone can teach. In 1960 Victorian government schools needed 1,460 permanent teachers of English, social studies, and modern languages at the current class sizes; the actual number available fell short by 500.

State departments are reluctant to divulge information which would clarify the extent of the shortage of qualified staff, and the information available was collected by the Australian Science Teachers' Association, the Australian Council for Educational Research, and the universities. The general findings are not reassuring for the future of secondary and tertiary education. The small number of graduate science teachers in secondary schools is related to employment opportunities in research and industry, the inadequate recognition given to a degree holder, the relatively low salary paid to well-qualified graduates, heavy teaching loads, absence of laboratory assistants, large classes, insufficient equipment and laboratories, lack of opportunity for further study, and frequent transfers. This depressing situation exists in the subject which enjoys the highest status in Australian schools, which is most in the public eye, and which provides the basic training for all scientific and industrial courses. No detailed study has been made of the distribution of qualified science teachers among schools of different size and in rural and urban areas.

In a survey of the academic qualifications of secondary school science teachers in Sydney, G. R. Meyer notes the tendency to place graduate teachers "in socially advanced areas where a greater proportion of the pupils would desire to complete secondary education and perhaps proceed to various forms of higher education".[18] Non-selective secondary schools in working class areas, however, are staffed by a majority of non-graduates. This is justified by the fact that in 1957 secondary education in these schools terminated at the end of the third year. Only four of twenty science teachers in the Catholic schools in his sample were graduates. Taking both independent and state schools, only 41% of science teachers were graduates, compared with 71% of English and history teachers.

That Meyer's sample of teachers was representative of New South Wales or Australia as a whole, was shown by the Australian Science Teachers' Association 1960 survey conducted in conjunction with the Australian Council for Educational Research, which shows that 59% of science teachers in Australia had no science degree, and 31% had no passes in any university science subjects. Some 32% of teachers of matriculation physics had passed

18 *The Australian Science Teachers' Journal*, vol. 8, no. 3, 1962.

no more than one unit of physics, and 24% of teachers of matriculation chemistry had passed no more than one unit of chemistry.

A study of trends in the supply of qualified teachers of science in Queensland, based on the reports of the Minister for Education for the years 1952–61, indicates that for the period 1952–6 the supply of teachers in secondary schools failed to meet the increase in the school population, being less than one-half the proportional increase, while the rate of increase of science graduates was only one-third of that required to meet the increased number of pupils; for the period 1956–61 the supply of secondary teachers was maintained at the same rate as the increase in the school population, but the rate of increase in the number of science graduates fell to less than one-tenth of that needed to keep up with the very large expansion in the numbers of pupils and of all teachers supplied. For the period as a whole, the rate of teacher increase was as high as five-sevenths of the rate of pupil increase, but the rate of science teacher increase was one-eighth of the pupil rate and only one-sixth of the rate of teacher increase. This trend is continuing in Queensland, and it seems likely that the position is deteriorating throughout Australia. Meyer showed that in 1952 61% of 191 biology teachers were graduates, whereas his 1957 sample had only 30%.

Tertiary education is under even greater strain than the primary and secondary schools. The problems of unprecedented student numbers, increasing at a rate in excess of the rate of population growth, have been discussed very frankly. New universities have been established, new courses in the sciences and humanities provided, and the social composition of the undergraduate body has changed. In spite of increased expenditure and the provision of more university places and staff, restriction has been applied in some universities and several thousand matriculated students excluded. Tertiary education has been recognized as a source of national power, as a means of national survival, but in most cases this has meant increased demands for technical education in the applied sciences and in commerce. The utilitarian attitude to university studies is still characteristic of the interests of governments, industry, and commerce, many parents and students. The universities are still undecided how to solve the problems of increased demand and large student population: by quotas and the exclusion of some capable students, by rapid expansion of the present university system, or by developing new tertiary institutions. The two reports of the Australian Universities Commission fail to present constructive solutions to these problems.

No uniformity exists between the educational systems of the Australian states. Transfer of children from one state system to another is difficult because of differences in curriculum, teaching methods, and organization. Transfer of teachers is rare because of lack of reciprocity of seniority and other fringe benefits between the public services of the states. The cultural content of many courses is not distinctively Australian, or designed to develop an appreciation of Australian culture as part of the school experience of children. This is gradually becoming less obvious, as attempts are made to modify the inherited culture of the West so that it becomes part of the Australian cultural environment and not hostile to it. Australian history and literature have gained a certain respectability, and a place in school courses. "Cultural" subjects generally are viewed with some suspicion because their content has until recently been largely imitative of formal education and culture in Britain, and also because of the high prestige attached to "practical" and scientific subjects.

The values implicit in the various systems of education are not accepted by all classes in society. This is reflected in the low status given to education by many Australians, and the widespread belief that while education lacks relevance to the main issues of life, material prosperity and happiness, it may be useful as the means of getting a good job. Finally, there has been little or no discussion of the aims of education so that there are no commonly accepted objectives for education in Australia. Most statements about education are statements of prejudice, and the range of agreement in a pluralist society is limited. The effectiveness of education depends not merely on the formal process of instruction in schools, but on the relationship between the formal process established by society and the primary social groups. Understanding begins only when the value judgments are placed beside research findings.

RESEARCH FINDINGS

The findings of research relating to non-academic factors in failure, the problems of wastage of talent, social factors in learning, and social attitudes to education, illustrate some of the weaknesses inherent in the claims made for Australian education, in the present structure of education, and in the quantitative approach to educational problems. It is clear that many educational problems are essentially social problems. If wastage, for example, is to be avoided, or if education is to be made available equally to all, social changes and social control are involved. Meanwhile, without change, most of the discussion of these important topics is merely platitudinous. The social changes taking place at present result from increased population, increased demand for higher education, and not from any prior policy for the improvement of education, although in meeting the demand improvements are achieved.

If the treatment of research findings given below seems limited in scope and lacking in balance, it reflects the nature of the research effort. Moreover, some overlap of concerns is inevitable in the reporting.

If the social factors in education were studied closely, adequate and appropriate educational services for all sections of the community could be provided, and near equality of opportunity achieved. The provision of opportunities for all students irrespective of place of residence—a recurring aspiration in Australia—has led to such interesting expedients as one-teacher rural schools, correspondence schools, and the School of the Air. More than 20,000 children of the outback, handicapped children and Australian children overseas, are at present taking lessons by correspondence. Little is known of the effects of education received in isolated areas without the normal contact with a large number of children in other grades in the school. It is likely to have effects on later adjustment to schooling and study under urban conditions. Generally, the curriculum is the same for urban and rural schools but performance varies. In a Victorian study[19] the variation in the performance in English, which was below the level "regarded as normal for urban children

[19] O. A. Oeser and F. E. Emery, *Social Structure and Personality in a Rural Community*, pp. 161 and 175.

in the same grades", was not traceable to intellectual backwardness, as the group was slightly higher than state norms.

The distribution of secondary pupils in different types of school, and in rural and urban areas, and the proportion of pupils from the various schools entering the university, are changing. More students are staying longer at state secondary schools and a higher proportion are now entering the university. The trend is illustrated by the results of an inquiry at the University of Queensland, reported in Schonell, Roe and Meddleton, *Promise and Performance*.

TABLE 4

Intake of First Year Students at the University of Queensland

	1955		1961	
Type of school	*Number*	*%*	*Number*	*%*
State high schools	103	25·75	419	37·44
Church schools	245	61·25	403	36·01
Grammar schools..	52	13	297	26·54

Type of school is a factor in the entry of students to honours courses, which are sources of potential university staff and of other highly trained graduates. As increasing demands are made for these highly trained specialists, the relatively small increase in the number of honours students which has taken place since 1950 becomes a major problem. Of the Arts undergraduates at the University of Melbourne in 1959, only 15% were in the honours schools, yet a study of potential honours students showed that in terms of ability the honours group could be more than double the size it was.[20] Some of the potential honours students were not interested in the honours course because of the extra time and work involved. Three main variables operated: type of school, level of matriculation result, and, for studentship holders, the policy of the Education Department.

TABLE 5

School attended	*Students enrolled in honours courses* *%*	*Enrolled for pass courses but potential honours* *%*
Major "Public"	26	17
Associated Grammar	19	15
Roman Catholic	19	15
Metropolitan State High	17	21
Country State High	3	9
Coaching College	5	2
Others ..	11	11

[20] D. S. Anderson, "Students of honours potential in pass courses in the University of Melbourne", *The Educand*, vol. 4, no. 1, 1960; and "Non-intellectual Correlates of Academic Performance", *Vestes*, vol. 4, no. 2, 1961.

Educational wastage, including the under-use of able people as well as failure in school and university courses, involves important non-intellectual factors associated with successful learning. "There is no doubt from our evidence that sociological factors of an important kind need consideration. . . ."[21] It is self-evident that ability is an essential factor in academic success, but large numbers of talented children do not take, or complete, courses to the limit of their ability. The progress of the upper 5% of Queensland children entering secondary education in 1952 was marred by a wastage of about one-third of the group, and influenced by the occupation, schooling, and income of the father.[22] The same factors are evident at universities. The educational standard of the parents of students in the 1955 intake at the University of Queensland was much higher than that of the general public.[23] The professional and administrative groups (8% of working males) produced 42% of the students' fathers; only 3.5% had fathers in the semi-skilled and unskilled groups (35.5%). The same problem exists in other states.[24]

A study of science graduates in Western Australia[25] in the years 1952, 1954 and 1956 indicates that about one-third came from families with a standard of education already above average.

The probability of a pupil's planning to go to a university is related to the level of the parents' education.[26] The parents of most students who plan to go to the university did not receive more than a secondary education. The sons of fathers in the professions have a greater chance of attending a university than do children of similar ability whose fathers are skilled workers. But educational level, occupation, and economic status together do not explain variation in educational plans and achievements. Indifferent parental attitudes to further education, and low educational and occupational aspirations of parents and students, both result in the erosion of talent.[27] In these cases increased grants alone would not suffice. Financial difficulties are often mentioned as a reason for leaving school, although the evidence of children from well-to-do homes who leave school early indicates the importance of parental influence.[28] Lack of information about university education is often as important as lack of finance.[29]

> Any attempt to explain school-leaving or continuing upon the basis of a single factor such as economic conditions will provide a distorted picture, and any attempt to alter the situation by giving attention to an inadequate number of conditions not only will fail but actually may be followed by socially undesirable consequences. . . .[30]

[21] F. J. Schonell, E. Roe and I. G. Meddleton, *Promise and Performance*, 1962, p. ix.

[22] *Bulletin No. 13, 1957*, Research and Guidance Branch, Queensland Department of Education.

[23] Schonell, Roe and Meddleton, *op. cit.*, p. 28.

[24] J. M. Wheeler, *The Educand*, vol. 2, no. 2, 1955.

[25] J. R. Greenway, B.Ed. Honours thesis, University of W.A.

[26] R. F. Berdie, *Manpower and the Schools*, ch. 4.

[27] *Bulletin No. 24, 1962*, Research and Guidance Branch, Queensland Education Department.

[28] E. R. Wyeth, *Interim Report on Wastage of Talent in Victoria* (1957).

[29] R. F. Berdie, *op. cit.*, pp. 97-8.

[30] *Ibid.*, p. 62.

For example, size of family is one factor contributing to wastage, but family limitation is unlikely to avert wastage. Of greater importance is the level of acceptance of the value of education. A child's acceptance of school depends in part on the parents' acceptance of school. People of lowly occupational status are habituated to early leaving, and employment does not depend on academic success. Low aspiration often results in low achievement. In higher occupational groups less able children are frustrated by formal learning, but the status of the school often influences the acceptance of education by a group habituated to a longer period of schooling.[31] On the whole, the educational attitudes of the upper and middle classes are more in accord with the values of the school than those of the working classes. Acceptance of the value of education is linked with the process of upward social mobility. Many able children from classes low in the social order appear to enter teaching as a stepping-stone to improved social position. Later, as parents, these same people assist their children to enter the professions offering high financial and social status.[32]

The pattern of recruitment for the Armidale Teachers' College over the period 1929 to 1957 indicates that almost half the students were recruited from a narrow range of occupational groups comprising small business men, small farmers and tradesmen. The students completed the full secondary school course before entering college. This is a commentary on the spread of ability in groups where a low level of acceptance of education might be assumed, and on the opportunities provided for developing ability by the state secondary school system.[33] Many students, however, who enter teachers' colleges because this matches their educational aspiration, could on the basis of ability manage university studies.

National origin of the family is related to the educational plans of pupils and is thus a factor in wastage. Children of parents born in Australia or other English-speaking countries are less inclined to consider attending the university than the children of parents born in Europe.[34] A higher proportion of children in urban areas tend to continue with education to the end of the secondary school than children in rural areas.[35] The entry of some students into technical and commercial courses in country schools, where these courses are valued for their practical value, probably represents a greater diversion of talented country students than that occurring amongst talented students in city schools.[36]

"We certainly should look at the leakage of large groups of really able students from the secondary schools. Why do so few able children, particularly girls, from the homes of skilled artisans, ever reach the university?"[37] Prejudice against girls being educated at the tertiary level is still quite strong —and against women continuing to practise a profession after marriage.

[31] G. W. Bassett, "The Retention of Zest in Learning", *Educational Values in a Democracy*, p. 196.
[32] G. W. Bassett, "The Social Role of the Secondary School in Australia", *The Australian Journal of Education*, vol. 1, no. 1, 1957.
[33] G. W. Bassett, "The Occupational Background of Teachers", *The Australian Journal of Education*, vol. 2, no. 2, 1958.
[34] R. F. Berdie, *op. cit.*, p. 60.
[35] J. M. Wheeler, *The Educand*, vol. 2, no. 2, 1955.
[36] E. R. Wyeth, *op. cit.*
[37] Schonell, Roe and Meddleton, *op. cit.*, p. x.

Little is known about the social utility of the curriculum offered in schools, although syllabus committees must make assumptions. The work in some courses—arithmetic, history, shorthand and English—seems to be achieving the results desired, but without relation sometimes either to the needs of employers, or the ability of students.[38] In other cases the school is not well related to the needs of a particular community.

The general conclusion drawn from a study[39] of the relations between a timber mill community and its school was that if schools neglect their communities it is because psychological and sociological factors are neglected, and not because the school is part of a centralized administrative system. This limits the extent of the school's responsibility in a community deficient in many ways—employment opportunities, people of limited capacities, attainments and resources, children as a group below the average of Western Australian children in ability, and more than usually dependent upon the school for educative experiences. The limitation of the school's responsibility in the social development of a community, typical of many in isolated areas of Australia, illustrates the uniformity of the normal education department approach to the socializing function of the school.

Some of the social factors which influence the education of aboriginal children apply to other special groups in the community—migrant groups and poor children—where lack of money and parental awareness of the value of education in personal development and social and occupational mobility make for school achievement and early leaving. Aboriginal education will need also to take into account the nature of social change involved, provide for adult education and, in the case of tribal groups, for extensive community education after the style of fundamental education. Because of the differences between the environment of tribal life, mission stations and government aboriginal settlements, and fringe-dwelling and the environment of a normal Australian community, aboriginal education must be directed toward social change to prepare for the transfer from one environment to another, whether the terms of the transfer be in terms of assimilation or integration. Children, adults and, in particular, the natural status-holders in the present environment, must be reached.

The future of technical education in Australia is under study by the engineering profession and university staff, and it appears that new specialist courses will be developed to meet the demands of industry, alongside more general training in the humanities.[40] The definition of different types of technical education ranging from technology to trade training remains a problem.

---

[38] G. H. Brown, "Decimal computation in industry in New South Wales and its educational implications", *Journal of Education, V.I.E.R.*, vol. 2, no. 1, 1955. L. M. Brown, "An enquiry into the teaching of the history of Britain and her empire in New South Wales secondary schools", *Educational Research being undertaken in Australia*, Commonwealth Office of Education, 1955. J. A. Davis, "Nature of English courses which will best meet the future needs of day diploma students at the Melbourne Technical College", *Journal of Education*, V.I.E.R., vol. 2, no. 1, 1955. L. J. Archer, "What do employers expect from Victorian secondary schools with regard to pre-employment commercial education", *Journal of Education*, V.I.E.R., vol. 2, no. 1, 1955.

[39] F. J. Hunt, "Milltown", unpublished M.Ed. thesis, University of W.A., 1961.

[40] C. E. Moorhouse, "Technical and Technological Education in Australia", *The Australian Journal of Education*, vol. 4, no. 3, 1960; D. H. Norrie, "Fundamental Problems of Engineering Education", *Vestes*, vol. 5, no. 2, 1962; H. S. Williams, "Higher Technical Education in Australia", *The Australian University*, no. 1, 1963.

The categories overlap, and courses which provide for the needs of research, industry and trades, *and* offer a high degree of flexibility to meet changing conditions, have yet to be established. The supply of qualified scientists, engineers and skilled workers is inadequate. Senator Sir William Spooner, former Minister for National Development, estimated in 1958 that the number of qualified engineers fell below that required by 500 a year. Facilities for expanded technological and technical courses are urgent. The task of increasing the supply of students at the upper end of the educational ladder is related to community attitudes to education as much as it is related to facilities. Only an analysis of the intake to various occupations, the reasons for choice of occupation, the potential for further study to prepare for employment in a higher category, and the level of education on leaving school, support a realistic assessment. If the demand cannot be met from the groups entering higher education at present, then plans will involve tapping the resources of those now under-contributing.

An understanding of the present pattern of educational opportunity, the hierarchy of types of schools and courses, the values held by parents and students, and the social factors involved in academic success clarifies some of the problems facing education in the future. Far-reaching changes are required before equality of educational opportunity and the use of ability irrespective of social class become realities.

APPENDIX
Religious Instruction in State Schools

THE variations in practice between the states are indicated by the following extracts from their Education Acts. In each case the information is up to date for 1961.

New South Wales

Section 17. In every Public School four hours during each school-day shall be devoted to secular instruction exclusively; and a portion of each day, not more than one hour, shall be set apart when the children of any one religious persuasion may be instructed by the clergyman or other religious teacher of such persuasion, but in all cases the pupils receiving such religious instruction shall be separated from the other pupils of the school. And the hour during which such religious instruction may be given shall be fixed by mutual agreement between the Public School Board in consultation with the teacher of such School and the clergyman of the district or such other person as may be duly authorized to act in his stead and any classroom of any Public School may be used for such religious instruction by like agreement. Provided that if two or more clergymen of different persuasion desire to give religious instruction at any School the children of each such different persuasion shall be so instructed on different days. Provided also that the religious instruction to be so given shall in every case be the religious instruction authorized by the Church to which the clergyman or other religious teacher may belong. Provided further that in case of non-attendance of any clergyman or religious teacher during any portion of the period agreed to be set apart for religious instruction, such period shall be devoted to the ordinary secular instruction in such School.

Section 18. Notwithstanding anything to the contrary in the last preceding section, no pupil in a Public School shall be required to receive any general or special religious instruction if the parents or guardians of such pupil object to such religious instruction being given.

Victoria

Section 23. (1) Subject to this section, religious instruction may be given in any State school but otherwise secular instruction alone shall be given in State schools.

2. When religious instruction is given in any State school during the hours set apart for the instruction of the pupils—

(a) such religious instruction shall be given by persons who are accredited representatives of religious bodies and who are approved by the Minister for the purpose;

(b) such religious instruction shall be given on the basis of the normal class organization of the school except in any school where the Minister, having regard to the particular circumstances of such schools, authorizes some other basis to be observed;

(c) attendance at any class for such religious instruction shall not be compulsory for any pupil whose parents desire that he be excused from attending.

(3) No teacher within the meaning of this Act shall give any instruction other than secular instruction in any State school building.

(4) Nothing in this section shall prevent any State school building from being used for any purpose on days other than school days, or at hours on school days other than the hours set apart for the instruction of pupils.

Section 25. (b) No such regulation shall authorize the exclusion of any pupil on any ground relating to the religious or political opinions or beliefs of the pupil or of his parents if such opinions or beliefs do not prevent the inculcation of a love of country, or the observance of any prescribed patriotic ceremony in the school.

Queensland

Section 22A. Instruction shall, in accordance with regulations in that behalf, be given in the primary schools during school hours in selected Bible lessons from a separate reading book to be provided for the purpose; but such instruction shall not include any teaching in the distinctive tenets or doctrines of any religious society or denomination.

Moreover, any minister of religion shall, . . . ,* be entitled during school hours to give to the children in attendance at a primary school who are members of the religious society or denomination of which he is a minister, religious instruction during one hour of such school day or school days as the committee or other governing body of such school are able to appoint:

Provided always that any parent or guardian shall be entitled to withdraw his child from all religious instruction if such parent or guardian notifies to the head teacher that he wishes so to do.

(The above was inserted in the Act in 1910, after a referendum. In 1948 an amendment provided that the head teacher, not the governing body, should determine the hours for religious instruction.)

South Australia

In 1915 the following section was inserted in the Act:

Section 62. (1) Subject to subsection (3) of this section, in no public school shall any instruction other than secular instruction be given.

(3) Any primary school may be open in the morning before the time fixed for commencing secular instruction, for the purpose of reading portions of the Holy Scriptures in the Authorized or Revised or Douay version, or any other version approved by the Governor, provided that:

(a) the attendance of no child at such reading shall be compulsory, and

(b) no sectarian or denominational religious teaching shall be allowed in any public school.

In 1940 the following was substituted:

Section 62. (1) Subject to the other subsections of this section, only secular instruction shall be given in a public school.

(2) Teachers shall give only secular instruction in public school buildings on days when the buildings are used for school purposes.

(3) Subject to the other subsections of this section four and a half hours at least shall be set apart during each school day for secular instruction in every primary public school.

(4) Clergymen may attend every public school for the purpose of giving religious instruction to the children of the school for one half hour in each week during the regular session of the school.

(5) The head teacher of each school shall agree with the clergymen who attend to give religious instruction upon the half hour or half hours which shall be set aside for such instruction, and, failing agreement, the Minister shall direct what half hour or half hours shall be set aside.

(6) The head teacher of each school shall, so far as the accommodation of the school permits, make such arrangements as regards the pupils and rooms as may be necessary to enable the instruction to be given satisfactorily.

(7) Every child shall attend religious instruction given by the clergyman of the Church to which the child belongs as appears from the enrolment book or from any later notification by the parent in writing, and no child shall be required or allowed to

---

* Provision made for regulations.

attend any other religious instruction: Provided that no child shall be required to attend any religious instruction

(a) if the child's parent has stated that the child shall not receive any religious instruction or

(b) if the head teacher does not know to which Church the child belongs.

(8) When religious instruction is being given to any children in a school, secular instruction need not be given to the other children.

(9) A clergyman shall be allowed to give religious instruction in a school only so long as he is authorized to do so by the person acting in the State as the head of the Church to which the clergyman belongs and so long as he gives the religious instruction authorized by the Church (or Synagogue added 1945).

In 1947 a further change was made, as follows:

Section 62. (2) Provided that a teacher, at his own request, may be authorized by the Head of a Christian Church or of the Jewish Synagogue, to give religious instruction on behalf of that Church or Synagogue; and if so authorized the teacher may give religious instruction under this section as if he were a clergyman of that Church or Synagogue.

Western Australia

Section 29. (1) In every Government elementary school a portion of each week may be set apart when the children of any religious persuasion may be instructed by clergymen or other religious teachers of such persuasion, accredited by the denominational authority, subject to the conditions following:

(a) The children receiving such religious instruction shall be separated from the other children of the school.

(b) The time during which such religious instruction is given shall be fixed by the head teacher of such school, subject to approval of the Director of Education.

(c) The religious instructions to be so given shall in every case be the religious instruction authorized by the Church to which the clergyman or other religious teacher belongs.

(2) If the clergyman or religious teacher does not attend during any portion of the period set apart for religious instruction, such period shall be devoted to the ordinary secular instruction in such school.

(3) In all Government schools the teaching shall be strictly non-sectarian, but the words "secular instruction" shall be held to include general religious teaching as distinguished from dogmatic or polemical theology.

(4) No child shall be required to receive any instruction in religious subjects if the parent of such child signifies his objection to such religious instruction by notice in writing to the head teacher of the school.

Section 30. (1) It shall not be required, as a condition of any child being admitted into or continuing in any school, that he attend or abstain from attending any Sunday school, or any place of religious worship, or that he shall attend religious observance or any instruction in religious subjects in the school or elsewhere, from which observance or instruction he may be withdrawn by his parent, or that he shall, if withdrawn by his parent, attend the school on any day exclusively set apart for religious observance by the religious body to which his parent belongs.

(2) It shall be no part of the duty of an inspector to inquire into any instruction in religious subjects given at any school, or to examine any scholar in religious knowledge, or in any religious subject, or book.

Tasmania

Section 6. (1) In all state schools the teaching shall be strictly non-sectarian.

(2) Not less than four hours each school day shall be devoted to secular instruction exclusively.

(3) A clergyman or other religious teacher of any particular persuasion may attend a school at a time arranged as prescribed with the head teacher of such school and may impart religious instruction to children who are of such persuasion during such time, not exceeding one hour in each week, as may be so arranged, but not more than one such clergyman or teacher shall attend any school on the same day.

(4) The children receiving such religious instruction shall be separated from the other pupils of the school while such instruction is given.

(5) No child shall be compelled to attend such religious instruction if his parents object to his so doing.

(6) If on any day so arranged, such clergyman or teacher fails to attend, the time set apart as aforesaid for instruction by him shall be devoted to secular teaching.

A. F. DAVIES and S. ENCEL

6   Politics

THIS is not another attempt at a short sketch of the Australian political system but, more modestly, an inquiry into how clearly it is mirrored by one line of present-day studies—those in political sociology. Their focus is the social environment of the political system, and research on these lines has grown with the development of political science at the universities.[1] Historians and lawyers launched the detached study of politics in this country many years ago, but their interest remained for long narrow and sporadic. Academic political science has thrown up a group of investigators whose sociological bent is manifested in the use of survey methods and living subjects, or in attempts to relate observations to explicit concepts derived from systematic thinking about social processes, or both. The majority preoccupation has been, and remains, to understand the recent workings of the political parties, including, of course, their immediate electoral fortunes.[2] In addition, examples of successful work overseas have influenced ideas as to what could well be studied locally, and how. In this chapter we shall be concerned especially with studies of organizations, social groupings and attitudes.

ORGANIZATIONS

The trend towards bureaucracy and "bigness" in both public and private organizations, first noted two generations ago by Weber, has stimulated the growth of organization theory into one of the most advanced and comprehensive branches of contemporary sociology. There is now an impressive body of systematic observation of, and reflection upon, internal processes of control, communication, decision-making and personal adjustment drawn from studies of government agencies, business firms, military formations, trade unions, churches, hospitals, prisons, research institutes, voluntary associations, schools and universities. To link these spheres, writers have tried hard to forge a common language for analysing organizational vicissitudes and improvisations, from which models can be built and testable hypotheses de-

---

[1] R. N. Spann, "Political Science in Australia", *Australian Journal of Politics and History*, no. 1, 1955; L. F. Crisp, "Political Science in the Australian Universities", *Vestes*, vol. 5, no. 2, 1962.

[2] S. R. Davis and C. A. Hughes, "The Literature of Australian Government and Politics", *Australian Journal of Politics and History*, vol. 4, no. 1, 1958.

rived.[3] The lesson of these attempts, as Spann observes, is that "structure, type of leadership, characteristic conflicts and co-ordination problems" are largely the result of the organizational objective and the "technology of the task".[4] In Australia the recruitment of influential public servants of a certain sort into regional groups of the Royal Institute of Public Administration has led to the accumulation of a useful stock of descriptive accounts of governmental organizations of every kind in broad plan, but has done little to advance sophisticated analysis. Identification with the office, as well as the somewhat competitive character of the audience at Institute meetings, has turned speakers regularly to the bland side of their material. The Pangloss role of the official was compounded until recently by academic neglect of the bureaucratic organizations whose influence permeates large areas of social life. Australians may, indeed, have "a characteristic talent for bureaucracy".[5] The key role of government enterprise in economic development, for long taken for granted, has only recently been demonstrated in detail by economic historians.[6] Government dominance in education and social welfare, which leaves an authoritarian mark on all social relationships, is analysed in chapters 5 and 7 of this volume.

The last ten years have seen much good work on the interplay between organizations and their environment. We select the outstanding themes. First, the pervasive influence of egalitarianism has been closely charted in the context of public service recruitment and staffing. Weber's comment that democracy "takes an ambivalent stand in the face of specialized examinations, as it does in the face of all the phenomena of bureaucracy—although democracy itself promotes these developments"[7] finds a gloss in Hancock's sardonic remark that "democratic sentiment applauds the sound argument that every office boy should have a chance to become a manager, and perverts it into a practical rule that no one shall become a manager who has not been an office boy".[8] The result, in Australia, is "a shotgun wedding between strictly egalitarian theory and strongly differential practice".[9]

In the Public Service Acts passed in the various colonies during the closing years of the 19th century, very limited recognition was given to special qualifications, and there was no suggestion that special training could fit a man for the duties of higher administration. Advancement was based almost entirely on seniority, the assumption being that length of experience and detailed

---

[3] Two outstanding recent examples are Amitai Etzioni, *The Comparative Analysis of Complex Organizations,* and Robert V. Presthus, *The Organizational Society.*

[4] R. N. Spann, "The Study of Organizations", *Public Administration* (London), vol. 40, no. 4, 1962. Two local contributions to organizational theory are N. F. Dufty and P. W. Taylor, "The Implementation of a Decision", *Administrative Science Quarterly,* vol. 6, no. 1, 1962, and R. N. Spann, "Large-scale Administration—Some 'Principles' and Problems", *Public Administration* (Sydney), vol. 21, no. 2, 1962.

[5] A. F. Davies, *Australian Democracy* (2nd edition, 1964), p. 4.

[6] See, *e.g.,* Noel Butlin, "Colonial Socialism in Australia", in H. G. J. Aitken (ed.), *The State and Economic Growth.*

[7] Max Weber, "Bureaucracy", in Gerth and Mills (eds.), *From Max Weber,* p. 240.

[8] W. K. Hancock, *Australia,* p. 57.

[9] S. Encel, "Recruitment of University Graduates to the Commonwealth Public Service", *Public Administration* (London), vol. 32, no. 3, 1954. Recruitment, promotion and classification are discussed in various chapters of R. N. Spann (ed.), *Public Administration in Australia,* and by V. A. Subramaniam, "Promotion in the Commonwealth, N.S.W. and Victorian Public Services", unpublished Ph.D. thesis, Australian National University, 1959.

acquaintance with all the routine duties of a department were the qualities above all which made a good administrator. "On this theory, professional qualifications are important but not decisive. In spite of this ideal picture the history of recruitment shows that methods of evading the results of this philosophy have been built into the system throughout."[10] The men who attain senior positions are frequently marked out at a relatively early age, which is contrary to the egalitarian myth but consistent with the orthodox teachings of public administration, and a large number were recruited by "exceptional" methods, especially in the Commonwealth service.[11]

Schaffer and Knight have pointed out the effect of "ideologies of promotion" on the advancement of officials in the public services of N.S.W. and Queensland.[12] In the Commonwealth, promotion ideology is reflected in the belief that special virtue attaches to training in economics.[13] In addition, professional officers have high status both as specialists and as general administrators, although this situation may be changing. Schaffer and Knight note examples of the appointment of lay administrators to positions once reserved for professional officers. The recent reorganization of the Second Division of the Commonwealth public service, together with new attempts to recruit university graduates for general administrative duties, suggest a deliberate move towards a new type of administrative "generalist".[14]

A second theme has been the derivativeness of Australian institutions. Though our politics can be comprehended only in terms of a distinctive constellation of social forces, formal institutions have mostly been copied from Britain. The apparatus of Cabinet government, departmental organization, internal co-ordination, Treasury control and audit is in most respects taken direct from Westminster.[15] So is parliamentary procedure. The results are sometimes good, sometimes comic, and sometimes costly. Defence planning has repeatedly failed to develop strategic or organizational concepts suitable to the special problems of a small, dependent country. Studies by Schaffer and Beddie have underlined the rigidity of local planning, overwhelmingly determined by financial limitations, and carried out with remarkable lack of criticism or informed argument.[16] Public corporations, for two generations the chosen method of operating government enterprises, were indeed developed in an atmosphere of innovation and experiment, but this has long since evaporated, and second thoughts about their problems have followed British con-

---

10 S. Encel, "Recruitment and Careers of Government Officials", *Public Administration* (Sydney), vol. 18, no. 1, 1959.

11 For a historical survey of "exceptional" or "lateral" recruitment see H. A. Scarrow, *The Higher Public Service of the Commonwealth of Australia.*

12 B. B. Schaffer and K. W. Knight, *Top Public Servants in Two States* (University of Queensland Papers, 1963), p. 34.

13 S. Encel, The Commonwealth Public Service and Outside Recruitment", *Public Administration* (Sydney), vol. 14, no. 1, 1955. The special role of training in economics is asserted, fairly cautiously, by Sir John Crawford, "The Economist in the Public Service", *Public Administration* (Sydney), vol. 22, no. 1, 1963.

14 J. C. Conway, "Training for Generalist Graduates", *Public Administration* (Sydney), vol. 22, no. 4, 1963.

15 S. Encel, *Cabinet Government in Australia*, esp. parts 1–3, 5.

16 B. B. Schaffer, "Policy and System in Defence: The Australian Case", *World Politics*, vol. 15, no. 2, 1963; B. D. Beddie, "Some Internal Political Problems", in J. Wilkes (ed.), *Australia's Defence and Foreign Policy.* Dependence on British strategic concepts is traced by the official war historian, Gavin Long, in *To Benghazi*, chs. 1–2.

troversy, with a lag. Many of the old-established corporations—notably the railways—have sunk deep in a rut; and even some of the newer ones have been led into financial and administrative difficulties by following traditional patterns.[17]

British empiricism has been compounded by Australian pragmatism, and the "technology of the task" remains fixed at a depressingly low level of sophistication. A recent account of a major reconstruction of departmental functions in the Commonwealth administration concludes that the results bore little relation to "the current propositions of administrative theory about the purposes and methods of departmental organization".[18] The lack is noticeable even where imagination and creative thinking are crucial, as in education and social welfare. Tierney's study of child welfare in Victoria shows how those responsible for administering an initially generous and far-sighted programme were led by the exigencies of day-to-day decision making to pervert it into a timid, legalistic and radically ineffective set of operating procedures. Bureaucratic distortion of public purpose has rarely been demonstrated so clearly.[19]

The administration of scientific research is another area which calls for a particularly delicate balance between the factors conducive to individual creativity and the requirements of a large organizational machine. Harrison's study of C.S.I.R.O. shows how these problems were, for a long time, not appreciated either by the scientists and even less by the lay administrators with whom they have to deal.[20] Close study of organizations often exposes the crucial role of the individual administrator, whose personality and performance can affect the whole structure of the organization and permeate its style of work. This gives us our third main theme. In countries with an egalitarian tradition, there is often a reluctance to admit the creative role of the outstanding individual. Selznick has criticized the long-established tendency of administrative theory in America to dodge the question of leadership by a "retreat to technology" which finds the secret of achievement in organizational devices or "management engineering".[21] In Australia, accounts seeking to give the individual his proper weight in the organizational drama are few and still hesitant to exploit their opportunities. L. F. Crisp's detailed account of J. B. Chifley as politician and administrator follows the tradition when it hedges on the crucial question of his role as leader rather than spokesman of his party, although it gives a vivid picture of the special relationship between Chifley and his "official family".[22] Heydon has recently contributed

---

[17] For the early development of public corporations see F. W. Eggleston, *State Socialism in Victoria* (1931), and the chapter by Geoffrey Sawer in W. Friedmann (ed.), *The Public Corporation*. Recent events are discussed by D. C. Corbett, "Airline Policy and Administration", *Public Administration* (Sydney), vol. 20, no. 3, 1961, and S. Encel, "Public Corporations in Australia: Some Recent Developments", *Public Administration* (London), vol. 38, no. 3, 1960.

[18] R. P. Deane, *The Establishment of the Department of Trade.*

[19] Leonard Tierney, *Children Who Need Help.*

[20] H. P. Harrison, "Aspects of the Administration of C.S.I.R.O.", unpublished Ph.D. thesis, Australian National University, 1957; Leon Peres, "Research Organization and Incentives", *Public Administration* (Sydney), vol. 22, no. 4, 1963; D. T. C. Gillespie, "Research Management in C.S.I.R.O.", *Public Administration* (London), vol. 42, no. 2, 1964.

[21] Philip Selznick, *Leadership in Administration*, pp. 74–82.

[22] L. F. Crisp, *Ben Chifley*, esp. chs. 10–21. The general problem is discussed by S. Encel, "Political Leadership in Australia", *Australian Journal of Social Issues*, vol. 1, no. 2, 1962.

a shrewd intimate assessment of the work habits and accomplishments of Sir George Pearce, who held the federal portfolios of Defence, Home and Territories, and External Affairs over a number of years during a long political career.[23] Dax's account of the highly successful reform of mental health administration in Victoria, which is largely an autobiography, showed modestly but in detail how the qualities of the administrator are manifested in his organization.[24] The work of Frank Tate and Peter Board in education illustrate creative leadership in another field.[25] Obituaries of Wallace Wurth, chairman of the N.S.W. Public Service Board for more than twenty years and popularly known as the "uncrowned king of N.S.W.", suggest how much remains to be written about this remarkable figure.[26] The influence of a leading South Australian public servant, J. W. Wainright, has recently been described.[27]

Studies of voluntary political organizations such as political parties and interest groups are numerous, although few of them have used sociological tools or concepts with much cutting edge. Some acquaintance with Michels and Ostrogorski informs the better works on Labour Party history.[28] Rawson has examined the different meanings of membership in the Labour and Liberal parties in the context of a thorough study of branch activity in two close polls in one electorate.[29] Wilson's pioneer study[30] of a year's activity in two A.L.P. branches in Melbourne, showing utterly dissimilar preoccupations, has had no successors, and most electoral studies confine themselves to reporting branch pre-selection practices.

Henry Mayer complained some years ago that "The analysis of Australian parties in terms of the interests behind them breaks off when it comes to the crucial question of policy."[31] Katharine West's recent account of the Liberal Party,[32] however, tends to bear out Finer's stimulating suggestion that conservative parties are best seen as peak organizations of their constituent trade associations.[33] Several explorations have now been made of the relation of interest groups to the urban non-Labour parties.[34] The links between the

[23] P. R. Heydon, "Sir George Pearce as Administrator", *Public Administration* (Sydney) vol. 22, no. 4, 1963.

[24] E. C. Dax, *Asylum to Community*.

[25] J. O. Anchen, *Frank Tate and His Work for Education*; A. R. Crane and W. G. Walker, *Peter Board: His Contribution to the Development of Education in N.S.W.*

[26] *E.g.* "Wallace C. Wurth: In Memoriam", *Public Administration* (Sydney), vol. 20. no. 1, 1961.

[27] T. J. Mitchell: "J. W. Wainright", *Australian Journal of Politics and History*, vol. 8, no. 1, 1962.

[28] V. G. Childe, *How Labour Governs* (1923); E. M. Higgins, "The Queensland Labour Governments 1915–29", M.A. thesis, University of Melbourne, 1954; D. W. Rawson, "The Organization of the A.L.P. 1916–41", Ph.D. thesis, University of Melbourne, 1954.

[29] D. W. Rawson and Susan Holtzinger, *Politics in Eden-Monaro*, pp. 44-65, 148-55.

[30] I. F. H. Wilson, unpublished B.A. thesis, University of Melbourne, 1956.

[31] Henry Mayer, "Some Conceptions of the Australian Party System", *Historical Studies*, no. 27, 1956.

[32] Katharine West, *Power in the Liberal Party* (1965).

[33] S. E. Finer, "The Political Power of Private Capital", *Sociological Review*, vol. 3, no. 2, and vol. 4, no. 1, 1955-6.

[34] B. D. Graham, "Finance Committees in non-Labour Politics 1910-30", *Australian Journal of Politics and History*, vol. 6, no. 1, 1960; R. S. Parker, "Group Interests and the non-Labour Parties Since 1930", unpublished paper, Section E, ANZAAS, 1958; Trevor Matthews, "Political Activities of Australian Employers' Federations", unpublished paper, A.P.S.A. conference, 1964.

Country Party and farmers' organizations, the legislative returns obtained by trade unions from state Labour governments, and the influence of organized Catholic groups on Labour policy have been examined in the last few years.[35]

The changing relations of interest groups to party machines in the years when these were still developing have been usefully schematized by Campbell. There is "a formative phase in which the party is structurally, financially or otherwise dependent on certain supporting groups; a phase of limited independence, when the party can play one supporting group off against another; and one of comparative maturity, as the party ceases to be dependent for resources on individual groups, and instead groups become dependent on the party for access to decision making". He shows, too, how party activities become progressively differentiated with the growth of other agencies catering for one or more of the social needs initially met by the party machine alone. Campbell also examines the pervasive federalism of Australian political organizations, and the growth in the early years of this century of new national associations on a more or less standard pattern.[36] Analyses of particular interest groups such as the Australian Medical Association, the Returned Servicemen's League, and the Associated Chambers of Manufactures, now in progress, promise further light on the problems of federal organization in politics and on the influence of such national bodies on policy making.

SOCIAL GROUPINGS

Political sociology has been fed by two important streams of 19th century social thought. Pluralism discovered the group as a political entity with legitimate functions, standing between the isolated individual and the leviathan state. The sociological tradition running through Marx, de Tocqueville, Weber and Pareto broke down the state into a set of institutions depending for their nature on that of the society in which they were rooted. Political sociologists are thus peculiarly interested in the different contributions made by social groups to the manning of political institutions like parties and bureaucracies. Equally, the widely accepted model of democracy as a system in which parties compete for the support of a mass electorate, most clearly formulated by Schumpeter,[37] creates a perennial interest in the processes by which a variety of groups can be used as building blocks for electoral majorities. Studies of the recruitment of "*élite* groups" have been slow to develop in Australia. A self-consciously egalitarian community entertains only with unease the notion of *élites* of any kind. Yet, as Keller has recently argued, every developed industrial community is characterized by "strategic *élites* . . . who man the positions of leadership"—a muffled version of Mills' power *élite* who occupy "command posts" in politics, the economy, and the armed

---

[35] B. D. Graham, "The Political Strategies of the Australian Country Parties to 1929", Ph.D. thesis, Australian National University, 1958; D. A. Aitkin, "The Organization of the Australian Country Party (N.S.W.), 1946 to 1962", Ph.D. thesis, Australian National University, 1964; R. M. Martin, "Trade Unions and Labour Governments in Australia", *Journal of Commonwealth Political Studies*, vol. 2, no. 1, 1963; Celia Hamilton, "Catholic Interests and the Labour Party", *Historical Studies*, no. 33, 1959; T. C. Truman, *Catholic Action and Politics*.

[36] Ian Campbell, "Groups, Parties, and Federation", in *Groups in Theory and Practice* (Sydney Studies in Politics, no. 1).

[37] J. A. Schumpeter, *Capitalism, Socialism, and Democracy*, ch. 22.

101

services.[38] Strategic *élites* proliferate with population growth, occupational specialization, bureaucratization, and "the growth of moral diversity".[39] Although these forces are at work in all industrial societies, different national communities obviously throw up quite different *élite* groups. The study of national patterns of *élite* formation is an important key to the character of each political system.[40]

The growth of public and private bureaucracies in Australia since the second world war has provoked a new concern over the possible development of a power *élite* in Australia. H. W. Arndt asked, some years ago:

> Are we in danger of allowing our lives to be controlled by a narrow class of "managers"—more or less benevolent, able, expert, powerful business executives, acting in concert with more or less benevolent, able, expert, powerful heads of government departments, public corporations, trade unions, primary producers' organizations, professions? . . . If you look around you, particularly at Canberra where few important decisions are made without consultation and negotiation between senior public servants and senior representatives of private interests, you can convince yourself that this is the most serious threat to democracy in Australia.[41]

No real counterpart to Mills' rather dramatic conception is likely to be found in Australia: our own power structure seems altogether too loose and too muted. Local studies have, however, made out well-established patterns of recruitment and mobility within political, administrative and business leadership. These patterns diverge both from one another and from accepted stereotypes.

TABLE 1

Father's occupational group	1947 census (males) %	Fathers of businessmen %	Fathers of Commonwealth officials %	Fathers of Ministers %
Rural proprietors	17·9	7	10	23
Professional and semi-professional	3·5	17·5	16	18·5
Administrative and business	5·6	33	11	9
Commercial and clerical	16·4	27	35	23
Manual workers	47·2	11·5	22	17·5
Other	9·4	4	6	9
	100·0	100·0	100·0	100·0

[38] Suzanne Keller, *Beyond the Ruling Class*, p. 67; C. Wright Mills, *The Power Elite*, ch. 1.

[39] Keller, *op. cit.*, p. 65.

[40] Raymond Aron, "Social Structure and the Ruling Class", *British Journal of Sociology*, no. 1, 1950; D. R. Matthews, *The Social Background of Political Decision-Makers*. For an acid sketch of the tone of the Australian "establishment" see H. A. Wolfsohn, "The Ideology Makers", *Dissent*, no. 1, 1964.

[41] H. W. Arndt, "The Dangers of Big Business", *Australian Quarterly*, vol. 29, no. 4, 1957. See also S. Encel, *Is There an Australian Power Élite?* (Chifley Memorial Lecture, 1961), and "Power", in P. Coleman (ed.), *Australian Civilization*.

One index of diversity is social origin in terms of father's occupation. This becomes apparent from Table 1 above, based on surveys made by Encel between 1956 and 1958, covering 91 Cabinet ministers, 63 state and 28 federal, holding office between 1945 and 1958; 327 senior Commonwealth officials, and 325 managers and directors occupying executive positions in industry.[42]

The influence of heredity among businessmen is accentuated by family connections, which had played some part in the careers of at least one-third of this group. Most of the businessmen had been educated at private schools affiliated with the Headmasters' Conference of Australia, compared to one-quarter of the public servants and the Cabinet ministers (nearly all, predictably, non-Labour). Some two-thirds of the public servants were university graduates, compared with less than one-third of businessmen who had had some form of tertiary education, and one-sixth of Cabinet ministers. Only 3% of the businessmen could be positively identified as Catholics, as against 16% of public servants. If Catholics are as numerous in the Commonwealth public service as a whole as in the community at large, then they are under-represented in the higher echelons. The reason is probably education, though discrimination is sometimes alleged.[43]

Among Cabinet ministers there is a sharp difference between parties. Of the 70 ministers in federal Labour governments between 1904 and 1949, 40 were Protestants, 27 were Catholics and three freethinkers.[44] In the mixed group of 91 postwar state and federal ministers, 44 were Labour men, of whom 17 were Catholics. As against this, out of a sample of 142 non-Labour ministers, state and federal, from 1901 to 1958, only eight were Catholics, and two of these were defectors from the A.L.P. Crisp, in a decade by decade analysis of the federal parliamentary Labour party during its first fifty years, demonstrates the "rise of the Irish-Australians", stimulated particularly by the schism over conscription in 1917.[45]

Labour parliamentarians are popularly thought to come overwhelmingly from the ranks of the working class, and particularly from trade union officials. In federal politics, at least, this conception has long been out of date. From 1901 to 1951, 41% of all members of the federal parliamentary party were manual workers. Before the general election of 1934 the proportion of manual workers at any one time was over half; they fell below this level in 1934 and have continued to decline. Trade union officials, too, fell to below half in 1917 and have declined gradually ever since. Moreover, union officials (and honorary officials) drawn from clerical and white-collar groups have gradually increased, in line with the general increase in white-collar representation. Up to the 1940 general election, less than 10% of the parliamentary party were white-collar workers; after the A.L.P.'s landslide victory in 1943 the proportion rose sharply and has gone on rising ever since. In the 1958-61 parliament almost one-third of Labour members were white-collar workers. Schoolteachers, making up 13% of the parliamentary party in the 1958-61

---

[42] For a full analysis of Cabinet ministers, see S. Encel, "The Political Élite in Australia", *Political Studies*, vol. 9, no. 1, 1961.

[43] Anon, "Catholics in the Public Service", *Australian Quarterly*, vol. 32, no. 3, 1960.

[44] L. F. Crisp and S. P. Bennett, *A.L.P. Federal Personnel 1901-54* (unpublished MS, Canberra, 1954).

[45] L. F. Crisp, *The Australian Federal Labour Party 1901-51*, appendix H.

parliament, have advanced rapidly. In 1949-51 there were only six teachers in the whole federal parliament; in 1958-61 the number was 15.[46]

Aspiring Liberal politicians differ somewhat from those who succeed. Katharine Holgate has analysed the occupations of aspirants for state and federal pre-selection in N.S.W. from 1950 to 1959. Table 2 compares the occupational backgrounds of the 710 aspirants, the 191 successful candidates, and the 142 non-Labour ministers already referred to.[47]

TABLE 2

Liberal Candidates and Ministers

Occupational Group	1947 census (all breadwinners) %	Candidates for N.S.W. pre-selection %	Successful candidates %	Non-Labour ministers %
Rural proprietors	8·5	9	13	28
Professional and semi-professional	5·2	31	16	44
Administrative and business	7·0	19	15	25
Commercial and clerical	20·0	30	39	2
Manual workers	47·6	4	5	1
Other	11·7	7	12	—
	100·0	100	100	100

Country Party ministers inflate the proportion of "rural proprietors" in the last column, but less than might be imagined, as over one-third of them came from non-rural occupations, and one-half of all the rural proprietors were Liberals. To abstract the C.P. ministers (a quarter of the total) would increase the importance of the "professional" and "administrative" categories even further. Lawyers form the largest occupational group of all. From 1901 to 1961, 97 members of the Liberal Party (or its precursors, the Nationalists and the U.A.P., and exclusive of Labour defectors) held portfolios in federal ministries; 32 of them were lawyers. A career at the Bar remains the best passport to a safe Liberal seat and to ministerial office.

The social origins of politicians are indicative of the social groups which support their parties, even if the relation is not simple and direct. Poll data on support for each party in the countryside are examined in chapter 16. Aitkin, in a close study of the rural vote in N.S.W., shows how country communities can be classified as Urban, Township or Rural by density of population and degree of urbanization. Country Party support is highest and most reliable in the Rural and least in the Urban communities. Its future, he concludes, depends on the possibility of changing "a political party founded by farmers, possessing a rural history and a rural mystique, and relying ultimately on farmer and grazier support, into an electoral machine capable of winning the country town wage-earner".[48] He also found that small farmers, especially in dairying and mixed farming, were Country Party supporters, whereas

[46] S. Encel, "Political Leadership in Australia", *loc. cit.*
[47] *Ibid.*; and Katharine Holgate, "The Structure of Liberal State Politics in N.S.W.", M.A. thesis, University of Melbourne, 1962, pp. 34-5.
[48] D. A. Aitkin, "Voting Trends in N.S.W. Country Electorates", paper presented to A.P.S.A. conference, 1961.

graziers tended to identify themselves with the Liberal Party. Similar findings are reported in other studies.[49] The rise of the Democratic Labor Party in 1955 and its obstinate persistence have led to several explorations of its social roots. Spann argues that, whatever its original composition, it is now a party of militant Catholics, although direct guidance from the clergy is not the main influence upon it. It attracts several types of Catholic voters—those whose party attachments are loose; those whose traditional allegiance is Labour and who see the D.L.P. as the legitimate heir to this tradition; and those who find in it new communal ties (which are important because of the disruptive effects of social mobility). "The party clearly asserts certain anti-rational values (in Max Weber's sense), which Labour, as it has lost its appeal as a movement, does less and less."[50] An example of the appeal of the D.L.P. to individual Catholics is given in a study by Davies. The D.L.P. activist, "Leonard East", whom he describes in detail, had taken little or no part in politics until the split in the Labour Party in 1954, which appeared to him as a great opportunity. His personal history reflects many of the frustrations and tensions which have affected the Catholic community as a whole because of post-war change.[51]

Jupp has described an electorate "index of D.L.P. predisposition" based on the percentages of Catholics and of European immigrants, and the political affiliations of the state and federal M.P.s. The social roots of the D.L.P., he concludes, are similar to those of the A.L.P., with the addition of immigrant and Catholic influences, but it is also serving as a "residual" party of protest like the British Liberals.[52] Recent voting trends lend some support to this speculation.

Burns, reporting on the D.L.P. voter in a federal by-election sample, found that he was typically "the skilled or white-collar worker, younger and better educated than the average and most probably a conscientious Roman Catholic. He tended either to think of himself as middle class rather than working class, or to be so bemused by his own social promotion that he had lost his earlier sense of working class identity without acquiring any clear substitute."[53] He identified four types of political history in the sample. One group had switched from the A.L.P. during the split; another between the general elections of 1955 and 1958; a few were new voters; and one-third were by-election converts, three-fifths of whom had previously voted Liberal. Rawson, in a national study of the 1958 election, gave religion the most weight. Outside Victoria, he pointed out, the D.L.P. vote is evenly distributed among various social groups. It is not *the* Catholic vote but *a* Catholic vote —"the vote of that section of the Catholic population which was not formally attached to any of the existing parties".[54]

---

[49] Rawson and Holtzinger, *op. cit.*; Henry Mayer and Joan Rydon, *The Gwydir By-Election 1953*; B. D. Graham, "Graziers in Politics 1917-29", *Historical Studies*, no. 32, 1959.

[50] R. N. Spann, "The Catholic Vote in Australia", in Henry Mayer (ed.), *Catholics and the Free Society*, pp. 133-5.

[51] A. F. Davies, *Private Politics: A Study of Five Political Outlooks*, pp. 117-73.

[52] James Jupp, *Australian Party Politics*, p. 84.

[53] Creighton Burns, *Parties and People*, p. 93.

[54] D. W. Rawson, *Australia Votes*, p. 238. A similar conclusion is reached by R. R. Alford, *Party and Society*, pp. 200-17. See also C. A. McCoy, 'Democratic Labor Party Support', *Jnl. Commonwealth Pol. Stud.*, Vol. 3, no. 3, 1965.

The history of the D.L.P. makes a major fault line in Australian politics, cutting across its apparently simple contours and exposing a range of problems which will occupy students for a long time. It fits into none of the traditional categories, and illustrates strikingly the impact of urban complexity on patterns inherited from a simpler era.

ATTITUDES

Two separate local streams had to merge to produce the standard electoral survey: the reflective journalism of the old *Round Table* (perpetuated in the seasonal commentaries of the *Australian Quarterly* and the *Australian Journal of Politics and History*) and the newer interview methods of the opinion pollster.[55] It took quite a struggle to convince the old stagers that conventional notions of voting habits and the influence of the campaign ought to be checked by inquiries among voters themselves. The pollster had to be convinced, first, that picking the winner was, in the long run, less important than clarifying predispositions based on age, sex, religion, education, occupation or social class,[56] and secondly, that one should also test the voters' awareness of the election and its issues. This confluence was achieved in books like Rawson's *Australia Votes* and Burns' *Parties and People* (both published in 1961). But they also made it plain that elections might not be the best occasion for seeking the kind of broad knowledge about political initiative demanded by this new level of analysis.

A striking illustration of the problem is the tendency of election "leads" to run out and end in bafflement. A campaign study might, for example, collect a batch of "floating voters" in its net,[57] yet they would turn out to be in confused motion, and not easily distinguished by age, occupation, or some other mark from the sample average. The same enigmatic ordinariness attached to those who "wouldn't vote if I didn't have to",[58] the "don't knows"[59] and the "late deciders" (those who only made up their minds in the last days or weeks before the poll).[60] The survey might disclose clear grades of concern about the poll, or of exposure to the campaign,[61] without any evident consequence in voting patterns. Again, if voters were asked directly their reasons for voting as they did, their replies, far from clearing anything up, merely indicated a variety of customary ways of acknowledging an inclination to one or other party, few of which had any connection with the campaign.[62]

The attempt, in short, to explain electoral happenings in terms of some more or less self-contained, input-output system proved unworkable, and

---

[55] The first election survey carried out by the Australian Gallup Poll (A.P.O.P.) was in 1943.

[56] See appendix to this chapter.

[57] Burns, *op. cit.*, ch. 11.

[58] Colin A. Hughes, "Compulsory Voting: History, Practice, Theory", paper at A.P.S.A. conference, 1964.

[59] Burns, ch. 10.

[60] Rawson, *op. cit.*, p 177; A.P.O.P. survey, 9 February 1962.

[61] Burns, ch. 6.

[62] *Ibid.*, ch. 12.

students were forced back on the study of the permanent and much slower moving processes of political communication and attitude formation. A typical finding of this disenchanted wisdom remarks that "Electoral activity is continuous rather than intermittent. . . . Groups which do not participate in elections may yet influence those that do. . . . The campaign may have less impact on the outcome of a current contest than on the shape of the one that will follow."[63]

Popular images of the parties, of party leaders, or of the political system as a whole form one line of analysis attempting to cope with these complexities. Mayer and others, by an ingenious classification of letters to the editor in the daily press at the time of an increase in Commonwealth parliamentary salaries in 1959, showed the prevalence of a disposition to see political leadership as fully analogous to business management. They also found considerable variety within pro-establishment and dissident images of politics.

Managerial thinking, a conception of politics as unproductive, a frustrated longing for popular democracy . . . are co-existing images of politics in Australia. It would be worth investigating how far images differ between various strata, how they are related to types and levels of political activity . . . and their relation to activities, associations and institutions and their role in and through these in influencing the process of political decision making.[64]

A classification of the La Trobe sample according to Riesman's categories of political "competence and affect" produced four main political styles: apathetic (66%), condescenders (7%), indignants (12%), autonomous (8%).[65] In striking contrast to overseas findings,[66] political interest and competence spread evenly over the occupational levels (and over the schooling that lay behind them). Suburban people fell into clearly marked grades of participation in political discussion: one in five seldom or never talked politics, one in two had intermittent exposure to but little personal taste for it, and one in three were regular talkers. A middle class pattern of caution at work and openness with friends contrasted with a working class pattern of openness at work and caution (or apathy) elsewhere.[67]

Hughes, in a study of three Brisbane suburban electorates at the 1963 state election,[68] explored the images both of the party leaders and of the parties as a whole. The Liberal leader was much less unpopular with Labour voters than vice versa ("Liberal supporters expect to find disunity and a narrow class preoccupation in their opponents . . . and cultural inferiority"). Hughes' findings support a distribution of partisanship of the following tepid order:

[63] Ian Campbell, *State Ballot*, pp. 7-8.

[64] Henry Mayer *et al.*, "Images of Politics", *Australian Journal of Politics and History*, vol. 6, no. 2, 1960.

[65] Burns, ch. 13.

[66] G. Almond and S. Verba, *The Civic Culture*, ch. 13.

[67] A. F. Davies, "Politics in the New Suburb", *Australian Journal of Politics and History*, vol. 8, no. 2, 1962.

[68] Colin A. Hughes, "The Brisbane Panel", unpublished seminar paper, Australian National University, 1963.

TABLE 3

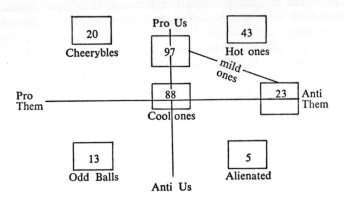

The same author traced party and leader images at the time of the 1963 federal election in a Canberra panel group exposed to the Prime Minister's opening speech on TV.[69] The speech could be shown not to have affected vote intentions at all; but replies allowed some fairly detailed charting of shifts in elements making up the two political schemata. Again, Labour voters were found to be relatively charitably disposed towards their opponents. One-third of them thought the Liberals "would make the country more prosperous"; one-half that they had a "fine record of achievement"; two-thirds that they had "brought a great deal of progress". Both groups agreed to call Sir Robert Menzies brilliant, eloquent, able, intelligent and vigorous. Labour voters insisted he was arrogant, immodest, pompous and snobbish, which Liberal voters were prepared to admit to some degree. Liberal voters insisted on his being honest, reliable, practical and good-natured, which Labour voters also admitted.

A second line of exploration has sought to relate partisan attitudes to deeper social and political beliefs. However, according to a small study made in Victoria in 1961, Labour and Liberal supporters appeared to differ little either in radicalism-conservatism or on Eysenck's "tough-tender"-minded scale.[70] "Authoritarianism" among local schoolchildren has also been found to be more weakly linked with "ethnocentrism" than in the United States.[71] In a sample of 400 Melbourne voters at the 1963 federal elections, Alan Hughes distinguished three clusters of attitudes which he dubbed "established radicalism", "conscience radicalism", and "new radicalism" (each with its conservative counterpart). These were spread evenly throughout both "middle class" and "working class" groups. But he argued that their distribution through age groups suggested a bright future for "new" and "conscience"

69 Colin A. Hughes and J. S. Western, "Televised Politics", unpublished seminar paper, Australian National University, 1964.

70 J. Collins, "Social Attitudes and Political Differences", *Australian Journal of Politics and History*, vol. 9, no. 1, 1963.

71 F. Knopfelmacher and D. B. Armstrong, "Authoritarianism, ethnocentrism and religious denomination among Australian adolescents", unpublished MS, University of Melbourne, 1962. Cf. T. W. Adorno *et al.*, *The Authoritarian Personality*.

radicalism.[72] Rawson, some years earlier, had argued for conscience radicalism as a future source of Labour support.[73] Concern with international politics seems certainly to have grown with the cooling of domestic issues. But the rise of libertarian concern—civil liberties, opposition to censorship, opposition to hanging, opposition to White Australia, pressure for safeguards against bureaucratic authority—though fairly clearly the result of the first tentative engagement of the new educated strata as such with public affairs, and a welcome counterweight to the cynicism and boredom with established political routines revealed elsewhere, is fairly sharply checked by the almost equal indifference, if not equal culpability, of the existing parties.

Finally, there has been some speculation about how individual political outlooks are structured and maintained, particularly in the context of the family and of group affiliations. A study of the membership of primary political groups, and the extent to which associational ties overlap or come into conflict is urgently needed. From the broad picture of anomic isolation that emerges from the standard survey of leisure activities, it may be that a concept of latent or vicarious membership of political groups is necessary to show how people at large can be involved in the analysis.[74]

The neglect of the broad problem of "political socialization", which does not fall comfortably into any of the settled social disciplines, has been unfortunate. We know little, indeed, about how children come by their formative prejudices—those "complexes" which, Freud said, "are legitimately what directs a man's conduct in the world"[75]—or the knowledge of political motives and dealings which follows in their train.[76] That this lack has only now come to seem important may be partly a reflex of political stasis, which makes it suddenly appropriate to explore the invisible but evidently coercive schooling that links political generations.

APPENDIX

Voting and Its Social Correlates

THE following tables represent the breakdown of figures obtained by the Australian Gallup Poll in a survey of voting intentions before the federal election of December 1961.

UM—upper middle class
M—middle class
LM—lower-middle class
W—working-class
LCP—Liberal and Country Parties
ALP—Australian Labor Party
DLP—Democratic Labor Party
DK—"Don't Know"

[72] Alan Hughes, "Political Attitudes in a Sample of Melbourne Voters", paper at A.P.S.A. conference, 1964.

[73] D. W. Rawson, "Labour, Socialism and the Working Class", *Australian Journal of Politics and History*, vol. 7, no. 1, 1961.

[74] A. K. Olley, *Post-Television Social Survey*, pt. 2; D. Scott and R. U'Ren, *Leisure*; Almond and Verba, *op. cit.*, ch. 11.

[75] Ernest Jones, *Sigmund Freud*, vol. 2, p. 188.

[76] But see "Children's Reactions to a Visit From the Queen", *Australian Pre-School Quarterly*, 1962; A. F. Davies, "The Child's Discovery of Social Class", seminar paper, Australian National University, 1964.

1a. *Religion and Class*

	Catholic (23·6%)	C. of E. (38·6%)	Presbyterian (14%)	Methodist (15·3%)	Other Christian (8·5%)
UM ..	5·5	5·9	7	4·3	3·8
M ..	38·8	43·5	50·4	47·4	42·4
LM ..	11·4	11	11·4	13·7	16·9
W ..	44·5	39·3	31·9	34·6	36·9
	100	100	100	100	100

1b. *Class and Religion*

	UM (5·5%)	M (44%)	LM (12%)	W (38·5%)
Catholic	23·5	20·8	22·3	27·3
C. of E.	41	38·3	35·4	39·5
Presbyterian	17·6	16	13·1	11·6
Methodist	11·8	16·6	17·8	13·7
Other Christian ..	5·9	8·2	12	8·1
	100	100	100	100

2a. *Vote and Class*

	L.C.P. (44·5%)	A.L.P. (43·5%)	D.L.P. (5·5%)	D.K. (6·5%)
UM	8	2	2	13
M	60	29	42	36
LM	11	12	16	11
W	21	57	40	36
	100	100	100	100

2b. *Class and Vote*

	UM (5·5%)	M (44%)	LM (12%)	W (38·5%)
L.C.P.	66	61	42	25
A.L.P.	16·5	29	45	65
D.L.P.	2	5	7	5
DK	15·5	5	6	5
	100	100	100	100

3a. *Rural/Urban—Class*

	Rural (34%)	Urban (66%)
UM	5·5	5
M	42·5	46
LM	14·5	11
W	37·5	38
	100	100

3b. *Class—Rural/Urban*

	UM (5·5%)	M (44%)	LM (12%)	W (38·5%)
Rural	34	32·5	40·5	33
Urban	66	67·5	59·5	67
	100	100	100	100

4a. *Electorate Type and Class*

	Solid Lab. (30%)	Mixed (32%)	Solid Lib. (38%)
UM	3	7	6
M	38	43	52
LM	13	9	13
W	46	41	29
	100	100	100

4b. *Class and Electorate Type*

	UM (5·5%)	M (44%)	LM (12%)	W (38·5%)
Solid Lab.	17	25	33	36
Mixed	43	30	27	34
Solid Lib.	40	45	40	30
	100	100	100	100

5a. Class and Occupation

	Managerial and Professional (11·9%)	Small Business (5%)	Working Class (24·4%)	Skilled (22·5%)	Semi-skilled (16·2%)	Un-skilled (6·8%)	Farmers (9·7%)	Farm Employees (3·5%)
UM	13	5	6	2	—	4	5	4
M	80	45	51	38	22	17	60	20
LM	5	21	15	14	10	2	17	17
W	2	29	28	46	68	77	18	59
	100	100	100	100	100	100	100	100

5b. Occupation and Class

	UM (5·5%)	M (44%)	LM (12%)	W (38·5%)
Managerial and Professional ..	34	22	5	1
Small Business	6	5	8	4
Working Class	30	28	30	18
Skilled	10	19	25	27
Semi-skilled	1	8	13	28
Unskilled	6	3	1	13
Farmers	10	13	13	4
Farm Employees	3	2	5	5
	100	100	100	100

6a. Age and Class

	20/30 (20·5%)	30/40 (26%)	40/50 (24%)	50/60 (16%)	60+ (13·5%)
UM	6	6	4·5	4	7
M	39	42	47·5	51	42
LM	10	15	10	14	11
W	45	37	38	31	40
	100	100	100	100	100

6b. Class and Age

	UM (5·5%)	M (44%)	LM (12%)	W (38·5%)
20/30	23	18	17	24
30/40	28	25	33	26
40/50	19	25·5	19	24
50/60	13	18·5	18	12
60+	17	13	13	14
	100	100	100	100

7a. Education and Class

	Prim. (30%)	Some Sec. (30%)	Higher Sec. (30%)	Tert. (10%)
UM	2	6	6	17
M	30	37	60	58
LM	11	13	11	14
W	57	44	23	11
	100	100	100	100

7b. Class and Education

	UM (5·5%)	M (44%)	LM (12%)	W (38·5%)
Prim.	10·5	20·5	28	45
Some Sec.	30·5	26	33	35
Higher Sec.	32·5	41·5	28	18
Tertiary	26·5	12	11	2
	100	100	100	100

8. Age and Vote

		% choosing:		
Voters' age	% of electorate	Lib.-C.P.	Lab.	Other (excl. D.K.)
20–29	23	44	50	1
30–39	21	46	48	6
40–49	20	48	47	5
50+	36	54	41	5

9. Religion and Vote

	Catholic %	C. of E. %	Presbyterian %	Methodist %	Other Christian %	Other %
A.L.P. ..	50·5	46·5	37·9	39·0	43·1	38·3
D.L.P. ..	13·8	1·8	1·9	2·4	3·9	5·5
L.C.P. ..	27·9	46·5	56·0	51·9	46·9	45·2
Ind. ..	—	—	—	1·2	0·6	—
D.K. ..	7·8	5·2	4·2	5·5	5·5	11·0
	100	100	100	100	100	100

N.B.—These figures understate the D.L.P. vote, which is a normal occurrence in polls and surveys. As indicated in chapter 3, D.L.P. voters are more evasive about their political stance than any other group. The Gallup Poll estimate of the D.L.P. vote in the 1961 election was 6%, compared with the election figure of 9%. The L.C.P. estimate was 47%, compared with an actual figure of 42%. Some or all of the D.L.P. percentages in the above table should therefore be increased, probably with corresponding reductions in the L.C.P. figures. For a detailed discussion, see R. R. Alford, *Party and Society*, pp. 202-17,

LEONARD TIERNEY

---

7 The Pattern of Social Welfare

AUSTRALIANS have a legend that their country is a social laboratory, and that if there had been some falling away in social innovation before 1939, the extension of social services during the second world war placed it again in the forefront of social advance. Yet Australia was not the first country to introduce major social services: Denmark introduced in 1891 an age pension system which was to become a model for many other countries, including Australia; New Zealand introduced an age pension several years before Australia. It is true that Australia introduced a comprehensive system of age pensions long before Great Britain or the United States and comparisons are usually made with these two countries, but compared with other advanced western countries Australia has not been distinguished in the usual range of social services. Since 1945 it is questionable whether it has kept pace with developments in the United States and Britain. Australia struggled through the depression without producing a system of unemployment allowances equal to the public assistance programmes in either country.

If Australians from 1900 prided themselves on having introduced pensions as a right, they overlooked their limitation to the aged and invalid only. There was no right to unemployment insurance, and the Children's Maintenance Act in Victoria in 1919 required applicants to apply for assistance before a police magistrate in an ordinary police court. The social services have yet to receive comprehensive study, but recent reports on child welfare and mental health in Australia give little cause for satisfaction. For forty years after the introduction of age and invalid pensions, no major changes were made in Australian social welfare. In 1941 child endowment began, but the value of these payments has gradually been eroded by inflation and changes in the standard of living. Between 1942 and 1944 a series of acts extended the principles and benefits of age and invalid pensions to a whole new class of beneficiaries: the widowed, the sick and the unemployed. Except for health services, Australia has emphasized income security. Experiments in social provision not clearly related to loss of income have been cautious and partial.

Nevertheless, the popular Australian belief that this country is socially advanced is not simply a function of insularity and local pride. In broad areas of social advance such as voting rights for women, adult suffrage and in a whole range of industrial legislation, Australia has been among the pioneers. Minimum wage legislation is clearly linked with income security programmes.

114

It has been said often enough that the first essential for income security is a guaranteed minimum wage. However, to argue from this legislation that all is well with the other social services is scarcely justified. The social services have come into being slowly and piecemeal. They now touch the lives of most people and absorb a large proportion of the national income. In 1961-2 the consolidated revenue of the States and Commonwealth amounted to a little more than £2,100m. The Federal government's expenditure on its major programmes (social services, health and repatriation) amounted to £466m., while the major welfare programmes of the States (education, health and welfare) cost a further £298m.[1] Expenditure on social services is approaching 40% of total revenue. There is, nevertheless, an extraordinary confusion of opinion about their role and purpose. For some, the social services represent an extravagant burden upon the community, for others, man's compassion for his fellows; they are seen now as palliatives, now as an end in themselves; they show a decline in individual responsibility, represent a response to the growing demands upon the individual.

Part of the confusion arises from the fact that there is no agreed list of items or activities which must be counted as social services. It is a rather nice question whether milk distributed to school children is a social service or a subsidy to the dairy industry. The student has to decide for himself what should be included. At the broadest level of definition, all activities of government or individuals which may be described as conducive to human welfare may qualify. For some the "welfare state" refers to all recent extensions of governmental activity in economic life; in particular, the preparedness of government to use its powers to regulate the economy and to effect a measure of income redistribution. Sometimes the term "welfare state" is used to refer specifically to income security measures, notably in the form of benefits to the aged, the widowed, the unemployed and the sick. This excludes from consideration the whole of the education and health services and a group of smaller services—including recreation, family and child welfare, penal and vocational counselling services—which, taken together, have a considerable impact on community life. Each attempt at definition has a certain validity, but the common feature which binds them together is that they all describe efforts at collective responsibility for matters once thought to be largely of private concern. To understand why there is so much confusion about the social services one must examine the peculiar situations which brought them into being and the factors which determined their particular shape.

The Nation State and the Social Services

The last century has witnessed a transformation of the relationship between the state and the individual. Indeed, the modern state as we know it did not exist one hundred years ago. To detail this development is outside the scope of this chapter, but the peculiar forms and purposes of the social services cannot be understood without taking the change into account. In the process new methods of administration have been forged and more and more responsibilities undertaken. These changes did not occur without compelling citizens to ask questions about the proper role of the state, the forms of social intervention and the responsibilities of citizens. Many social services have their

---

[1] Commonwealth Year Book, 1961-2.

origin in these early periods of uncertainty, and questions raised about the social services today still express these dilemmas. Controversies about the provision of social services have involved the most fundamental questions about the nature of man and the nature and working of society. Today the state has developed vast social institutions, it has become a significant employer of labour to service the institutions, and whereas the economy was once largely directed by the operations of private finance, the operations of public finance are now critical in directing the flow of goods and services.

With the federal system of Australian government established as recently as 1901 and with the Commonwealth government not firmly asserting its primacy until after 1939, most of the issues relating to the early development of the social services were debated within the framework of the responsibilities of the six individual states which comprise the federation. Until 1946 the Commonwealth government's mandate in the field of social services was restricted to the provision of age, invalid and maternity benefits. In 1946 a referendum transferred the following definite power: "The provision of maternity allowances; widows' pensions; child endowment; unemployment, pharmaceutical, sickness, and hospital benefits; medical and dental services (but not so as to authorize any form of civil conscription); benefits to students; and family allowances." It should also be recalled that the age and invalid pension legislation, regarded as the shining jewel of federal action, represented little more than a transfer of functions already accepted by New South Wales, Victoria and Queensland—the Commonwealth legislation was almost a replica of the N.S.W. provisions.

The early development of the social services is not well documented, althought some useful insights can be gained from brief studies by Dora Peyser, A. W. Greig and Thomas Kewley.[2] Reference will be made largely to Victoria and New South Wales, but there are interesting variations between all states. Social welfare problems began to emerge within a short time of the founding of each settlement. In N.S.W. the Female Orphan School was established in 1800, and the Society for the Promotion of Christian Knowledge and Benevolence in 1813. Five years later the latter Society was reconstituted as the Benevolent Society of New South Wales. In Victoria the first recorded welfare services grew out of the activities of the congregation of the Anglican Church of St. James. In 1842 the St James Dorcas Society began welfare work with children, and in the following year the St James Visiting Society commenced outdoor relief to the poor in their own homes. In both states, although many other organizations were established, two key agencies emerged. These were the N.S.W. Benevolent Society, which came to be known as the Government Almoner, and the Immigrants' Aid Society in Victoria (founded 1853) which was frequently described as the "workhouse of the colony". In their earliest stages both institutions had a wide charter to cover the needs of the sick, the poor, the homeless, the aged and orphans. The method of administering these and similar agencies provides a clue to early attitudes about the social services.

---

[2] Dora Peyser, "A Study of the History of Welfare Work in Sydney from 1788 till about 1900", *Journal of the Royal Australian Historical Society*, 1939; A. W. Greig, "Early Melbourne Charitable and Philanthropic Organizations", *The Victorian Historical Magazine*, 1936; Thomas Kewley, "Social Services in Australia, 1900-10", *Journal of the Royal Australian Historical Society*, 1947.

Australian social institutions were fashioned in a time when industrial society was beginning to become an established fact. There was no slow transition from subsistence farming to commercial farming. There was no slow transition from rural to urban life; rather settlement spread outwards from the towns. Central government was established before local government, although there was a transition from military and quasi-military government to civil government. In addition, welfare problems in Australia presented the special problem of the person in distress, often without family or a bond with a particular locality. The early social agencies express a special concern for the traveller, the stranger and the immigrant. In the absence of existing services, the first crucial issue was the pattern of organization that should be adopted. Who would accept responsibility for the distressed? In England this class of need would have been covered under the Poor Law, but in Australia there was no system of local government, and the semi-nomadic nature of the population would have made such a scheme unworkable.

The solution to this problem of organization was to be found in the government-subsidized voluntary agency. In a limited fashion, the colonial authorities accepted responsibility for the care and welfare of convicts and military personnel, but the settlers were expected to make provision for themselves through their own civil bodies. In his study of the Royal Melbourne Hospital, Inglis cites Governor Gipps's reluctance to provide a general hospital for Port Phillip: "Such institutions are properly the object of private charity."[3] Should this method fail, he suggested, a local rate could be struck. The latter suggestion was never taken up, but under the Victorian Municipal Act of 1854, the care and maintenance of the destitute sick and poor was devolved upon the municipal corporations. Gradually there came into being a loose network of voluntary agencies throughout Victoria and N.S.W. These included visiting societies, hospitals, orphanages and benevolent homes. Voluntary organizations with the approval, support and quite frequently with the direct sponsorship of the government, were assigned the task of providing many of the community's essential social services.

It was some time before governments came to realize that the voluntary agency had special advantages. There is considerable evidence that this development was regarded at first as a temporary expedient. In Victoria, from the passage of the original Municipal Act in 1854 until 1891, it was expected that local government would at some stage become responsible for social services. In 1878, when Graham Berry was Premier and Treasurer of Victoria, he stated in reply to a question asking whether his government intended to bring down a Bill for the better management of charities, "The subject is one of wide policy involving the consideration whether the State should continue to support these institutions or whether their maintenance should be made a charge on the localities in which they existed."[4] A belief that local government would eventually undertake more responsibilities occurred again and again throughout the second half of the nineteenth century. This belief was not borne out by circumstances. At first municipalities made some efforts to discharge their charitable functions, but abandoned them as the system of voluntary organizations became an accomplished fact.

[3] K. S. Inglis, *Hospital and Community.*
[4] *Victorian Parliamentary Debates*, Vol. 28, 6/7/1878.

Local government remained generally dependent on grants from central revenue. In Victoria these grants had been expected to taper off, but this was not to be the case, and central government had little financial inducement to change the system. In any case the municipalities were reluctant to accept more responsibility. As part of the Royal Commission inquiry on Charitable Institutions, 1890, a circular was sent to all Victorian municipalities seeking their opinion on local responsibility for welfare. The Commissioners concluded[5] that there was practically no support for the proposal that the burden of charity should be entirely borne by municipalities, which were numerous, small and debt-ridden. They had little of the authority and none of the traditions of English local government. They lacked its judicial functions, and there was no magisterial class. The weakness of local government affected the administrative organization of social welfare in several ways. For many years the only administrative organization which covered the whole country was the police force, and policemen were widely used as welfare officers. In New South Wales, the Bank of N.S.W. was the agent for paying old age pensions.

The development of social welfare administration in Victoria and N.S.W. can be seen as a response to local exigencies, frequently in conflict with established practices in Britain. But this conflict can be exaggerated. At first glance there is a picture of small voluntary organizations being in close touch with central government, in a remarkably free and democratic manner. An English visitor, the Reverend Dean Latham commented, "It is amazing to a man who has lived in England to see how much the State comes into the life of the ordinary citizen here. The State and the citizen out here seem to work hand in hand in a way in which I am not yet accustomed."[6] What was significant, of course, was the way in which voluntary committees were used as an administrative organ of government. The significant democratic aspect of this arrangement was that central government exercised no detailed supervision of the agencies. At the same time the vital relationship between the state and voluntary organizations has not always been clearly grasped. The voluntary agencies existed instead of the Poor Law Authorities, and did not, as in England, represent an alternative or supplementary form of assistance. Therefore they were not likely to become the target of the same kind of criticism as the English Poor Law Authorities. Critics of the spread of welfare programmes frequently attacked the voluntary agencies on the ground that they were not truly voluntary, but largely dependent upon statutory funds.

From time to time efforts were made to control and co-ordinate the voluntary welfare agencies, particularly in defining the categories of those eligible for assistance, but these efforts were largely unsuccessful. The role of the voluntary agency was to meet minimum needs and not to provide a comprehensive welfare programme. If the state had moved far in co-ordinating voluntary agencies, it would thereby have accepted responsibility for a comprehensive welfare service. The main control imposed was the condition that the agency raise a proportion of its funds: the requirement of raising one-

---

[5] *Report of the Royal Commission on Charitable Institutions,* Victorian Government Printer, 1891.
[6] Reverend Dean Latham, "Institutional System in Western Australia", *Dependent Children: Interstate Congress of Workers,* 1909.

third or one-quarter of its income placed a brake on requests for Treasury assistance. As they had very limited funds it was unnecessary to supervise the agencies in detail to ensure that they assisted only the most needy.

This pattern of welfare services where the favoured method of organization was the encouragement of relatively uncontrolled voluntary agencies has slowly changed over a century to a pattern of government-accepted responsibility for providing a uniform minimum service to all citizens. In some services the government acted, in others it has yet to. Services have been transferred from voluntary agencies to the individual states, then later from them to the Federal government.

This development has been accompanied by changes in attitude, changes in knowledge about the causes of welfare problems and, above all, changes in administrative and economic theories and techniques. These changes are evident in the structure of the whole community, but they apply in a special way to the social services. Because the various factors interlock it is difficult to estimate whether one aspect is more crucial than another. However, to assert that changes in knowledge and attitudes are a sufficient explanation of the long term trend towards collective responsibility ignores the massive alterations in society itself, examined in other chapters of this book. When the social services are studied programme by programme, those established with a particular philosophy seem to have persisted beyond a point when they were attuned to later thinking and to changes in society. Changes in community attitudes have tended to be influential only at points when there was gross disparity between the social services and the changed needs of the community.

The Changing Purpose of the Social Services

One hundred years ago, the visible evidence of illness, unemployment, widowhood or old age was likely to be utter destitution, and as the size of towns increased, poverty began to appear as a mass problem. Poverty was sometimes mistaken for the whole disease and measures for its relief permitted little differentiation. The immediate problem was destitution as such. Despite a more practical and democratic social climate in Australia, measures for the relief of poverty were not, in practice, so remarkably different from those taken in Britain. Until the introduction of age pensions in 1900, differences were mainly in organization and perhaps in the spirit in which the services were rendered. As in Britain, Australians were perplexed by the problem. There was, however, an important difference in the status of the poor. In Australia the rigours of poverty were softened by the climate and the conditions of settlement. The poor could live more easily in rough shacks and provide for some of their own needs. In New Zealand, where circumstances were similar, it was found that when age pensions were first introduced, many old persons emerged from the bush, not having been in contact with people for years.

The nineteenth century, throughout the western world, may be viewed as a period of tumult in social welfare. The Poor Law had not been designed to deal with poverty in an industrial society, but no new methods had been devised. The causes of poverty were not understood and the notion of state responsibility had yet to be forged. Social services were regarded as artificial creations—for persons who could not satisfy the basic needs of shelter, sustenance and health through the normal channels of the market, the family and personal charity. The 1891 Royal Commission on Victorian Charities opposed the trend of government acceptance of responsibility for the poor:

> In most parts of the world, the burden of charity is locally borne and there are manifest reasons why this principle should be maintained. In an earlier state of society, neighbour is helped by neighbour. Institutions that arise to take the place of individual help are the result of action by neighbours. Though in a new country where settlement is unequal, it is natural that larger places should help the smaller, local support should be regarded as the normal system. . . .[7]

If neighbourly and local help were to be regarded as the normal methods of assistance, what was to be the basis for intervention? For many years the answer to this question was straightforward and uncomplicated. The state was justified in assisting where a person was utterly destitute through no fault of his own; or where he represented a danger to himself or to others. The first class of persons were assisted through the subsidized voluntary institutions, the second through custodial provision in gaols, lunatic asylums and reformatories. In practice it was difficult to distinguish the two classes, particularly as the voluntary agencies could not always provide a minimum even for the most destitute. Magistrates then had no choice but to commit the destitute to gaol under the vagrancy laws. One of the more dramatic events which led to the passing of the age pension legislation was the increase in the aged sent to gaol because of the shortage of accommodation in the benevolent homes.

Despite this very limited acceptance of responsibility, destitution was sufficiently widespread for large numbers to apply for help. To the practical administrator and politician of the nineteenth century the central problem was how to minimize costs, and much thought was given to the imposition of new social controls for those no longer subject to the control of the market place and the family. The nineteenth century was alive with specific theories of destitution, its causes and prevention. One of the most popular was that the social services destroyed incentive, and fostered and perpetuated a hereditary pauper class. This theory was widely held in Australia and it was also argued that as destitution was an artificial disease, the proper cure was to establish restrictions and prohibitions so that only the most desperate would apply for help. Common suggestions were that assistance should be below the lowest prevailing community standards, that recipients should be institutionalized in work houses or benevolent homes, that they should lose the right to vote, and that they be required to undertake arduous or unpleasant tasks of work. Rigorous character investigations were proposed and it was frequently suggested that relatives should be required by law to assist the indigent members of their families. Another significant rule was that applicants for assistance should have resided for a minimum time within the locality where they applied for assistance.

Most of these restrictions were applied at one time or another by the voluntary agencies in New South Wales and Victoria, though the commonest was to

[7] *Report of the Royal Commission on Charitable Institutions.* Melbourne, 1891.

refuse regular assistance to people living in their own homes. From time to time fears were raised that the welfare agencies were assisting persons other than the completely destitute or that they were being tricked by rogues. In 1862 a Royal Commission[8] recommended more adequate investigation and scouted the possibility of introducing something like a workhouse test which in other countries had "been found essential, to preserve a spirit of independence among the labouring classes". On the positive side, the Commissioners proposed that Friendly Societies should be encouraged as they led to "provident habit and moral improvement". In many respects, however, a workhouse test was unnecessary. No one had a presumptive right to assistance and in the final analysis the assistance rendered had to be geared to the limited funds of the charities and not to the needs of the applicants. The Commissioners of 1862-3 observed:

> The institutions have in all respects adhered to their vocation as charities, *no absolute right to relief* being conferred. But while preserving this distinctive feature, which, from its tendency to discourage pauperism, we regard as the most valuable in their constitution, we have found very few instances in which objects of compassion have been turned away from their doors.

In retrospect, it is evident that before the turn of the century communities were singularly ill-equipped to understand the nature of indigence or to design programmes for its prevention or relief. Little was known about actual living conditions or about the extent of poverty. The degree by which people, by the exercise of thrift, could protect themselves against poverty was overestimated. One of the major contributions to social reform was a spate of late nineteenth century surveys which illustrated the widespread incidence of poverty and the desperate shifts adopted by the poor. *How the Other Half Lives,* by Jacob Riis (1890) and *Life and Labour of the People of London* (1891-1903) by Charles Booth were landmarks among many similar publications. These were eagerly read in Australia. A picture began to emerge of a large landless class congregated in towns and entirely dependent upon earnings for self-maintenance. For large numbers, self-maintenance was precarious, and fluctuations in economic conditions or the normal vicissitudes of life quickly reduced them to destitution and misery.

The problem posed by poverty and affliction required national and even international policies, but the machinery, resources and sophisticated attitudes associated with the working of the nation state have developed slowly. In their absence small local or voluntary bodies were limited in what they could achieve; their charters and resources both worked towards the introduction of discriminatory measures to keep down costs.

Almost without a plan but as a slow response to changed circumstances and attitudes, the social services began to reflect a new purpose and philosophy towards the end of the nineteenth century. The passage of old age pensions legislation in Victoria, New South Wales and Queensland between 1900 and 1908 is a significant bench mark. This legislation did not stand alone but was accompanied by the extension of democratic rights, early closing of factories, and the beginning of wages legislation.

---

[8] *Royal Commission on Municipalities and Charitable Institutions, 1862-3,* Melbourne, 1863.

The most common way of describing the change in philosophy represented in the new legislation is to refer to the availability of pensions "as a right, not a charity". Because the Australian pensions embody a means test this distinctive feature is sometimes misunderstood and confused with the investigation of means under voluntary welfare, the poor law legislation and public assistance. The difference between the age pension legislation and voluntary charitable relief is, however, fundamental. With a system of voluntary charitable relief, the applicant had no legal right to assistance at all, and even where he could establish his destitution, the voluntary agency might lack the funds to offer a minimum level of assistance. Almost inevitably the general morals of the applicant came under review. Attempts to distinguish between the deserving and the undeserving poor proved humiliating to applicants, particularly as the ordinary habits of the poor were sometimes thought to be enough to label them as undeserving.

The distinction between the age pensions legislation and poor law and public assistance programmes is less obvious but just as fundamental. For the greater part, assistance under the latter programmes was conditional on proof of destitution, personal investigation of the character of applicants and on the willingness of relatives to assist. In the older programmes, assistance was available only where the applicant was prepared to enter a workhouse or benevolent home. No specified amount of assistance was available, but in each case the payment was left to the discretion of the administration. The legislation of New South Wales and later the Commonwealth applied only one significant condition of eligibility for the age pension; namely, income. The amounts to be received were specified and not subject to administrative discretion.

One of the foremost analysts of social welfare programmes has characterized the Australian pension as the "income-conditioned or flat grant-minus system".[9] The benefit is fixed as a sum based upon assumed average minimum need and it is thus possible for the beneficiary to have a reasonably accurate idea of what benefit he might expect. The person with no income would know that at the age of 65 years he was entitled to a fixed weekly payment. After being granted the pension the only further activity required, by him, was to forward an annual statement of income. While it is true that some actively resent the operation of any kind of means test, there is no evidence that the Australian kind of means test has aroused the bitter feelings of shame and resentment which accompanied the operation of the public assistance programmes in the United Kingdom and other countries. Many pensioners profess to see no difference between the operation of the means test and the operation of a taxation de_rtment, referring to their annual statement of income as their "tax return".

In the context of the late nineteenth century the income conditioned pension gave legal status to the poor, although their social status as "the poor" still remained. This marked a revolution in social policy which reflected new understanding of the causes of poverty and a new attitude to collective responsibility. The debates of the time reveal some of the uncertainty of the cause of need in old age. Perhaps the most remarkable statement—surprisingly modern—is contained in the report of the Victorian Royal Com-

9 Eveline Burns, *Social Security and Public Policy*, pp. 22-3.

mission on Old Age Pensions, 1898, which bears the unmistakable imprint of its Chairman, Joseph William Kirton.

At the very outset we were impressed with the magnitude and complexity of the question. The evidence elicited deepened this feeling. It is not so much a disease as the symptoms of a disease which has its roots deep down in social, industrial and political conditions. It embraces the whole labour question in its sweep . . . the social and industrial revolution has brought, in its turn, new responsibilities. The national conscience has been pricked and it is recognized that the ethics of this question make clear the obligation of the State to insure that the worn-out wealth creating human machines who have contributed to its development and enrichment receive the means of sustenance and support.

The implication was that a new permanent social institution was necessary. This was certainly not perceived by everyone. At the same Commission, Commandant Booth of the Salvation Army suggested that the State of Victoria could solve its problem by dividing the aged poor into two portions, the Protestant and the Roman Catholic, and that the individual churches should be asked to tender for their support. These proposals make strange reading today, but they indicate the puzzlement of people who faced large-scale destitution under what were not always recognized as changed social conditions. Suggestions ranged from a return to greater stringency and a compulsory billeting of the aged with members of the public, to the payment of universal pensions regardless of age.

The precipitants of the new approach in the social services are difficult to disentangle, but the strong egalitarian elements in Australia society have sometimes been thought to be alone responsible for the very considerable changes.[10] However, this interpretation over-estimates the political influence of beneficiaries and tends to ignore the pressure for change resulting from the sheer inefficiency of the previous range of services.

In times when the social services were regarded as marginal and secondary, more enlightened attitudes and increased prosperity did not automatically lead to their revision, although other areas of social living were profoundly affected by these changes. The precipitants of change in the social services have tended to be associated with the manifest failure of existing services to provide even a minimum standard. The introduction of statutory education followed upon the failure of voluntary education to meet the minimum needs of children, and the introduction of state child welfare programmes was associated with a belief that voluntary organizations could not provide a sufficient service. In the case of age pensions, the emergence of a significant number of the aged poor placed too great a strain upon the resources of the charitable institutions. One of the earliest measures specifically for aged persons was an 1897 amendment to the conditions of grant-in-aid to the charitable institutions of Victoria, which enabled the Treasurer to require Benevolent Homes to accept the destitute aged and infirm without the necessity for them to appear in gaol. An effective solution to this crisis required a new social invention, and in Australia the popularizing of the new technique appears as much as

[10] For an example of this interpretation, see J. F. Cairns, "The Welfare State in Australia", unpublished Ph.D. thesis, Melbourne University, 1957.

anything to have been due to individuals. The effort and initiative of J. C. Neild appears to have been outstanding.[11] By and large, the student of Australian social services seeks in vain to find sufficient attention paid to the devising of techniques to solve the social problems of industrialized society, and antiquated methods and philosophies have tended to continue even though the climate of social opinion has changed.

When the old age pension legislation was proposed, there was surprisingly little opposition and a general readiness to accept important amendments advanced by the organized labour movement. It was generally agreed that the poor had no margin of savings and that even for others, savings were not secure. Australians were aware that the earliest settlers had fashioned a nation under difficult circumstances, and could not accept the notion that the aged poor were poor solely because of faulty character, or that pensions would encourage thriftlessness. The preamble to the New South Wales Act of 1900 stated: "It is equitable that deserving persons who during the prime of life have helped to bear the public burdens of the Colony by the payment of taxes, and by opening up its resources by their labour and skill, should receive from the Colony pensions in their old age." A social obligation was asserted. Attempts to build in character qualifications received mixed support and did not survive the test of public opinion. With a philosophy of social service based upon earned rights, moral behaviour came to be regarded as secondary. Persons who were by no means identified with the emerging Labour Party were ready to declare that in their experience hard drinkers had often been the hardest workers and that the latter was the significant criterion of eligibility for assistance.

The changed purpose of the social services embodied in the age pension legislation surprisingly remained an almost solitary achievement for nearly 40 years. Minor measures such as invalid pensions (1910) and maternity allowances (1912) were introduced by the Commonwealth, and from time to time individual states experimented with restricted programmes of unemployment assistance and allowances to widows and children, but for the greater range of social services the traditions embodied in the system of voluntary welfare services prevailed until 1945 and later. Age pensions had been introduced under favourable circumstances, the needs of the beneficiaries excited sympathy, their numbers were relatively few, and the technique of the income conditioned pension was relatively simple. Until 1939 most of these favourable circumstances were absent. The Commonwealth lacked financial resources and constitutional powers to legislate for further services. The conservative governments in power saw the need to act but made only abortive efforts to introduce national insurance. Conservative spokesmen had become increasingly aware that the expansion of the income conditioned pensions would interfere with existing social arrangements. Taxation would be increased and there would be a change in the relationship between the state and the individual. Hence, in 1929, the Royal Commission on Family Allowances entered a majority report opposing family allowances. "Beneath the claim seldom avowed, there was in many instances a clearly perceptible hope that the appealing suggestion of child happiness would make Child Endowment an

[11] For Neild's views, see J. C. Neild, *Report on Old Age Pensions*, 1898.

easy means of bringing about a virtual re-distribution of wealth."[12] However, if little was achieved, the idea that social services were necessary in the modern industrial state was accepted by conservative governments. The key issue that emerged was the method of financing.

Methods of Financing the Social Services

Advocating a system of contributory national insurance in 1939, Mr R. G. Menzies (shortly to be prime minister) said: "The enormous burden of free pensions in Australia cannot be indefinitely increased. There is a great moral principle in the proposition that if we desire to obtain benefits from the community, we must be prepared to contribute towards the cost of those benefits."[13] In opposing the contributory system Mr Forde, deputy leader of the Labour party, objected that "as a social measure it is retrogressive in that it ignores a cardinal principle of taxation under which those best able to pay, shall bear the burden".[14] The opposing "principles" epitomize one issue in the modern debate about the social services. Both concede the necessity for social services, but differ about the way they should be related to the existing social order.

The possibility of introducing a contributory system of insurance had been considered when age pensions were introduced, but had been rejected on the grounds that the most needy were excluded, that the poor had no margin of savings, and that a contributory scheme promised benefits to future generations but offered nothing to the present generation of aged persons. Instead, age pensions were financed from consolidated revenue, and to the extent that taxation was progressive, effected a transfer of income from the more to the less wealthy. The result was a form of assessment insurance with the premium being part of the expected tax burden and a charge upon the whole community. Yet it is clear that this approach disturbed the more conservative elements in the community, and between 1913 and 1938 a series of inquiries examined the feasibility of introducing contributory insurance schemes for the sick and unemployed. Unemployment insurance was introduced in Queensland (1923), and twice the Commonwealth drafted national insurance legislation, and once (1938) passed a National Insurance Act.

Insurance schemes had a definite appeal to those who were concerned that a widespread programme of social services might interfere with existing social arrangements. There was a specious analogy with private life insurance and it was widely believed that even a partial contribution gave the contributor a sense of responsibility. However, before 1939 a contributory system of pensions did little to come to grips with the pressing problems associated with unemployment and in large part the original objections to the insurance type programmes remained valid.

Between 1941 and 1945, largely under the leadership of the Labour party, a comprehensive social security programme came into being based on the age pension method of finance. The Labour party was committed to a policy of redistribution of income, but at the same time wished to preserve the notion

[12] *Report of the Royal Commission on Child Endowment and Family Allowances*, 1929.
[13] *Commonwealth Parliamentary Debates*, vol. 158, p. 1821.
[14] *Ibid.*. p. 1807.

that financial benefits were earned rights. It set out to achieve this by designating part of the income tax as a social services contribution which was paid into a separate national welfare fund. However, this legislation was to be repealed and the Labour government was unsuccessful in its attempts to extend this principle to the field of health services.

Since 1945 the pendulum has swung away from assessment insurance and a system of social services based upon redistribution and from any schemes which tended to enhance the state with respect to the individual. This has been most obvious in housing and health. In 1955, when the first Commonwealth-States Housing Agreement legislation (1945) came up for review, housing policy was revised to reduce the functions of the state as a landlord and to pour more finance into home ownership schemes. One conservative government member commented that the previous programme had features which resembled "the Marxist concept of society", while another commended the legislation because "it represented a step away from socialism".[15]

The most impressive attempt, however, to introduce a comprehensive social welfare service with a minimum of government control and a maximum contribution from beneficiaries, has been in the field of health. Between 1950 and 1955 the Commonwealth government introduced what is probably the most sophisticated legislation of this type. The government accepted responsibility for a general guarantee of quality health services. The worst features of previous insurance programmes were averted by a mixture of direct government subsidy and voluntary contributions to approved societies. The special classes of pensioners and the chronically ill were covered by separate provisions, thus enabling the approved societies to remain financially sound, but ensuring the same service to all. In praising the plan the chief architect of Australia's National Health legislation, Sir Earle Page, quoted with approval a comment by a fellow medical practitioner, "It may not be easy to stop the progress towards socialism, but it is far easier and more realistic to halt it than to try to eliminate it after it has become an established fact."[16]

In other ways post-war trends indicate a reluctance to conceive of social welfare programmes as being solely operated by the state. There has been a willingness to subsidize voluntary welfare bodies to provide marriage counselling (1960), residential care for the aged (1954), and for the disabled (1963). Even more important has been the revival of interest in meeting social welfare needs through industrial programmes. Recent surveys of employer operated retirement programmes suggest that more than 20% of persons in the work force are now covered by these schemes.[17] As these plans qualify for tax exemption, the Commonwealth government forfeits considerable revenue and without this support employer operated programmes would not be viable. Industry also provides other fringe benefits in the form of paid holidays, sick leave, long service leave and various health services and amenities. In both Britain and the United States there is interest in the provision of annual wages and redundancy payments.

[15] Commonwealth Parliamentary Debates, 4 Eliz. II, H. of R. 6, pp. 281, 863.
[16] Sir Earle Page, What Price Medical Care? 1960, p. 87.
[17] See (i) Survey of Private Pension and Retiring Allowance Schemes 1955-56, Commonwealth Bureau of Census and Statistics, 1957; (ii) Government and Semi-Government Pensions and Superannuation Schemes, Bulletin no. 44, Commonwealth Bureau of Census and Statistics, 1952-3.

This trend is so significant that it is now scarcely possible to define social welfare in terms of direct governmental provision. Richard M. Titmuss,[18] in his important essay, "The Social Division of Welfare", suggests that social services should be defined in terms of aims and not in terms of the particular methods employed to achieve them. He draws attention to the fact that, apart from individual pensions, social welfare needs are met not only through statutory services, but through taxation policies whereby the taxpayer is given a certain amount of relief through deductions for dependants and health expenses, and through payments to private retirement schemes.

The vital social needs of a modern industrial community can be satisfied through a wide range of institutional devices, with maximum or minimum direct governmental control. In an affluent society, the conditions which once made the prospect of insurance type programmes illusory have now largely passed away. There is a real danger that private welfare programmes will lack accountability to the community, but the development of these programmes marks a revolution in understanding of the causes of need and the acceptance of social responsibility. This revolution is typified in the movement away from the idea that destitution should be financed from charitable sources to the idea that pensions are simply a labour cost item and should be regarded as no more than deferred wages.

There has been a slight revival of Australian interest in changing the method of financing the most costly of the social services, namely retirement pensions. The chairman of the present government parties' social services committee[19] is a keen advocate of a national contributory scheme, while R. I. Downing has proposed a contributory plan to supplement the present age benefit.[20] The main grounds of opposition to reform are twofold. First, that the income conditioned pension is simple to administer and is easily adjustable to changes in economic conditions; but ease of administration should not be the significant criterion and it is not beyond human ingenuity to devise contributory schemes which are sensitive to economic change. Second, a contributory scheme does not favour redistribution of income; but the social services are not the only method of achieving greater equality—there is room for further tax reforms and it should prove socially more desirable to aim at greater equality before taxation.

The criterion to apply in allocating funds is a special problem in financing the social services. They must compete with the other public services, and both together with the requirements of the private consumer. Even the most ardent advocate of extension will concede that there never can be enough service and that decisions must be made about priorities. Because provision does not depend upon the profit motive other stimulants to action are necessary. Carefully controlled surveys may disclose the need for action in some fields. Experiments with new approaches may show what can be expected in others, *e.g.* delinquency prevention or mental hygiene programmes. With the gradual removal of mass poverty, more subtle methods of analysis will be needed to disclose what social services are required and to measure their

---

[18] R. M. Titmuss, *Essays on the Welfare State.*

[19] K. Cameron Wilson, "Financing Our Later Years", in *Economic Security in Old Age,* Old People's Welfare Council, Melbourne, 1960.

[20] R. I. Downing, "Reforming the Australian Tax System", *Economic Record,* 1962.

costs. When such knowledge is brought to public attention, the question becomes an ethical issue. Are taxpayers prepared to forgo certain amounts of marginal consumption in order to get social services? This will then depend upon scales of values and the quality of life that people seek. It should be remembered that economic welfare is related to personal welfare. Where people believe that society as a whole cares for them they are more active in their response to society. Thus how much can be spent on the social services cannot be determined by the methods of "pure" economics.

Australian Social Services and the Affluent Society

The acceptance of national and collective responsibility for the welfare of citizens and the development of broad programmes and specialized services constitute the idea of the welfare state. Its achievements have been considerable although there is ample scope for further progress. Fears that these changes would lead to bureaucratic regulation of individuals or to a decline in initiative and responsibility have, so far, proved largely unfounded. In 1926 the secretary of the Victorian Employers' Federation could claim:

> Compulsory (unemployment) insurance must paralyse the initiative of men seeking employment and it certainly cannot tend to aid the formation of character and self-reliance. It is safe to prophesy that, whatever scheme may be introduced, and whatever amount of money be estimated for such a purpose, as time goes on and the self-reliance of recipients becomes weaker, the cost must enormously increase.[21]

Men who lack inspiration should, perhaps, eschew prophecies. In this case the prophecy was unfulfilled. Since 1945, when unemployment benefits existed for the first time, unemployment seems to have disappeared as a significant characteristic of the industrial state. Men have begun to think rationally about the social environment as something which can be governed and ordered to fit man's needs and values. Before the second world war, a figure of no more than 4% unemployment seemed a barely realizable goal; since the war governments are likely to be unseated if unemployment exceeds 2%.

The social service solutions introduced in Australia have been surprisingly pragmatic and have had their origins in efforts to provide minimum well-being without dramatic changes in social structure or economic arrangements. Despite the lack of drama, the changes represent important new social inventions. The *laissez-faire* theorist of the nineteenth century might well regard present day interferences with the working of the market as little short of rank collectivism. Industrial, social, and economic changes have, however, left little room for the unregulated society. The doctrinaire collectivist viewing the changes is inclined to take pride in the observation that some of the rapaciousness of capitalism has been curbed and to consider that the social services are imposed upon the free enterprise society. However, this is to regard the nineteenth century version of capitalism as the normal type of free enterprise. It would be more accurate to describe the present welfare state as the modern version of the free enterprise society.

---

[21] James R. Fraser, in evidence to the Royal Commission on National Insurance, 1926, p. 970, *Report of the Royal Commission on National Insurance 1925-1927*, Commonwealth Parliamentary Papers.

Remarkable as the achievements of the welfare state have been, there is evidence that much of the thinking about the role of the social services is in need of revision. Assumptions about the purpose of the social services were embodied in social welfare legislation at a time when the emphasis was upon the relief of symptoms and when financial exigencies demanded services geared to minimum needs and in large part available to the working classes only. These assumptions are becoming increasingly less valid. The last century has witnessed the relative emancipation of the working class, a rise in the standard of living and changes in general taste. As basic subsistence needs tend to be taken for granted, the community is directing its demands towards qualitative improvement in the existing services. Drawing attention to the inadequacy of age benefits, the British Labour movement insisted, "The time has now come to rise above the concept of fair shares in poverty."[22] In post-war Australia a generation is growing up which did not know the insecurity and deprivation of earlier generations. For them the present level of cash social services represents not so much a defence against poverty, but their first real encounter with poverty. The notion of a minimum benefit will need, in the near future, to comprehend not only what is necessary for health and efficiency, but also what is necessary for social participation and the maintenance of self-respect and respect of others. Rising levels of expectancy are rapidly condemning the present system of cash social services to obsolescence.

The same changes in aspiration are affecting other social services. In vivid language, Dr Cunningham Dax has described the state of the Victorian mental hospitals in 1952. Staff were demoralized, wards were dirty, smells were abominable and inmates were often mechanically restrained. These depressing circumstances continued despite much public sympathy and concern..[23] Public education and imaginative professional leadership has changed the concept of mental health from that of asylums to a community service. Minimum housing and education standards are rising. In the fields of general health, behaviour difficulties, and mental health, the demand is now for high quality individualized services. The general health field is responding rapidly to this demand but the mental health and protective services are moving more slowly.[24]

The gradual defeat of mass poverty has also highlighted intractable areas of poverty and misery which cannot be reached by broad policies of full employment, subsidized health services and free education. A survey of unemployed persons in 1963 suggested that 25% of the unemployed suffered from physical or mental illness, while in another 20% personal characteristics and attitudes to employment were serious barriers to finding work. Other significant reasons for unemployment were age restrictions and the lack of suitable work within daily travelling distances.[25] The Commonwealth Department of Labour has introduced advisory and counselling services and there will be a greater demand for vocational rehabilitation in the future. Sheltered

---

[22] *Labour's Policy for Security in Old Age,* 1957.

[23] E. Cunningham Dax, *Asylum to Community,* pp. 15-20.

[24] See Alan Stoller, *Mental Health Facilities and Needs of Australia;* and Leonard Tierney, *Children Who Need Help.*

[25] *Characteristics of Persons Registered for Employment with the Commonwealth Employment Service,* Department of Labour and National Service news release, 2/1/64.

workshops already exist for small groups of physically and mentally handicapped persons. In 1959 Mr David Scott drew attention to the existence of a group of socially handicapped families, designated as the "multi-problem family". Mr Scott estimated that there might be 25,000 such families in Victoria alone.[26]

The notion that the social services might have a rehabilitative and preventive function is indicated by a number of small but significant changes. In 1942 the Commonwealth government introduced a vocational training programme for invalid pensioners, and in 1960 a programme of marriage counselling for those who might be seeking divorce. State hospitals have programmes of physical rehabilitation and more attention is being given to the rehabilitation of the offender. Early in 1957 the first stipendiary probation and parole officers were appointed in Victoria, while the new Victorian Social Welfare Act (1960) authorizes the Social Welfare Department "to promote family welfare in the community, to prevent its disruption and to mitigate the effects thereof".

Taken together, these new services indicate a positive interest in the nurturing aspects of society. In the past, statutory interest in the problems of behaviour was largely expressed by legal prescription programmes of custodial care. In the debates about health and destitution the social policies governing the services had been heavily influenced by prevailing attitudes to the role of the state and proper relationships between property and labour. In the debates about crime and delinquency, family problems, leisure activities and mental health, other factors become important. Yet the notion that people are motivated by a free choice after considering all possible lines of action has had a powerful influence. Historically the effort to impose social controls through punishment, incarceration and shame has been a factor in all of the social services.

It is of special interest that in the provision of the nurturing and rehabilitative services public action has been slow because of a lack of tested procedures. New developments in knowledge and professional skill are now becoming available. Perhaps the most important findings from the social welfare viewpoint are those which have established a relationship between the environment and individual and family problems. A body of knowledge is being accumulated which indicates that the manner of providing a social service can be critical in remedying or worsening the situations. More concern is being given to all those factors which tend to lead to social isolation and to the institutionalized personality. In the field of mental health the day hospital enables people to receive psychiatric help but to return to their own homes in the evening. Emergency housekeeper services enable children to remain at home when their mother is ill. Home nursing and "meals on wheels" enable the old person to remain in his own community. Day centres for retarded children have largely developed since the war.

The desire for greater personal achievement is focusing attention on the social changes which have accompanied urbanization and industrialization. The family has changed and its functions are greater. Long term demographic trends are altering the composition of the population. There are more older

[26] "Multi-Problem Families as a Concern to the Community" in *Proceedings of Conference on Multi-Problem Families, 1959.*

people, families are smaller and women are no longer so preoccupied with child-bearing. More women are going to work and parental roles are being affected. The growth in the size of cities raises new problems for the individual trying to find a meaningful place for himself in society. It is in response to those changes that many new social services are called into being.

Governments have shown some interest in recreational programmes, balanced town planning, and personal services, but there is still a tendency to regard the social services as a burden on the private sector of the community, as something for nothing; a transfer of income from the hardworking and provident to the idle and improvident. Sir Robert Menzies could recently answer an interjector's query whether he could live on the age pension, "Never having had any money I didn't work for, I wouldn't know."[27] The notion that social services can play a dynamic, rather than a static role in social betterment has still to sink in.

Organization and Administration of Social Services

The social services may be defined as new institutional arrangements which have come into being as a response to long secular changes, notably urbanization and industrialization, accompanied by rising standards of living, increased literacy and a revolution in knowledge and attitudes. In recent years there have been indications that the social services may play a dynamic and integrative role in community life. Their scale and the interrelatedness and complexity of social needs now require more attention to organization, administration and technique. Most services came into being as *ad hoc* arrangements to deal with special problems, and have been grafted into a public service administration which has stressed legal and financial accountability rather than social accountability. In the past the most frequent question was whether a person was eligible for the service provided; in the future it will become, are services adequate, or does the community need new ones? Community care programmes often require co-operation from labour and industry and the ordinary citizen, and their structure will need clarifying to achieve meaningful relationships with the community. Instead of a conservatively stated bureaucratic accountability, administrations will need to present a clearly stated social purpose.

Part of this reform has already been achieved. The following legislative changes in Victoria show how recent has been the acceptance of statutory responsibility for co-ordinated services. The Hospitals and Charities Act, 1948, gave increased authority to the state for planning and budgetary control of hospital services and at the same time placed the Hospitals and Charities Commission under professional direction. The Mental Hygiene Authority was established in 1950 to carry through a thorough revision of existing services. The Social Welfare Act, 1960, co-ordinated the efforts of voluntary and statutory bodies operating in the field of child care, welfare assistance, youth, and crime and delinquency programmes. In each case the new legislation has led to schemes of staff training, research and planning.

At the same time efforts to provide adequate service have been bedevilled by a necessary focus upon transforming the existing services, finding enough

[27] Melbourne *Age*, 27 March 1963.

qualified staff,[28] and securing adequate funds. There is evidence of timidity and failure in social advance because of the lack of administrative skill and shortage of professional staff. Many worthwhile new projects are over-burdened by long waiting lists of applicants for assistance. The importance of these factors is not always realized. From one point of view, for example, it is possible to consider the inadequate approach to the welfare of aborigines as indicative of apathy and prejudice, but it is probably more valid to consider this failure in terms of the lack of administrative insight and associated skills. In far too many services, failure at this level makes a mockery of the stated purpose of the organization.

A feature of the present pattern of social services has been departmentali-zation. Human needs have tended to be fragmented between different welfare agencies. The Association of Social Workers (Victorian Branch) has stated a strong case for the multi-purpose family welfare agency which can see total family needs in a decent perspective.[29] One antidote to departmentalism is the development of central co-ordinating councils and greater citizen partici-pation. Since the war there has been a rapid increase in the number of voluntary co-ordinating councils. The most important are probably the various State Councils of Social Service and the Australian Council of Social Service, although there are numerous other bodies operating in such diverse fields as youth welfare, old people's welfare and mental health. Unfortunately these bodies are inadequately financed and in some cases unable to employ paid staff.[30]

Because the social services can play such a significant role in the community life, there is an urgent need to review the part played by local and voluntary activity. Local government is in a key position to develop and administer a whole range of personal and environmental services, but is hampered by too frequent elections, inadequate staff and poor leadership. The ordinary citizen has played a small part in social policy and administration. The education, health and economic security programmes have little direct citizen represen-tation or beneficiary representation. This problem will not be overcome by introducing into management only those private citizens who do not see them-selves as past, present or future beneficiaries. Citizen representation is far too often of the conspicuous charity type, where it is primarily important that one's charitable activities be publicly known.

There has been some fear that the role of the citizen volunteer might become insignificant as the state accepts more responsibility. To many this is regarded as a favourable trend because voluntarism has been associated with private charitable action in areas where it was inappropriate. The attempt of private voluntary bodies to provide an alternative to community action was doomed to failure and the very preoccupation with providing alternative basic services has, in the past, militated against the pioneering functions often assumed by the voluntary agency. The distinction between citizen partici-pation and the private organization of welfare needs to be made clear. Private

[28] See, e.g., R. J. Lawrence, "Development of Professional Social Work in Australia", Ph.D. thesis, Australian National University, 1962.
[29] Family Welfare: A Guide to Developing Local Services, Association of Social Workers (Victoria), 1963.
[30] See Financing of Voluntary Welfare Agencies in Victoria, Victorian Council of Social Service, 1961, pp. 36-8.

welfare organizations are often equated with democracy, but they have frequently ignored community needs and it is rare for private organizations to be managed by beneficiaries or at least by persons who do not see a sharp cleavage between themselves and beneficiaries.

As the issues become more complex and the technical procedures more esoteric the ordinary citizen may find himself excluded from policy making unless he can gain an effective voice in community organization. The community welfare council can give him this voice. In the last few years several of the voluntary associations have demonstrated that they can play an important part in instituting changes. The Brotherhood of St Laurence pioneered the elderly citizens' club in Victoria. In New South Wales the Council of Social Service undertook a survey of the economic and social condition of widows and dependent children.[31] Its revelations stimulated political demands which resulted in the enactment of legislation providing for substantial increases in benefit rates for this group. In South Australia the Service to Youth Council has pioneered a method of working with street gangs. In Victoria the Helping Hand Society pioneered retarded children's centres. Future policy may well be to encourage private citizens to avoid undertaking costly maintenance programmes and to devote more time to programmes of research, discussion of social policy and small pilot programmes of new services. For some, the voluntary agency is seen as a corrective to large dehumanized statutory services, but any approach which admits that statutory services must be dehumanized is a policy of despair and fails to recognize the need for clear policies, better administration and better staffing.

---

[31] Jean Aitken-Swan, *Widows in Australia.*

PART III

D. W. McELWAIN and W. J. CAMPBELL

8   The Family

INTRODUCTION

SOME form of family life has been found in virtually all known human societies, and many charming myths and legends attempt to explain its origins.[1] However, biological factors, such as mating impulses, the handicaps of pregnancy and the long helplessness of the young have probably contributed most.[2] The existence of powerful forces encouraging the development of the family has not led to a common pattern of family structure or behaviour. In the kibbutzim of Israel, we find married couples whose family behaviour, as we understand it, is at a minimum.[3] On the other hand, the traditional Chinese family[4] and the ancient Roman one[5] are examples of multi-functional units of great stability. The Todas who are found in small villages scattered across the plateau of the Nilgiri Hills in South India are polyandrous in their marital relationships,[6] while the Baganda in Central Africa are polygynous.[7] Cooking, housekeeping and baby-tending are proper male occupations in the Marquesas,[8] and among the Tasmanian natives the difficult work of seal-hunting was done by women.[9] These examples, which could be multiplied a thousandfold, suggest that no single form of family life can be regarded as inevitable or more "natural" than any other.

Our aim in this chapter is to present an account of research on the white Australian family and, in the main, we refrain from making our own generalizations. The focus is the intact *nuclear* family, sometimes called the conjugal group, comprising husband and wife together with their blood or adopted children, but we begin by looking briefly at the network of nuclear families which form the the *extended* family or kinship group. We next look briefly at

---

[1] For example, the Sanskrit myth as reported by F. W. Bain in *A Digit of the Moon*, pp. 32-4.
[2] H. S. Jennings, *The Biological Basis of Human Nature*, p. 253.
[3] M. E. Spiro, *Kibbutz: Venture in Utopia*.
[4] Lee, Shu-Ching, "China's Traditional Family. Its Characteristics and Disintegration", *American Sociological Review*, vol. 18, 1953.
[5] S. A. Queen, R. W. Habenstein and J. B. Adams, *The Family in Various Cultures*, pp. 159-79.
[6] W. H. R. Rivers, *The Todas*.
[7] J. Roscoe, *The Baganda*.
[8] A. Kardiner, *The Individual and His Society*.
[9] R. Linton, *The Study of Man*.

certain demographic features of the nuclear family—age at marriage, number of children and divorce (treated more fully in Chapters 10 and 11 below)— then more closely first, at the unity or emotional solidarity which it displays, and then at the roles taken by mothers and fathers. This leads to an exploration of socialization practices within the family: responsibilities accepted for child development, parental division of labour; behaviour expected of children, and nature of the training. Finally, we examine the effects of the home experiences as revealed in children's behaviour, attitudes and values.

Our plan reflects both the type of research that has been undertaken and our own particular interests. If, at times, we appear to ignore class, religious and regional differences, this is due partly to the fact that these are discussed elsewhere in this volume, and partly to the paucity of Australian research on these differences.

STRUCTURE

The extended family group, as traditionally conceived, is not a prominent feature of Australian life. Nevertheless, in rural communities one can find vestiges of the kinship structure. Thus Campbell reports in a study of a small dairying community:

> Whatever disagreement there might be concerning the importance of distant relatives in day-to-day affairs, there is strong agreement on the significance of relationships within cousin boundaries. Adult siblings often work, or even live, together on family farms or in family businesses, and they support one another strongly in community organizations. They and their children visit together, go on picnics together, and sit together at local functions. There have, of course, been several examples of quarrelling within close kinship groups, but in times of crisis the ranks are not only quickly closed but are swollen by more distantly related recruits.[10]

That extended kinship relationships are less intense in metropolitan areas is clear from the reports of several investigations. In a detailed study of twenty professional and eighteen tradesmen families, Fallding found that:

> To the parents of all save one of the families of the sample relatives were far more close than the friends of choice. This was so although, verbally, relatives sometimes suffered devaluation in comparison with friends and some were regarded as diabolically difficult. They were cherished more, helped more, depended upon more, seen more, and spoken of more than friends—and usually much more.
> Contacts with relatives, however, seldom carried much intensity beyond those with the parents' families of origin and their siblings' families.[11]

Certainly within urban communities we get a picture of distinct nuclear units which have varying amounts of contact with one another. While in some of these communities the extent of contact approaches that described by Campbell, in many others it is very small. In a study of thirty families who were

---

[10] W. J. Campbell, "Television in a Rural Community", unpublished MS., University of Queensland.

[11] H. J. Fallding, "Inside the Australian Family" in *Marriage and the Family in Australia* (ed. A. P. Elkin), pp. 58-9. D. Scott and R. U'Ren, *Leisure,* has an account of family visiting in a new Melbourne working class suburb.

135

moving upwards in the social scale, Tugby and Crook, for example, found that, although each adult had approximately 200 kinsfolk whom he recognized, only about one-quarter of these could be named. The families in this study had relatively little contact with their kin and there was a sharp reduction in the intensity of contact as genealogical distance widened. Distant kin were rarely contacted and even immediate kin did not feature prominently in the daily rounds of life of those interviewed.[12]

Let us now begin our closer study of the nuclear family by examining the time in the life of the individual when he establishes such a group. In the 1920s the average age of women at marriage was about 25, and of men about 28. In 1961 these figures were 24.7 for women and 28 for men. In the 1920s one-third of all women had been married by the age of 25. By 1947 this proportion had risen to 49%; in 1954 to 59%; and in 1961 to over 60%. A similar increase has taken place in the proportion of women married by the age of 35: three-quarters in the 1920s, 87% in 1947, 90% in 1954, and 92% in 1961.

Although husbands still tend to be older than their brides, the difference has been narrowed during this century. By 1954 the average difference was 3.3 years, ranging from 5.2 for teenage brides to 2.5 for women in their late fifties. In the same year 16% of wives had husbands younger than themselves. In 1961 the average difference in ages was also 3.3 years.

Commenting upon the pattern of family-building within the new nuclear groups, Borrie in 1957 wrote:

> Prosperity since the war has encouraged early marriage; but many of these young people have also been taking some pains to establish themselves economically before they have started to raise their families. They are starting to have their children at an earlier age than the depression generation of the thirties; but the important question is whether they will cease having children after two or three births when they are still at the comparatively young age of about 30 or 35, or whether they will go on to have a larger family. The answer to this question is not at all clear from Australian data, but so far as American data can be a guide it appears that this tendency to begin to have families at a younger age and to cease childbearing at a younger age is a phenomenon of the post-war situation there.[13]

The wife's age at marriage is clearly an important correlate of family size, as may be seen from the following table, based on the 1954 census.[14]

In 1954, 13% of married women were working, and this figure can be further analysed as follows: Australian-born 11%, United Kingdom-born 15%, and other-born 29%. The largest group of working wives was that married less than five years, of whom 21% were in the work force (29% of the total). The average issue of all working wives (1.3) was considerably lower than the Australian average (2.3), but after five years of marriage more

---

[12] D. J. Tugby and A. E. Crook, "Kinship and Social Mobility in an Australian City: An Interim Report", unpublished MS., University of Queensland.

[13] W. D. Borrie, "Australian Family Structure: Demographic Observations" in A. P. Elkin (ed.), *op. cit.*, pp. 13-14.

[14] Commonwealth Bureau of Census and Statistics, *Families,* chap. 18 of Statistician's Report, vol. 8, 1954 census.

TABLE 1

Marriage Age and Family Size

Age at Marriage	Average Issue at Age 45-49	Percentage Childless
15–19	3·94	2·77
20–24	2·95	6·41
25–29	2·30	12·95
30–34	1·64	27·89
35–39	0·80	54·26
40–44	0·23	83·89
45–49	0·02	98·28

than half the working wives were mothers, and the proportion rose to over 90% among those married for 35 years or more.[15]

The subject of divorce has acquired additional interest in recent years because of the passage of uniform national legislation by the Commonwealth parliament.[16] As Enid Campbell points out, the social policies implied in the new Act are of considerable importance:

It is assumed that the bonds of marriage are not lightly to be shed, that stability in marriages is to be fostered and that marriages should be saved from disintegration wherever possible. In the second place, the Act seeks to give effect to the principle that where a marriage has disintegrated and is beyond redemption, the parties should be absolved completely from the marriage bonds. One of the most important innovations in the federal Act is the place accorded to accredited marriage guidance organizations . . . the Act clearly intends to encourage spouses to utilize the services of the organizations whenever a marriage is in danger of disintegration. . . . Of the grounds for divorce, one requires special mention, that is, five years' separation. Inclusion of this ground represents a significant departure from the traditional conception of divorce as a remedy for matrimonial fault (or even "guilt") and a step in the direction of recognition of an opposing principle, namely that marriages in name only should be dissolved, regardless of the relative blameworthiness of the spouses.[17]

The introduction of this principle brings the law closer to the conception of marriage as a human relationship and takes it a step further from Pauline Christianity, with its rigid doctrine of marriage as a sacramental union that no man may put asunder.

INTERACTION WITHIN FAMILIES

The preceding comments on divorce will suggest that not all Australian families reveal high levels of unity. Several studies which have explored the emotional solidarity between parents and their children confirm this. Thus,

[15] *Ibid.* For survey data on the family income of working wives, and the numbers and ages of their children, see Scott and U'Ren, *Leisure*, pp. 17-20.
[16] See chapter 4.
[17] N. MacKenzie, *Women in Australia*, pp. 394-6.

137

in a large study of nearly 10,000 Sydney adolescents, Connell[18] found that approximately 2,000 were experiencing considerable anxiety and dissatisfaction in their family relationships. Nevertheless, as these figures suggest, the majority of families were moderately to strongly united. Mother and father, for example, were nominated as "most influential associates" throughout the adolescent years, and there was strikingly little disagreement between parents and children on such controversial matters as betting, dancing, and "having bodgie or widgie haircuts".

Similarly, W. J. Campbell[19] in a study involving 1,200 adolescents reports that typical family behaviour includes: much common participation in home chores, and evening and week-end leisure activities; close sharing of confidences about school, peer and personal activities; and general acceptance of home standards. Campbell's rural study of 81 families told a similar story and suggested that among pre-adolescents family behaviour was even more cohesive.[20] In all cases about 20% of Australian families have been rated as displaying a low level of unity.

It appears that family solidarity, at least in its more superficial aspects, has increased with the introduction of television. Overseas investigations suggest that television brings the family together more often, but that the members go along "parallel" rather than truly "interactive" lines. The two Australian studies give some support to these conclusions, although many case studies in which the contrary trend develops could be cited. Campbell[21] reports that time spent at home after television increased for younger adolescents in particular and that "solidarity" behaviour and values which were already high, were strengthened. In addition, the various adolescent age and sex groups tended to adopt a common pattern of family actions. Before television, the family behaviour of young adolescents differed from that of older adolescents, and girls behaved differently from boys. After television, these differences tended to disappear as a result of a general shift towards the type of behaviour previously found mainly in families containing young adolescent girls. It is probably no coincidence that older adolescent boys reported less satisfaction with family relationships after television than they had before.

Olley[22] reports very similar findings, and summarizes the position as follows:

An average of 58% of persons (N = 994) claim to spend about the same time at home as they did before television. Another 38% claim to spend more time at home. Thus, for 96% of the television sample, television is perceived as either maintaining or strengthening home ties for individuals. This trend is recorded for each of the age levels and for each period of television ownership.

In the opinion of Olley's respondents, the two major changes wrought by television are the reduction of time available for other or former activities, and staying at home more often because of a new interest in television.

18 W. F. Connell, et al., Growing Up In An Australian City.
19 W. J. Campbell, Television and the Australian Adolescent.
20 W. J. Campbell, "Television in a Rural Community", loc. cit.
21 Television and the Australian Adolescent.
22 A. K. Olley, The Effects of Television on Interests and Activities of Families and Persons in Sydney, unpublished MS., University of New South Wales, 1962.

It is clear that the Australian family has become slightly more housebound during the last few years, but it would be wrong to imagine that we are developing into a nation of sedentary non-participants. By any standards, the participation of Australians in outdoor activities is very high.

The studies mentioned above can be viewed as introductions to more penetrating analyses of family life. The first of these was undertaken by Oeser and his associates as part of the UNESCO Tensions Project beginning in 1949. By means of a "Day-at-Home" questionnaire, data were gathered from 80 Melbourne children and adolescents[23] and from a similar age group in a rural community.[24] Information was sought on: (a) participation of mothers and fathers in various specified home activities; (b) decision making in these activities; and (c) level of tension generated.

Each activity could be classified according to who decided about, and who acted on it. The classification was as follows:

(a) Husband dominance (husband decided and wife or both husband and wife acted);

(b) Wife dominance (wife decided and husband or both acted);

(c) Autonomic (where husband and wife decided and acted in separate autonomous areas);

(d) Syncratic co-operative (both decide and both act over the whole area).

It was then possible to classify the families by considering the extent to which these patterns were present in the whole range of activities being considered. This gave rise to definitions of families as Syncratic, Average, Autonomic or Autocratic. For instance, a family where the syncratic co-operative pattern appeared for less than 20% of the activities and the wife dominant pattern more than 30% and the autonomic pattern more than 30%, was classified as Autonomic with Wife Dominance.

These Melbourne studies introduced original and promising techniques into research on the family and other investigations were soon launched. In Perth, Taft[25] set out to explore the generality of the Melbourne findings with respect to sex of respondents, socio-economic class, type of school attended, religion and geographical location, and concluded that each of these "subcultural" variables was likely to affect the pattern of family behaviour. A consolidation of results for the various comparisons made by Taft is shown in Table 2.

As well as defining patterns of family behaviour, both Oeser and Taft considered the amount of "tension" generated and agreed that:

> The optimum would appear to lie somewhere between the syncratic and the autonomic family structures, to have social and economic activities largely co-operative, and some proportion of separate work activities, thus achieving a healthy balance between co-operative group activities and autonomous individual activities.[26]

[23] O. A. Oeser and S. B. Hammond (eds.), *Social Structure and Personality in a City*.
[24] O. A. Oeser and F. E. Emery (eds.), *Social Structure in a Rural Community*.
[25] R. Taft, "Some Sub-Cultural Variables in Family Structure in Australia", *Australian Journal of Psychology*, vol. 9, no. 1, June 1957, pp. 69-90.
[26] Oeser and Hammond, *op. cit.*, p. 172.

TABLE 2

Sub-Cultural Variables and Family Behaviour

Pattern	High	Low
Syncratic Co-operative	Catholic, Middle class, Melbourne.	Protestant, Working class, Perth.
Husband Dominant	Boys, Perth.	Girls, Melbourne.
Wife Dominant	Protestant, Boys, Working class, Perth.	Catholic, Girls, Middle class, Melbourne.
Husband Autonomy	Boys	Girls
Wife Autonomy	Protestant, Girls, Working class, Melbourne.	Catholic, Boys, Middle class, Perth.

The most extensive application of the "Day-at-Home" technique was carried out in 1957-8 by Adler. Adler's results are of special interest because of the large size of his sample, and also because he had earlier used the technique in America, so that direct comparisons were possible. In addition, his sample included a large number of migrant families, and his results are therefore of particular interest as an exploration of the problem of assimilation of immigrants which has been one of the major themes of Australian social life since the second world war. Adler's report, which also describes the development of the "Day-at-Home" method, appears below (ch. 9), but comments on his main findings may usefully be given here.

Adler investigated a total of 1,313 primary school children in 25 different schools in five capital cities. Of these 537 were children of migrant families: 137 British, 52 Dutch, and 348 of other nationalities.

Adler was able to distinguish a series of interaction patterns similar to those already described. He found that by far the most frequent pattern was that where the mother both decided and carried out activities. Taken over all activities, mothers were responsible for 50% of all decisions and 40% of all actions, compared with only 2% of decisions and 15% of actions taken by fathers. What Adler calls the "MeMo interaction pattern"—*i.e.* where the mother both decides and carries out activities—predominated. Joint activities were at a discount compared with autonomous activities by either parent.

The Australian family thus appears as even more "mother-dominated" than the American family, where the father has been described as a back-seat driver. The application of the "Day-at-Home" technique to American families brings this out very strikingly. Where Australian mothers carried out 50% of decisions and 40% of actions, the corresponding figures for American mothers were 30% in each case. Moreover, co-operative action between parents seems to be much commoner in the American family. 90% of American fathers participated in virtually all the regions of family activity, while no Australian fathers were found to participate in every one of the regions of activity identified by Adler. The disparity was not due, moreover, to some kind of structural difference between families in the two countries which meant that some activity regions were not available to Australian fathers.

Adler's conclusion is that the apparent predominance of the mother's role in the Australian family, for which he suggests the name *matriduxy,* may be due to an absence of full father-participation in family activities. In the American family there is more joint participation, making the mother-leadership role appear to be less important. Adler's results give more weight to the mother's role than the Melbourne study described above, where the "autonomic" pattern of both parents acting separately is the most important one, with "wife dominance" close behind.

The analysis of responses obtained from the migrant children in the sample shows two significant differences from the Australian pattern among recent migrants. On the one hand, the pattern of mother-dominance was markedly less evident, and on the other, there was markedly more joint decision/action by both parents. However, the differences between "indigenous" and migrant families were rapidly reduced with increased length of residence in Australia, the results agreeing closely with those of studies made by Taft in Perth. Like Taft, Adler regards this as evidence of successful assimilation, though he does not seem to consider the possibility that the migrant children themselves may have adjusted their answers to what they perceive as the accepted patterns of response among their schoolmates.

These studies all rely heavily on the testimony of children, and for this they have been criticized. However, in all cases the researchers were primarily interested in the reactions of children to their family life, and in a study of these reactions it is particularly important to know how family behaviour is seen and interpreted by children. Perhaps the accounts have not been entirely "objective", but reports of parents and trained observers are not always so either. One study which escapes the criticism mentioned above was undertaken by Fallding and involved a detailed examination of 38 families. "The overall picture", Fallding writes,[27] "is one of patriarchy being challenged by a pattern of partnership." In 21 of the 38 families patriarchy was observed, and in 14 of these it could be said to be "rightful" in so far as it occurred with the consent of all concerned and had been adopted on principle. In these 14 families there were clear and well-accepted divisions of responsibility; the mother was the homemaker and the father fought the battles with the outside world on behalf of his family. The other main type of family discovered by Fallding was a partnership in which husband or wife assumed the right of direction in any matter in which he or she had the greater competence.

FAMILY SOCIALIZATION OF CHILDREN

Despite encroachments on family functions made by schools, government agencies, and other institutions, a number of studies have suggested that the family still retains important responsibilities for ensuring the development of its young members. Middleton, for example, writes that in Australia the family is supported and reinforced by other institutions,[28] and Campbell's Karribee study[29] illustrates this clearly. The adults in this small community (279 in number) were asked to list the achievements which young people

[27] H. J. Fallding, *op. cit.*

[28] M. R. Middleton, "Trends in Family Organization in Australia", in Oeser and Hammond, *op. cit.,* p. 113.

[29] W. J. Campbell, *Growing Up in Karribee.*

ought to have before being regarded as adult citizens. They were also asked which agencies or institutions should be responsible for ensuring that these achievements are gained. In all of the aspects of development listed, except *personal adjustment* and *knowledge and skills,* the home was assigned prime responsibility, and even in the two exceptions it was a close second to the church and school respectively. It was judged to be particularly important for the development of *good health and efficient use of the body, morality, appropriate attitudes concerned with marriage and family life,* and *social responsibility.*

There is, moreover, evidence to suggest that Australian mothers, in particular, accept these responsibilities. Thus, when children in Melbourne[30] were asked who rewarded or punished them for specific acts, their replies could be classified as follows:

						Boys %	Girls %
Sources of Praise							
Parents	..	..	..	..	..	19	20
Father	..	..	..	..	..	22	8
Mother	..	..	..	..	..	54	65
Other	..	..	..	..	..	5	7
Sources of Punishment							
Parents	..	..	..	..	..	27	38
Father	..	..	..	..	..	22	11
Mother	..	..	..	..	..	49	48
Other	..	..	..	..	..	2	3

Both boys and girls see the mother as the most important source of pressure. Fathers exert more pressure on boys than on girls, and mothers slightly more on girls than on boys. Children see their parents as a joint authority more frequently in the punishment situation than in the reward situation.

The rural study by Oeser and Emery endorsed the importance of the mother as the rewarding agent, but suggested that the father punished sons more than the mother did.[31] Connell's study of Sydney adolescents found they had many more conflicts with their mothers than with their fathers.[32]

In both the Melbourne[33] and Karribee[34] studies, children and parents provided independent evidence of behaviour expected at various ages. In general:

(i) very young children encounter parental pressures concerned with obedience, morality, good manners, cleanliness, independence and happiness;

(ii) during the pre-adolescent years, parents show slightly more concern with the development of morality and independence and slightly less with obedience;

(iii) during adolescence, many of the former influences continue, but new ones concerned with the acquisition of knowledge and personal pride spring into prominence.

[30] Oeser and Hammond, *op. cit.*
[31] Oeser and Emery, *op. cit.*
[32] W. F. Connell, *op. cit.*
[33] Oeser and Hammond, *op. cit.*
[34] W. J. Campbell, *op. cit.*

These general findings obscure some important sex differences. Herbst[35] has shown that boys and girls participate in different daily experiences, and a careful study by Scott[36] of Brisbane families with pre-school children reveals that differentiation of training appears very early in most cases. The percentages of mothers who reported varying attitudes and behaviours with respect to the training of boys and girls were:

Rejects differentiation of boys and girls in principle and practice: 10.
Rejects in principle but reveals in practice: 22.
Believes in differentiation: 51.
Not involved: 17.

Support for the prevalence of this sex-differentiation is forthcoming from studies by Campbell and by Middleton in which it is shown that, almost invariably, girls are expected to achieve maturity levels slightly ahead of boys,[37] and that parents are concerned more with conformity of character and super-ego characteristics in girls, whereas in boys they expect conformity of behaviour in specific situations.[38]

Although a variety of methods have been used to gather information, all the studies of family training practices agree that Australian children grow up under rather strict supervision. Thus Scott in her Brisbane study[39] reports that most parents were either strict or middle of the road (74%) and the remainder were inconsistent rather than lenient; physical punishment was prevalent (92%) and in most cases (64%) clear limits were set on behaviour; parents allowed little expression of aggression towards adults or set clear limits (93%). Similarly, Campbell[40] summarizes his findings from a "discipline" study in the following terms:

1. Parents are more often authoritarian than democratic or permissive, though they treat their pre-school youngsters more permissively than their older children and adolescents.

2. Parents are generally reluctant to let go the reins of control, and tend to treat their adolescents in much the same way as they do their younger pre-adolescents.

Oeser found also that girls receive "ethical" praise and punishment more than boys; material rewards and deprivations are used more with boys.[41]

Sooner or later, of course, the rather strict and formal training period does come to an end. Connell shows in his report of interviews with a sample of mothers and daughters in a middle-class residential area in Sydney[42] that in matters of personal appearance, clothing and general grooming, near-adult status is granted to the daughter at about the age of 16, with full independence at about 18. In personal behaviour at home and away from home, near-adult status is also granted at about 18. Thereafter she is responsible

[35] P. G. Herbst, in Oeser and Hammond, *op. cit.*
[36] P. M. Scott, "Personality Development in Children of Working Mothers", unpublished Ph.D. thesis, University of Queensland, 1962.
[37] W. J. Campbell, *Growing Up in Karribee.*
[38] M. R. Middleton, *op. cit.*
[39] P. M. Scott, *op. cit.*
[40] W. J. Campbell, *op. cit.*
[41] Oeser and Hammond, *op. cit.*
[42] W. F. Connell, *op. cit.*

for keeping herself, possessions, bedroom, and so forth in the manner of her choice. Household jobs, which had been done more regularly and under direction at an earlier age, became voluntary and irregular during later adolescence. The 17- and 18-year-olds are given considerable freedom in the choice of leisure activities, reading matter and friends, although mothers still insist on knowing their away-from-home movements. "Disciplining" ceases after the age of 18.

FAMILY AND DEVELOPMENT

For a number of reasons, the family can be expected to have an important influence upon the development of the children: it is the first social group entered; relationships are particularly intense and intimate; the family accepts prime responsibility for the majority of the developmental tasks; time spent within the family is greater than that spent in any other group until late adolescence.

In the metropolitan study directed by Oeser,[43] children's responses to the Thematic Apperception Test were used to provide measures of adjustment, and these were then related to family behaviour and to the children's own participation in family life. Well adjusted youngsters tended to come from homes which encouraged high levels of participation and which were classified as syncratic or autonomic. Poorly adjusted youngsters, on the other hand, reported low levels of home participation and came from autocratic or anarchic types of family. Of the 82 children in Oeser's sample, nine had parents who were divorced and six of these were poorly adjusted.

Campbell's study in Karribee[44] was concerned less with structural aspects than with quality of family life. He used ratings based on: richness of experience, warmth and affection of family relations, appropriate and realistic expectations and aspirations, democratic discipline, willingness to foster independence, and child-centredness of behaviour goals. Adjustment was rated on a 5-point scale after an examination of individual profiles showing scores on a variety of adjustment measures. The relationship between the two variables was clear, as shown in the table.

TABLE 3

Distribution of Adjustment Ratings According to Home Environments
(significant beyond 1% level)

	Adjustment Ratings		
Home Ratings	High	Medium	Low
Superior and Above Average	23	6	0
Average	21	37	12
Below Average and Inferior	7	13	25

The effect that "working mothers" have upon the personalities of their children has been a lively and controversial issue for many years, but it was not until Scott completed a careful empirical study that any worthwhile Aus-

[43] Oeser and Hammond, *op. cit.*
[44] *Op. cit.*

tralian data were available.[45] As many writers have stressed, employment status is only one of a number of factors which distinguish "working" from "non-working" mothers, and Scott has shown the prime importance of:

(a) attitude to present pattern of living (in particular where mothers value self rather than family goals);

(b) attitude to the traditional role ascribed to women;

(c) child-rearing practices (some of which, of course, might stem from the employment status of the mother);

(d) conflicts associated with the particular role being taken by the mother.

"These aspects of personality", writes Scott, "outweigh working status in their effect on a number of areas of children's behaviour." Nevertheless, this study also shows that when mothers work for 30 hours per week or more this, on its own, is sufficient to produce a number of dependency symptoms in the children: more displaced aggression; more frequent thumb-sucking, nail-biting and nose-picking; greater apathy; more frequent fantasies associated with a frustrated need to belong and be cared for; greater tendency to avoid competition; and more frequent self-oriented rather than task- or goal-oriented behaviour.

Scott is careful to point out that it is impossible, in our present state of knowledge, to determine the precise long-term significance of these effects. We know from child development research that children are remarkably resilient. Nevertheless, if deprivation is severe, prolonged and present during especially critical periods of personality formation the damage could persist through adult life.

Support for Scott's conclusion about the significance of mothers' attitudes and values, as distinct from employment status, is forthcoming in the Canberra study by Pentony. In this, the home environments of 109 four-year-olds attending pre-school play centres were assessed with respect to "Democracy" and "Dependence Encouraging", as these are defined in the Fels Parent Rating Scales. Social behaviour was rated on the Fels Nursery School Behaviour Scales by the teachers in charge of the centres. The principal findings suggested the importance of home environment in various aspects of social behaviour — co-operation, dominance, and constructiveness — but Pentony cautiously concludes that the relationship is very complex, since children from "democratic homes" may benefit in the following respects:

(i) Their parents tend to encourage freer group association not only by sending them to play centres, but also by inviting other children to the home and providing facilities for play in the home.

(ii) Their parents tend to be more actively interested in play centres and to participate more fully and more willingly in their functioning. This may result in the child feeling more at ease in the play centre.

(iii) Their parents as a group tend to have more formal education, to be of higher socio-economic status and presumably to be more intelligent. Hereditary factors would seem to favour these children.

---

[45] *Op. cit.*

(iv) Finally, there is the direct effect on the child's personality of a "democratic" home environment. . . . The present study does not allow us to discriminate its effects from those noted above.[46]

So far we have mentioned studies involving pre-school children (Scott, Pentony) and school-age children and adolescents (Oeser, Campbell); we propose now to refer to a study of the effects of family life upon the adjustment of adolescent boys in employment.

In this, Palmer[47] reports that more than 50% of the boys judged social adjustments as being the most difficult for them, and they mentioned in particular: feeling shy and ill at ease with other workers; being left alone during the lunch break; not being able to make friends, and being unsure of how the bosses and other workers expected them to behave. From our point of view, the most interesting part of the study concerns the relationship established between these adjustment problems and certain features of the boys' family relations. If the parents enjoyed harmonious relationships, the son tended to enjoy his work experiences and to get along well with his boss and colleagues. On the other hand, if the parents indulged in continuous warfare with one another the son tended to find work life unsatisfying. In addition, the relationship between father and son seemed to be particularly closely related to job adjustment. Detailed analyses of selected cases suggested that boys from inadequate family backgrounds may have favourable attitudes to work, and adjust in a satisfactory way if the working conditions are relatively nonstressful, the other workers friendly and so on. The boys from adequate family backgrounds are more likely to meet job stresses in a positive way, by, for example, turning the initially hostile attitudes of other workers into friendly ones.

A number of the studies of socialization referred to above have suggested that girls experience somewhat different pressures from those that boys do, and a thorough study by Harwood[40] has demonstrated how this is reflected in certain adolescent behaviour and values. A sample of 1,493 boys and girls, aged 14 to 19 years, completed a Social Maturity Scale (based upon the Vineland Social Maturity Scale, but standardized on a Queensland population), and an adaptation of the Allport-Vernon Test of Values.

Boys' scores exceeded those of girls in tasks which are strictly preparatory for full adult civic responsibility, such as use of money and forethought for future needs; freedom of movement and responsibility for arrangements; involvement in national and world affairs; and in making appointments for attendance at interviews personally. The items on which the girls surpassed the boys were almost all concerned with domestic or social tasks.

The study of values supported the above findings and suggested that the adolescent boy was being successfully conditioned to prefer personal-social, economic, theoretical and political values, whereas the adolescent girl was being influenced by the cultural expectation that she will pursue social, religious and aesthetic interests.

[46] P. Pentony, "Home Environment and Nursery School Behaviour", *Australian Journal of Psychology*, vol. 8, no. 1, 1956.

[47] V. Palmer, "The Transition from School to Work", unpublished Ph.D. thesis, University of Melbourne, 1959.

[48] E. Harwood, "Social Development in Adolescence", unpublished Ph.D. thesis, University of Queensland, 1956.

146

Although most of the studies referred to in this section have related specific family behaviour to development—participation, working status, democratic control and the like—the researchers cautiously suggest that these specific matters are best regarded as indicators of a more intangible family atmosphere which is particularly influential. This atmosphere is subtle and all-pervasive in scope, but as yet our techniques seem incapable of measuring it directly.

SUMMARY AND COMMENTS

In the preceding sections we have looked at some of the findings from studies that have been undertaken on white Australian family life. Although we have been able to cite several references, the reader, like the authors, will be painfully aware that many important aspects have not been studied at all, and that the data that do exist are far from conclusive. It is only in recent years that the white Australian family has been studied. Moreover, most of the studies have been carried out by social psychologists, rather than by sociologists, and, although the two disciplines are particularly close, this is reflected in the type of data reported.

It will be clear to the reader, too, that the trends found in Australian family life are shared by families in most other countries with Western type cultures. With improvements in transport and communications generally, members of extended families are now less likely to be found living close together and so the nuclear unit becomes of paramount importance. New occupational opportunities, too, have led to greater mobility, especially on the part of younger family members. In addition, in a non-static society like Australia, changes in social class status lead to a weakening, and often a deliberate cutting, of extended family ties. This emerges clearly in the study carried out by Tugby and Crook. Further contributing factors have been the growth of social services, which have to some extent freed the younger generation from the responsibility of caring for the older; and the general shift from primary to secondary industries.

The trend towards small nuclear units is more than an interesting sociological phenomenon. It has important implications for the development of the children. To an outside observer the large extended family gives the impression of authority, power and rightness while the small nuclear family, living in its own detached style, gives an impression of puniness and uncertainty. This view is, however, superficial. Close study reveals that the small family still exerts intense and compelling pressures. Interaction is restricted to only a small number of persons, and, in this interaction, the children are in subordinate but central positions. Obviously, in such cases, much depends upon the quality of the relationships existing between the parents and between parents and children.

The evidence suggests that the majority of families remain intact during the child-rearing years. In 1960 divorces were at the rate of 8.9%, and in a substantial proportion of these no children were involved. This, on its own, does not furnish us with a good measure of the quality of family relationships, but from other studies we know that, in the great majority of cases, the emotional cohesiveness of the families is rated as medium or high, and that only in about 20% of cases do the children and adolescents express, or give other evidence of, concern with the nature of family relationships. Again, however, emotional cohesiveness can be beneficial or deleterious depending upon the stage of development achieved by the children. Sooner or later the young member of the family must be able to cast aside the mantle of the family. There is some evidence to show that many Australian families are failing to make continuous adjustment. They provide a good environment for the younger children but do not or are not able to modify this to meet the different demands and needs of their adolescent children.

Another area in which there is a need for family adjustments is that of paternal responsibilities. For a variety of reasons, Australian mothers have taken, or had thrust upon them, most of the responsibilities for socializing the children, and, at least in this sense, the role of the father is becoming vestigial. This may be only superficial. It is probable that fathers still provide strong identification figures for their children, and, in this way, exert considerable influence upon the development of personalities. Perhaps for the sake of his own personality needs if not for those of his children, the Australian father might need to take a more active part in family life. This is not to advocate a return to roles which served an earlier society—law-giver, arbiter and disciplinarian—but rather to suggest that all might gain if fathers cultivated new roles of nurturer, companion and model.

The need to make adjustments of this kind is greater in Australia than in America where a number of studies have shown that encroachments of the school, in particular, have stripped the family of many of its responsibilities. In Australia, schools, churches, clubs and the community at large are still seen as supporters of the home. With the withdrawal of the father from many areas of family living, a heavy burden is imposed upon the mother, and, despite the introduction of numerous labour-saving units, she is probably now working harder and under greater strain than her own mother and grandmother did. The task of mothers is still burdened by the tendency to advocate and practise differential treatment of boys and girls. In his study Herbst showed that while both sexes enter family activities through the social region, they then take symmetrically opposed paths. In addition, different levels of participation, different freedom of movement, and different specific behaviour are expected. The participation of fathers in the decisions and training associated with this differential socializing could ease the mother's load.

The importance of the family for the healthy development of the children is obvious from the several studies reported. In general, those children who are developing satisfactorily come from families characterized by warmth and affection in family relations, encouragement to excel, realistic expectations and aspirations, and a rich background of cultural experiences. On the other hand, children whose development is inadequate often come from families in which these characteristics are absent. It is encouraging to find on the best evidence available, and somewhat contrary to popular opinion, that most of the young generation do develop adequately.

DAN L. ADLER

9   Matriduxy in the Australian Family[*]

In the comparative study of cultures it has often proved convenient to describe national groups as being matriarchal or patriarchal in character. The authority role of the dominant family figure is derived, in such instances, from appropriate inheritance lines and is often maintained by a supportive legal structure and formal social organization. In cultures where the line of control is not clearly drawn or supported, it is common, nevertheless, to maintain a stereotype which attributes familial control to either the husband or wife. The Australian culture is of this type, and subscribes to the stereotype of male pre-eminence.

Although male authority does not appear to be an insistent theme in Australian *mores,* it is clearly expressed in Australian literature and folkways. It is particularly clear when Australians compare themselves with other national groups. Americans are frequently the foil in such comparisons, since they are thought to be female-dominated, with the reins of decision and control in the hands of the wife as the real head of the household. In contrast, Australian men and women believe the husband to be the real head of household in their culture.

Recent studies of family life in Australia and the United States suggest a discrepancy between the stereotype and the conditions which actually exist. The material reported herein is concerned with the latter. Since the study utilizes a particular technique of investigation—the *Day at Home* questionnaire—we first outline its development and report some data obtained by earlier investigators.

The development of the "Day at Home" technique

In 1952 P. G. Herbst[1] reported the use of a "Day at Home" questionnaire designed to explore the interaction of family members in their everyday pursuits. Applied to the nuclear family (*i.e.* a family with both parents and one

---

[*] The study reported here was done while the author was a Fulbright Research scholar attached to the Canberra University College (now the School of General Studies, Australian National University), in 1957-8.

[1] P. G. Herbst, "The Measurement of Family Relationships", *Human Relations,* vol. 5, no. 1, 1952.

or more school-age children living at home), the instrument sought answers to questions in the following format:

1. Who *decides* what is to be done? (*e.g.* Who decides when the windows are to be washed? Who decides how much pocket money the children will get?)

2. Who *does* what is to be done? (*e.g.* Who washes the windows? Who gives the children pocket money?)

3. Do mother and father *disagree* about what's to be done? (*e.g.* Do they agree about washing the windows? Giving pocket money?)

This trio of questions was asked for each of 33 different items of family behaviour addressed to a sample of 86 children, 10-12 years old, in the Kew and Hawthorn State Schools in Melbourne. The children's responses indicated for each item whether the mother alone, father alone, or both mother and father were responsible for the decision or action. In addition, the children's responses indicated whether the parents "often", "sometimes", or "never" disagreed about the activity in question.

The analyses of these responses produced considerably more information than the mere cataloguing of parental interactions in diverse aspects of a family life. It demonstrated the existence of clear groupings of activities within which a definite pattern of parental interaction prevailed. Thus in the category of "child care and control", the wife typically not only decided what was to be done but was also the one who did it. Both husband and wife decided "social activities"—and carried them out; the same was true of "economic activities". "Household duties" had to be subdivided into: "husband's" (where he both decided upon and did things, like mowing the lawn), "wife's" (which she decided upon and dispatched autonomously—ironing, dusting) and "common" (jointly performed, like washing up).

In 1957 Taft[2], sampling Perth children, and in 1958 Bollman[3], sampling Brisbane children, found evidence of small sub-cultural variations in item-responses, but in general their studies substantiated the main trends established by Herbst.

The first application of the *Day at Home* technique outside of Australia was reported by Cooper[4] and Adler and Cooper[5] in the United States. Using 100 children in each of two widely separated California communities, they administered an expanded questionnaire adapted to family activities in the suburban American home. In both samples, only five activity categories could be distinguished; these paralleled the Australian family regions except that the category of Husband's Household Duties did not emerge. The predominant parental interaction pattern was a co-operative one in which both father and mother decided upon and did the activities. This pattern was typical of all but the Wife's Household Duties category.

[2] Ronald Taft, "Some Sub-Cultural Variations in Family Studies in Australia", *Australian Journal of Psychology*, vol. 9, no. 2, 1957.
[3] Lorna Bollman, "Australian Urban Family Structure: A Brisbane Sample", unpublished B.A. thesis, University of Queensland, 1958.
[4] A. M. Cooper, "Measurement of Family Relationships", unpublished M.A. thesis, Claremont Graduate School, Pomona, California, 1955.
[5] D. L. Adler and A. M. Cooper, "Family Structure, Interaction and Tension", paper read at Western Psychological Association, Berkeley, California, March 1956.

The *Day at Home* questionnaire was also translated into Spanish and, with the addition of items appropriate to Mexican family activities, was administered by Cooper[6] to children in Guadalajara, Mexico. Again, only five activity categories could be distinguished, of which one had no counterpart in Australian or American samples; this was a category of Economic Activities autonomously controlled by husbands. Another Economic Activity category appeared, jointly controlled by husband and wife. The categories of Husband's Household Duties and Common Household Duties were not found in this population.

In 1957, when a comparison of Australian and migrant family life was undertaken by the author, the questionnaire was revised to make it a more sensitive instrument and to avoid certain response ambiguities. The questionnaire was expanded to 45 items and the response alternatives to each item became the following:

1. *Mother usually* (decides or does an activity).
2. *Father usually* (decides or does an activity).
3. *Sometimes mother and sometimes father* (decides or does an activity).
4. *Mother and father together* (decide or do an activity).
5. *Someone else* (decides or does an activity). Children were taught how to identify the other person, *viz.* as a sibling, themselves, or someone else in the home.

It should be noted that there are now 25 possible combinations of responses (5 x 5) to the question "who decides" and "who does", and that it is possible to distinguish more easily between divided parental functions (alternative 3) and co-operative parental functions (alternative 4).

Parental interaction in Australian families

The selection of an appropriate sample for the study was somewhat limited by the need to control all variables that might distort the legitimate comparison of Australian and migrant families. It was deemed essential to pick migrant and Australian child-respondents from the same geographic areas of Australia, and preferably from the same community, same socio-economic background and of the same general level of intelligence. It soon became clear that the location of migrant families—restricted as they were to industrialized city-centres and fringe suburban zones where low rents prevailed—would determine the source of the sample population.

With the help of state Directors of Education, sixth and seventh grade school classes were selected which met the requirements (a) that they contain 20% or more migrant children, and (b) that their modal age be 12 years. The *Day at Home* questionnaire was administered by the author to 1,525 children in 25 different schools (see Table 1).

No significant geographic differences appeared so that it was possible to treat the 776 Australian families as a single sample.

---

[6] A. M. Cooper, "Tension, Structure and Interaction in Mexican and American Families", paper read at Western Psychological Association, Monterey, California, April 1957.

TABLE 1

Geographic Distribution of Sample

City	Total respondents	Usable respondents*	
		Australian	Migrant
Melbourne	480	158	265
Sydney	440	218	106
Brisbane	225	153	69
Perth	200	115	54
Hobart	180	132	43
	1525	776	537 *Total* 1313

* Cases which did not meet the nuclear family criteria set by Herbst were discarded.

The basic data with which we are concerned are the combinations of responses to the questions "who decides" and "who does". They take the following form for each questionnaire item:

Me					Fe					Ee					Be					Oe				
Mo	Fo	Eo	Bo	Oo	Mo	Fo	Eo	Bo	Oo	Mo	Fo	Eo	Bo	Oo	Mo	Fo	Eo	Bo	Oo	Mo	Fo	Eo	Bo	Oo
41	5	5	14	5	1	1	0	0	0	3	2	5	0	0	4	2	3	8	1	.4	.6	1	0	0

Key: M—Mother usually; F—Father usually; E—Either (*i.e.* sometimes Mother, sometimes Father); B—Both (*i.e.* Mother and Father together); O—Other person (*e.g.* respondents themselves); e—decides; o—does. Numbers refer to % of total responses. Significant percentages are underlined (see text).

Since the chance distribution for any one of the 25 combinations is 4%, a primary parental interaction pattern is said to exist when 12% (*i.e.* 3 x 4%) or more of the total responses to an item fall into any single box. In the example given above, the per cent. distribution of the 776 responses shows two primary patterns, *viz.* Me Mo (Mother decides and does this activity) according to 41% of the respondents, and Me Bo (Mother decides upon and both parents do the activity) according to 14% of the respondents.

The response distribution of each of the 45 items was determined in the same fashion. Each item was then allocated to a "region" on the basis of similar content and primary interaction patterns. Eight such regions (as against Herbst's six) were identified and appear in Table 2 with their characteristic interaction patterns.

TABLE 2

Activity Regions and Their Primary Interaction Patterns

	No. of Items	Patterns and % occurrence
Household Duties (Father)	2	FeFo 50%
Household Duties (Mother)	7	MeMo 66%
Household Duties (Mixed)	4	FeFo 28%; MeMo 18%; MeFo 15%
Household Duties (Mother and Children)	6	MeMo 38%; MeOo 26%
Child Care and Control (Mother) ..	7	MeMo 40%; MeOo 12%
Child Care and Control (Mixed).. ..	6	MeMo 21%; EeEo 21%
Expenditures	5	MeMo 22%; EeEo 15%; BeBo 14%
Social-Recreational	8	BeBo 17%; EeEo 14%; MeMo 11%

The frequency of occurrence of the Me Mo interaction pattern, *i.e.* where the mother decides and carries out activities, is strikingly high. While it might be reasoned that the larger proportions of regions defined as Household Duties, or Child Care and Control, lead to this preponderance of mothers' involvement, there are lines of evidence which tend to discount such an explanation. It should be noted (Table 2) that all but one of the regions (Household Duties—Father) have a significant component of Me Mo responses. Even the regions *not* directly associated with household and child care facets of family life show an appreciable pattern of mother autonomy.

The mother's role as leader in the family is further corroborated in the analysis of "regions" in terms of individual responses. Table 3 shows how mothers' autonomous decisions and actions compare with fathers' in each "region".

TABLE 3

Mothers' and Fathers' Involvement

(as % of total responses for each region)

	Me	Fe	Mo	Fo
Household Duties—Mother	85%	5%	70%	11%
Household Duties—Mother and Child	69	8	45	2
Child Care and Control—Mother	58	9	56	9
Household Duties—Mixed	40	41	27	49
Expenditures	34	19	32	16
Child Care and Control—Mixed	33	21	35	20
Social-Recreational	29	13	15	4
Household Duties—Father	16	62	7	62
All regions combined	50%	2%	40%	15%

The action role of the mother is clearly only a little less developed than her decision role: and both are pervasive. In Australia, since family leadership by the mother is clearly not a function of inheritance, legal structure or formal social organization, it would be misleading to refer to it as matriarchal. One might, instead, coin the term *matriduxy* to denote her powerful leadership functions.

Although mother-leadership in some aspect of family activity consistently appears in almost every culture, the strong matriduxy pattern is unusual. Comparing the situation in Australia with some other western cultures will help to establish the degree of difference. Table 4 affords such a comparison, using the Adler-Cooper and Cooper studies of American and Mexican populations.

It is immediately apparent that matriduxy, in so far as it is reflected in this type of comparison, does not occur in the Mexican family, and that it is most marked in the Australian family. It would also appear that matriduxy characterizes the American pattern but to a lesser degree than is the case in Australia. To reach this conclusion, however, one must compare the non-autonomous interactions as well. Here the differences between Australian and American culture patterns are placed into sharp focus by the preponderance

153

of *co-operative* interactions in the American group and their negligible occurrence among the Australians.

Further, if we compare (in our samples) the *participation* of American and Australian fathers in their respective family regions we find that 90% of the Americans, but none of the Australians, take part in all or all but one of these regions. To emphasize the fact that this differential is not a function of the difference in regions "available" to each, we note that half of the Australian fathers participated in not more than three of the eight available regions; 70% participated in not more than four of them.

TABLE 4

Mothers', Fathers', Autonomous Involvement—Australia, U.S., Mexico

(as % of all involvements)

	Australian	American	Mexican
Mother decides	50%	30%	27%
Father decides	2	6	27
Mother does	40	30	30
Father does	15	5	20

Thus, in the Australian family, the mother plays a strong leadership role in the absence of full father participation. In the American family, where co-operative patterns predominate, the mother-leadership role is less strong, probably because full participation of the father has made him more nearly a co-equal. It would appear then, that despite the impression of "mother directedness" in the American culture, the term matriduxy is inapplicable to it and should be reserved for the case exemplified in the Australian culture.

One shortcoming in the analysis of cultural differences by comparing interaction patterns is the failure to establish the differential dynamics involved. A hint of what such knowledge would add is afforded by an examination of a selected sub-group occurring in our Australian population. It will be recalled, first, that the *Day at Home* questionnaire required respondents to report parental disagreement for each activity item. The regions, "Expenditures", "Social-Recreational", and "Child Care and Control—Mixed" had disagreement levels of 35%, 37% and 36%, respectively; other regions showed less discord (from 20-24%).[7]

A large group of working mothers in our Australian population (29%) allowed us to test the hypotheses that disagreement would be greater where both parents worked, and that this might be due to an intensified division of parental function in such cases. Some corroboration was found for both hypotheses. Significant increases in disagreement responses, ranging from 1-6%,

[7] The highest disagreement occurs in the only two regions (Table 2) that have a distinctive BeBo pattern. Further, high disagreement appears to be mainly correlated with an EeEo pattern. The inference is that the division of parental function, where each parent's obligations are less clearly defined (or more haphazard), is apt to lead to parental disagreement. As a corollary, there is less likelihood of parents' acting at cross-purposes, and less basis for disagreement where each parent acts autonomously (MeMo or FeFo). It is conceivable, of course, that the higher inter-personal contact inherent in BeBo interactions is itself the basis of heightened disagreement.

154

characterize each of the eight regions, the increase being greatest in "Expenditures", "Social-Recreational" and "Child Care and Control—Mixed". These three regions were then examined for an increase in EeEo responses. Two of them ("Expenditures" and "Social-Recreational") showed significant overall EeEo increases and an increase of EeEo responses *for every item*. The "Child Care and Control—Mixed" region showed an overall increase in EeEo responses which was not statistically significant, with increases in only four of the six items constituting the region.

One might interpret these changes as evidence that matriduxy is the acceptable way of family life in Australia, and that alterations in the mother's role accompanied by increasing father participation tend to be disruptive and tension producing.

In addition to the comparisons with Mexican and American groups, we may consider here the evidence available from the migrant sub-portion of the Australian study. In all, there were 537 migrant respondents from 41 different countries (Table 1), of whom 137 British respondents made up the largest single group. Since this sample of migrants is not representative of their national distribution, we will confine our comparisons to the British migrants and to the migrant group as a whole.

Although the regions represented in the migrant family structures do not differ from those characterizing Australian families, there *are* significant differences between the parental interactions of the migrants and the Australians. Almost without exception, recently arrived migrants (1-2 years in Australia) show less mother-directed family control. The autonomous Me-Mo pattern occurs significantly less often in seven of the eight family activity regions, and Me responses occur 10% less often than in the Australian population. At the same time, the overall occurrence of co-operative interactions (BeBo) is 10% greater among both British migrant and total migrant groups and in both the FeFo pattern is augmented. These differences taken together indicate the lack of a pervasive matriduxy in the families of recent arrivals to Australia.

Summary

Close attention to the family *mores* of a culture may easily enable one to identify the dominant family figure as either the husband or wife. In some cultures, however, there is a difference between the true dominant family member and the one projected as a stereotype or national image. It was our intent, in this study, to determine whether such a discrepancy existed in the Australian culture. The *Day at Home* technique was employed to determine the conditions existing in Australian families, migrant families in Australia, and among Americans and Mexicans in their own countries. From these data, it appears that not one, but two examples of mistaken identity are involved. First, by virtue of underestimating the co-operative function of the *American* father, he is erroneously perceived as almost completely subordinate to his wife. Then, by overstating the independence of the *Australian* father, he is erroneously perceived as superordinate to his wife. In fact, however, the wife's leadership role in Australia, compared with other western cultures, is so prominent that it requires identification as the special social phenomenon which we call matriduxy.

LINCOLN H. DAY

10 Family Size and Fertility

THE main group differences in the size of Australian families are that rural dwellers have more children than city dwellers; Catholics more than non-Catholics; the Dutch-, Greek- and Italian-born more than the Australian born; and the British- and Polish-born fewer. European and other demographers have long noted such fertility differences by generation, place of residence, religion and country of birth, but have rarely been able to isolate pure differences in childbearing in these groups from differences in proportions marrying or in age at marriage or in incidence of divorce or separation. This study, designed to avoid these limitations, concentrates on women of the greatest potential fertility to throw group contrasts into strongest relief.

We drew from the 1954 Census a random sample of 88,428, *i.e.* 20% of women 40 years of age and over, currently married and living with husbands of at least 15 years' standing.[1] Cross tabulations covered age, duration of marriage, residence, country of birth, and religion. (No occupational, schooling, or income data were collected in this census, making social class analysis impossible.)

I

We outline first the main findings, then in Part II discuss their possible origins. The most general differences related to age. The older the woman, the more likely was she to have borne a large number of children. In one generation median family size was halved; the proportion with five or more children fell by some 40 to 80% (Table 1).

This massive decline occurred within each religious and residential category,[2] and the main country of birth[3] categories. Just when this decline

[1] This eliminates the effect of any group differences in proportions marrying, or in widowhood or divorce—temporary separations, except among certain immigrant groups, are unlikely to have been very numerous or long. It confines analysis to women who have completed or virtually completed their child-bearing (3.2% of all births 1950-4 occurred to women over 40), and achieves a reasonable standardization for infecundity (physiological inability to bear children).

[2] Metropolitan in 1954 comprised 54% of the population; Other Urban (of which two-thirds lived in middle-sized towns of 3,000 to 40,000) 25%; and Rural 22%. Residence given as of the date of the census probably reduces the size of rural-urban differences since the dominant flow has been out of rural into urban areas.

[3] Only Australia and British Isles (including Republic of Ireland) give large enough groups in each cell (minimum of 100 women) to assure that findings are not due merely to random variation.

156

TABLE 1

Australian Wives over 40 (1954)*

A—Median Issue

Minimum Duration of Marriage	Age of Wife	Residence			Religion			Country of Birth					
		Metro.	Other Urban	Rural	Catholic	Non-Cath. Christian	Other	Australia	British Isles	Italy	Poland	Nether-lands	Greece
15–19	40–44	1·89	2·36	2·84	2·55	2·12	2·12	2·20	1·91	2·53	1·36	2·94	2·40
20–24	45–49	1·88	2·47	2·92	2·56	2·14	2·18	2·23	1·96	2·64	—	2·89	—
25–29	50–54	1·92	2·57	3·04	2·68	2·20	2·29	2·28	2·05	2·54	—	—	—
30–34	55–59	2·14	2·86	3·44	3·00	2·42	2·69	2·54	2·24	2·72	—	—	—
35–39	60–64	2·57	3·33	3·93	3·41	2·87	3·04	2·95	2·28	—	—	—	—
40–44	65–69	2·87	3·79	4·63	3·85	3·25	3·29	3·35	2·76	—	—	—	—
45–49	70–74	3·17	4·37	4·89	4·24	3·86	3·68	3·89	2·87	—	—	—	—
50–54	75–79	3·67	4·66	4·97	4·76	3·99	—	4·22	3·61	—	—	—	—
55+	80+	4·08	4·65	—	—	4·51	—	4·61	3·54	—	—	—	—

B—Percentage with Issue of 5 +

Minimum Duration of Marriage	Age of Wife	Residence			Religion			Country of Birth					
		Metro.	Other Urban	Rural	Catholic	Non-Cath. Christian	Other	Australia	British Isles	Italy	Poland	Nether-lands	Greece
15–19	40–44	12	20	29	25	16	19	18	13	24	11	30	17
20–24	45–49	14	23	33	26	18	21	20	15	22	—	37	—
25–29	50–54	16	28	36	29	21	25	23	20	27	—	—	—
30–34	55–59	19	32	41	35	25	29	27	22	28	—	—	—
35–39	60–64	26	39	49	42	32	35	34	24	—	—	—	—
40–44	65–69	31	47	58	47	39	42	41	29	—	—	—	—
45–49	70–74	39	54	62	53	48	47	49	31	—	—	—	—
50–54	75–79	45	59	63	63	50	—	53	45	—	—	—	—
55+	80+	51	57	—	—	56	—	58	42	—	—	—	—

* The wives recorded in the table were all married to the husbands they had at the time of enumeration at the age of 25 or less. *Issue* describes all children, living or dead (except stillbirths) born to the *existing marriage*.

started cannot be determined from the data at hand; but certainly it was well under way by the mid-1890s, when our women over 80 would have begun their childbearing. The earliest data suggest, in fact, that it was under way as early as the 1860s.[4]

The most prominent feature of this fertility change is the decline in frequency of the large family of five or more children and the rise in the proportion of families of two to three. The proportion of childless tended to fluctuate round 5%; the proportion bearing only one child, though undergoing a substantial secular increase also, fluctuated round a fairly low level. But the two dominant trends—*away* from the large family and *toward* the medium-sized one—continued uninterruptedly throughout.

At the same time the fertility differences apparent at the beginning of the period also continued in force. Rural wives continued to bear more children than did Other Urban wives who, in turn, continued to bear more than Non-Catholic wives, while the issue of wives in the "Other"[5] religious classification —probably reflecting the heterogeneity of this grouping—continued to fall somewhere in between. A similar consistency is found in the differentials by country of birth—at least as far as can be determined from data for the younger ages only: the issue of wives born in the Netherlands, Greece and Italy regularly exceeded that of wives born in Australia; while the issue of wives born in the British Isles and Poland regularly fell short of it. In each instance these differences showed both in family size medians and family size distributions.

Among the Australian-born (which happens to be the only group numerous enough to permit a firm assessment of relative magnitudes) there is more variation by residence than by religion. To be sure, Catholic fertility consistently exceeds Non-Catholic: within each residential category and at every age level, typical (*i.e.* median) family size is larger among Catholics than among Non-Catholics, and so also is the proportion with large families of five or more children. Yet this Catholic/Non-Catholic differential is not so great as that between the different residential classifications: the fertility of metropolitan *Non-Catholics* is consistently closer to that of metropolitan *Catholics* than is the fertility of either to that of their rural co-religionists. Differences in Catholic and Non-Catholic typical family size are of about the same magnitude within each of the three residential groupings: the median issue of Catholic wives exceeds that of Non-Catholic wives by approximately the same amount in Metropolitan areas as in Other Urban and Rural areas. Place of residence differences in typical family size are of about the same magnitude among Catholics as among Non-Catholics: the degree to which the size of the typical Rural or Other Urban family exceeds that of the typical Metropolitan family is approximately the same among Catholic wives as among Non-Catholic, though Catholic fertility is consistently higher in all residential categories. Third, at least for the one-generation period represented by the childbearing of women between ages 40-44 and 65-69, there occurred little change in the differentials by either religion or residence. Declines in median issue were about as extensive in one group as in the other.

---

[4] 1911 *Census*, Vol. I, p. 285.
[5] Catholic in 1954 comprised 21%; Non-Catholic (claiming adherence to some other religion or denomination) 69%; Other (no answer, atheist, agnostic) 10%.

In short, during this generation of extensive over-all change in fertility, the religious and residential differentials—so far as *typical* family size is concerned —neither grew nor contracted. Median issue among Rural wives was about as far in excess of that among Metropolitan and Other Urban wives at the end of the period as it was at the beginning; median issue among Catholic wives about as far in excess of that among Non-Catholic.

TABLE 2

Catholic and Non-Catholic Wives

A—Median Issue

Minimum Duration of Marriage	Age of Wife	Catholic			Non-Catholic		
		Metro	Other Urban	Rural	Metro	Other Urban	Rural
15–19	40–44	2·18	2·84	3·34	1·84	2·26	2·76
20–24	45–49	2·22	2·96	3·53	1·82	2·34	2·83
25–29	50–54	2·34	3·08	3·68	1·85	2·43	2·94
30–34	55–59	2·57	3·59	4·13	2·01	2·69	3·30
35–39	60–64	2·91	3·92	5·02	2·49	3·21	3·80
40–44	65–69	3·45	4·39	5·08	2·78	3·64	4·53
45–49	70–74	3·44	4·83	—	3·15	4·27	4·74
50–54	75–79	—	—	—	3·49	4·45	4·85
55+	80+	—	—	—	3·81	—	—

B—Percentage with Issue of 5 +

Minimum Duration of Marriage	Age of Wife	Catholic			Non-Catholic		
15–19	40–44	17	30	37	10	18	27
20–24	45–49	21	32	43	12	20	30
25–29	50–54	22	36	45	14	25	34
30–34	55–59	26	43	52	17	29	39
35–39	60–64	33	49	61	24	36	47
40–44	65–69	40	55	62	30	45	57
45–49	70–74	43	60	—	38	53	60
50–54	75–79	—	—	—	42	56	61
55+	80+	—	—	—	47	—	—

Though the proportion with 5 + children in all groups fell, the depth of the fall varied inversely with the level of each group's fertility. Thus, the groups with the deepest falls already had the lowest fertility. Within each *residential* category the proportion with 5 + children declined further among Non-Catholics than among Catholics. Similarly, within *each* religious category, the fall was greater in Metropolitan than Other Urban, and in Other Urban than Rural.

In other words, though the relationships between the various *median* family sizes remained virtually unchanged during this period of extensive fertility decline, the relationships between the various *distributions* of family size changed considerably, and did so in such a way as to enlarge the differentials already in existence. By the time women aged 40-49 had completed their childbearing, those with large numbers of children were more than ever likely to be Catholics rather than Non-Catholics, Rural dwellers rather than Other Urban, Other Urban rather than Metropolitan. This was despite the fact that

159

over the period under consideration large families became steadily less common within each of these categories.

In the face of these changing relationships the differential by residence continued to exceed that by religion—at least among the Australian-born. In family size distributions, as in family size medians, the religious groupings remained closer to one another than did the residential. However, the Rural/Metropolitan differential was consistently greater among Non-Catholics than among Catholics, and the Catholic/Non-Catholic differential was consistently greater in the Metropolitan and Other Urban areas than in the Rural: both of which relationships support an American finding of greater Catholic/Non-Catholic differentials in urban than in rural areas,[6] presumably because rural dwellers exercise a lesser degree of conscious control over their fertility.

To get much out of the limited data on fertility differentials by country of birth it is necessary (particularly with the Polish-, Dutch-, and Greek-born) to depart from our rule of limiting analysis to cells of over 100. Where smaller denominators are used (sometimes as low as 40) the degree of confidence we can have in the findings must, of course, be correspondingly reduced.

As already noted, the fertility of wives born in the Netherlands, Greece, and Italy was consistently higher than that of wives born in Australia, while the fertility of wives born in the British Isles and Poland was consistently lower. As with the Australian-born, however, there seems to have been a considerable drop in family size within each of these country-of-birth groupings (with the possible exception of the Netherlands-born), most of this drop being accounted for—as also with the Australian-born—by declines in the proportion bearing 5 + children.

Standardizing for religion and residence—where the number of cases is large enough to permit it—adds considerably to an understanding of these relationships, particularly in the case of the Italian-born. Holding these two variables constant, their generally higher fertility is found to be closely related to their Catholicism; for if comparison is limited to Catholics, the fertility of these women, relative to that of the Australian-born, turns out to be about the same in Metropolitan areas, and very substantially lower in Rural areas. It seems likely, in fact, that among these Italian-born women there is no real Metropolitan/Rural differential at all in median issue and only a very small differential (relatively speaking) in the proportion bearing 5 + children—a relationship in direct contrast to that obtaining within the other country-of-birth categories. The British-born pattern—unlike the local-born—reveals a differential that is generally greater between religious groupings than between residential, or which is, at least, no greater in the one direction than in the other. Moreover, quite apart from its relationship to the residential differential, this religious differential is pretty considerably greater among the British-born than it is among the Australian-born. Among Non-Catholics (the only British-born group numerous enough to permit this additional comparison) the Metropolitan/Rural differential, though larger than among the Italian-born, is far smaller than among the Australian-born. In short, so far as fertility is concerned, Catholics are *further* removed from Non-

[6] T. L. Smith and H. Hitt, *The People of Louisiana,* pp. 153-7, cited in H. E. Brooks and F. I. Henry, "An Empirical Study of the Relationships of Catholic Practice and Occupational Mobility to Fertility", *Milbank Memorial Fund Quarterly,* vol. 36, 1958, p. 254.

Catholics, and Rural-dwellers *less far* removed from Metropolitan-dwellers, among the British-born than among the Australian-born.

*   *   *   *   *

We have here, then, a case of very considerable declines in fertility over a period of little more than a generation. Each residential, religious and— so far as can be determined from the relative paucity of data—country of birth grouping (save possibly the Netherlands) experienced these falls. The major source of these changes was a very substantial drop in the incidence of large families, a condition characterized by relative concentrations of family size in the middle range of 2-4, and particularly, 2-3, children.

Where the number of cases permits such analysis, there seems to have been no appreciable change in the relationships between any of the various residence/religion categories, so far as *typical* (*i.e.* median) family size is concerned. But with the *distribution* of family sizes there occurred a steady enlargement of the differentials already in existence: the general and consistent decline in the incidence of large families was participated in less by those groups with higher fertility at the beginning of the period under study than by those already characterized by lower fertility.

II

To find that Catholics or Rural-dwellers, women born before 1885 or Dutch immigrants, have higher fertility than Non-Catholics or Metropolitan-dwellers, women born after 1900 or Polish immigrants, narrows considerably the range of conjecture concerning the character of fertility differentials without telling us much about their actual causes. No such gross categorizations as those by age, religion, residence, birthplace will ever yield monolithic entities—with respect to fertility or any other manifestation of social behaviour. If some of these groups are generally more fertile than others, there is still no one-to-one relationship between any particular characteristic and any given level of fertility. The number of one's offspring results from the interaction of many factors: physiological attributes, aspirations, values, hopes, fears—in short, from the whole of the human condition. To seek explanations of human behaviour in terms of single causes fails to take account of the high level of causal complexity that does, in fact, underlie it. We now present a brief summary discussion of what, in the absence of direct evidence, appear to have been the major determinants of the fertility differentials described above.

It can be noted, first, that the decline in fertility, and the various group differentials accompanying it, *cannot* be attributed to any change either in the proportions ultimately marrying or in the age at which they marry: confining analysis not only to wives, but to wives married at or before 25, effectively rules out both of these possibilities. Nor is the explanation one of differences in fecundity (*i.e.* in the physiological capacity for reproduction): there is no reason whatever to suppose, for example, that Rural Catholics are, as a group, any more physiologically capable of reproduction than are Rural Non-Catholics, or that the latter are any more capable than their Other Urban or Metropolitan co-religionists.

Nor is there any reason, either, to suspect that the *general* level of fecundity has experienced a decline over time sufficient to explain that which has occurred in fertility. For this to be so, there would have to have been a steady increase in childlessness, and this has not occurred. The childless have not only remained a consistently small proportion, but have decreased at times and increased at others. Changes, like the improvement of prenatal care, that might have had some effect on reproductive capacities, would seem in fact to operate in a direction opposite to that followed by the pattern of fertility and, for that reason alone, to be incapable of accounting for it.

However, involuntary factors may have depressed fertility somewhat in the case of at least two of the foreign-born groups: the Italians and the Poles. Among the former this could have resulted from the fact that their migration to Australia frequently involved a separation of husband and wife—certainly for months, and quite possibly even for years. The fact that young adults constitute the largest proportion of migrants only heightens the depressant effect these separations might have on fertility.[7]

Such separations attending migration may also have depressed Polish-born fertility, though the timing of most of the Polish immigration and the group's unusually low median issue suggest that here the main involuntary depressant of fertility was the second world war, and conditions in the displaced persons' camps thereafter.

Even with these two groups, however, other—more voluntary—determinants appear to have predominated. Where involuntary factors have been at work, it has largely been to produce more, not fewer, children than were wanted, and therefore to postpone the general decline in fertility and reduce its rate.

Can any of the observed differentials be ascribed, therefore, to the fact that unwanted births are more common in some groups than in others? Certainly this seems likely—though here, as elsewhere, there is no direct evidence either of the existence of such differentials in Australia or of their extent. That family limitation of some sort is an almost universal practice in Australia is obvious from both the sales of contraceptives[8] and the extensive decline in fertility. This does not mean, however, that the various groups share equally in either their success with family planning or their concern over the possibility of experiencing an unwanted birth. Group differences in resort to the more effective means of controlling births, in the extent to which couples take "chances", and in the general degree of success with family planning have been found in several studies of American and European experience.[9] Similar differences undoubtedly exist here also—though in the absence of any studies of local practice it is impossible to say to what extent the various fertility differentials actually originate in this way.

But if involuntary determinants have been of some consequence in establishing fertility differentials, surely the most important have been those that work through essentially *voluntary* practices. There can be little doubt that

[7] This is discussed in more detail in the author's "Differential Fertility among Catholics in Australia", *Milbank Memorial Fund Quarterly*, April 1964.

[8] See below, pp. 166-7.

[9] See, e.g., C. F. Westoff *et al.*, "The Use, Effectiveness, and Acceptability of Methods of Fertility Control", *Milbank Memorial Fund Quarterly*, 1953; R. Freedman *et al.*, *Family Planning, Sterility, and Population Growth*, ch. 4; C. F. Westoff, *et al.*, *Family Growth in Metropolitan America*, ch. 5; D. V. Glass, "Family Limitation in Europe: A Survey of Recent Studies", in C. V. Kiser (ed.) *Research in Family Planning*, pp. 252-61

the generality of Australians—in all major categories of the population—have borne progressively fewer children because they *wanted* to, and not because they were, in any direct sense, *forced* to. Differences over time, and between the various categories of the population at the same time, are (with the possible exceptions already noted) to be explained in terms of differential resort to the various methods of family limitation. Whatever in individual instances may have been the degree of success or failure in achieving one's goals, the total result was the creation of those differentials described above.

To note that family limitation is a virtually universal practice in a country is not to suggest, however, that group differences in the distribution of family sizes would disappear if each couple had the exact number of children it wanted.[10] Some earlier students, noting that the (then) substantial group differences in knowledge of the more effective means of family limitation coincided with differences in fertility, concluded that group fertility differentials would probably disappear once every couple learned how to control the number of its offspring and succeeded in doing so. But more recent studies, which have found a persistence of certain group differentials despite widespread knowledge—and practice—of family limitation,[11] have forced a rejection of this conclusion. No more is it a question of how long group fertility differentials will persist, but, rather, of why some groups want (or at least permit themselves to have) larger families than others. With reference to Australia, what, in short, are the essential differences between Catholics and Non-Catholics, or between Rural-dwellers and Metropolitan-dwellers, or Dutch-born and Australian-born, that cause them to have families of different size?

Any answer to such questions must rely largely on inference. There is no direct evidence on the matter. The formidable difficulties of designing and carrying out research into social questions are in this instance only compounded by the multiplicity of interrelated variables and the fact that any couple's family-building will take place over a period of years and be subject, therefore, not only to a variety of influences, but to influences whose intensity may vary markedly over time.

Certain factors are likely nevertheless to have been of prime importance. At the highest level of generality: the likelihood of different fertility "norms". As the result of training and experience, most people, most of the time, do what others around them expect them to. Their behaviour is, in that sense, "rule-conforming". Families of, say, five or six children will be less usual if defined as "large", than if defined as merely "normal", particularly under conditions of extensive fertility control; and, conversely, families of one or two children will be more usual if defined as "typical" than as "small". The high level of Dutch fertility both at home and in Australia strongly suggests the operation of just such a fertility norm; as does the finding in some studies

---

[10] See A. A. Campbell, "Concepts and Techniques Used in Fertility Surveys", in *Emerging Techniques in Population Research*, pp. 26-30.

[11] Freedman *et al., op. cit.,* note on the basis of their detailed study of a random sample of 2,713 white married women in the United States that "attempts to avoid conception at some time are virtually universal among couples who have no fecundity impairment" and that the proportion doing so increases with duration of marriage and number of children (pp. 61-8).

that among urban dwellers the fertility of the farm-born generally exceeds that of the city-born.[12]

Even when (as seems to be the case in Australia for the period under study) there is considerable agreement that the most desirable number of children lies within but a narrow range (in this instance, 2-3, or at most, 4), there are conditions that can incline the fertility of one group towards the upper extreme and the fertility of another towards the lower. To many couples—particularly in the groups with higher fertility—it must seem at times as though everyone were having babies. When "everyone" is, not only is the example set, but the children have readier access to playmates and the parents themselves have the opportunity to share with acquaintances both the duties and the joys of raising children. Bearing and rearing children in such a setting conforms to the behaviour and, probably, expectations of one's fellows, and is easier in fact because the instrumentalities for child care are likely to be more fully developed.[13]

Fertility norms do not just happen, however. Nor do they operate in a vacuum, or remain unchanged in the face of changes elsewhere in the social setting. Historically, declines in both fertility and mortality have been associated with the process of industrialization. Why families should have become smaller in industrializing societies admits of no single explanation. Improvements in contraception appear to have coincided in these countries with a number of social changes that served to intensify what must already have become a widespread desire for control over the frequency and timing of child-bearing. The Royal Commission on Population's account of this development in England may be taken as descriptive of what, in general, happened in all countries undergoing this change:

The explanation lies . . . in the profound changes that were taking place in the outlook and ways of living of the people during the 19th century. The main features of these changes are well-known. They include the decay of small scale family handicrafts and the rise of large scale industry and factory organization; the loss of security and growth of competitive individualism; the relative decline in agriculture and rise in importance of industry and commerce, and the associated shift of population from rural to urban areas; the growing prestige of science, which disturbed traditional religious beliefs; the development of popular education; higher standards of living; the growth of humanitarianism, and the emancipation of women. All these and other changes are closely inter-related; they present a complex web, rather than a chain, of cause and effect . . . [14]

Just as changing conditions have brought changes in fertility norms over time, so can it be presumed that different conditions produce and support different fertility norms between various subgroupings of a population. What, then, might be the group differences supporting the different fertility norms apparently existing in Australia?

[12] See D. Goldberg, "Another Look at the Indianapolis Fertility Data", *Milbank Memorial Fund Quarterly*, 1960, pp. 23-26.

[13] W. D. Borrie, "The Family", in G. Caiger (ed.) *The Australian Way of Life*, 1953, p. 30.

[14] Royal Commission on Population, *Report*, H.M.S.O., 1949, p. 38.

To begin with, there are probably *no* group differences in actual liking for children. There probably are, however, fairly substantial differences in the levels of aspiration parents entertain for their children—and incidentally for themselves as well. This seems one of the more plausible explanations for the lower fertility of the cities—and also of the Italian-born. Total fertility in Italy itself has declined considerably since the early 1930s; which suggests a period of substantial fertility differentials, with certain sectors drastically limiting the number of their offspring while others remain at or near the earlier levels. Since migration to Australia is more likely to attract those who want (or think they want) to break with tradition, to "get on" in the world,[15] a preponderance of migrants may be those who had broken—or would be willing to break—with traditional childbearing practices in order to attain ends which a large family may preclude.

Group differences in what is thought to be the functional value of children may also play a part. For Rural and to a lesser extent for Other Urban parents, for example, children may well offer certain economic rewards not ordinarily available to city parents, and may fulfil a larger share of their parents' needs for companionship.

Degree of contact with frankly pro- or anti-natalist teachings may also differ. Surely in the official Catholic opposition to the more effective means of birth control there exists at least a strong implication of pro-natalism (birth encouragement),[16] whatever may have been the original intent of the doctrine's promulgators. Of the Catholic/Non-Catholic fertility differential found in recent American studies, it has been asked:

> Could it be due to the encouragement of high fertility by priests and other representatives of the Catholic Church? We know that the Catholic wives who are most devout are those whose fertility values and expectations are highest. Perhaps their fertility values are high not because the structure of their families or their personalities differ in important degree from those of other Catholic wives, but because they are more aware of the Church's emphasis on the procreative function of marriage.[17]

This may well apply in Australia, too, and even account for some of the group differences among Catholics themselves. A recent study of fertility *indications* in a sample of city mothers with two children in the United States[18] shows Italians to be rather less attached than other ethnic groups to the broader Catholic value system. This looser attachment—together with palpably higher levels of aspiration—compensates for counter-pressures arising from their higher concentration in groups of ordinarily higher fertility (*e.g.* rural-born, working class). Couples of Irish extraction, on the other hand, cluster at the high end of the fertility indications scale. The extent to which schooling was obtained in Catholic institutions was shown to be significant.

---

[15] See W. D. Borrie, *Italians and Germans in Australia*, pp. 79-80; and C. A. Price, *Southern Europeans in Australia*, chs. 2 and 4.

[16] See chapter 4.

[17] Campbell, *op. cit.*, p. 35.

[18] C. F. Westoff, *et al.*, *Family Growth in Metropolitan America*, pp. 202-211. The indicators used were: (1) mean number of children desired by husbands and wives; (2) proportion of husbands and wives claiming to have been "successful" in planning their pregnancies; (3) mean number of months between date of marriage and date of second birth.

Of the regular church attenders among Irish Catholic women in the white collar class, for example, 92% received some of their schooling in church-related schools, compared with 43% of Italian women.[19] In Australia also, children of Italian immigrants attend church schools much less than local or British-born Catholic children.

Intertwined with all these other possibilities is the likelihood of group differences in values and attitudes. Even where religious influences come most into play, the determination of family size is likely to depend less on simple compliance with official pronouncements than on a weighing of these pronouncements against concrete personal values: values which will, in turn, be affected by the social and cultural norms surrounding family life in the groups with which a couple identifies. From the standpoint of behaviour, values will be indicated by attitudes towards religious dogmas, ethical principles, political ideas and styles of life.

Though certain value preferences are suggested by studies of family planning differentials, explicit research into these preferences has nowhere been carried out. However, I should say that, in terms of values, higher fertility in populations practising extensive control over childbearing is generally associated with: a greater emphasis on life after death and a lesser emphasis on the condition of man here and now; a greater emphasis on the necessity of complying with absolute moral laws to fulfil supernatural designs or historical "necessity" and a lesser emphasis on the freedom and obligation of man to improve his lot through rational action; a greater emphasis on the negative consequences of sexual indulgence and "excess" and a lesser emphasis on the positive contributions of harmonious sexual relations to marital accord; a greater emphasis on married women as helpmeets and childrearers, with few (if any) needs apart from those that can be fulfilled within the family environment, and a lesser emphasis on a varied role for women as individuals.[20]

The first three affect willingness to practise birth control consistently and effectively, and, we suggest, help maintain the Catholic/Non-Catholic differential and possibly—though much less strongly—the ethnic and rural/urban differences as well. The fourth, affecting the likelihood that a wife may have interests outside the home, will go far to explain rural/urban differences.

The extent to which contraception is actually practised in Australia may be deduced from figures regarding the sale of contraceptive devices. The following figures are derived from a commercial survey made in 1963. They are based on sales per month by pharmacists throughout Australia.[21] (Months used for survey purposes are indicated in each case.)

---

[19] *Ibid.*, pp. 207-8.

[20] For an extended discussion, see Lincoln H. Day and Alice Day, *Too Many Americans*, chapter 5.

[21] These figures were quoted by Dr W. K. Whitten of the National Biological Standards Laboratory, Canberra, at an ANZAAS symposium on human fertility in January 1964. The figures are reliable except in the case of condoms, which are affected by sales through mail orders, rubber shops and perhaps bulk supplies for the purposes of prostitution. On the other hand, condoms do not appear to be available from barbers, as in Britain, or from service stations, as in the U.S.A. The survey also does not include the use of the Grafenberg ring, which requires insertion by a doctor. From the reports of the International Planned Parenthood Federation, it appears that this device is still used widely in Australia by comparison with other countries, and there is some evidence that the practice is most widespread in the city of Melbourne.

TABLE 3

Monthly Sales of Contraceptives, 1963

1. Oral contraceptives ("the pill"), packets of 20, July 1963	180,000
2. Vaginal chemical contraceptives, single doses, mean of September and October 1963	410,000
3. Condoms, mean of September and October 1963	560,000
4. Diaphragms, mean of sales in September and October 1963, plus those supplied by Australian Family Planning Association	1,600

Two of the figures in the above table represent considerable underestimates. The figure for condoms is regarded by the principal manufacturer as an underestimate, by as much as 50%, so that the true figure may be 900,000. In the case of oral contraceptives, the rate of growth has been very rapid. By the middle of 1964 it was estimated that close on 250,000 packets were being sold monthly; by that stage there were at least fourteen separate brands of pill on the market. It is probable that Australian sales represent the highest pro rata figure for consumer acceptance of oral contraceptives anywhere in the world.[22]

This discussion has relied perforce on inferences from overseas studies and on reasonably well informed guesses about comparable Australian conditions. I have examined conditions that seem of first importance only, emphasizing that a multiplicity of factors will be at work in any given instance, some serving to restrain, others to add force to, the thrust of the dominant ones. Our discussion underlines the persistence of group differentials in fertility, despite a general context of extensive control over fertility and the emergence of the average family with two to four children.

[22] This topic is discussed in a report on contraception prepared by the N.S.W. Humanist Society in December 1963. The report estimates that annual expenditure on contraceptives, excluding medical fees, is £5,000,000. An analysis of contraceptive devices available in Australia was published in November 1964 by Canberra Consumers Incorporated.

LINCOLN H. DAY

11   Divorce[*]

DIVORCE is almost universally condemned in the Western world, and its
incidence nearly always defined as "high"—with the implication that there is
something peculiarly bad about a high rate and, conversely, something peculiarly good about a low one, or, better still, no rate at all.

By definition, divorce involves the dissolution of the nuclear family of
husband, wife and their children. Because of the importance of this type of
family unit in Western society it follows that divorce represents at least a
potential threat to society itself. Not only does it involve a redistribution of
property, but, most importantly, it necessitates a change in the behaviour of
spouses, a change in the environment and training of their children, and a
change in the rights and duties of each member of the family. Without alternative ways of satisfying the emotional, economic, and social needs met by
the nuclear family, or with only scant opportunity for remarriage (that is, for
the formation of a new nuclear family), divorce could be highly disruptive
of any society as firmly grounded as ours is in the beliefs and practices of
this family system.

Yet the condemnation of divorce seems to be based less on an understanding of its possible social consequences than on two misconceptions as
to what it is and what it means. There is a common failure to realize, first,
that the state, in granting a divorce, merely gives recognition and legal status
to an already accomplished fact. Divorce does not cause broken families;
broken families cause divorce. By requiring a legal procedure the state
emphasizes society's interest in the family, and, at the same time, removes
the restrictions originating in its rules governing marriage: once divorced, the
individual is free to set about forming a more perfect—or, at least, less
*im*perfect—legally sanctioned union with someone else. But the family is
broken (though not necessarily beyond repair) well before the couple appears
in any divorce court.

The second misconception concerns the meaning of divorce rates. These
are commonly read as measures of marital disharmony, or at the very least
as *indicators* of it. Yet they most certainly are not the first; and need not
even be the second. Obviously, where divorce is, there, also, is marital disharmony. But beyond this we cannot go. We cannot say that an absence of

[*] A preliminary version of this contribution appeared in the *Australian Quarterly*, vol.
35, no. 2, 1963.

divorce indicates an absence of marital discord; or that there is necessarily twice as much marital discord in a country whose divorce rate is double that of another. If there are ways of measuring such a condition, comparing divorce rates is not one of them.

Marital discord itself is ubiquitous. Divorce is simply one of a number of possible "adjustments" to this condition. To account for differences in the incidence of divorce, either between different populations, or over time in the same population, it is necessary to assess the relative importance of three interlocking determinants: the availability of divorce, the alternatives to divorce, and the extent of marital discord.

By "availability" is meant not only the actual existence of divorce or other "remedy", but also the extent to which the divorced person can adjust to the condition of being divorced, and the extent to which the various alternative "remedies" for marital discord are available and acceptable to the parties concerned. Access to divorce is greatly restricted in nearly every Western country; so much so, in fact, that one can hardly avoid the conclusion that Western society is but little concerned with the happiness of individuals in marriage, that it would much prefer a couple to remain married, though unhappy, than that they should ever resort to divorce. Some Catholic countries—Spain, Portugal, the Republic of Ireland, for example—prohibit divorce altogether; which is not to say their populations are devoid of marital discord, but only that they "adjust" to it in different ways. In at least the first two there is, for example, a long tradition of separation, desertion, and concubinage. Of all Western countries, only Norway has divorce laws so liberal as to permit divorce on grounds of mutual dislike—or, for that matter, mutual indifference. Nowhere else in the Western world is the absence of love, affection, respect, comradeship—so widely regarded as essential to the successful marriage—considered a sufficient legal ground for dissolving a marriage.

But not all limitations on divorce are codified in law. To take an extreme case: divorce does not exist at all as an available alternative for one whose religious or moral scruples entirely preclude it—whatever may be the degree of legal availability. Fear for one's reputation, doubts (on the part of the wife, at least) of one's ability to support oneself, a shortage of suitable housing, insufficient funds for legal expenses, worries about its effect on children, are but a few of the conditions that act in some measure to lower the incidence of divorce by keeping "together" many a couple whose marriage has come to possess little more than legal reality. How many more divorces would there be in Australia if women were given more equitable treatment in the job market, if housing were less restricted to one-family dwellings in sprawling suburbs, if childbearing were not begun so soon after marriage, or if marriage occurred at an earlier age so that a person divorcing 3-5 years later would still be young enough to think he had a good chance of remarrying? The possibility exists, of course, that differences in the incidence of divorce, either over time or between groups, will have originated to some degree in differences in the extent of marital discord. But, in general, the statistical analysis of divorce is less a study in the incidence of marriage failure than it is a study in the relative availability of divorce and alternative remedies for marital discord.

What, then, can be said of the patterns of divorce in Australia? No one way of measuring divorce will meet all research requirements. As with the measurement of most other social phenomena, the particular method used will depend, first, on the nature of the available data and, second, on the interests of the investigator. Though unusually comprehensive, the Australian data are still too sparse to permit any precise determination of changes occurring in the incidence of divorce. Moreover, there are no Australian data on the incidence of divorce within various sub-groupings of the population, such as those by religion, occupation, rural-urban residence, or country of birth. All available data pertain solely to the total population.[1]

Nevertheless, there are certain dominant patterns of divorce in Australia about which there can be no question, whatever the limitations of the data that reveal them. The most obvious of these is the general increase in the frequency of divorce. At the beginning of this century, some 4% of Australian marriages could be expected to end in divorce; two generations later, this proportion has risen to some 12%.[2] Such a considerable secular increase was not without its fluctuations, however. The likelihood of divorce in the depression of the 1930s fell somewhat below that during the relatively good

TABLE 1

Divorces per 1,000

Year	Population		Married Women	
	Australia	*U.S.A.*	*Australia*	*U.S.A.*
1911	0·1	1·0	0·7	4·8
1921	0·3	1·5	1·5	7·1
1933	0·3	1·3	1·5	6·1
1947	1·2	3·4	5·0	13·9
1954	0·7	2·3	3·2	9·5

Sources: Australia: Calculated from data in Census and *Demography Bulletin.* Denominator is population as of 30th June. Numerator includes nullities of marriage and judicial separations —about 1% of the total.

U.S.A.: Paul H. Jacobson and Pauline F. Jacobson, *American Marriage and Divorce*, N.Y., Table 42, p. 90. Numerator includes annulment and dissolution of marriage decrees—about 3% of the total.

[1] Australia is no worse off in this respect than most countries. Such analyses have been attempted but in nearly every instance the attempt has been based on a misuse of census data: differences between proportions enumerated as currently occupying the status "divorced" have been taken to represent differences in the incidence of divorce itself, despite the fact that differences between the various sub-groups in rates of remarriage or in the interval of time between divorce and remarriage could seriously affect the relative sizes of these ratios.

[2] Though higher than in the United Kingdom, the incidence of divorce in Australia is considerably below that in the United States where, at current levels, one out of four marriages ends in divorce. For a discussion of the method of calculating this proportion, and the rationale behind it, see Lincoln H. Day, "A Note on the Measurement of Divorce, with Special Reference to Australian Data", *Australian Journal of Statistics*, vol. 5, no. 3, 1963, pp. 140-1. For a discussion of the reasons for the differences between Australian and American divorce patterns see Alice Taylor Day, "Divorce Down Under", *Columbia University Forum* (Summer, 1964), and Lincoln H. Day, "Patterns of Divorce in Australia and the United States", *American Sociological Review* (August 1964).

economic conditions of the 1920s; while the peak rates after the second world war were perhaps as much as 40-50% higher than those characteristic of the next decade. Nevertheless, however great the fluctuations, the general trend of divorce in Australia—like that elsewhere in the Western world—has been decidedly upward.

For example, the overall ratio of divorces to existing marriages was only three-fifths as high in 1954 as in 1947, yet this 1954 ratio was still more than twice as high as the 1933 and 1921 ratios, and more than four times as high as the 1911 ratio.

TABLE 2

Divorces per 1,000 Marriages in Specified Years

Year	Australia	U.S.A.
1891	8·0	60·0
1901	14·4	82·2
1911	13·1	93·4
1921	32·0	134·5
1931	50·3	173·1
1936	42·9	167·7
1941	44·6	168·5
1946	91·0	264·4
1951	94·8	230·4
1956	90·4	233·0
1960	88·9	—

Sources: Australia: Calculated from data in *Demography Bulletin*.
United States: Calculated from data in Paul H. Jacobson and Pauline F. Jacobson, *American Marriage and Divorce*, Tables 2 and 42, pp. 21 and 91 (excluding annulments and New York dissolution of marriage decrees).

More detailed information on the character of this trend is available in the data on divorce by duration of marriage. One might reasonably expect an increase in the frequency of divorce to be accompanied by a shift in incidence toward the earlier years of marriage; that as divorce became more common, less opprobrium would attach to it, with the result that it would be resorted to earlier in marriage. However, this has not happened in Australia. There have been some fluctuations, to be sure: the upsurge after the second world war involved new marriages rather than those of longer standing, while the general decline in rates after this peak did not extend to couples married 20 years or more. For the present, however, it seems safe to conclude that there has been little tendency for divorce to occur either earlier or later in the course of a marriage.[3]

The likelihood of divorce in Australia increases rapidly from the third to the sixth year of marriage and then more or less levels off until about the twelfth, after which it declines slowly. In the United States, on the other hand, there is no levelling off in the rates and the peak incidence occurs much earlier—in the third year of marriage—after which, as in Australia, there is

[3] This point is discussed more fully in Day, *Australian Journal of Statistics*, 1963, p. 139.

171

a steady decline with increasing duration (see Table 3). The American rate is higher than the Australian at every duration, however, which may be attributed partly to differences in divorce laws (notably the virtual absence of divorce in Australia in the first three years of marriage), in the acceptability of divorce, in the availability of alternatives to divorce, and (possibly) in the extent of marital disharmony.

TABLE 3

Divorces per 1,000 Wives, by Duration of Marriage

Duration (years)	New South Wales				N.S.W., Vic., S. Aust. and Queensland	Aust.	U.S.A.
	1901	1921	1933	1947	1947	1954	1954
Under 5	·61	·46	·64	3·64	3·45	1·61	21·8
5–9	2·26	2·58	3·89	10·75	9·30	5·60	13·3
10–14	1·90	3·34	2·86	9·07	8·36	4·69	8·1
15–19	1·40	2·24	2·32	7·56	6·68	3·69	6·3
20–24			1·83	4·49		3·27	5·2
20–29	·70	2·49	1·52	3·87	2·65	2·77	4·5
25–29			1·08	3·14		2·23	3·7
30–39	·34*	·84	·50	1·27	1·13	1·14	2·0

*Calculated on the basis of only 12 divorces.

One consequence of the Australian pattern is that divorce here is quite likely to involve children. In 1954, for example, children had been born to 57% of the couples who obtained a divorce after less than 15 years of marriage, and to 78% of those who obtained one after 15 to 19 years of marriage. The corresponding proportions among Americans were 40% and 62% respectively. Because of the lower divorce rate, however, the proportion of *all* children affected by divorce is substantially lower in Australia than in the United States. Were the 1954 rates to continue, divorce would directly affect some 2% of all Australian children before they reached the age of 15, and just over 3% before they reached the age of 20. The corresponding American proportions (for 1948—the only year for which such data are available) would be 8% and more than 10% (see Table 4).

But if Australian divorces are more likely than not to involve children, those couples whose marriages end this way have, nevertheless, a consistently lower average family size and a consistently higher incidence of childlessness than does the married population generally. This is true of each marriage duration. Divorce involves many young children in Australia, but the number affected is far smaller than it would be if divorcing couples had the same childbearing patterns as non-divorcing couples.

The incidence of divorce by age is what could be expected from a knowledge of its incidence by duration of marriage: the highest rates are at ages when couples are most likely to have been married some 5-15 years. Unfortunately, there are no data by which to determine the possible relationship

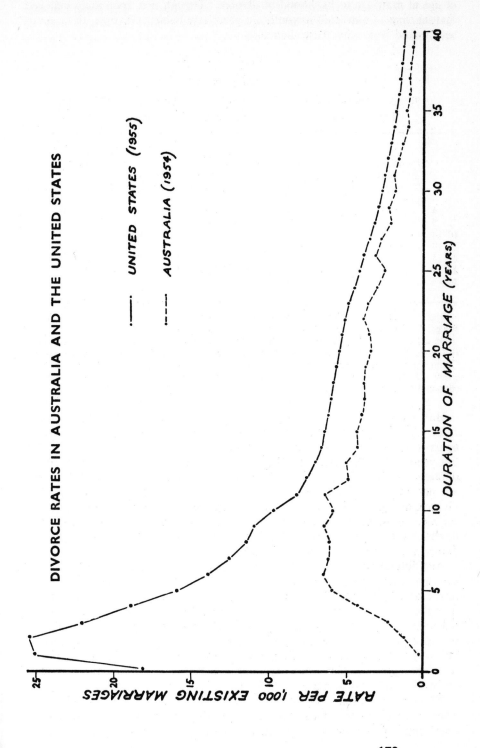

DIVORCE RATES IN AUSTRALIA AND THE UNITED STATES

UNITED STATES (1955)

AUSTRALIA (1954)

DURATION OF MARRIAGE (YEARS)

RATE PER 1,000 EXISTING MARRIAGES

of age at marriage to likelihood of divorce. Though it is commonly believed that marriages contracted in youth are peculiarly liable to divorce, this cannot be checked from any Australian data.

TABLE 4

Divorce and Family Size

Average Issue and Proportion Childless, by Duration of Marriage. Divorcing Couples Compared with All Couples: 1954

Duration of Marriage (years)	Average Issue		% Childless	
	Divorcing Couples	All Couples	Divorcing Couples	All Couples
0– 4	·36	·75	68	44
5– 9	·75	1·82	45	17
10–14	1·23	2·27	30	14
15–19	1·67	2·54	22	12
20–24	1·98	2·69	17	12
25–29	2·13	2·73	16	12
30+	2·74	3·47	—	—

Sources: Data for couples obtaining a divorce calculated from Government of New South Wales, *Statistical Register of New South Wales*, 1953-4, p. 424, Table 9.

Data for all couples are for the entire Commonwealth, *not* merely New South Wales. Rates for New South Wales in previous years were virtually identical with those for the Commonwealth, however, so there should not be much difference between them in 1954 either. Calculated from Commonwealth Bureau of Census and Statistics, census of 1954, chapter 18, "Families", tables 13 and 14.

But age *differences* between spouses *are* associated with higher divorce rates. A marriage in which the ages of husband and wife are 10-14 years apart is more likely to end in divorce than is one in which the difference is 5-9 years; while the latter, in turn, is more liable to divorce than one with a difference of less than 5 years. The data on which this conclusion is based are not entirely satisfactory, however, since age is given as of the time of divorce, not marriage (though an age difference of, say, 10 years is doubtless far more important to persons marrying in their teens or twenties than it is to those who marry in their thirties or forties), and cannot be related to duration of marriage or number of children.

Age differences may indicate divergences in interests and personalities; but they may also indicate the extent to which the parties to a marriage conform to the norms of the society, since divorce rates are lower for husbands older than their wives (a condition more in keeping with the norm) than for wives older than their husbands. As long as divorce remains outside the bounds of fully acceptable behaviour, we can expect it to occur more frequently among those whose marriages were themselves contracted outside the range of full social acceptance. Marriages involving substantial age differences between husbands and wives would seem to be just such "abnormalities".

To study any social phenomenon is to ask three general questions about it: what is the character of its incidence? has this undergone any change over time? and what causes it? Answers to the first two questions depend on the availability of data; but for the third, this can do little more than limit the range of conjecture and suggest some of the more valuable lines of approach for inquiries based on other types of evidence. Of course, any meaningful causal hypotheses will have to take account of patterns revealed by the available statistics, and they will also have to be based on a full recognition of what divorce is and of what is meant by the various measures used to determine its incidence. But the type of data discussed here can tell us nothing about the actual causes of divorce. Nor will any study of the grounds on which divorces are granted. Between 1953-5, adultery was the official ground in 28% of the decrees granted in Australia, desertion in 62%, and cruelty in 5%.[4] The corresponding proportions in England and Wales were: adultery 42%, desertion 41%, cruelty 16%.[5] Are we to conclude from this that the English and Welsh are given more to adultery and cruelty, and less to running away from their spouses? Or is it, as various students of the subject have pointed out, that the legal grounds for any particular divorce action will be largely a function of the relative barriers (legal, administrative, and normative) lying in the path of the couple seeking an end to their marriage? Study of the allowable grounds for divorce may tell us something of the moral standards of the legislators who write divorce laws[6] (in many jurisdictions, only adultery—particularly on the part of the wife—is considered an offence heinous enough to justify dissolution of a marriage), but there is nothing about family structure, nothing about actual social behaviour, to be derived from summarizing the numbers of petitions based on these various "matrimonial offences". Those who use such figures for bewailing an increase in immorality or in domestic irresponsibility do so out of ignorance of their actual meaning. Desertion, adultery, cruelty, drunkenness are, at most, the symptoms or end products of marriage failure. They are not its underlying cause. As Milton remarked three centuries ago, no court is capable of inquiring into "the secret reason of dissatisfaction between man and wife". A statistical inquiry into the incidence of divorce is very different from an inquiry into the causes of marital discord.

[4] Calculated from data in *Demography Bulletin*, 1957, Table 68, p. 46.
[5] O. R. McGregor, *Divorce in England*, Table X, p. 43.
[6] See, for example, McGregor, especially chs. 1-2.

PART IV

J. M. MAIN

12   Painting: Taste and the Market

IN February 1963 the B.B.C. television programme "Tonight" showed the "Ten Top Prints" for 1963. Some of these pictures are unfamiliar to Australians, but among them there were three or four which may be as popular here as they are in Britain. Tretchikoff's "Lady from the Orient", "Low Tide, Polperro" by Shepherd, "Incoming Combers" by Andrews are all displayed in the shops of Sydney or Adelaide, Melbourne or Perth. Popular taste in pictures is to a considerable degree international, but in this country the indiscriminating or unsophisticated buyer of a picture is more dependent on what is produced overseas than similar purchasers in other countries. We do not have our own Tretchikoff, and Australian landscape pictures similar in tone and content to "Incoming Combers" or "Low Tide, Polperro" have not been reproduced in this country. Often, it seems, it is the foreign element in the imported colour print which makes it most appealing; the manufactured exoticism of Tretchikoff's oriental ladies or the simple romantic quality of Claver's Paris cafés are attractive to people precisely because they are not Australian.

. Until very recently there were only a few colour reproductions of pictures by Australian artists available—one or two water colours of red gums by Sir Hans Heysen; a Namatjira print of central Australian ranges in bold blue and red ochre; a landscape of Victorian hills and forests by Buckmaster or Rowell were exclusively representative of Australian art reproduced in any quantity. And even these were confined to small shops with closed doors whose customers are required to possess a social assurance not demanded of those who usually buy in the large department stores. Only now are there signs of change. The aboriginal artist, Albert Namatjira, had become a public figure before his death and his water colour landscapes are reproduced and sold in large numbers. One department store with branches in many parts of the country has discovered a demand for a series of "Australiana" prints and has purchased 42,000 of them to sell at half a crown each. A popular magazine offering its readers large and well-made copies of paintings by William Dobell and Russell Drysdale was surprised by a demand for more than 4,000 of Dobell's "Wangi Boy", and for nearly 4,000 of Drysdale's "Sofala". But while Australian painting is becoming familiar to more and more people in this country, taste is usually confined to pictures of the landscape painted in the representational or "realist" manner, and even then art of this kind has

176

not displaced Tretchikoff or Andrews from their positions of prominence in the living rooms of thousands of Australian houses.

Those who sell colour prints in the shops have informed us that their customers' first desire is that a picture should be colourful; they also demand that the colours should be simple and the variations of tone uncomplicated. One or two pictures of Renoir and Utrillo have a steady sale, but other pictures of the French impressionists and post-impressionists are difficult to sell, even though customers very frequently ask for a "Paris scene". There are of course many people who do buy reproductions of the work of well-known European artists, and every Australian city has those small specialized shops in which one finds Sienese saints and Etruscan musicians lying beside fantasies of Chagall. In these places, however, the range of choice is confined and the stock would appear to a foreigner as rather behind the times; their sources of supply are European firms who have discovered or established a safe market for particular colour prints. One may find a Jackson Pollock print in an Australian shop, but the search is long and difficult.

There is one great difference in this country between those who buy colour prints and those who possess or buy original paintings, prints or drawings; while the former are buying copies of pictures of European origin, those who buy original works of art confine their purchases almost exclusively to works by Australian artists. To all but a few of the wealthiest, overseas markets for pictures are closed to us, and the work of foreign artists has been virtually excluded from the Australian art market. The distance between Australia and the rest of the world, transport costs and other charges, the risks and difficulties of importing pictures, have all given the local artist a natural protection which is fortified by the imposition of a sales tax, 15% at the moment, on the work of foreign artists imported to this country. A very few of the largest collectors have brought in pictures purchased overseas and we have recently been offered for sale some collections of paintings and colour prints from abroad; nevertheless, the Australian artist has an all but exclusive monopoly of his home market. Our knowledge and appetite for paintings or sculpture from America or Europe may be occasionally whetted by the official showing of imported exhibitions, but otherwise we are dependent on travellers' tales, or books reproducing the work of overseas artists. In the recent past the Commonwealth government imposed a heavy duty in addition to other charges on imported works of art, with the justification of assisting artists in Australia. But even this aroused little public protest, and it seems that most collectors in this country accepted without rancour the restrictions imposed on their tastes and purchases.

Since the last war, painting in Australia has won respect and attention of a kind which none of the other arts can rival. While there has been a similar new interest in the visual arts in Europe and North America since the war, this is not, like so many of our fashions, one which we have imported from overseas. Our new enthusiasm for painting is partly due to causes which are common to this and other parts of the world, but there are particular reasons why painting among all the arts should have attracted so much public and private patronage. In Australia the art of painting has a history and a tradition which is closely bound up with national consciousness. It has always been concentrated upon the landscape, and partly because of the way in which artists have portrayed the landscape, we have come to believe that the pecu-liarity of our natural environment has determined most of the unique qualities in our "character" and "culture". Not only do many Australians see their landscape as the painters of the last century interpreted it, but we have more recently been persuaded that the artist is capable of exploring the subtle relationships betwen our environment and character. Even today, most painting in Australia is either of the landscape or inspired by it, and those of us who have ceased to look for recognizable Australian figures or images in painting have nevertheless been ready to discern the quality in the painter's work which may be identified as Australian. It is here, even more than in literature that we have chosen—or have been instructed—to find our distinc-tive culture. Moreover, since collections of the work of Australian artists have been shown and sometimes admired overseas, they have become ambassadors, charged with the responsibility of demonstrating to the world that our society has now come of age. We are half proud of our artistic parochialism and would resent a mass invasion of our galleries by the artists of America and Europe.

Even so the development and rapid expansion of a national art market in this country is comparatively recent, and it is not just a reflection of intellectual or emotional attitudes to painting. In Australia, as in other countries, the purchase of works of art has become an increasingly common form of luxury expenditure as incomes have risen and social values have changed. Personal spending has risen very sharply in the last decade,[1] and there has been a con-spicuous jettisoning of the more austere conventions which once governed our use of time and money. A generation ago the purchase of works of art was the privilege of the rich or confined to small coteries among the educated and devoted. Today, the ownership of one, two or three original paintings or drawings is commonplace among those who can afford to spend money on things other than acknowledged necessities. Moreover, houses are regarded as very significant indicators of wealth and status: with changing habits and values they have become centres of entertainment and social life, and the decoration and adornment of the home is a testimony to the taste as well as the wealth of the householder. To this testimony the artist can add a unique contribution.

Modern taste and convention in interior design have recently given the artist a new function, and an all but indispensable role. Architects have pro-vided those flat and featureless surfaces which demand the compensating colours, decoration, and centres of interest which the artists and manufac-turers of fabrics can so effectively provide. Australian cities are being torn apart at their centres and recreated in a form which is international; modern steel frame buildings with their concourses and piazzas are decorated with sculpture and mosaic panels, indoor gardens, and sometimes too with pictures. In hotel decoration, as in housing, the influence of professional interior de-signers and the luxury home and garden magazines is increasingly apparent. The visual lessons learned in public places are rapidly applied in private ones. These informal and indirect influences in our tastes have focused attention

---

[1] A recent survey estimates that retail sales in Australia in 1961-2 had increased by 76.5% over sales in the year 1951-2. *Ten years of Personal Earning and Spending in Australia,* published by Herald Research, May 1963.

on the artist and his work, but they have been assisted by active agents. The prices paid for better known pictures at public auctions have become front-page news; secretarial courses sometimes add "art appreciation" to the curriculum they teach; women's magazines devote pages to reproducing pictures and telling "personality" stories about the artist's daily life. The artist has become a public figure, no longer thought of as alien to our society, but one who is especially endowed to comment upon it, and to brighten and enliven it.

Among the new schools of fashion, taste, and knowledge, the new small commercial art galleries are now very important. In most Australian cities these galleries have multiplied, and their entrepreneurs have been influential in persuading their clients and visitors of the pleasure and profit associated with owning pictures. In Sydney there are now reckoned to be twelve commercial galleries holding regular exhibitions; in Melbourne there are at least nine; Brisbane has two; and Adelaide has the advantage of one of the country's best informed and most adventurous collectors and dealers. These new galleries sometimes differ in the paintings which they show, but they all differ more remarkably from those cheerless halls in which we attended exhibitions in the 'thirties and 'forties. White-washed cottages, renovated terraces or smart facades in once frowsy and out-of-the-way corners, now attract the picture buyers and the picture viewers. The new gallery owner combines the role of connoisseur, host and salesman; he instructs the ignorant, lends confidence to the uneasy, or guides the taste of the assured and knowledgeable. On opening days the galleries take on something of the character of a salon in which the smartly dressed jostle with bohemia, and where the earnest talk about art and the shrewd watch to see who buys.

Some of the new gallery proprietors are dealers who buy pictures speculatively, though most of them are merely concerned to sell for commission on behalf of the artist. Sometimes they have contracted to take all the work of an artist for a given period; occasionally they assist by "keeping" him in return for his work, or give him help in managing his financial affairs. The gallery owners have undoubtedly persuaded more and more people to buy paintings and they have encouraged and enabled more artists to paint and to show their work. While it would be difficult to prove conclusively that the prices paid for pictures have been increased by the policies of the galleries, they have undoubtedly established a high market value for the work of a considerable number of Australian artists.

A keen interest in prices which the work of better known artists can command has been stimulated by recent auctions in Sydney and Melbourne of large private collections. Not until 1963 has there been a journal in this country publishing the current prices of pictures, and these grand occasions —the public auctions—have attracted attention to the art market. They have also given emphasis to the fact that the purchase of pictures may be a secure form of saving for the discriminating and a profitable investment for the more adventurous. The Australian art market is still an imperfect one compared with those of Europe and America, but these imperfections are rapidly disappearing. The commercial galleries are showing the works of interstate artists; there is a great movement of dealers about the country; communications are being established more and more firmly. All these are very important developments since the reputation and esteem commanded by an artist in this country among the larger collectors is now, as never before, reflected by the prices which he can command.

The new galleries and some of the older ones are devoted exclusively, or all but exclusively, to showing the work of those painters whose styles are variously described as "figurative", "abstract" or "expressionist". The "modern" movement in Australian art has a history extending back to the pre-war years, but in the period between the wars experiment or innovation in painting which reflected trends in European art was often ignored, and not occasionally criticized with contempt, before the public and in the press. Even in the immediate post-war years many of the young artists whose works are now eagerly sought were little known and they received only meagre public and private patronage. Now, however, there has been a reformation and re-direction of public taste; it no longer lags in the rear of the painters' changing modes. Nevertheless, there is still a lively demand for the work of those artists whose reputations were established before the end of the last century, a demand which has been enhanced simultaneously with the new favour won by "contemporary" painting. The landscapes of Streeton and McCubbin, and some of those of Tom Roberts and a few others, command prices comparable to those paid for the most highly priced paintings of the best known con-temporary painters.

Moreover, there still remains considerable respect and admiration for those who claim, or on whose behalf it is claimed, that they paint within the tradition of the nineteenth century. Some of these artists, who are often de-scribed as "realists", paint portraits under public and private patronage and occasional "still lifes" and flower pieces, but most of them are known as landscape painters. In both Sydney and Melbourne there are dealers who sell only pictures of these kinds, and these dealers and their clients are generally convinced that artistic standards have decayed in recent years. The apologists and protagonists of the "traditional" school have been at war with the spokesmen for "contemporary" art for more than a generation, the last public outburst occurring in 1962 when the portrait painter, William Dargie, accused a Melbourne "establishment" of having captured the National Gallery of Victoria and of using its power to cripple the efforts of "young realists". The periodic condemnation of modern art wins considerable support from people who insist that art should represent or reflect nature, and this conflict between admirers of "realist" and "contemporary" painting still represents the great division of taste among those who buy pictures in Australia today. A more recent debate on the relative qualities of abstract and figurative painting was confined to a narrower circle, and aroused none of the passion so regularly called forth in the other, older controversy.

We have endeavoured to establish what kinds of people buy pictures in Australia today: whether they are predominantly men or women; whether the wealthy are the most important patrons of the artist; and whether represen-tatives of different occupational groups differ in their tastes. We sought answers to these questions among the dealers and those concerned in the management of commercial galleries in Sydney, Melbourne and Adelaide, and in many of these places our questions were answered with encouraging assurance. Those dealers who sell pictures of a more conservative kind have told us that their clients are predominantly, though not exclusively, men. In Melbourne, where the works of the "Heidelberg School" and those artists who immediately followed them are very much sought after, we were informed by the best known dealer that it is rare for a woman to buy pictures of this kind. The highly valued and highly priced pictures of artists like Streeton, Roberts, McCubbin, Bunny and Penleigh Boyd are sought by members of the medical profession, lawyers and businessmen, and occasionally too by the directorates of the bigger industrial and commercial companies. Many of these men are collectors, but others are also quite frankly speculating in the work of "Australian masters" in the expectation that the prices they now fetch will soon go very much higher.

Those dealers who show and who sell "contemporary" paintings are insistent that independent women buyers are not only numerous among their clients but have tended to become more so during recent years. Some painters, we have been told, attract more women buyers than they do men, probably because women are quick to see the ways in which they might employ the decorative qualities of the work of some artists. In Melbourne one gallery proprietor guessed that men and women buyers of "contemporary" paintings are evenly balanced, and he kindly checked his books over a number of years to confirm his guess.

Many of the gallery proprietors in those cities we visited did suggest that their clients might be described in terms of occupation, status, or social "style". At one of the newer Sydney galleries selling abstract and semi-abstract paintings, we were told that the most numerous of its buyers were businessmen and their wives, people in young middle-age, with incomes in the range of £3,000-£5,000 a year. They buy their first picture as an adventure and experiment, then another, until they own four or five; even then they continue, discarding their early purchases in favour of new ones, enhancing the pleasure they derive from their possessions with the knowledge that they are spending soundly and safely. In this gallery, we were told that professional people, whether doctors, lawyers or lecturers in the universities, are remarkably indifferent to contemporary art. In Adelaide our informant described his clients in quite a different way. Here, it appears, younger professional people—university teachers, doctors, dentists and architects—are the most regular and discriminating buyers, while representatives of the wealthier and established families of the city cling to tastes of a more conservative kind. But we were also told that new clients who cannot be assigned to any certain class or category do appear: his example was a racing driver who is one of his most selective buyers. In Melbourne the proprietor of one of the busiest galleries was insistent that the most numerous among his purchasers were drawn from the older families of Victoria, many of them substantial land-owners and some with two or even three houses in which to hang their pictures. Such people, it was suggested, have been brought up in a family tradition of patronage of the arts, and the security of their social position emancipates them from the more conservative conventions which dominate those who are uneasy about their social status. But some of the dealers whom we questioned were hesitant in describing their clients in these terms; indeed, we were finally tempted to suppose that sometimes our informants were telling us about those among their clients whom they most esteemed, or those among their potential buyers whom they would most like to attract.

In the search for more specific information concerning the tastes of those who buy pictures, we prepared a questionnaire which we were permitted to circulate among members of the National Gallery Society of Victoria. In both Sydney and Melbourne the societies affiliated with the National Art Galleries have a large and varied membership: in Melbourne there are some sixteen hundred members of the society and in Sydney rather more. These are not the only art societies in the two cities, but unlike others they are not committed to supporting particular schools, nor do they attract large numbers of artists or those who live on the fringe of the artist's world. Our questionnaire, addressed to the members of the Victorian society, asked them to list the names of those artists whose paintings or drawings they had bought since 1950. They were also asked to name three Australian artists whose pictures they would buy if they were given complete freedom of choice. Members were requested to state their occupations and to nominate the age group to which they belonged. Three hundred and seventy-eight members replied to our questions, two hundred and ninety-four of whom had purchased original pictures since 1950. We grouped the occupations of those who replied to this question in the following way:

(a) Medical practitioners. Of forty who replied, thirty-five were purchasers.

(b) Other professions, including lawyers, dentists, architects, engineers, university lecturers and professors. Of sixty who replied, fifty-two were purchasers.

(c) Those in professional and semi-professional occupations who are usually less highly paid than those in the professions listed in (a) and (b). Of eighty-two who replied, fifty-four were purchasers.

(d) Businessmen whose occupations are usually considered to give them relatively high incomes: company directors, stock-brokers, merchants, accountants and managers. Of forty-four who replied, forty-one were purchasers.

(e) Those in other commercial occupations usually less highly paid or earning lower incomes than those in (d): salesmen, self-employed retailers, secretaries and stenographers. Of forty-five who replied, thirty were purchasers.

(f) Housewives: of forty-seven who replied, thirty-six were purchasers.

(g) Miscellaneous: of fourteen who replied, thirteen were purchasers.

(h) Those who did not state their occupation. Of forty-four who replied, thirty-three were purchasers.

It was then necessary to attempt to assign the artists whose pictures had been purchased by members into various categories corresponding to their period, type or style. These were defined in this way:

(a) The works of aboriginal artists (*i.e.* Namatjira and his followers who paint in water colours).

(b) "Historical" paintings: pictures painted before 1880 by artists such as Martens, Gill, Buvelot and Russell, whose work possesses both historical and artistic interest.

(c) Paintings and drawings by artists of the "Heidelberg school" and others whose reputations were established before 1900.

(d) Paintings and drawings by artists in this century whose work is in the "realist" or "representational" manner.

(e) Paintings and drawings by those artists who, since the 1930s have usually been regarded as "contemporary" or *avant-garde* in their work. This group includes both figurative and abstract artists.

(f) Those artists whose names were unknown to us and whose work we were unable to classify. Most probably part-time painters or students who do not and did not exhibit commercially.

(g) Paintings and drawings by overseas artists.

Our calculations of the way in which those in each occupational group have distributed their purchases among the various categories of paintings and drawings as we have defined them, are set out in the following table. The purchases made in each category are shown in figures and as a percentage of the total number of purchases made by those in each of the occupational groups.

We are aware, in presenting these figures, that they represent the purchases of pictures among a limited and self-chosen number of people: members of the National Gallery Society in Victoria who were willing to reply to the questionnaire. We cannot pretend that they reflect either the range of tastes or the character of picture-buying in the community at large. Many of those whose tastes are of a more radical kind may not join a society; its activities and the atmosphere in which it meets may appeal to many of those with rather traditional attitudes to art. Even so, this sample does indicate that there are a considerable number of members who have bought the works of contemporary painters, and the society appears to contain people of a sufficiently wide range of occupations to give some meaning to the conclusions drawn from these figures.

As one would expect, those among the wealthier occupational groups are stronger buyers of pictures than those among the poorer. Doctors, professional people, and wealthier businessmen, stand out as the largest buyers. Secondly, doctors and businessmen have been more often purchasers of paintings of the "'Heidelberg" artists and others of the later nineteenth century. The more conservative purchasers, those who have revealed considerable demand for painters called "realists", are those in commercial occupations, members of the medical profession, and those in semi-professional occupations. The reason for assigning members of the medical profession to a separate category in our analysis was not only that a considerable number replied to the questionnaire: it had been suggested to us that they are generally conservative in their tastes, a suggestion which is partially confirmed by the response which they made to our questions.

Businessmen were the largest picture buyers among our sample, and they have bought more "contemporary" paintings than those in any other occupational group. Those assigned to the category "other professions" have been strong buyers of contemporary pictures, but these were the weakest buyers of the works of "realist" or "representational" artists.

Many of these members of the Gallery Society had purchased considerable collections of pictures since 1950. Seventy of them had bought five or more; thirty-four of the seventy had bought ten or more. Among the seventy large purchasers there are eleven doctors; sixteen belong to "other professions";

TABLE 1

Occupations	Number of Purchasers	Works by Aboriginal artists	Works of artists of historic interest	Works of the 'Heidelberg School' and the late nineteenth century	Works by artists who are called 'realist' or representational	Works of Contemporary artists	Works of overseas artists	Works of unknown artists	Total Purchases
Medical Profession ..	35	1 / 0·54%	2 / 1·08%	18 / 9·73%	65 / 35·14%	72 / 38·92%	3 / 1·62%	24 / 12·97%	185
Other Professions ..	52	5 / 1·96%	3 / 1·18%	14 / 5·49%	43 / 16·86%	150 / 58·82%	22 / 8·63%	18 / 7·06%	255
Semi-Professional Occupations ..	54	10 / 5·99%	0	1 / 0·60%	44 / 26·35%	64 / 38·32%	11 / 6·59%	37 / 22·16%	167
Business-men ..	41	4 / 1·36%	4 / 1·36%	18 / 6·12%	62 / 21·09%	164 / 55·78%	17 / 5·78%	25 / 8·50%	294
Commercial Occupations ..	30	1 / 1·28%	1 / 1·28%	2 / 2·56%	34 / 43·59%	14 / 17·96%	4 / 5·13%	22 / 28·20%	78
Housewives and Housekeepers ..	36	5 / 4·03%	1 / 0·81%	2 / 1·61%	31 / 25·00%	48 / 38·71%	1 / 0·81%	36 / 29·03%	124
Miscellaneous Occupations ..	13	2 / 2·06%	0	2 / 2·06%	20 / 20·62%	69 / 71·13%	2 / 2·06%	2 / 2·06%	97
Occupations not stated ..	33	2 / 1·25%	4 / 2·50%	2 / 1·25%	35 / 21·88%	99 / 61·88%	1 / 0·62%	17 / 10·62%	160
TOTAL ..	294	30 / 2·21%	15 / 1·10%	59 / 4·34%	334 / 24·56%	680 / 50·00%	61 / 4·49%	181 / 13·31%	1,360

nineteen are businessmen. Thirty-seven of the larger purchasers who stated their occupations had bought collections which were either predominantly "conservative" or predominantly "contemporary" in character.

Their choices may be represented thus:

	Conservative purchasers	Contemporary purchasers
Medical profession	7	4
Other professions	4	11
Businessmen	2	9

In general, the number of pictures by foreign artists bought by members of the Gallery Society has been few. Even in the collections of the seventy "larger purchasers", pictures by foreign artists are comparatively rare, and they are almost without exception the work of painters who are little known.

In analysing the answers to the question concerning three Australian artists whose pictures members of the Gallery Society would most like to purchase, we used those occupational groups we defined in analysing purchasers, with the exception that instead of using the category "housewives", we made a separate count of all women who replied to our question. Artists' styles were distinguished in the same manner; but since the names of Dobell, Drysdale, and Nolan appeared frequently on members' lists, we not only counted them among "contemporaries" but also made an additional calculation of those who expressed a preference for their work. Our results are as follows:

Many of the patterns of choice and taste which are revealed in the table of pictures purchased by each occupational group are reflected in these figures showing the kind of artists whose work the members of each group would like to purchase. Those in commercial occupations and in the medical profession show a greater liking for "realist" artists than other groups; those in "other professions" and businessmen compose the two groups who most prefer the pictures of contemporary artists. But every occupational group indicates a greater preference for the paintings of contemporary artists than their past purchases suggest, and this variation between the two tables may be interpreted as a general change in taste in favour of "contemporary" artists, whose popularity has grown at the expense of "realist" painters. It may also be noticed that the paintings of the late nineteenth century and the "Heidelberg School" are more popular with each group than their purchases suggest, but most popular with medical practitioners and with businessmen.

The replies to our second question, concerning the artists whose work members would like to purchase, indicates the very general appeal of the pictures of Dobell and Drysdale. Both are painters who have been working for a considerable time, both have been given great publicity in the press, and at recent auctions their pictures have brought record prices. Among the Gallery Society members, those who put the names of Dobell and Drysdale on their list of preferences included those who had bought many pictures and those who had bought none at all; thirty of the seventy larger purchasers listed Dobell as an artist whose work they would like to own, and twenty-seven named Drysdale. Not only do the paintings of these two artists appeal to those who buy or who aspire to buy pictures; we have also remarked that some thousands of reproductions of their paintings have recently been distributed by a popular magazine. A liking for their work would thus appear

TABLE 2

	No. of Replies	Pictures of aboriginal artists	Historical Pictures	Pictures of 'Heidelberg' and late nineteenth century	Pictures of 'Realist' artists	Pictures of contemporary artists	Total score	Drysdale	Dobell	Nolan
Medical Profession ..	38	0 0	0 0	26 22·81%	29 25·44%	59 51·75%	114	16	17	2
Other Professions ..	50	2 1·33%	1 0·67%	23 15·33%	14 9·33%	110 73·33%	150	21	30	10
Semi-Professional..	50	—	4 2·67%	25 16·67%	34 22·67%	87 58·00%	150	12	14	8
Businessmen ..	32	1 1·04%	3 3·13%	20 20·83%	15 15·63%	57 59·38%	96	8	11	9
Commercial Occupations ..	37	1 0·90%	1 0·90%	19 17·12%	38 34·23%	52 46·85%	111	10	10	4
Women	90	1 1·11%	5 1·85%	41 15·91%	69 25·56%	152 56·30%	270	28	36	10
Total	297	7 0·78%	14 1·57%	154 17·28%	199 22·33%	517 58·02%	891	95	118	43

to bridge a wide social and cultural gap in the Australian community. Sometimes, we suspected, those who put the names of these two painters on our
questionnaire did so because theirs were the first to come to mind, or perhaps because they believed that in nominating them they were giving evidence
of their knowledge and discrimination. The esteem in which they are held
reflects rather more than their talent as artists, though undoubtedly it is in
part a response to the kinds of subjects which they generally choose to paint.
Drysdale is best known for the way in which he depicts aboriginals and the
Australian "outback"; Dobell for the way in which he portrays "typical"
Australian types in their robust vulgarity or their sinewy and sinister character.
It is remarkable too that both painters, while they have been admired overseas, have not been dependent on foreign acclaim in establishing their reputations in this country. Nolan's paintings, however, while no less "Australian",
are apparently much less esteemed by those who answered our questionnaire.
There have been fewer opportunities to become familiar with his work, but it
is also possible that many people think of him as an experimental painter, or
find themselves uneasy before his allusive and occasional jesting qualities.

The replies to our question concerning members' preferences among Australian artists did not suggest that there are striking differences of taste
between the sexes. If it is true, as some gallery proprietors suggested, that
men's taste is more conservative than that of women, this is not revealed in
our survey, though it may nevertheless be accepted that women buyers of
pictures are now more numerous than in the past, and moreover, that they
more often buy the works of particular contemporary artists than do men.
Finally, we may say that our survey showed no variations of taste according
to age, either in the purchases of members of the Gallery Society, or their
preferences for particular artists. We had few replies from members under
35 years of age; those who replied were for the most part 45 or more, and we
have no reason to suppose that the older members of the society are more
conservative than younger members.

It is difficult to offer detailed and convincing explanations of the varieties
of taste in pictures which our survey has illustrated. The hypothesis on which
some of our questions were based, that taste is to some degree influenced by
occupation and income, we believe is confirmed by the results which we
obtained, but in commenting further on the social factors which influence
taste we are handicapped by the lack of detailed analysis of the structure of
the Australian community. Moreover, while many attempts have been made
to establish a sociology of art which relates the work of the artist to the society
in which he lives, these theories have been applied to the very broad artistic
movements of the past, and they are of far too general a nature to assist an
interpretation of the kind with which we are concerned.

Among the wealthier groups of picture buyers in our sample, the numbers
of the medical profession were distinguished from businessmen and those in
other professions by the conservatism of their taste. A surgeon, commenting
on the pictures he has purchased in recent years, said that he believed that
the nature of his work and his professional training led him to look for craftsmanship in art and that this he found wanting in a great deal of contemporary
painting. But he agreed that his range of tastes is in general conservative—
in furniture, in motor cars and in dress—and that this was also true of most

187

of his professional friends. Indeed casual observation would suggest that medical men in Australia, members of a strongly corporate profession, choose the accepted and traditional in the general style of living they adopt.

It was to be expected that those we assigned to the group "other professions" should have evinced more radical tastes in painting. This group included a number of university teachers and architects, as well as a few lawyers and engineers. Both university teachers and architects we would suppose to be readier to accept innovation and experiment in the arts than others, though the lawyers who replied to our questionnaire were not a conservative enclave in the general professional group. That the wealthier businessmen should have been almost equally strong as purchasers of "contemporary" art is more difficult to explain. An American writer has suggested that abstract painting, and more particularly "action" painting, is essentially an urban art form, expressing the movement and tensions of modern city life. Further, this kind of painting appeals most to those belonging to high income groups whose wealth has been recently acquired and whose claims to commensurate social status are uncertain or unacknowledged; unable to purchase "old masters" as the rich of past generations purchased them, the new rich have adopted novel art forms as their own. The theory is ingenious but it is difficult to relate to artistic taste in this country. It may be questioned whether we have developed an "urban" art, and furthermore, if the demand for abstract painting in America represents a form of self-assertion on the part of the new rich, we in Australia have never had an *élite* whose exclusiveness has been fortified by the patronage of the arts and the collecting of pictures by the acknowledged masters. Nevertheless, here as in other countries, those whose wealth is new are usually obliged to equip themselves for a social or domestic life which reflects their affluence and changing status, and people of this kind are likely to be susceptible to the persuasions of the supporters of contemporary art forms. But it should be remembered that art dealers are giving great publicity to the speculative advantages of buying pictures, and this aspect of collecting may appeal most to those who are used to calculating risks and who are more alert than others to the fluctuations of a market.

The relative conservatism of the two groups, "other professions" and "commercial occupations" may be related to the fact that these two groups included those who had bought fewest pictures. Not being larger or regular buyers, it is unlikely that they attend the sales and exhibitions as regularly as others, and they have less opportunity to become familiar with the work of contemporary artists than those who are more active purchasers. But these two groups include the less wealthy; those who are less often engaged in rebuilding and refurnishing, those who are less sensitive to changing fashion, and more often content to live among the accumulated possessions of the past.

Those who are selling pictures in Australia today are very confident that the art market in this country will continue to expand as it has done in recent years. This confidence is shared by very many artists who feel assured that their work will find purchasers and patrons. Some of our critics and prophets, however, now suggest that Australian artists will meet increasing competition in this country from their contemporaries overseas, and there are already signs and promises that our isolation will be broken down. Should the wealthier and more discriminating purchasers in this country attempt to build collections giving representation to European and American art we may find that the differences between taste in popular art and taste in the fine arts which we have described in time will be reversed. Popular taste, reflected in the colour prints which are sold in greatest numbers, has hitherto been of an international kind, but it is nevertheless moving a little towards pictures with Australian themes; perhaps in the next decade the art of Australian artists will have turned away from the brolga birds and the "you beaut country" of John Olsen, and art in Australia will cease to be Australian.

13   Drama

THE major contributions to this symposium are concerned with what is manifest in Australian society. This chapter discusses something that has not happened. It is about Australia's failure to produce a culturally significant drama and about some of the reasons which may account for that failure.

One reason which is often advanced is the timidity of Australian entrepreneurs about investing in local plays of unknown box-office appeal when confronted with the strong competition of films and television. This explanation, though just as a description of a cultural problem since the first world war, takes no account of the failure of dramatists before films began to compete with the stage. By 1900 the theatre in Australia was thriving. Sydney and Melbourne each had seven large central theatres—a number commensurate with those of Dublin and Manchester, cities which were then producing, or would soon produce, an indigenous or provincial drama of merit. From the 1880s, painters and writers had begun to produce a lively indigenous art and literature; after 1900 they began to win a widening public for their works. From about 1910 dramatists, often exploiting themes like those which had helped win recognition for Henry Lawson and the other Sydney *Bulletin* writers, strove to develop an indigenous drama. They failed completely to interest entrepreneurs or, in amateur performances, to attract better than coterie audiences. Why, when interest in a national culture was quickening, did entrepreneurs—whose predecessors had commissioned Australian plays —rely more and more on importations and so help to cripple the development of a national drama? It is not sufficient to say that the new plays had serious technical faults. Some, like the one-act plays of Louis Esson, were praised by competent critics such as St. John Ervine when eventually they were published in London; and one engaging three-act comedy, *Mrs. Pretty and the Premier,* by Arthur H. Adams, achieved a run in London. To answer the question we need to examine the nature of drama ("the most social of the arts"), the nature of Australian experiments in drama, and the nature of the society which, except for coteries, ignored these experiments until recently.

There is an essential difference between theatrical entertainment ("theatre") in which performers supply the main attraction, and drama, in which the play itself compels. The appeal of theatre is ancient and universal. Its origins lie in primitive human impulses towards "play", a mimetic impulse involving "dressing up", from which there evolved the theatre of ritual and pageantry; and an exhibitionistic impulse ("showing off") from which there evolved the theatre of fairs and circuses. From both sprang the folk-mummings and other enactments of stories and jokes which contributed towards the development of plays mimed, danced, spoken and sung. All these forms developed in communities both large and small, and appealed to all kinds of men—including, eventually, the Europeans who came to Australia and their descendants.

Australians, despite their climate and vaunted informality, have never been shy about "dressing up" (witness the regular historical pageants celebrated in both small towns and cities) or about "showing off" (witness the floridly theatrical character of surf carnivals or Australian Rules football). From the earliest years of colonization there was hunger for stage entertainment. In the first four decades this was mainly supplied by amateurs.[1] The first professional theatre was opened in Sydney in 1833. Already Australians had developed a passion for sport—a clergyman, John Dunmore Lang, was among the first to denounce it—but the attraction of indoor entertainment was such that in 1838 Sydney's first Theatre Royal, seating nearly 1,000 persons, was replaced by the Royal Victoria, which seated 2,000. After the gold-rushes the entertainment industry boomed—in the 1860s Melbourne's Royal Theatre seated 4,000—and continued to thrive until after the first world war. The cinema first began to compete with stage farces and extravaganzas and with music-halls about 1911, when it was estimated to be attracting a Saturday night audience of about 15,000 in Melbourne.[2] Its popularity forced the theatre industry to contract; by the 1930s it was alleged that Australia had the highest number of cinemas relative to population in the world. Playhouses catered almost exclusively for middle-class audiences. Vaudeville, however, until the arrival of television, continued to flourish in what was claimed to be the biggest chain of variety theatres in the world, the Tivoli circuit established by an immigrant, Harry Rickards, from 1893 onwards. As late as the second world war, comedians like Roy Rene ("Mo") and George Wallace, masters of an indigenous brand of low comedy, tart and topical in its satire, with a bias "offensively Australian", continued to attract mass audiences.

Drama, though owing much to folk theatrical forms and skills, did not develop universally. Its origins were in cities, the Athens of Aeschylus and the London of Shakespeare, where there existed the material resources to build versatile playhouses, the division of labour which enabled professional companies to be trained and maintained, and the permanent audience sophisticated enough to welcome and large enough to support entertainment more elaborate, intelligent and artistic than that which villages enjoyed. In the 17th century, drama, though often depending on the patronage of courts for its legal right to exist, catered also for the taste of urban merchants, master craftsmen and their dependants. From the 18th century, drama, when it thrived, addressed itself to the urban middle class, and particularly the upper middle class. When it did not thrive, as in the England of Wordsworth and Byron (i.e. the early years of the Australian colonies), its decline coincided

---

[1] Watkin Tench in his *Complete Account of the Settlement at Port Jackson* (1793) describes how Farquhar's "The Recruiting Officer" was performed on June 4, 1789, by eleven convicts "in a mud hut, fitted for the occasion".

[2] *The Argus*, 17 January 1911. Quoted by C. M. H. Clark, *Sources of Australian History*.

with the desertion of playhouses by the middle class. Evidently, in examining Australia's failure to produce a significant drama in contrast with its success in organizing a prosperous entertainment industry, we must consider the relationship between the urban middle class and its would-be playwrights. Conflicting attitudes towards nationalism provide one reason for the dramatists' failure; the other important one is their own inability, because of a preoccupation with naturalism, to find appropriate forms to express their nationalist themes effectively.

The American experience suggests that there are broadly four stages in the emergence of a national culture in a society with colonial origins: first, a period of transplantation when the colonists import a parent culture; a period of adaptation when they attempt to modify imported forms to accommodate their novel environment and experience; a period of revolt and experiment when imported forms are rejected as inadequate; and, finally, a period when the self-reliant indigenous culture establishes itself alongside the parent culture as an integral part of a wider civilization. The history of Australian literature offers Kendall and Harpur as characteristic figures in the period of adaptation, Lawson and Furphy in that of revolt, and Patrick White in the fourth period which may now be emerging. The history of Australian drama, such as it is, is out of phase.

The early period of transplantation saw many imports of popular entertainment but few of drama, apart from ranted travesties of Shakespeare.[3] This was, presumably, partly because Australian towns did not have a middle class large enough to support drama; but it was also because London—with its two giant, monopolistic theatres, both of which were compelled by their size to cater for mass tastes in spectacle and melodrama[4]—had little drama to export. The period of literary adaptation in the second half of the century saw some writers (*e.g.* Harpur in *The Bushrangers*) attempt to treat local subjects in the style of the 19th century pseudo-Shakespearian verse drama. More frequently, serious writers who were attracted to the drama wrote verse plays on European historical and romantic themes for publication rather than performance (*e.g.* Alfred Deakin, whose *Quentin Massys*, about a Renaissance Flanders artist, was published in 1875.[5] Writers who were serious only about royalties collaborated with actor-managers in devising local imitations of Drury Lane spectacle or Shoreditch melodrama (*e.g. The Wreck of the Dunbar* and *The Streets of Melbourne*). In the last years of the century imported companies, many of them of high standard, began making frequent appearances. The

[3] Sydney's Theatre Royal was opened with a melodrama, *The Miller and His Men,* preceded by an Irish farce. The Royal Victoria was opened with *Othello,* presented by Conrad Knowles.

[4] Allardyce Nicoll's *British Drama* contains an informative discussion of the reasons for the decay of drama after the rebuilding of Covent Garden and Drury Lane at the end of the 18th century. What the Australian colonies did import from England in the 19th century was a tradition of grandiose theatre-building which was abandoned in London after Covent Garden and Drury Lane lost their monopolistic licences in 1843 and entrepreneurs began to seek middle-class audiences by building intimate playhouses staging sentimental comedies. Today, of the 29 central London theatres which regularly stage plays, only six seat more than 1,000 and sixteen seat less than 800. Most Australian theatres seat more than 1,200, and are in fact not playhouses but music-halls or small opera-houses.

[5] Leslie Rees, *Towards an Australian Drama,* describes *Quentin Massys* in some detail, as well as other early plays mentioned in this chapter.

192

best of them introduced Sydney and Melbourne audiences to the reviving English drama. In 1885 Dion Boucicault dared offer nothing better than the popular and sentimental *The Colleen Bawn,* written by his father in 1859, but in 1893, when he joined forces with the Broughs at the Melbourne Bijou and Sydney Criterion, he staged plays by Robertson, Pinero and Wilde as well as some by Shakespeare, Sheridan and Goldsmith. About the same time Janet Achurch appeared in *A Doll's House.* There could be no clearer evidence that the expanding middle class was becoming a factor in theatrical economics.

This period, the 1890s, famously saw the beginnings of cultural revolt. "During (this) decade", C. Hartley Grattan has written, "there was a great upsurge of creative idealism among the masses and the intellectual classes. Australian literature flourished as never before. The painters, under the stimulus of impressions (*sic*) brought home from Spain by Tom Roberts, for the first time began to get the Australian scene on canvas."[6] In fact, as Vance Palmer and others have pointed out, the artistic stir of the 1890s—reflecting, especially in the *Bulletin* writers, the radical political and social philosophy arising from a developing sense of national identity and national destiny— made only a limited impact on the public. The most popular of the *Bulletin* writers was A. B. Paterson, but his bush ballads were "concerned less with the future than with a romantic pastoral past".[7] Henry Lawson eventually became widely known. But Joseph Furphy's *Such Is Life,* published in 1903, sold only a few hundred copies in the next two decades; C. E. W. Bean, author of the outback classic, *On the Wool Track,* has written that not until 1944 did he hear of Furphy's book, let alone read it.[8] Vance Palmer relates that Roberts, before he went abroad again in 1900, offered his landscapes at only a few guineas compared with the 100 guineas which he asked for *The Young Queen.* Nevertheless, although public interest in "the creative upsurge" grew only slowly (and although the next "generation" of artists, including Henry Handel Richardson, Christopher Brennan and Norman Lindsay, tended once again to look abroad for elements in their inspiration), the Heidelberg painters and the *Bulletin* writers had demonstrated by their rejection of imitations of overseas forms and fashions the possibility of an indigenous culture. After the first world war and the experience of Gallipoli this possibility was widely accepted, and the works of Lawson and Streeton began to be popularly recognized as Australian classics.

Unfortunately for the dramatists, this period of cultural revolt, establishing traditions which persisted as influences in the tepid atmosphere between the wars, coincided with a period of cultural transplantation in the theatre. While writers like Lawson and Furphy, in A. A. Phillips' words, were "setting fiction free from the cage of a middle-class attitude and a middle-class audience",[9] the theatre, emerging from a century of subordination to mass-supported popular entertainment and depending on the support of the emergent middle class, looked exclusively abroad for plays to stage. Louis Esson ("the father

[6] Quoted by Vance Palmer, *The Legend of the Nineties.*

[7] *Ibid.*

[8] From the preface to *On the Wool Track* (republished, Sydney, 1963).

[9] "The Craftsmanship of Henry Lawson", in *The Australian Tradition.* This volume of essays includes a sensitive study of Douglas Stewart's *Ned Kelly,* referred to later in this chapter.

of the Australian drama"),[10] had his first one-act plays staged by amateurs in Melbourne in 1910 and 1911. The second play, *Dead Timber*, skilfully extended to the stage the realism of Henry Lawson; so did his later one-act, and with much less artistic success, his three-act, plays which the Pioneer Players (founded by himself, Stewart Macky and Vance Palmer in 1922, and surviving until 1923) produced in Melbourne. By 1911 entrepreneurs like Alfred Dampier and Bland Holt,[11] who had been accustomed to commission many of their melodramas from local writers,[12] were no longer active. Their mass audience, which once had thrilled to *The Breaking of the Drought* and *Robbery Under Arms,* was beginning to turn to the cinema. On the other hand the new middle-class audience, for whom J. C. Williamson[13] and his

---

[10] Thomas Louis Buvelot Esson (1879-1943) came to Australia from Scotland as a child. He was educated at Scotch College, Melbourne, and the University of Melbourne, became a journalist and visited India in 1908 for *The Lone Hand.* In 1917 he travelled to America and then to the British Isles where he met Yeats, Synge and Lady Gregory. Esson then believed that Australia "was crude, materialistic, Philistine", and offered no opportunities to a writer. Yeats persuaded him that, like the Greeks, he must "keep within his own borders". He returned to Australia in 1921 and then helped found the short-lived, now legendary Pioneer Players. His wife, Hilda Esson, gives an interesting account of him in her introduction to *The Southern Cross and Other Plays.*

[11] Alfred Dampier arrived in Australia in the 1870s, and from then until his retirement about 1905 staged melodramas and from the handsome profits he made from them, occasional seasons of Shakespeare. His great successes were adaptations of *For the Term of His Natural Life* and *Robbery Under Arms.* He presented *All for Gold,* a melodrama which he commissioned from the Australian writer F. R. Hopkins, in London. *All for Gold* was based on the Wandering Jew myth. In 1898 he also took *Robbery Under Arms* to London. Bland Holt, his great rival, arrived in Australia in 1876 and opened his very successful Australian career by presenting burlesques at the Victoria Theatre, Sydney. His later fame was derived from his spectacular productions of melodramas including *The Breaking of the Drought,* by himself. He retired in 1909.

[12] Most of them were hacks. Playwrights with artistic ambitions went abroad. The most successful of these was Haddon Chambers (1860-1921) who persuaded Beerbohm Tree in 1881 to play in his drama, *Captain Swift.* It was Swift, turned gentleman, who coined the phrase "the long arm of coincidence". Chambers continued to write successfully for the West End until 1917. His later plays all had English themes. It is a characteristic irony of Australian stage history that *Captain Swift* was one of the contemporary English plays presented by Dion Boucicault in his brilliant seasons in the nineties. No other Australian playwright has had the consistently successful career abroad that Chambers enjoyed. Those who have had one or two plays successfully produced in London include W. J. Turner (*The Man Who Ate the Popomack*), Alex Coppel (*I Killed the Count*), Hugh Hastings (*Seagulls over Sorrento*) and Ralph Peterson (*The Square Ring*). Of the playwrights who have had successes in Australia since the second world war, Sumner Locke-Elliott is an American citizen and Ray Lawler and Alan Seymour have not returned to Australia since their plays, *Summer of the Seventeenth Doll* and *The One Day of the Year,* were staged in London.

[13] James Cassius Williamson (1845-1913), an American actor, came to Australia with his wife, Maggie Moore, in *Struck Oil!,* a comic melodrama which he bought from a Californian miner and re-wrote to serve his own talents. He scored a great success which he repeated in London. He returned to Australia in 1879, playing Sir Joseph Porter in *H.M.S. Pinafore* less than a year after its first London success. Few other Australian showmen have equalled his flair for recognizing and exploiting a box-office success. After 1882, when he entered a partnership—which lasted nine years—with Arthur Garner and George Musgrove, he organized Australia's leading entertainment organization. The many famous artists and personalities whom he brought out included Sarah Bernhardt in 1891 (and immediately after her, the prize-fighter John L. Sullivan in a play written to exploit his talents). He died in Paris. Following mergers with other entrepreneurs and the retirement of his partners, J. C. Williamson Pty. Ltd. in 1931 came under the control of E. J. Tait and his three brothers and then, following losses during the depression, under that of the New Zealand chain store organization of Sir John McKenzie who invested in it for the real estate which it owned. For the financial history and ramifications of J. C. Williamson Ltd., see "The Musicale Score" in *Nation,* 4 May 1963.

successors catered, had tastes markedly different not only from those of the Bland Holt audience, but from those of the country-wide and largely country-based audience whom Lawson and the *Bulletin* writers addressed. Esson and his friends were not the only dramatists to fail. Arthur H. Adams[14] published three plays with local neo-Shavian themes in 1914. The best of these, *The Wasters,* exposing the hypocrisy of a city store-owner, achieved production only by the amateur Adelaide Repertory Company (founded by Bryceson Treharne in 1908). *Mrs. Pretty and the Premier,* a political comedy, though produced in London in 1916, gained only an amateur performance in Melbourne. Apparently J. C. Williamson's new audience, though delighted by Julius Knight in *Arms and the Man,* unlike Shaw's middle-class London audience had not sufficient confidence in its own credit or in the stability of its society to enjoy criticism.

Of course there were other, aesthetic, reasons for the dramatists' failure. Their temper was that of revolt, but their methods were those of adaptation. Their attempts to apply the naturalistic methods of the early Abbey Theatre playwrights (whom some of them, including Esson, had met)[15] to the epic themes of the outback were analogous to Kendall's attempt to apply a Keatsian vocabulary to the austere Australian bush. Why did Esson and his successors in the 1920s and 1930s, while seeking to attract city audiences, turn to the bush for their subjects? Presumably, since they were nationalists seeking like the Abbey playwrights what was distinctive in their country, the answer lay in part in the nature of cities dominated by what Francis Adams had called "the appalling strength of British civilization".[16] Even city-dwellers deplored the lack of national individuality in their surroundings: a contributor to the *Sydney Morning Herald* in 1907 criticized the "civilization in the Australian cities" as "old, hoary-headed, decrepit" and pointed to the "civilization up country as "more or less *a new thing*" where the people were "vigorous and healthy and strong".[17] But the answer lay also in the nature of the artistic problems confronting them.

A South African, Dan Jacobson, writing in 1962[18] of the conditions which inhibit literary activity in the British Dominions and colonies, has said that "for anybody with a literary bent who grows up" reading a literature which is about other countries, "the consciousness of a gap or gulf between his reading and the world around him . . . produces even in children . . . an almost metaphysical preoccupation with 'reality'. Which is 'real'—the world of books or the world around one?" This search for "reality" can be seen as a central preoccupation of artists in colonial periods of cultural revolt. Its artistic results include a romantic resort to descriptions of local nature. It produces an art tending towards naturalism. But naturalistic playwriting, using Ibsen's realistic "well-made play" with its "fourth-wall" convention as

---

[14] Arthur Henry Adams (1872-1936) was a New Zealander who became "literary secretary" to J. C. Williamson in 1898. He left Williamson to become a journalist. He was editor of the Red Page of the *Bulletin* from 1906 to 1909, and later edited *The Lone Hand* and the Sydney *Sun*.

[15] For further discussion of the Australian playwrights' incomplete understanding of the Abbey playwrights' ideals, see my introduction to the Penguin *Three Australian Plays* (1963). The volume includes *Ned Kelly* and *The One Day of the Year.*

[16] From *Australian Essays,* quoted in *Sources of Australian History.*

[17] From the *Sydney Morning Herald,* 8 June 1907; quoted, *ibid.*

[18] *Encounter,* April 1962.

a model, could not accommodate the scene, or the epic themes of wandering and endurance of the outback, and its stories and mythology. In a typical play by Ibsen or Synge the audience look *in* upon a domestic scene of drama or comedy between characters representative of a tightly-knit society. The Australian realists used their methods for plays which looked *out* upon a scene dominated by a vast landscape. Conflict in that landscape was not between men but between man and his environment. It could not realistically be isolated in time in terms of dilemma and *dénouement* as in an Ibsen play in which the action—though it may have been developing for years (e.g. *John Gabriel Borkman*)—is compressed into a few hours of crisis. Because the antagonist in the bush was the bush itself, conflict developed episodically, through flood and fire and drought and good seasons and bad seasons, and it persisted as long as men endured it. Moreover, the characters representative of the bush were not members of a village or a town, with their social relationships and tensions, as were the characters of Ibsen and Synge; they were vagrants enjoying only casual relationships with each other and employing, for that reason, language expressing idiomatically, and monotonously, the ideas and experiences which its speakers had in common rather than, idiosyncratically, the differences of mind and temperament on which drama thrives. In the event, Esson and Vance Palmer produced a few excellent one-act plays *illustrating* aspects of outback life. In three-act plays, attempting to *dramatize* the outback through conflict, Esson tended to substitute contrived human violence—communicated through the impoverished and inflexible idioms of bush speech—for the violence of the land, and produced melodramas almost as unconvincing as those of Dampier and Holt.

The absence of "established and highly-developed social forms" (one of the inhibiting conditions of which Jacobson writes) was not peculiar to the outback. The cities also lacked such forms. D. H. Lawrence noted as late as 1922:[19] "The minute the night begins to go down, even the towns, even Sydney, which is huge, begins to feel unreal, as if it were only a day-time imagination, and in the night it did not exist. That is a queer sensation: as if life here had never *entered* in: as if it were sprinkled over and the land lay untouched. . . . " What Lawrence was describing was a city situated on the edge of a continent, a port housing a population existing in the main as middlemen—money-changers and porters—between the producers of the country's wealth, in the interior, and their markets abroad. The middle class of such a city did not derive its main wealth from secondary industry but from the industry of others. Its dynamic element consisted of bankers, speculators, wool-buyers, wheat-traders, importers and exporters, ship-owners and retailers—descendants of the *arrivistes* with whom Richard Mahony rubbed shoulders when he first became prosperous, men who regarded Australia as a vast paddock on the outskirts of the civilization of Europe. Until after the first world war industrialists were few and relatively unimportant. America, before its period of cultural revolt by Melville, Whitman, Twain and others, had already developed, from the discoveries of the British industrial revolution, thriving secondary industries based on local materials, local experiments and inventions, and locally improvised patterns of manpower organization.

---

[19] In a letter to his sister-in-law. From *The Collected Letters of D. H. Lawrence*.

Around such industries, as historians like Hofstadter[20] have shown, there matured distinctive urban economies which in turn produced distinctive responses from intellectuals and artists. But the secondary industries which existed in Australia before about 1930 were derived from overseas industrial techniques and models. Like the cities' social forms and institutions they were imported from the societies upon whose markets the country as a whole depended. In their origins and in their dependence on overseas countries for assistance ranging from spare parts to technical advice, Australia's early experiments in industrialization tended only to reinforce the cities' orientation towards Europe and their alienation, as far as the practical matters of living were concerned, from the "civilization up country".

This alienation began in the 19th century after town and country, in alliance, had sought and won political independence. Thereafter the interests of the city middlemen naturally diverged from those of the producers inland. City folk no doubt admired all that was romantic about the bushman; as C. E. W. Bean has said,[21] they were proud of the "bush arts", the horsemanship for instance of "the man from Snowy River". But they scorned a nationalistic culture derived from the bush and its legend, and they deeply suspected the radical, reformist faith which helped to organize shearers and miners into militant trade unions challenging their mastery of the economy. Businessmen, as they won more and more economic independence from London and Bradford, embraced not nationalism but Imperialism as a faith. As the Labour Party emerged amid the turmoil of the 1890s, the urban Liberal Party, its appetite for reform diminished, looked defensively towards alliance with the squatter conservatives. By the Edwardian decade, when Esson began writing plays, the urban middle class was in no mood for either the old melodramas, with their reminders of convicts and bushrangers and an unsavoury past, or for the new bush realism. The only bush plays which succeeded with city audiences in the first half of the century were *On Our Selection* and its successors, travesties of outback life.

These features—an artistically unconvincing, naturalistic bush drama and apathetic London-oriented city audiences—persisted until after the second world war. From the 1920s, amateur "little" theatres began building small audiences for local playwrights. From the 1930s, the Australian Broadcasting Commission produced many locally written plays. Until the appearance in 1943, however, of Douglas Stewart's verse drama, *Ned Kelly*—a brilliant experiment—radio had no noticeable success in helping playwrights to solve the technical problems posed by the outback from which, stubbornly, they continued to take most of their subjects. Commercial entrepreneurs, deprived of mass audiences by films and radio, found by painful trial and error that musical comedies whether newly imported or revived paid the best dividends, so that drama, even as an importation, had declining cultural importance. Many talented performers (*e.g.* Judith Anderson, Robert Helpmann, Cyril Ritchard, Cecil Kellaway and Coral Browne) went abroad.

The change, such as it is, became apparent in the 1950s. It had four main features: a turning by playwrights from the bush to the cities for subjects; the

[20] Hofstadter's *The Age of Reform* is particularly interesting on the emergence of an urban culture.
[21] In his discussion of the Anzac archetype in his war history volume, *The Story of Anzac*.

commercial success of some of these urban plays; the investment of public money in the patronage of the theatre arts; and a resumption of theatre-building.[22] This revival of interest in the drama and new concern for an indigenous drama coincided with a growing middle class interest in a national culture. Presumably this change was due to changing middle class attitudes towards nationalism. These, one supposes, were at least partly due to the development, before and during the war, of a more diversified economy and of a quickly expanding secondary industry. The cities which, a generation earlier, seemed to Lawrence to be "sprinkled over" the edge of the continent began to put down economic roots. More and more of their inhabitants depended less and less on the enterprise of the bush or on overseas markets. This process coincided with the weakening of real and sentimental ties with Britain. The expansion of industry produced increasing competition between local and British manufacturers. The depression, for which "foreign devils" could be blamed, left to employers as well as unemployed a legacy of distrust of overseas financial institutions and their policies. During the war the fall of Singapore, the quarrelsome exchange of cables between John Curtin and Winston Churchill over the British plan to divert an A.I.F. division from the direct defence of Australia to Burma, and the greater importance of the United States to the defence of Australia, all helped to erode the traditional image of Britain as protector. The post-war breakdown of British imperialism destroyed the political, and some of the sentimental, basis of Anglo-orientation. The compulsions towards real, as against formal, political and economic independence, feeble in the 1920s, gathering strength in the 1930s, were widely acknowledged after the war. It is not surprising that the years which saw Australian governments of both Left and Right seek to develop an independent foreign policy, culminating in the ANZUS Pact from which Britain was excluded, also saw increasing popular sympathy with efforts by cliques and coteries to establish the cultural forms and institutions through which the search for national self-expression could proceed. One of the most conspicuous forms of a nation's culture is its theatre, as Britain demonstrated in the later 1940s when it sent its Old Vic and Stratford-upon-Avon classical companies to tour Australia. In due course the call for a "national theatre" (a catch-cry which begged far more cultural questions than it pretended to answer) began to attract a good deal of influential middle class support.

Those who assumed leading roles in this movement, mainly businessmen, though seeking to promote a national culture, nevertheless looked abroad for models of the institutions through which it might be imposed on Australia. In 1947 Tyrone Guthrie, the eminent British director, came out as guest of the British Council, which had been requested to provide an expert who could examine the local scene and advise the Prime Minister, J. B. Chifley, about the establishment of a "national theatre". His report produced no immediate result. He has written:[23]

---

[22] The most ambitious projects are Sydney's Opera House and Melbourne's Cultural Centre. Other new theatres include the Playhouse in Perth and the New Fortune, a reconstruction of the Elizabethan Fortune Theatre, at the University of Western Australia; the Union Theatre at the University of Adelaide; the Union Theatre at the University of Sydney and the (temporary) Old Tote Theatre at the University of New South Wales; a playhouse at Wagga; and a still uncompleted complex of auditoria at Canberra.
[23] Tyrone Guthrie, *A Life in the Theatre.*

... it was no surprise to find Australia an extraordinary mine of talent. There was at that time no satisfactory organization for its expression, no considerable public appreciation to develop it, and little enlightened criticism to lead the public. My report to the Prime Minister suggested that the time to *build* a national theatre had not yet arrived. But it suggested several practical ways of developing Australian talent and taste as a preliminary. It was my view that before spending great sums on a building, a much more moderate sum should be spent on equipping the human material of a national theatre.

In fact, he suggested the formation of a permanent touring company or companies to provide experience for players and to develop loyal audiences for a local drama. Shortly after his report was received, a Liberal government took office. The report itself was unpopular with those who had long campaigned for a national theatre and with the public generally. Guthrie himself commented later:[24]

> The suggestion that Australian taste might not be entirely perfect and that Australia might, in certain matters, be a decade or two behind certain other communities, aroused a tremendous head of steam. Persons who would not otherwise have given a snap of their fingers to support a national theatre felt a passionate eagerness for Australia to possess such an institution, and a passionate rage against the sneering, bloody Pommy who dared suggest that the time was not quite yet.

This "head of steam" found its outlet in 1954, following the enthusiasm aroused by the first tour of Queen Elizabeth, when a group of businessmen headed by the Governor of the Commonwealth Bank, Dr. H. C. Coombs, launched the Elizabethan Theatre Trust[25] with a publicly subscribed capital of £80,000, mainly from business houses, and with promises from the Federal and State governments and some city councils of annual subsidies amounting to about £100,000.

The Trust's proclaimed objective was to foster an indigenous drama, opera and ballet. Dr. Coombs expressed the idealism behind its formation:

> Australian life, splendid as it is in its physical and material aspects, is deficient in many of those things which mark the civilized community. How many Australians visiting abroad have sighed after having experienced and participated in the magnificent presentation of some theatrical masterpiece —thinking how good it would be if in Australia, too, we could have a vigorous, mature Australian theatre. . . . And even more splendid if, at the same time, we could create an environment in which the truly creative artists among us—the playwrights, the composers, the choreographers, many of them now mute and inglorious—should come to flower. . . . This is a great Australian venture, a piece of practical idealism in keeping with the Australian character.[26]

---

[24] *Ibid.*

[25] John Douglas Pringle, who was then editor of the *Sydney Morning Herald*, states in *Australian Accent* that the organization of the Trust also owed much "to the ideas put forward privately by Ernest Burbridge, the British Council representative in Australia from 1952 to 1957".

[26] It is fair to explain that Dr. Coombs' inspirational statements of intentions were made in a broadcast at the beginning of the Trust's public appeal for funds.

The venture had several novel features. Australia's first large-scale experiment in public patronage of the theatre arts assumed the form of a private company not answerable for its expenditure to any of the tax-raising bodies which financed its operations, and with a board of thirty members consisting mainly of businessmen with a sprinkling of academics. Its model was the Arts Council of Great Britain, a body responsible to the British Treasury, through which the government channels its subsidies to long-founded institutions, such as the Old Vic, Covent Garden and Sadler's Wells, which serve an identifiable public and its needs. Unlike the Arts Council, the Trust had a federal constitution with each of its members sitting primarily as the representative of his state.

From these features there flowed results inappropriate to a realistic attempt to foster arts which elsewhere have matured from city-based institutions. The Arts Council model was inappropriate because from the beginning the Trust —"a great Australian venture" which immediately employed an Englishman, Hugh Hunt, as its executive director—largely ignored the long-struggling and admittedly amateurish "little" theatres and other institutions which already existed. It followed logically from this decision that its first task should be the establishment of the new institutions—theatre companies and an opera company—which could develop a theatre culture. This became Hunt's ambition; but his task became increasingly difficult as the representatives of the smaller states—some of them with scattered populations smaller than those of English and American provincial cities which rely utterly on London and New York for their theatrical culture—demanded conspicuous, parochial returns for their contributions. Since the Trust's resources were too small to permit the simultaneous establishment of companies in all states, the result was increasing compromise. The opera organization which came into being from the merging of earlier state bodies was disbanded, and a policy of presenting biennial tours by companies assembled *ad hoc,* and dispersed after each tour, was substituted for the original grand aim of creating an indigenous opera. In Melbourne the Trust fruitfully subsidized the Union Repertory Theatre, a local university initiative; in Sydney, at the large suburban theatre which it leased (on the model of the Old Vic?) an attempt was made to establish a permanent drama company, but this was abandoned after the smaller states' representatives objected to the losses—some £67,000 over two years—which it incurred. Following Hunt's departure in 1961, the Trust reverted to a policy of assembling impermanent companies for occasional tours. After eight years' heavy losses it became evident that these policies, aimed at serving up drama and opera as commodities to be consumed by widely dispersed audiences whose taste for them was shown to be capricious, were not building audiences, were not training or maintaining artists, and were only randomly serving the theatre arts. Hugh Hunt expressed his views about these vacillating policies before he left Australia. Emphasizing the need for institutions, he declared that theatre "needs solid roots, it needs careful planning. . . . It is not—and I cannot say this too strongly—a hobby to indulge the surplus energy of people whose main interests are centred in other activities, or who seek easy access to social position."[27] He also rejected in the formation of a theatre culture the usefulness of "the shop-

27 From *The Making of the Australian Theatre.*

200

keeping mentality—to pursue what appears to be the majority taste and to provide a variety of plays which follow this fickle will o' the wisp in the hope that one success will pay for many failures, much as the gambler who backs the favourite". The point of these remarks[28] sharpened by two years of financial and, in the main, artistic failure after Hunt's departure, was recognized in 1963 when the Trust, with trebled financial grants to help it cope with the additional responsibility of a national ballet company, embraced under Stefan Haag new policies aimed at the support of regional theatre institutions brought into being by local initiatives (though sometimes at Trust prompting) to serve identifiable community cultural needs. This, at the moment of writing, seems a realistic approach to the problems of developing the organizational context in which a theatre culture may grow organically.

The sociological interest in these vacillations is in the way they illuminate the middle class attitude to a national culture—the middle class preoccupation with the conspicuous culture of Britain and its standards and judgments; the businessman's amateur approach to art; his concept of art as a commodity to be manufactured and distributed; his expectation that an under-capitalized enterprise would be capable of paying artists and creative talents even the modest rewards which he regards as their deserts. Robin Boyd comments:

> . . . constructive talent of the kind essential to the initiation of ideas in all fields is given lower rewards, proportionately to the country's richness, than almost anywhere else. While every man who prints a magazine and every boy on the corner who sells it receives fair payment for his labours, the man whose writing appears in the magazine is often lucky if he clears the cost of his paper and postage. Australian newspapers with respectable circulations—half a million or so—are in the habit of paying the national oracle on any subject five or six guineas for a special article. The highest paid Australian actors or actresses receive, while a season lasts, less than a competent carpenter is paid continuously. . . . [29]

Above all, there is the grandiosity of the cultural forms envisaged, the result, one feels, of a materialistic philosophy impatient with the need for the organic growth of art and its institutions from regional, realistically modest roots.

If the leaders of the middle class audience tended still to look abroad for models of institutions for a national theatre culture, so also did many of the new generation of playwrights seek to impose the forms and methods of English and American realists upon their Australian subjects. The significant change in play-writing has been from country to city subjects and from an orthodox acceptance of the bush legend to criticism from urban points of view of many of its assumptions. Sumner Locke-Elliott's *Rusty Bugles*, which enjoyed considerable popular commercial success throughout Australia in 1948-49, comically described the boredom of mainly urban characters with their life in an army camp in the Northern Territory: though not questioning

[28] Criticisms of Trust policies were summarized in the *Sydney Morning Herald* in an article by a special correspondent on 17 June 1961. An eloquent reply by the executive director, Neil Hutchison, published by the *Herald* on 20 June 1961, pointed out the difficulties of providing drama and opera in six states on an income derived from subsidies amounting to 2½d. a year per head of population. For other criticisms of Trust policies, see *Nation*, "The Case for Trust-busting", 16 December 1961, and "The Bit Players", 12 August 1961.

[29] Robin Boyd, *The Australian Ugliness.*

the heroism of the "digger", it gleefully stripped away something of the glamour which orthodoxy associated with his uniform. Ray Lawler's *Summer of the Seventeenth Doll,* which had an unprecedented success under Trust management in 1955 and which subsequently ran for nearly a year in London, questioned the social validity of mateship and exposed illusions engendered by the traditional veneration of the "bush arts". Richard Beynon's *The Shifting Heart,* which had a comparable success in Australia in 1957-8, studied an Italian migrant family's tribulations in a Melbourne slum and assailed Australian xenophobia. *The One Day of the Year,* by Alan Seymour, first produced in 1961, used controversy between father and son about Anzac Day and its ideals as a departure for criticism of Australian isolationism and anti-intellectualism. Patrick White's *The Season at Sarsaparilla* (1962) included an acid commentary on suburban materialism and conformism, and yet another unfavourable comment on mateship.

These plays (with *The Season at Sarsaparilla,* which is anti-naturalistic, as an exception) represent a growth of realism about what the realistic drama can achieve convincingly. Technically, they represent a very marked advance. Nevertheless, they share inadequacies with the bush plays. Many of the new playwrights are still preoccupied with the differences between Australians and other kinds of men (compare O'Casey, who takes the distinctiveness of his Irish characters for granted and dramatizes the differences between men). Three of these plays, and many others less assured, are set in working-class or slum suburbs because, one feels, working-class characters permit comic exploitation of the vernacular and of the "dinkum" Australian-ness of the scene—and because slum life makes more plausible the introduction of violence as an often arbitrary method of achieving a climax or *dénouement.* The murder which is the central event in *The Shifting Heart* would be difficult to make credible if the author had chosen Kew instead of Collingwood as the scene of his study of xenophobia. This frequent resort to low life as a setting for violence, though not peculiar to Australian playrights, seems to indicate an almost desperate response both to audience apathy (no other play has had the success of those by Lawler and Beynon) and to the "undramatic", non-violent and homogeneous character of the suburbs in which the great majority of Australians live. Even Patrick White introduced a working-class family, a sanitary collector and his wife, into lower middle class Sarsaparilla. Their presence, living next to "a minor executive" and a shop salesman and their families, offers a valid comment, perhaps, on the homogeneity of suburbia and the social effects of a uniform "high standard of living". What is unexpected is that this family generates most of the play's warmth and that their crisis, dramatically overshadowing all else in the play, provides its suspense. The resort to low life also surely indicates a contemporary example of the "almost metaphysical preoccupation with 'reality' " of which Jacobson has written: the search for "reality" constrains the dramatists to write naturalistically, the naturalism produces genre studies of "dinkum Australians", and an injection of violence becomes necessary to jolt the genre studies into dramatic movement. Yet one has only to consider the leading features of the contemporary affluent urban Australian community to see that this preoccupation with naturalism is leading playwrights away from reality as it exists. An Alf Cook, in Seymour's play, or a Clarrie, in Beynon's, though embodying roughly recognizable Australian attitudes, and therefore acceptable in the theatre as colourful archetypes, are in fact of only marginal social significance: much more significant are Jan's prosperous father, who never appears, and Hughie Cook and Jan herself, university students, whom Seymour—critical opinion seems to agree—was quite unable to endow with life.

Why is it that even the best of contemporary playwrights (again, with the exception of Patrick White) seem unwilling to dramatize the tensions which exist in the main body of reasonably educated, reasonably articulate, affluent, suburban, middle class people? There are tensions between what John Pringle[30] has called the old, privileged class, which "was inherited, more or less intact, from England" and which is now "rapidly fading", and the "new-rich"; between the generation which had either a nationalistic or an Imperialistic faith and the new one which is "internationalist"; between conformists and intellectuals, with their sense of alienation from the culture; between masculine careerists and the educated women who feel excluded from public life. The results of these and many other tensions may not be drama as theatrical as that provided by violence (unless juvenile delinquency be considered), but they could be the subject of comedy, the kind of comedy which most of the best dramatists from Jonson and Molière to Chekhov and Shaw produced in response to the significant pressures and movements in their essentially urban, middle class societies. Consider the dramatic riches yielded, from *Le Bourgeois Gentilhomme* to *Pygmalion,* by the results of social mobility such as we see in Australia, the efforts of the newly rich to be accepted into "society" and the still more strenuous efforts of members of "society" to marry their sons and daughters to the newly rich. Consider the ambiguous comedy which Chekhov distilled from the spectacle of three provincial sisters and their yearning for "Moscow", or the "black" comedy Ibsen found in the frustrations of the house-bound intellectual, Hedda Gabler. One would not wish local authors merely to copy these playwrights. But the search for "reality", for archetypes, and for rather hackneyed public issues (colour, immigrants and other "problems") seems to be diverting them from the areas —the private homes and private lives of articulate human beings—where drama most obviously resides and upon which dramatists from Shakespeare (*Hamlet*) to Arthur Miller (*Death of a Salesman*) have seized.

Are playwrights, aware of the possible hostility of the middle class to comedy at its expense, deliberately playing safe? If they are, they can cite the hostility which *The Season at Sarsaparilla* aroused in certain quarters as a kind of commercial justification, although truckling to that hostility must eventually involve artistic abdication.[31] Audiences will not become more

---

[30] J. D. Pringle, *Australian Accent.*

[31] After the first performance of *The Season at Sarsaparilla* in Sydney in May 1963, the *Daily Mirror,* having thoughtfully sent a reporter to the premiere to supplement the notice by its drama critic, decorated the streets of Sydney with a placard declaring "NEW PLAY STINKS". After the Trust production in Sydney in July 1962, of *The Ham Funeral* (Patrick White's first play, written in London in 1947), Mrs Marcel Dekyvere, a well-known member of Sydney society and a member of the board of the Trust, informed the readers of her weekly article in the *Sunday Telegraph* that she found it "in very bad taste with its sordidness and bad language". In 1961 the Governors of the Adelaide Festival refused to accept *The Ham Funeral* as a Festival attraction. It was later produced by the Adelaide University Theatre Guild and was highly praised by the critics of the *Sydney Morning Herald,* the Adelaide *Advertiser, Nation* and the *Bulletin.* In 1959 the Governors of the Adelaide Festival also refused to accept *The One Day of the Year.*

sophisticated if they are invited only to laugh at characters and situations remote from their experience. On the other hand, do the playwrights—the best of whom (Patrick White again is the exception) are writers only for the theatre—have the knowledge or the critical awareness which can show them dramatic themes in the "undramatic" suburbs? Ray Lawler's *The Piccadilly Bushman* with its comic-strip cartooning of upper middle class characters; George Kerr's *Hunger of a Girl*, with its alcoholic father, gigolo-supporting mother and delinquent daughter; and Alan Seymour's unconvincing Hughie and Jan—all these suggest a gap between the professional theatre-writer and the real audience whom he is trying to interest. Dot Cook, the mother in *The One Day of the Year*, though dramatically vivid in her staunchness and sanity, remains virtually an observer of the conflict between father and son, characters who cannot communicate with each other. Another chapter in this book cites evidence which suggests that in fact the mother is the decision-maker in the typical Australian home and that it is more likely to be mother and father who cannot communicate with each other than parent and child.[32] The reader can decide for himself whether Dot Cook remains convincing (her theatrical effectiveness is not in doubt) in the light of that evidence. What the evidence does indicate is the possibilities for dramatic exploration which exist in the Australian family, a subject which has hardly been seriously discussed on the stage since the success of *The Shifting Heart* persuaded playwrights to view the home primarily as an arena in which public issues could be dramatized.

These attitudes, of playwrights adapting fashionable realistic methods, of local genre studies, and of businessmen attempting to impose imported cultural models, suggest some lack still of national confidence and of critical self-awareness in the Australian urban community. It seems probable, whatever conclusions may be drawn about the other arts in Australia, that the drama—despite the original successes of Esson, and (in one play only) of Lawler, and despite the varying kinds of revolt against naturalism by Douglas Stewart and Patrick White—is still in its period of adaptation.

[32] See D. L. Adler on "Matriduxy in the Australian Family", above.

A. F. DAVIES, S. ENCEL and others

14   The Mass Media

PROVINCIAL and monopolized—two words sum up the structure of the Australian Press, and its offshoots. But it is a task, indeed, to characterize its performance and the peculiar satisfactions and dissatisfactions it affords. Our discussion will be critical and discursive, seizing on selected topics, passing many others by. The dissemination of ideas, however, is our focus; we take for granted a dependable flow of entertainment.

The chapter is a composite; it was put together by the editors with the assistance of several other people working in journalism, radio and television, who for professional reasons wish to be anonymous. Apart from the annual Arthur Norman Smith lectures in journalism, hardly read outside the profession, accounts of the mass media rarely reflect the first-hand attitudes of those working in them. We have tried to combine these with the sociological analysis of outsiders.

I

How much is the thinking of Australians limited by factors stemming from the sheer economics of the newspaper world?

The daily press is privately owned; television and radio have a small public sector. Pressures towards the concentration of press ownership into fewer and fewer hands, economic in the main and seemingly ineluctable[1]—though personal ambition has played a part, too—have not brought any efforts at public (or governmental) remedy. The twenty-one separately owned metropolitan daily newspapers of the early 1920s have shrunk to fifteen, controlled (or influenced through investment) by seven companies. Three out of every four newspapers sold in Australia are printed by the *Herald & Weekly Times* or the John Fairfax companies. Only Sydney, Melbourne and Canberra offer a choice of morning papers. The accompanying chart shows the present pattern of ownership.

Concentration of ownership may mean much or little depending on how the owners behave. In ordinary commodity production there may indeed be positive advantages in monopoly. The newspaper industry developed in a period when papers were small enterprises started by groups whose main capital was ideas. While they were numerous it was possible to claim that

---

[1] See W. M. Corden, "The Economics of the Australian Press" (M.Com. thesis, Melbourne, 1951) and "Towards a History of the Australian Press", *Meanjin*, vol. 15, no. 2, 1956.

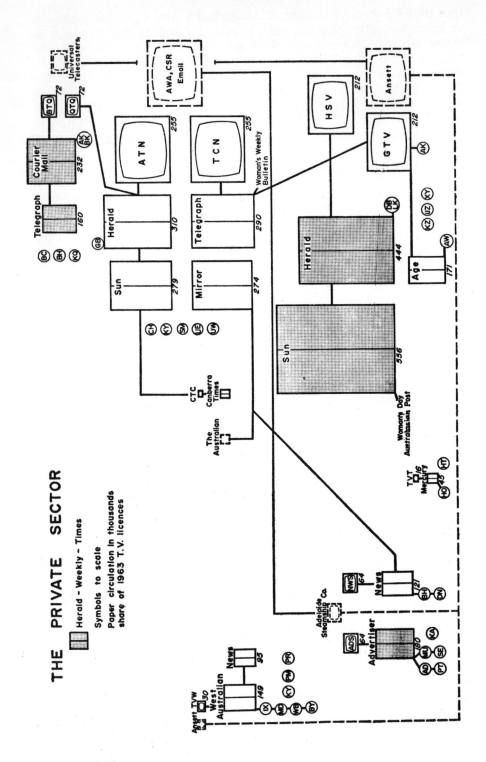

THE PRIVATE SECTOR

Herald – Weekly – Times

Symbols to scale

Paper circulation in thousands
share of 1963 T.V. licences

their rivalry guaranteed freedom of information to readers, and of expression to journalists. Proprietorial control, however, of undertakings so big or so entrenched that competition is ruled out is clearly a public danger. The creation of the Press Council in Britain is one significant reaction: the self-denying Trust form of management perhaps a more hopeful one. The captive audience of the single firm (now the rule in Australian cities) who cannot be liberated except by unforeseen advances in technology is not a happy sight. Their plight is hardly alleviated by the fact that proprietors in modern conditions tend to be persons distinguished only by the accident of their possession of wealth rather than men of definite outlook. (For some individual profiles see Section II.)

The advent of television opened a choice between decisively loosening the grip of the private proprietors and confirming it. Rather alarming expectations about the new medium's power to persuade were current. But the challenge fell on an apathetic and cynical public, the Labour opposition proved incapable of agreeing on a policy, and the Government, failing to see the advantages of the British commercial television scheme in which *stations* were owned and operated by a public authority and *programmes* provided by private companies under contract, simply handed the press proprietors the new toy on a platter, while undertaking to provide a minority non-commercial supplement.[2] Section IV attempts to characterize the service that has developed, and the dissatisfactions and efforts at public remedy provoked.

Abstract defects in the structure of press ownership and control take on flesh when read as the discomforts of the profession of journalism in Australia. It is not altogether pleasant to belong to a dowdy profession, low in social prestige, unable to recruit first-raters or to retain mature members against the lures of "public relations", or to give to its most gifted and senior members the full sense of accomplishment.[3] But one should watch in the account that follows for the "points of pressure", too—the places where a concerted heave, or even a dashing solo run, could turn the tables.

II

Until 1964 at least, the Australian press had not been a tremendously exciting or vital institution, throbbing with intellectual life. It is not, of course, the only institution in this country about which this could be said. The press has not even shown great vitality by its own historical standards. It is ironical that the Melbourne *Age,* for example, owes its existence to a man who, if he were alive today, would despise the *Age* as it is, and would certainly think about starting another paper in opposition as he did a century ago. Newspapers often go safe in this way when they pass into managerial and executive hands in the second and third generations. Whether one agreed or disagreed with David Syme, an intolerant and despotic personality, he gave his newspaper a character possessed by no newspaper in Australia today. Similarly, it is interesting to go back to the early issues of the Sydney *Herald* when it

---

[2] See Leicester Webb, "The Social Control of Television", *Public Administration*, vol. 19, no. 3, 1960. The granting of the *third* commercial licences in four cities to non-newspaper capitalists may mark a turning point in the industry's development.

[3] See W. S. Holden, *Australia Goes to Press*, Ch. 11, for details of the imperfections of the cadetship system; and W. J. Hudson, "Metropolitan Daily Journalism in Australia" (M.A. thesis, University of Melbourne, 1963) for an interesting discussion of stages of the journalist's career. Hudson notes (p. 75) signs of hereditary recruitment.

was a weekly and not yet the *Sydney Morning Herald*. The leading articles of that time are striking in their freshness and boldness.

Discussion of the Australian press is frequently conducted in terms of an implicit or explicit contrast with the British press. This is sometimes beside the point for economic reasons. The obvious point of contrast is the absence here of a distinct separation between "quality" papers and mass circulation papers. This can largely be explained by the wide scatter of a relatively small population in Australia. The London *Times* is published in an enormous metropolis, is read nationally, and has a considerable number of readers outside the United Kingdom. Even so, its circulation is less than 300,000. This figure should be divided not by five, which is the population quotient as between the two countries, but a higher figure which is due to the practical problems of distribution in a scattered population. The divisor might then have to be ten, and the result puts the possibility of such a journal for Australia out of the question. One of the things about the Australian press which irritates the observer is the relative sparsity of publications, but this also is practically inevitable in view of the population scatter. It leads to a lack of that intimacy between the press and the intellectually sophisticated middle classes which is an important reason for the existence of the quality press in London or in Paris.

Comparisons with America can also be misleading, although even America does not have a quality press on the British or European pattern. The New York *Times* might be regarded as basically an advertising vehicle in the sense that its enormous volume of advertisements *compels* it to carry "all the news that's fit to print", and often in too diffuse and unedited a style. This news coverage undoubtedly has great value for specialized readership. But the New York *Times* is not representative of the American press, and even its leading articles are often of a lower standard of precision and hard thinking than many of the leaders published in Australian papers. The same could be said about its discussion of the arts, which is certainly no better and sometimes worse than in the Australian press. On the other hand, America has a system of medium sized provincial newspapers of real value which is absent in Australia. This, too, may be explained partly in terms of economics and population. If the vast empty middle of Australia was filled with industry, agriculture, mining and towns as in America, we too could have a continental sweep of provincial newspapers, because the physical problem of distribution would be to their advantage.

Concentration of Control

To working journalists, the overwhelming characteristic of the press is the way in which it is controlled by very few hands. Although this is by now a platitude, its impact on the practice of journalism is of the greatest importance. From the point of view of a working journalist, the concentration of ownership has effects which are of daily significance. There is lamentation among journalists when any publication, no matter how bad, closes down, since it means that one more avenue of employment is closed. The demise of *Smith's Weekly* in 1950 was widely regretted among journalists, although most journalists probably never looked at it because it was thought to be old hat.

Concentration goes so far that in some cities there is only one proprietor with whom the working journalist can deal, and in the particular case of the

Herald and Weekly Times group the same proprietor dominates in several cities. Sydney alone has three distinct newspaper firms. The lack of alternative employers is one reason for the continuing exodus of journalists into the fields of public relations and advertising, and the men who leave in this way are often of a type most needed in the profession. Mobility out of the profession is related to lack of internal mobility, which is discouraged by the actions of employers. Superannuation is an important example: journalists either have no superannuation provisions, or else they are of a kind which tie them to the one employer. Cases have occurred where journalists leaving a newspaper were not only cut off from the employer's contribution to the superannuation fund built up in their years of employment, but were not permitted to take over the superannuation policy themselves and to finance it out of their own pockets. This gives the employer a large reserve fund to attract new men, without enabling corresponding severance benefits to be given to the employee leaving his company, and the employer can offer the accumulated contributions as an inducement to the new man. Even in Sydney, where there is the greatest possibility of movement between papers, the two largest enterprises have for some years observed a "no poaching" agreement. By not taking one another's staff, they act to their mutual benefit in keeping down salaries and in weakening the sense of independence of the journalists.

This problem adds greatly to the inherent hazards of the profession of journalism. Journalists as a class are a curious combination of innocence and cynicism. In a way, they never grow old and retain some boyish enthusiasms, accompanied by a typical pessimism about their ideals ever being realized. Journalism appeals to individuals with a taste for excitement, and in a dull and small country like Australia it provides a passport into unusual and diverse sections of the community. However, the profession is in bad standing, exemplified by its inability to attract many of the boys from the expensive private schools who came into the profession before the war. It is also a hazardous occupation because of the special problems of survival in middle age and late middle age. A journalist, like an actor, lives on what he does today, not on the accumulated service of past years. The journalist who has no specialized field, but works as a reporter, encounters great problems as he gets on in years. He may give up reporting to work as a sub-editor, as a number of able men do, but even so the exodus continues to be high.

Concentration of ownership makes it easy for newspaper managements to stifle discussion of controversial topics. In this respect there may be little difference between Australian practice and that which applies in Britain or the United States, where there is equally no clear dividing line between the rights of the executive management and those of the editorial writers. When differences of opinion come into the open, the management's view will almost invariably prevail. During the Tait murder trial in Melbourne in 1962, there was a conflict inside the *Age* over its attitude to capital punishment. The result was a weakening of the editorial line by comparison with that of the Melbourne *Herald,* which opposed the execution of Tait as the result of a direct decision of the managing director, Sir John Williams.[4] The *Sydney*

[4] A detailed analysis of press influence on this occasion is given in Creighton Burns, *The Tait Case.* A parallel series of incidents in Adelaide a few years earlier is analysed by K. S. Inglis in *The Stuart Case.*

Morning Herald group has been unusual in Australia for allowing expression of differing points of view among its publications.

Another well-known limitation on newspaper freedom of discussion has been the power of the retail advertisers, specially in the evening papers, which draw a large part of their revenue from this source. A well-known instance was the playing down of news about the approach of war in Europe in 1939 because of pressure from these advertisers. Similarly, policies adopted by the Commonwealth government during the war to conserve scarce materials were distorted and ridiculed in the daily papers because they involved restrictions on retail trading. D. H. Lawrence observed in 1922 that the retail traders were the aristocracy of Australia, and even today, when a well-known merchant dies, he may get more spectacular funeral notices than a prime minister.

The advent of television has had its effect of reducing the sharpness of press competition. In 1963, for example, two of the newspaper proprietors in Sydney, Sir Frank Packer and Mr. Rupert Murdoch, became associated in a television company. Up till then there had been keen rivalry between them, but recently their newspapers have come to exchange full-page advertisements for one another's publications. As television companies frequently involve shareholdings by several different newspaper firms, it has become necessary for newspaper proprietors to hesitate before incurring the displeasure of other proprietors. This extends to relationships between newspapers in different cities.

In Australia, as elsewhere, the hope is often expressed that the introduction of new and cheaper methods of producing newspapers will make it possible to break down the rigidly entrenched positions. At present the costs for a new entrant into publishing are prohibitive. The late Sir Keith Murdoch said fifteen years ago that it would cost at least a million pounds to start a new daily paper in Australia. Murdoch's estimate might have to be multiplied by five at the present day, and this means, in effect, that the only entrepreneurs with the resources to do it would be those who already own newspapers. Sir Keith Murdoch's own son, Mr. Rupert Murdoch, starting from a small newspaper inheritance in Adelaide, has done more than anybody in recent years to break the established pattern of the newspaper industry (see postscript).

Concentration of control has led to a very marked degree of syndication of news. The ownership of papers in several cities by the *Herald and Weekly Times* group is the outstanding example. In addition, there is Australian United Press which gives its news to a wide range of provincial papers. Syndication of cable news from overseas is also notorious, leading to the publication of the same cable news in all papers, whether in one city or various cities. Finally, there are the liaison services between newspapers in different cities. These liaison services are all the more important because of the failure of daily papers headquartered in one city to maintain a staff of any size to report the news from any other city. The most important instance is the transmission of news between Sydney and Melbourne. No Sydney newspaper has a staff of more than two or three in Melbourne, and these tiny staffs are not concerned with transmitting first-hand news to Sydney; their job is simply to cut the Melbourne press for their own papers.

The liaison service works in curious ways. Thus, the *Daily Telegraph* in Sydney—a tabloid—is linked with the *Age* in Melbourne, a broadsheet.

Contrariwise, the *Sydney Morning Herald* broadsheet is linked with the Melbourne *Sun News-Pictorial,* a tabloid. However, the *Sydney Morning Herald* also publishes the *Sun,* a tabloid evening paper, obtaining essential reciprocal services with the Melbourne broadsheet *Herald,* which owns the *Sun News-Pictorial.* These links are sometimes related to television, where there are connections between the *Sydney Morning Herald* group and the Melbourne *Herald* group. The natural newspaper connection would be between the *Age* and the *Sydney Morning Herald,* but this is ruled out because of the arrangements just described. An interesting recent example of the effect of dependence between the newspapers of these two cities was the treatment of the report by a team of investigators appointed by the Victorian State government into the affairs of the Reid-Murray group of companies which had been placed in receivership. The Melbourne *Herald,* although it gave a large amount of space to the report, omitted the strong criticisms of the management of these companies made by the investigators. In particular, no reference was made in the *Herald* to a long section of the report which criticized the role of a leading Melbourne trustee company, the Equity Trustees Company, which had acted as a trustee for the debenture holders in the Reid-Murray group. It was subsequently pointed out that the chairman of directors of the *Herald* was a director of the Equity Trustees Company.[5] The *Age,* on the other hand, gave a detailed and accurate summary of the report, and the account in the *Age* formed the basis for the account given in the Sydney *Daily Telegraph.* The Melbourne *Herald's* account was repeated in Brisbane, where both daily papers are owned by the *Herald and Weekly Times* group, in Adelaide, where the only morning paper, the *Advertiser,* is owned by the same group, and in other cities where the group had indirect interests. The *Sydney Morning Herald* was also left in the same position, though it gave space on subsequent days to the publication of further extracts from the report of the investigators.

The Role of the A.J.A.

The great power of proprietors is unfortunately not balanced by any corresponding organization on the part of the journalists themselves. The Australian Journalists' Association, the A.J.A., is a trade union body in a narrow and short-sighted sense. It has not taken up such important questions as the transferability of superannuation. It does little to promote the independent status and self-respect of journalists as a profession. The A.J.A.'s monthly paper is concerned with nothing but industrial awards and their application, personal paragraphs about journalists who are getting married or going overseas, long and detailed accounts of what the officials of the A.J.A. have been doing in the last month, heavily illustrated with photographs of those officials which are carried in issue after issue. Until lately, a great deal of its space was devoted to a dispute between the Sydney and Melbourne branches as to where the federal headquarters of the A.J.A. should be located. (Sydney, after constant battling on this subject, finally won.)

In principle, the A.J.A. should take vigorous action when, for instance, there is evidence that a journalist is being made to write at his employer's whim, or that material not of his writing is appearing under his by-line. It

[5] *Nation,* 14 December 1963.

might be too much to expect the A.J.A. to take direct action successfully against a particular employer in such cases. What they could do is to raise the standing of the profession with members of the public so that no employer could take the risk of being publicly upbraided for such an action. Although this is a more difficult task, it could be done if journalists took more trouble to communicate with the public about their problems. The A.J.A. has not done such things as endowing research into the press, or making provision for public lectures. The annual Arthur Norman Smith Memorial Lecture on journalism is supported not by the A.J.A. but by the newspaper proprietors, and the speakers only rarely give utterance to real criticism. The A.J.A. has not looked at the press as a whole, and has not become widely known as a public body. With more public prestige, it might be able to stand up and openly attack a proprietor for abusing what journalists would consider the prerogatives of an editor. Although agreement in principle is occasionally reached that these things should be done, there is no sign of action.

The Newspaper and Its Public

The difference in character between the daily papers in Sydney and those in Melbourne is striking. It may be said that journalism in Melbourne has an old world, provincial flavour, and that there is a frequent tone of complacency as to what a great place Melbourne is. On the other hand, this genteelism probably contributes to the strong undercurrent of dissent which can be noticed in the intellectual life of Melbourne. Radical and independent journals, such as the monthly *Voice* (1951-6) and the fortnightly *Nation* achieve a striking response in Melbourne. Their Melbourne readers show, by their letters, that they welcome outlets which give an alternative to the placid, dull picture painted by the daily newspapers. This staid quality is all the more marked by contrast with the relative raucousness and extravagance of the newspapers in Sydney, which also possess a streak of radicalism that has been absent from journalism in Melbourne since the death of David Syme. There was a fleeting period in the career of Keith Murdoch, for many years managing director of the Melbourne *Herald,* when he adopted a favourable attitude towards the Labour Party. This was during the late 1920s, when the depression was looming, and is shown by extracts from his private "house" memoranda to the *Herald* staff which were recently published.[6] This phase was exceptional, and in the 1930s Murdoch played a large part in politics on the non-Labour side.[7] In Sydney the tone of the press and the fact that there are three separate newspaper firms means the Labour point of view has more chance of expression, and Sydney has provided a vehicle for this viewpoint more consistently than any other city.

Forthrightness about scandals is another long-standing feature of the press in Sydney. It is unlikely that key sections of a report like that on the Reid Murray group of companies would have been suppressed in that city. The difference between newspapers in the two cities reflects the different characters of the two cities. It is related to what Mr Walter Stone once described as the "Bostonian" air of Melbourne. He was referring to the group around the novelist and short story writer, Vance Palmer; another good example of the

[6] *Nation*, 29 June 1963.
[7] S. Encel, *Cabinet Government in Australia,* pp. 231-4.

same kind of high-mindedness and intellectualism was the circle of which the late Sir Frederic Eggleston was the central figure. Individuals like these represent the highest manifestations of a strain which has long been typical of Melbourne. The University of Melbourne has never gone through the phase of nescience and reaction against constructive social thinking which happened at the University of Sydney in the 1940s and 1950s. Radical thinking in Sydney has been much more negative, destructive, sceptical and libertarian in character. Recent signs of concern about Asia and Africa, like the Immigration Reform Movement and the plan for setting aside 1% of the national income for foreign aid, typically emanate from Melbourne. By contrast, opposition to nuclear armaments, which is essentially a protest movement, has been Sydney-based. In Sydney, with its beaches and its outdoor life, more importance is placed on personal liberty of behaviour. The atmosphere in Melbourne is more stuffy and confining, but it seems to breed as a counterpart a more positive and constructive kind of radicalism.

The tendency of the Melbourne papers to play safe is well illustrated by their fondness for taking up a campaign about some safe issue of public concern. One of the campaigns of recent years dealt with the lopping of trees in St. Kilda Road, Melbourne's main thoroughfare, which was carried on by the *Herald*. The *Age*, on the other hand, has concentrated on shocking people with the statistics of road accidents. These two instances illustrate how newspapers can find innocuous substitutes for campaigns about real issues. On the other hand, the campaign against capital punishment conducted by the Melbourne *Herald* during the Tait murder case does not fit into this picture, and it remains a striking exception to the general rule. There is no doubt that the papers were responding to the prevailing mood among the intellectual public in Melbourne, but this cannot be the whole explanation because such moods have existed before and the press has been notably reluctant to reflect them.

Reaching the Audience

Most Australian newspapers aim for a mass circulation, and therefore for the same readership. There is no very marked attempt to distinguish between potential audiences. There is a general unspoken assumption that each newspaper is writing for everybody. One consequence is that long sentences and long paragraphs are very much discouraged in all newspapers. Only two minor factors influence this situation. One is that evening papers strive for a different character, since they cannot afford to repeat what has appeared in the morning papers. The evening paper's problem is to dress up the news, since it cannot hope to be a paper of record. The other factor is that in battles for circulation it is the marginal readership of about 10,000 people which counts, and it is at these that the paper has to be aimed.

One of the few editors who could be regarded as deliberately pitching the character of his paper to attract a particular type of person was Brian Penton, editor of the Sydney *Daily Telegraph* from 1941 to 1951. In his day the *Telegraph* appeared to be shaped for an ideal reader: a man who lived near the surf of Bondi Beach, a sun-tanned out-of-doors character, with a cynical, sport-loving mind, who read the *Telegraph* on his way to work from Bondi to the city in the morning. It was at this type of smart, hard-headed person

213

that the *Telegraph* was aimed. The *Telegraph* has changed its character since then, and so for that matter has Bondi.

Surveys of content and readership show that there is little real difference between the *Sydney Morning Herald* and the *Daily Telegraph,* although people often think there is.[8]

TABLE 1

Content analysis—Sydney Morning Herald 1962

Advertising	.. ..	64·3%
Editorial ..	.. ..	35·7%

Main content categories expressed as %s of editorial space

1.	Foreign news	.. ..	7·4%
2.	Domestic politics ..	.. ..	11·8
3.	Political etc., features	.. ..	3·0
4.	Leaders ..	.. ..	1·9
5.	Letters to the editor	.. ..	2·1
6.	Sport ..	.. ..	15·3
7.	"Services" (weather, mails, ships, T.V. programmes, exam. results, court lists, advice columns)		15·3
8.	Pictures ..	.. ..	14·8
9.	Finance ..	.. ..	11·4
10.	Cartoons, comic strips	.. ..	3·3
11.	Book reviews, theatre, etc., criticism ..	.. ..	2·9
12.	Women's page	.. ..	2·5
13.	Court reports	.. ..	2·1
14.	Other ..	.. ..	6·2

(Adapted from Hudson, *op.cit.* pp. 35–6, 192–8).

The character of these papers suggests how these impressions of divergence between the two papers arise. The *Telegraph* is a young person's paper. Its size makes it more convenient. It does not carry pages of classified advertisements like the *Herald,* and this has a profound effect on its character. The public conception of the *Telegraph* is still influenced by its chequered history since the early 1930s, before it was taken over by its present proprietor, Sir Frank Packer. For a time it even ceased publication, and it had to fight its way back by the sheer briskness and brightness of its presentation. In those days the differences between the two Sydney morning papers were more marked.

As a matter of policy, Sir Frank Packer decided that the *Telegraph* was not to go too far in a popular direction. He has never achieved, or really sought, the kind of tabloid mass circulation enjoyed by Melbourne's *Sun News-Pictorial.* When the *Telegraph* overtook the *Herald* in circulation, the *Herald* fought back and has been waging a circulation battle ever since. At present, the margin between the two papers appears to be almost 30,000 in the *Telegraph's* favour, which is the biggest lead the *Telegraph* has had for decades.

[8] An exhaustive analysis of the differences between the two "quality" papers, the *Sydney Morning Herald* and the *Age,* and the rest of the press is given by Henry Mayer, *The Press in Australia,* pp. 218-19. Mr Mayer shows that there is little difference in content. The two papers have slightly more international news but also more sport than the average of the rest.

The *Telegraph* has endeavoured to compete with the *Herald* in one of its traditional strongholds, the North Shore suburbs of Sydney. This appears to have inspired the *Telegraph's* attempts to improve its presentation of financial news, and it may also have impelled it towards a strongly conservative political position. Its conservatism also appears, on some occasions, to have been dictated by the strategy of adopting the contrary approach to the *Herald*.

The readership of the *Herald* appears to be older than that of the *Telegraph*, and this may mean among other things that the *Herald* cannot go too far in attracting the large number of school leavers caused by the post-war "bulge" in the birthrate. If it did, it would be likely to alienate some of its traditional public. One of the objections which readers of the older generation apparently have towards the *Telegraph* is based on their impression that it is a sensational paper. In fact, some of the headlines and news stories in the *Herald* are no less sensational, but the impression is mitigated because, as a broadsheet, it does not devote the whole of its front page to the one story. Nevertheless, the *Telegraph* will lead on an overseas subject as frequently as the *Herald*, e.g. a new move by President de Gaulle. In Melbourne, a corresponding distinction is sometimes drawn between the *Age* and the *Sun News-Pictorial*. The latter is often regarded as more sensational, although by standards other than those of Melbourne this is probably a misleading description. A more important characteristic of the *Sun News-Pictorial* is its concentration on the "human interest" aspect of a story. Its outlook is similar to that of the mass circulation London daily papers, although the *Sun News-Pictorial* does not go nearly so far as the London *Daily Mirror*, which failed in its attempt to adopt London methods after taking over the Melbourne *Argus* in 1949. The *Sun News-Pictorial* will devote almost the whole of its front page to a photograph of a baby which escaped burning in its home the previous night through the good sense of the next-door neighbour, or its front page lead story may be a human interest story about a mother going overseas, again holding her baby. The *Sun News-Pictorial* makes a speciality of "warmth" and Dickensian jollity.

The relations between the *Sun News-Pictorial* and the *Age* in Melbourne are quite different from those between the *Herald* and *Telegraph* in Sydney. The *Sun News-Pictorial* was originally launched as something of a decoy. It was started by a Sydney newspaper proprietor, Hugh Denison, in the early 1920s as a preliminary in a battle to break the monopoly of the Melbourne *Herald* in the evening field, which he tried to do by producing the *Evening Sun*. The *Evening Sun* failed and was liquidated, but the *Herald* bought the *Sun News-Pictorial* and developed it. At that time there were two long-established morning papers, the *Argus* and the *Age*, both of them broadsheets and both conservative in their methods. The management of the *Age* either did not realize, or did not act on the realization, that the rival was no longer the *Argus* but this strange new form of journalism. The *Argus* management did realize this and tried various ways of combating the rise of the *Sun News-Pictorial*, but ultimately it went under in the struggle. The *Age* did nothing about it, perhaps because its proprietors felt they could not stoop to doing what the *Sydney Morning Herald* did in its battle against the *Telegraph*. The *Herald*, for instance, was the first to put its news on the front page, to introduce a cartoon and comic strips, and to give sport considerable space. The

Age was much slower in doing these things, which in the end it was forced to do in any case, and by its slowness it may have "missed the bus". This is probably a case where the great influence of the proprietors, in this case the Syme family, prevails over the professional views of the journalists.

The contrast between the policies of the *Age* and the *Sydney Morning Herald* is paralleled by the different aims of the *Telegraph* and the *Sun News-Pictorial*. Sir Frank Packer has been interested in power and influence and not only in readership, and clearly he does not see the *Telegraph* as another *Sun News-Pictorial*. The *Telegraph* has taken an interest in different things, and has always been relatively free of the chatty tone which is so characteristic of the *Sun News-Pictorial*. For that matter, even the *Age* is much more chatty than the *Sydney Morning Herald*. The conclusion would seem to be that the *Age* has retained a core of readers who correspond to the hard core of the *Sydney Morning Herald* readership. What it has not attracted are the people who read the *Herald* for less serious reasons, as it were, and whose faithfulness cannot be taken for granted.

The Melbourne *Herald,* on the other hand, is unique. Because of its monopolistic position as an evening paper, it could claim to be the best evening paper in Australia, and one of the best in the world. Its position did not lull Sir Keith Murdoch, but on the contrary gave him the means to seek excellence in all departments, and to indulge the desire for power and influence which is shown by various incidents in his lifetime, such as his activities as a war correspondent in the 1914-18 war and his role in politics in the 1930s, when he is credited with the making of two prime ministers—J. A. Lyons and R. G. Menzies.[9] The Melbourne *Herald* still runs largely on the Murdoch impetus, but remains a remarkable paper. There were glimpses of the skill at its command during the Tait case, and also in its masterly handling of the attempt by the Federal government to ban the broadcasting of a television interview with M. Georges Bidault in 1963. But basically the paper is run as a business.

Postscript

Since this was written, two noteworthy events have occurred. The first was the publication, early in 1964, of Henry Mayer's *The Press in Australia,* the first major study of the subject (apart from W. Sprague Holden's *Australia Goes to Press,* which is largely concerned with the mechanics of newspaper production). Mr. Mayer takes up, in detail, a number of the points dealt with above. Although his analysis is devastating, his conclusions are quite mild. The choice offered by the daily press is too narrow; the absence of Labour newspapers and of a genuine quality press is a serious failing. But, in general, irritation and disgust with the press are "part of the price one pays for living in the sort of society Australia has". A change in the press is only possible as the result of other changes in society, some of which might be unwelcome. In any case, the influence of the press is comparatively small, and it is too often a scapegoat for criticism which should be aimed elsewhere.[10]

---

[9] Victorian newspapers acting together secured the defeat of legislative councillors opposing reform in 1936, and the return of the Hollway independent Liberals in 1952 (though they could not repeat that performance in 1955).

[10] *Op. cit.,* pp. 270-3.

On 15 July 1964 there appeared the first issue of *The Australian,* proclaimed as Australia's first national newspaper. *The Australian,* published in Canberra but distributed nationally, is owned by News Ltd., which controls *The News* (Adelaide), the *Daily Mirror* (Sydney), a string of suburban newssheets in Sydney, and *The New Idea* and *T.V. Week* in Melbourne. It also has TV interests in three states, magazine interests in Hong Kong, and a large share in a leading New Zealand daily, *The Dominion.* The head of this chain is Mr. Rupert Murdoch, son of Sir Keith Murdoch.

In a lavishly produced volume announcing the appearance of the new paper, its management declares that it will be "a newspaper of intelligence, of broad outlook, of independent spirit and of elegant appearance . . . dedicated to the attainment of the highest standards of reporting and analysis". Time will tell. At the date of writing, *The Australian* had shown striking resemblances in format and general style to the London *Daily Express* (which alone would make it a novelty among local dailies), and its standards were marked by considerable variation. Its coverage of both local and overseas news was, however, appreciably greater than that of any other daily, and its use of overseas book reviewers, feature writers, and news correspondents was much more enterprising.[11] It may provide a corrective both to the lack of competition and the provincialism which we have emphasized.

III

How different is the picture within the public sector of journalism? Does the absence of the private proprietor remove all the constraints examined above? Are some inseparable from organizations of a certain scale, whether public or private? Are there fresh hazards and handicaps? The A.B.C., which has produced a sound radio service since 1932, and a television service since 1956, is an institution with a distinct climate and tone; old enough to have its own mystique and its own way (often baffling to the outsider) of doing things. It can hardly be said, however, to be "winning the fight against commercialism"—if indeed it is holding its own. It has certainly failed signally to collect about it a devoted following, who could do without it only with difficulty. (Its TV audience is estimated at 16% of the total in Melbourne and Sydney; its radio one at 24%.)[12] It *does* provide, however, an often valuable additional choice of programme; and has succeeded with certain special services like the news service,[13] the country hour and kindergarten of the air.

The working of the A.B.C. can largely be understood in terms of its organizational structure. The Commission itself, which is the policy-making body, is responsible for deciding the areas of artistic taste and political controversy within which programmes are permitted to function. It consists of seven commissioners appointed by the Federal government (technically by the Governor-General). One of these commissioners is named as Chairman,

---

[11] K. S. Inglis, in *Nation,* 24 July, and 12 December 1964.

[12] McNair Survey of Radio and Press Audiences, Sydney, March 1963, p. 7. This last figure is a cumulative average for a sample week, *i.e.* one person in four will have tuned in to an A.B.C. station sometime in that week. The great majority are listeners merely to the breakfast news.

[13] Which employs 173 full-time journalists. Holden, *op. cit.* p. 139, and see M. F. Dixon, "Bold Experiment in Nationally-Owned News Service", *Meanjin,* vol. 14, no. 1, 1955.

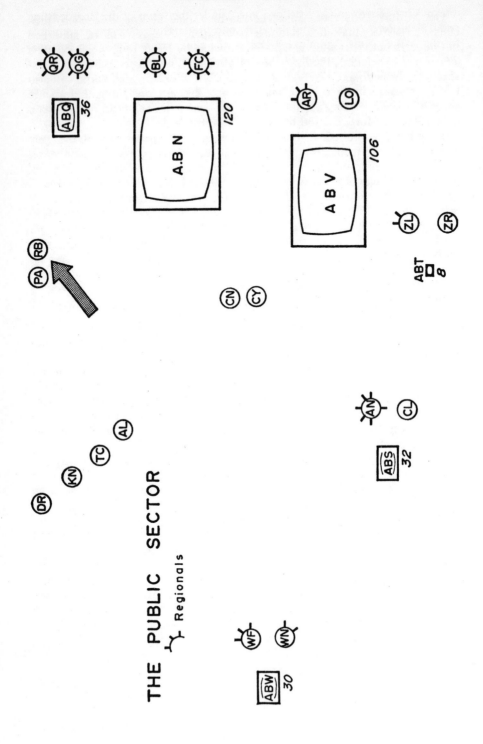

THE PUBLIC SECTOR

Regionals

one as Vice-Chairman. At least one must, under the terms of the Broadcasting and Television Act, be a woman. Although the minister officially responsible for the A.B.C. is the Postmaster-General, the chairman is usually the personal choice of the Prime Minister of the day, acting either on his own decision or on recommendations submitted to him. The period of appointment for all commissioners is three years, though some seem to have achieved, by renewals, a fairly permanent status; *e.g.* Mr E. R. Dawes, the present vice-chairman, was appointed in 1945 by a Labour government, and is the only remaining Labour appointee on the Commission. In practice it seems that commissioners are chosen, firstly to give each state in the Commonwealth a voice in the Commission's deliberations, and secondly because they are regarded as satisfactory representatives of leading pressure groups.

Mr H. B. Halvorsen, from Western Australia, is a public accountant with a wide range of company connections. Mr J. T. Reid, the Victorian commissioner, is an industrialist who is also on the board of the Y.M.C.A.; he could be said to exemplify the role of Protestant Christianity in a business civilization. The Tasmanian commissioner, Mrs Dorothy Edwards, succeeded Dame Enid Lyons, a former minister in the Liberal government and the widow of a former Prime Minister, in 1962. She is an alderman of Launceston, president of the Australian National Council of Women, and is close to the Country Women's Association and similar women's organizations. Mr A. G. Lowndes, from New South Wales, is a former Sydney businessman who also owns a pastoral property, and has had a long association with the Australian Institute of Political Science and with local government. The commissioner from Queensland, Miss Rhoda Felgate, is a drama producer and speech teacher, who represents the arts in a conventional manner acceptable to the respectable middle class. Mr Dawes, who comes from South Australia, was formerly a trade union official, but has been involved in government service of some kind since 1940. The present chairman, Dr J. R. Darling, a former headmaster of Geelong Grammar School, might not unfairly be described as a High Church evangelical, by turns the Sydney Smith and the Hildebrand of the Victorian Western District feudalities.

On these commissioners collectively, and on the chairman particularly, rests the responsibility of deciding the broad aesthetic and political patterns of the A.B.C.'s programmes. The Commission are the inheritors of a rather polite "Establishment" tradition in programme making, but they can exercise an independent power. They did so during the 1961 Federal election campaign when, under the acting chairmanship of Mr Dawes, they inspired and launched "The Candidates", a programme which broke new ground in broadcast discussions of politics. The opinions and attitudes of the commissioners filter down through the A.B.C., creating a framework for programme operations. Dr Darling's public statements, frequently reported in the press, indicate the nature of his concerns. For example, the Commission has tried to emphasize the importance of religion in the community.[14] Dr Darling is dissatisfied at the traditional way of treating religion as a special department of the A.B.C.'s programmes, and would like to see more awareness of re-

[14] The Act directs that "divine worship and other matters of a religious nature should be broadcast for adequate periods and at appropriate times". See I. K. Mackay, *Broadcasting in Australia*, pp. 93-7.

ligious issues in all programmes. He was concerned that the A.B.C.'s treatment of the assassination of the late President Kennedy did not sufficiently stress the religious problems, and is quoted as having expressed this concern in the form of a rhetorical question: "Why did God let it happen?"[15] In this concern over religion he is apparently supported by Mr Reid, with whom he has close contact as a fellow Victorian. He has expressed some distress at the use of freethinkers and atheists on the "Any Questions" programme, unless their views are "balanced" by orthodox Christian views. He also expressed regret over the news commentaries given by well-known left-wing speakers such as Dr J. W. Burton and Dr Peter Russo at the time of the Cuban crisis in October 1962. (An analysis of the news commentaries given at this time suggests that there were eight "pro-American" as against two "anti-American" commentaries.) This attitude is apparently justified on the grounds that the times were abnormal, and considerations of "national responsibility" were more important than freedom of speech. It is also apparent that Dr Darling and most of his fellow commissioners were not happy at the trend of the popular television programme "Four Corners" in August and September of 1963, when the programmes, whose control had recently been reorganized, dealt with topics such as nuclear weapons, book censorship, aboriginal co-operatives, the rise of discount houses, the cult of the teenager and the social role of the Returned Servicemen's League. A year later, the freedom of the production team associated with this programme was again invaded over a film dealing with capital punishment. Frequent and conflicting public denials of interference by Dr Darling and other executives of the A.B.C. served only to weaken any remaining public confidence in the Commission's management of its affairs.

The cultural climate of an organization like the A.B.C. is largely set in this way, not through the issue of specific directives, which appears to be rare, or by insistence that particular programmes should be presented, but by creating a general atmosphere. In other words, though the Commission does not interfere with the content of the A.B.C. programmes in the way in which the management of a newspaper interferes directly in deciding content of each day's issue, the general effect is the same. The Commission does not, on the whole, remove programme officers from positions of control, although this was done in the case of the "Four Corners" programme on the R.S.L., following a public outcry from the R.S.L. and subsequent pressure from the government.[16] Even without such actions, programme officers clearly respond to the understanding of what the Commission wants. Pirandello's play, *Six Characters in Search of an Author*, was recently "cleaned up" in its A.B.C. presentation to remove the suggestion in the original text that a father might commit incest with his daughter.

The Commission includes no person who would normally be regarded as an "intellectual", and equally, it contains no one with any first-hand knowledge of the mass media. Thus, it contains neither practical experts in mass communication nor people accustomed to the world of ideas.

---

15 *Nation*, 10 January 1964.
16 This episode is discussed by G. L. Kristianson and P. B. Westerway in the *Australian Quarterly*, vol. 36, nos. 1 and 2, 1964.

Against the tepid composition of the Commission must be set the dominant role of the general manager, Sir Charles Moses, who held the post for 30 years from 1935. His role was greatly strengthened by his long direct personal experience of broadcasting. He first made his mark in the A.B.C. in Melbourne as a general announcer and sports broadcaster, and developed, through radio, certain popular and respectable community interests—*e.g. cricket*, stock exchange reports, news, children's sessions (which later extended into direct teaching through school broadcasts) and talks (particularly the potted lecture, "Armchair Chat" and "Guest of Honour"). In particular, Sir Charles has shown himself to be a first rate entrepreneur in the field of music, skilfully selecting visiting celebrity artists. He has sought to make the A.B.C. one of the largest of concert organizations, and it is through its concerts more than anything else that the A.B.C. has become a respected cultural institution. Music critics have occasionally attacked the continual emphasis on "popular classics", and deplored the scant representation of contemporary music either in A.B.C. programmes or public concerts. The stress on music programmes has been for long an A.B.C. peculiarity. A programme planner, asked for special radio time on the night after the assassination of President Kennedy, allegedly replied: "Oh, no, we can't interrupt the Sibelius."

In recent years, the organization of the A.B.C. has given more prominence to administrative officers and less to members of staff who are actually concerned with creating programmes, particularly in TV. The A.B.C. has about 50 senior officers, of whom no more than five or six have worked directly in television. Organizational changes which have increased the numbers and the importance of senior administrative staff also contribute to this tendency; of the six divisional heads immediately responsible to the general manager, only one is directly concerned with programmes. The most important post at the state level, that of manager for Victoria, was filled in 1961 by the appointment of an "outsider", whose previous experience was that of an administrative officer in the Air Force. This growth of administrative control over A.B.C. affairs may lead to the development of a managerial counterpart to the Commission itself, which would be in line with tendencies observed in other large organizations. This is also indicated by the growth of a committee system; *e.g.* in 1964 an editorial committee was appointed to oversee "Four Corners". Interstate producers regularly complain of Sydney domination.

The A.B.C.'s reluctance to permit free discussion of ideas, its conformity to standards of "safety" and familiarity (even in its musical programmes), does not encourage the notion that publicly-controlled mass media can act as a countervailing force against a monopolistically controlled press. A.B.C. discussion programmes and talks are rarely broadcast before 9 p.m.; until then, programmes suitable for "family" listening or viewing are the rule. The wish seems to be to cultivate an average listener (or viewer) who, like Barry Humphries' Mrs Everage, wants a "nice night's entertainment".

IV

One of the tasks of sociology is to make out what the effects of reading the papers or watching television really are. Though much patient, and some ingenious work has been done in the last thirty years, this has proved extraordinarily difficult. The steps are plain: to find out exactly what is sent out—the content of columns and programmes; exactly what is taken in—audiences

221

B.B.C.

Board of Governors

Director General

Board of Management
Director General
Director of Sound Broadcasting
Director of Television
Director of External Broadcasting
Director of Engineering
Director of Administration
Chief Assistant to Director General
Secretary

A.B.C.

COMMISSION

Executive Liaison Officer

General Manager

MANAGEMENT COMMITTEE
General Manager
Deputy General Manager
A.G.M. (General)
A.G.M. (Programmes)
Controller, News Services
Director Publicity & Concerts

Organisations & Establishments Officer

Overseas Representatives

A.G.M. (General)

A.G.M. (Programmes)

Deputy G.M.

Controller News Services

Controller Engineering

Controller Finance

Director Publicity & Concerts

State Managers

The diagram illustrates the large administrative overhead of the A.B.C. A chart of B.B.C. organization is shown for comparison.

222

are selective, and their attentiveness even more so; and (it sounds so simple) what difference the exposure has made.

A brief review of recent studies will illustrate some of the intrinsic difficulties. Connell in 1957 studied the reading habits of Sydney adolescents.[17] He found nine out of ten of them were newspaper readers; a taste normally acquired by the age of thirteen. They preferred the *Sun* to the *Mirror,* the *Mirror* to the *Telegraph,* and the *Telegraph* to the *Herald.* Suburb lived in, and type of school attended, made for minor variations in choice: the *Herald* was a shade more popular in genteel, less in rougher districts; but the four papers sold very evenly through all suburbs. The top forms of secondary schools turned solidly to the *Herald.* He analysed the content of each paper for a week in 1953, and gave a rough impression of how young readers attacked it. "Usually it appears they would start with the front page, turn over to the sporting news, glance at the general news, and then settle down to the comics." Connell's discussion follows a similar course—not lingering over the question of what their reading gave them, but plunging forward into the details of their taste in strips (they preferred *Blondie*).

Brown, in an unpublished study of the *Sydney Morning Herald* readership in 1962[18] confirmed the even social spread of Sydney dailies. (Almost one man in two read both morning papers and almost one woman in three.) People in high status jobs, however, tended to value their daily paper more than others (they were asked how much they would miss it, if it failed to appear "one day this week"). We shall see why in a moment.

Brown was equally concerned with the audience for different parts of the paper. Everyone read "news about Sydney", less than one person in five the art reviews. Behind the staple items of news and features of general interest lay pretty distinctly a man's world and a woman's world. Both sexes concurred in reading—in roughly descending order of enthusiasm—the general news (Sydney, Australia and overseas), the news pictures, the leader page articles, the letters to the editor, and among the features, the TV news, special supplements, do-it-yourself and gardening hints, the classified advertisements, court cases, magazine features and serials and book reviews. But differences of more than 10 percentage points separated out a male realm of political news, cartoon, editorial comic strips, sports (62% to 27%), car testing reports (52% to 11%), financial news and racing (31% to 12%)—in order of interest; and a female world of large advertisements, woman's page (72% to 9%), births, deaths and marriages, film and play reviews, social column (52% to 12%) and horoscopes.

Social classes, too, dug out their distinctive nourishment, beyond a shared concern for Sydney and Australian news, pictures, cartoons, special supplements, large advertisements, sports, women's pages, film reviews, gardening and cars, births, deaths and marriages, and magazine features. While the upper middle class, for example, knuckled down to the serious columns—overseas, political, financial, news, leader page and reviews; the working class settled back with the TV news, comic strips, do-it-yourself hints, small advertisements, court cases, horoscopes, racing news and serials. The social column interested all strata equally.

[17] W. F. Connell *et al., Growing Up in an Australian City,* Ch. 12.
[18] Morven S. Brown, *Sydney Readership Survey* (unpublished MS, 1962).

Political students have at intervals examined the imperfections of the press coverage of particular elections,[19] by-elections,[20] and referenda;[21] or of particular subjects.[22] At some polls they have had fairly lurid stories to tell of partisanship and smearing but the general verdict is closer to this—"apart from editorial matter the parties received equal treatment and spent much the same on advertising".[23] They have, however, hardly attempted to relate content systematically to impact, and thus to effect. The two electoral studies based on surveys showed at least the rough importance of different media for voters: in Parkes at a general election half the women but only a quarter of the men ignored the campaign in the papers;[24] in the La Trobe by-election, nearly half of the voters did not follow the campaign in the metropolitan or the local papers, and only 13% did in both.[25]

A market research survey in 1958 disclosed the readership of the principal local magazines.[26] The *Australian Women's Weekly* went into every second home, and was read by one husband in three as well. Half the *Women's Weekly* wives also took *Woman's Day*. If the men poached their wives' magazine (they usually read it in one 45 minutes burst, while women spent four times as long in five or six dips), wives retaliated by looking regularly into the barber shop magazines, *Australasian Post, Pix* and *People*. It is disheartening to find that three out of five university graduates take the *Reader's Digest*.[27] The circulation of overseas journals like the *Observer, New Statesman, Time* and *New York Times* (Weekly) is of some significance and subject to wide swings of fashion. In 1962 the *Bulletin* surveyed and reported (somewhat barely) on its own readership,[28] in transition from Dad and Dave to the city slickers.

Though nearly every home has a radio set (it used to be all), they are now used mainly at breakfast time; less than one in ten will be on after 8 p.m.[29] Commercial stations, as if to thoroughly earn the old nickname of "the poor man's juke box", have reacted by doubling the time given to hits in the last three years.[30]

[19] T. C. Truman, "The Press and the 1951 Election", *Australian Quarterly*, vol. 23, no. 4, 1951; D. W. Rawson, *Australia Votes*, ch. 7; I. F. Wilson, *The 1958 Federal Election in Yarra* (A.P.S.A. monograph, 1959); F. K. Crowley, *State Election*, passim.

[20] Henry Mayer and Joan Rydon, *The Gwydir By-Election 1953* (includes some general expostulations about the difficulty of establishing bias); D. W. Rawson and Susan Holtzinger, *Politics in Eden-Monaro*, pp. 73-4; Creighton Burns, *Parties and People*, pp. 172-3.

[21] L. C. Webb, *Communism and Democracy in Australia*, ch. 8.

[22] *E.g. International affairs*: see W. M. Ball (ed.) *Press, Radio and World Affairs*, 1938; I. Wilson, "The Australian Press and Foreign Affairs" (M.A. thesis, University of Melbourne, 1959); *State politics*—which tends to be skimped: no Victorian paper for example, has used a first-class man as state roundsman in the last 20 years; *Financial analysis and criticism*, see T. M. Fitzgerald, "The Role of the Finance Editor" (A. N. Smith Memorial Lecture, 1962); and the sketchiness of *Science* reporting is well-known.

[23] J. Jupp, *Victoria Votes*, 1962, p. 12.

[24] Rawson, *Australia Votes*, p. 185.

[25] Burns, *op. cit.*, pp. 61-2.

[26] McNair Survey of Readership of *Reader's Digest* and Competitive Magazines (1958), p. 7.

[27] *Ibid.*, pp. 2, 10.

[28] *Bulletin*, 31 March 1962.

[29] *Australian Broadcasting Control Board*, Report, 1963, p. 25.

[30] *Ibid.*, p. 23.

Television transmission, beginning in Sydney and Melbourne in 1956, now covers nearly the whole country. Programmes have, however, changed little in that time in form, or popularity. At peak viewing times commercial screens show only drama or light entertainment;[31] over 12 months they provide:

Drama	55%
Light entertainment	23%
Children	8%
Sport	5%
News	4%
Current affairs	3%
Documentaries	2%

(excluding advertisements, which fill every seventh hour).[32] Programme ratings by general category follow this order closely.[33] The A.B.C. more soberly supplements the standard fare as follows:

By 8%—documentaries, sport
By 5%—education, the arts
By 3%—current affairs, news and children

mainly at the expense of westerns, quizzes, panel games, and police drama.[34] Stations are required to give two hours of Australian material weekly at peak viewing times, and a rising proportion, which will be 50% in 1965, in aggregate; and they must put at the disposal of religious bodies 30 minutes (free) weekly.[35] Political broadcasts are regulated more closely: no dramatizing of political matter, all parties to be offered space, no programmes on polling days.

Federal elections have become largely TV occasions since 1961 (it was of minor importance in 1958)[36] without notably changing their character. The dramatic promise (or threat) which the medium seemed to offer in its early days of opening a whole new audience to politics with incalculable results (carrying Big Daddy into every hearth? selling personable young aspirants like toothpaste?) was not borne out. Television's impact on politics has not been much studied,[37] but Trenaman and McQuail's analysis of its part in the British 1959 election will no doubt guide future local work, if only because of the ingenious methods devised to measure voters' images of the parties. In an election in which two-thirds saw some of the campaign on TV, and just over half any of the parties' special programmes, it was clearly the main element: far more than the press, or any campaign devices, it educated electors about the parties, the issues and the policies. But there was *no* evidence of persuasion: the only demonstrable result of the whole TV coverage was to improve Mr Gaitskell's standing with his own supporters.

What changes in attitude there were could not be related to exposure to television (or to any medium at all). However one splits the sample, or

---

[31] *Ibid.*, p. 55.

[32] *Ibid.*, pp. 54 and 62.

[33] *E.g., Broadcasting Control Board*, 1959 Report, p. 34.

[34] 1963 Report, p. 89. It holds the allegiance of 12%-16% of viewers—A. K. Olley, *Post-Television Social Survey*, 1962, p. 75.

[35] *Ibid.*, pp. 59 and 61.

[36] D. W. Rawson, *Australia Votes*, Ch. 8, and Parkes Survey, Table 11.

[37] An A.N.U. study of the reactions of a middle-class Canberra panel to the 1963 policy speeches is in progress.

isolates groups like changers, or those heavily exposed to propaganda during the campaign, no direct connection can be traced between the message and the effect. Political change was neither related to the degree of exposure, nor to any particular programmes or argument put forward by the parties.[38]

Baffling though this may be, the study offered the reassurance that "matter is more important than manner"[39] and that it is "highly unlikely that parties can bring about any important modifications of their images in the short and artificial period of an election campaign".[40]

A novel desire to emphasize the local choice of candidates—giving each five minutes' time in joint programmes electorate by electorate—launched by the A.B.C.[41] in 1961 was boycotted by the Liberal Party on the Prime Minister's initiative, and not repeated in 1963. Did this help electors to a clearer choice, or merely distract them from the business of deciding on a government? Here the controllers of the medium simply fell into line with the assumptions of those already managing the political contest.

The Broadcasting Control Board has farsightedly and generously subsidized studies of the social effects of television, but the reports so far published, though they describe with care changed patterns of leisure since its introduction, and Australians' broad viewing habits, have not gone very deep.

Australians watch a lot of TV—about two hours a night with one night off a week[42]—it has replaced radio listening, thinned out night classes, brought the evening meal on earlier[43] and cut into reading, as Olley's figures show.[44]

TABLE 2

Adult reading:

	No books	1 or 2 a month	3 or more a month
With T.V.	34%	44%	22%
Without	33%	35%	31%

But it is a mistake to see the television audience as homogeneous and monolithic; it has been succinctly broken up (for the U.S.) as follows:[45]

TABLE 3

Acceptance of TV in U.S.A.

Age	Upper middle class	Lower middle class	Working class
–12	Embraced	Embraced	Embraced
13–20	Protested	Protested	Protested
20–55	Protested	Accommodated	Embraced
55+	Embraced	Embraced	Embraced

[38] J. Trenaman and D. McQuail, *Television and the Political Image*, p. 191.
[39] *Ibid.*, p. 206.
[40] *Ibid.*, p. 224. The loudest complaints about electoral TV in Australia so far were made by the Victorian A.L.P. against the D.L.P.'s programme in the 1963 election.
[41] It was copied from Granada's *Marathon* (1959). Trenaman and McQuail, *op. cit.*, p. 71.
[42] A. K. Olley, *op. cit.*, pp. 6 and 32.
[43] *Ibid.*, pp. 32 and 50; and see W. J. Campbell, *Television and the Australian Adolescent*, ch. 5.
[44] Olley, p. 121 (rearranged)—Magazine reading has kept steady.
[45] I. O. Glick and S. J. Levy, *Living with TV*, p. 45.

Australian categories, as set out in Olley's thorough and valuable study, seem to match this. Taking selectivity of viewing, he found that 34% selected their programmes, the remaining 66% said they "leave the set on for most of the evening". He also related intensity of viewing with age and occupational level, with results similar to the American study; unfortunately, he did not construct a composite analysis similar to Table 3. He found that 25% of his sample "wouldn't miss it", compared with 39% of an adolescent sample studied by Campbell.[46] Television appears as a magic box for young and old; it goes uneasily with the high energy and sociability of teenagers, and is also identified with home and family life, from which they wish to disengage; its use by the broad body of adults is a reflex of cultural level.

Campbell, after a determined search, failed to find any deleterious effects on Sydney adolescents: homework and neighbourliness (as far as this can be measured by pencil and paper test) were unaffected; they were a bit more home-bound and apt to trot out saccharine stereotypes of ideal family relations; they showed no sign of making heroes of television stars. The "absurdly simple"[47] exercise establishing this last point (*"The person I would most like to be is . . . ?"*) should warn us not to treat the problem of viewer identification—or others of a similar complexity—as closed.

Emery, in a subtle and delightful report on 12-year-olds and Westerns,[48] pointed out that they shift the "silent framework" to a bleaker world of powerful and hostile forces, but they also heighten the posture of action.

> The Western says Beware, and then Take Action, and then Beware. . . . It is a readiness for defence and not aggression. . . . It is not violence at all which is the point of the Western, but a certain image of man, a style which expresses itself most clearly in violence. Watch a child with his toy guns and you will see what most interests him is not (as we so much fear) the fantasy of hurting others, but to work out how a man might look when he shoots or is shot.

Addicts, he points out, are little affected: they are accustomed to seeing the environment as threatening.

We have said that the audience for television is not monolithic: any deeper study of its appeal might do well to concern itself with the "core audience" for each distinctive programme—the group responding most fully and reliably to it.

The popularity of the main types of programmes with different social strata, and with the sexes, is roughly indicated in the following table, which is based on Olley's figures for sex and occupational differences.[49]

In Table 4, male and female preferences are shown in rank order in each case; there is a clear distinction at both ends of the ranking scale and an overlap in the middle. Olley's "professional" and "craftsmen/manual" categories have been used to construct average differences of those demanding "more" programmes of each category, so that the horizontal lines represent "marginal" and not "raw" tastes.[50]

[46] Olley, *op. cit.*, pp. 27-28, 61, 101; Campbell, *op. cit.*, p. 16.
[47] Campbell, p. 60, and Appendix D.
[48] F. E. Emery, "Psychological Effects of the 'Western' Film", *Human Relations*, vol. 12, no. 3, 1958.
[49] *Op cit.*, pp. 65-75.
[50] Cf. Glick and Levy, *op. cit.*, p. 112.

TABLE 4

Popularity of TV Programmes

Type of Programme	Social Class of Viewers		
	Upper-Middle	Lower-Middle	Working
Most popular (Males) Sport		———————————————	
Westerns	—————————————		
Adventure	——————————————————————		
News and News Features	———————————		
Crime		—————————————————	
Comedy	————————————————————————————		
Old films		———————————————	
Science, Nature, Animals	—————————————————		
Interviews, Talks	———————————		
Variety	————————————————————————————		
Quizzes		—————————————————	
Most popular (Females) Family drama		—————————————————	

The top 10 programmes in Sydney in early 1961 were: *The Untouchables, Pick-a-box, Perry Mason, Perry Como, Mobil-Limb Show, 77 Sunset Strip, Bonanza, I Love Lucy, Wagon Train, Desilu Play House.* Thematic analyses made by David Martin of *77 Sunset Strip, Perry Mason,* and *I Love Lucy* are given by Campbell. Olley also made a study of TV personalities liked and disliked.[51] In Melbourne in mid-1963 the top 10 were (excluding old films and children's shows), *The Untouchables, Mitch Miller Show, Alfred Hitchcock Hour, Dick Powell Show, Bonanza, Pick-a-box, Coles Quiz, Father Knows Best, Sunnyside Up, Steptoe and Son.*[52] Programmes get their special character (and audience) from the way they handle basic familial themes, from their subtlety, superficiality, intensity, candour, and dominant figures. They feed curiosity or national pride or cultural aspirations, or prove "success". Television in America has already passed its peak of interest, and is moving to a consolidation of these core audiences—"in coming years there may be less TV watching, but the quality of viewing may become more intense".[53]

[51] The popularity list appeared in the Sydney *Sun,* 21 February 1961; see Campbell, **pp.** 25-30, and Olley, pp. 82-5. *Cf.* Glick and Levy, ch. 6.
[52] McNair Survey of Television Audiences, Melbourne, 1963, p. 33.
[53] Glick and Levy, p. 38.

An assessment of the impact of television which stands back from the detail of its performance as a carrier of the entertainment arts and looks at the image of their society that viewers absorb, must surely stress two features: its pressure towards the standardization of tastes (already far gone, as the leisure studies show brutally)[54] and the spread of a lower middle class classlessness, or non-style[55]; and its solidary or socially conservative effects. The division between studio and house is deliberately blurred, and the "personalities"—"namby-pamby" paragons of middle class virtue with decently modest intellectual capacities[56] drop their hints on behaviour and opinion from a position half-way inside the family. Television woos and socializes the lonelies, and treats ordinary people as persons of consequence. It affirms the fundamental generosity and good-will of one and all. Conflict, aggression, deviance, madness, creativity are ignored, or shown as bad form. The good thing viewers learn is to be sociable, affable, relaxed, moving easily into and between pleasant small circles. The bland beam on at a mirror they take for a window.

---

[54] See especially Scott and U'Ren, *Leisure*, for the constriction of experience in a TV-soaked (new) working class suburb of Melbourne; Clark and Oliey, *op. cit.*, esp. vol. 1, chs. 3 and 7.

[55] Richard Hoggart, *The Uses of Literacy*, pp. 276-8.

[56] D. Horton and R. R. Wohl, "Mass Communication and Para-Social Interaction", *Psychiatry*, vol. 19, 1956, pp. 215-229.

229

PART V

MAXWELL NEWTON

15   The Economy

A MAJOR barrier to understanding the problems and needs of the Australian economy is the existence of myths about how the economy has performed in the past and how it works now. The existence—and widespread public acceptance—of these myths also colours and confuses political debate and inhibits constructive thinking about the adequacy of our political institutions for the tasks of the time.

There are three broad strands to current myths about the Australian economy. They are that it is:

(1) "a rapidly developing economy". Thus, in his 1959-1960 Budget speech the Federal Treasurer, Mr. Holt, talked of "the immense expansion and diversification of industry which has taken place (over the previous ten years) and . . . the gains in efficiency which have been made";

(2) highly egalitarian, with no great extremes of wealth and income;

(3) "a preponderantly free enterprise economy, in which the great bulk of goods and services are provided in response to demand, local or foreign". This quotation is from the Annual Economic Survey produced by the Federal Treasury. The Survey went on to say that:

> Governments, on their part, provide facilities to aid current production and future development and to meet the social and civic needs of the community. The Government goes beyond this, however, to encourage and assist private enterprise in particular directions, through, for example, tariff protection, bounties and subsidies, tax concessions, overseas trade promotion, special developmental works and the like. The underlying assumption is that, given the right facilities and economic climate, private enterprise will advance growth further, and along lines more acceptable to the community, than any alternative system could.[1]

These are the dominant myths. But there is another strand of thinking which has been of considerable importance during the period of growing industrialization since the end of the second world war. That is the general pride in the "development of Australian industry" and the willingness in the community to make the sacrifices needed to facilitate this development. What is only dimly understood is that Australian manufacturing industry is falling

[1] *The Australian Economy, 1962.* Treasury Report to Parliament, Government Printer, Canberra.

230

steadily under the control of foreign enterprises and that the ownership and control of great tracts of Australian industry are steadily passing out of the control of Australians. There will be more about this process later on in this chapter. For the time being, let us see what substance there is in the dominant three myths about Australia's economy.

They are comforting myths, but they beg most of the interesting questions about the Australian economy today. On closer examination, the Australian economy looks very different from what one would assume to be the case if prevailing myths were taken at face value. In fact, the Australian economy has grown at a relatively modest pace in the last decade when compared with other advanced countries; there are very wide differences in income; and there is an enormous range of regulation of economic activity in Australia. The existence of regulation of markets has long been recognized by economists, and theoretical explanations of how this regulation works have formed an important part of academic economic writing in the last three decades. Most attention by economists has been devoted to the explanation of how deviations from the "competitive norm" operate in the business sector, and here there has been the well known analysis of imperfect competition, oligopoly, monopoly and the like. The authors of a recent text state that their object is "to examine the Australian economy with the special task of determining the extent to which it diverges from the competitive *laissez-faire* model, both with respect to market organization and to the activities of government".[2]

In part, Australian experience fits neatly into these categories. Australian manufacturing industry, the monetary system (through the banks and the hire purchase companies) and the fields of privately-controlled communications (including press, radio, television) are all distinguished by oligopoly, with occasional examples of monopoly. The characteristic pattern in Australia in these fields is for a very few enterprises to control the majority of the industry's output. Some examples of this concentration of power, and hence of ability to regulate markets through control of output and price, are given below. For the moment, it is sufficient to say that in manufacturing industry, the monetary system and privately-owned communications the Australian markets are regulated markets, where "normal market forces" have little bearing on levels of output and price. There is nothing startling in this discovery, which has been long discussed in this country and elsewhere. The surprising fact is that the myth of "free enterprise"—a myth which would have us believe that normal competitive forces are the significant ones in deciding prices and levels of output—still commands such support outside academic circles. A more accurate description of the actual arrangement of the Australian economy—in manufacturing industry, money and banking and communications—would be that it is a system of "monopoly capitalism". The same goes for mining. In the case of retailing, there is a high degree of concentration in buying, *i.e.* "monopsony" rather than "monopoly".[3]

But regulation in the Australian economy extends far beyond the well known phenomena of oligopoly and monopoly. Government intervention is a most important form of regulation, often grafted on to a pattern of regulation of prices and output imposed by business itself. The Australian tariff is a powerful instrument for regulating output, investment and prices. Regu-

2 P. H. Karmel and Maureen Brunt, *The Structure of the Australian Economy*, p. 4.
3 *Ibid.*, pp. 72-6.

lation of transport is wide-ranging. Similarly, regulation of primary product markets is a major force, if not *the* major force, in the determination of prices, investment and output in the primary sector, where taxation policies also have a marked effect. In the field of money and banking, there is a system of complicated and detailed control by governments.

In addition to the effects of regulation there is the influence of public enterprise itself on pricing and output policies in individual industries, and on pricing and output policies in industries buying goods and services from government-owned enterprises. We need only think of the influence of government policies in the fields of electric power, water, land development, railways and air transport to understand that into the simplified analysis of oligopoly and monopoly there must be inserted a consideration of the role of governments before any approximation to the true balance of forces deciding levels of output, investment and prices can be reached. When this consideration is brought into the discussion, it is clear that it is very difficult indeed to decide whether the pattern of output and allocation of resources is the most efficient one. Simple invocation of textbook analysis of "monopoly capitalism", as a deviation from the "competitive norm" on the one hand, or of the disruptive effects of government intervention on the other side, are neither of them satisfactory benchmarks for judging the efficiency of the arrangements actually in being in the Australian economy.

This leads us to the next distinguishing feature of the Australian economy. It is that most of the regulation of the economy, whether by business itself—through oligopoly or monopoly—or by government, through taxation, tariffs, outright control of prices and output—or by government and business combined, as in the case of air transport—is haphazard. Regulatory measures often result from *ad hoc* political pressures, including wars, depressions, the desire for "national development" through forced industrialization, and particular crises such as the failure of Australian National Airways, which gave the Ansett interests the opportunity to move into domestic trunk air transport in a big way. The resulting patchwork of regulation may bear little resemblance to what could have been achieved if the issue of regulation had been squarely faced as a fact of life, and policies designed accordingly.

It is true, of course, that it is not possible to decide *a priori* which allocation of resources is the most desirable one. It is also difficult to decide *a priori* whether more regulation or more competition is the correct answer, right across the board, largely because things have gone far beyond that point. In some cases more competition may be desirable. Thus, more competition from imports is desirable in fields like dairy products, vegetables and textiles, where Australia's comparative advantages appear to be small. In the field of money and banking, the pattern of government regulation has reached a stage of confusion and anomaly where sweeping reforms in the pattern of regulation are necessary. The same goes for road and rail transport, where enormous confusion prevails. In other areas, such as the behaviour of unregulated enterprise in the securities markets and in the field of restrictive trade practices, more regulation is desirable, in order to improve the honesty and efficiency of current practices.

Again, in the field of fuel policy there is the difficult issue of competition between coal and oil, where "leaving it to the market" may not be the most efficient policy to adopt. Little or nothing is known of the cost patterns of oil refineries, of the transport costs of oil companies, of the effects on the future of coal as a fuel, of the regulation of coastal shipping. There is nothing to suggest that for Australia the most desirable solution to this problem is the current one where residual oil fuel sales are making steadily growing inroads on coal markets. These great issues of national policy are not open to solution by the adoption of a general policy of more or less regulation, no matter who does the regulating of markets. At the moment, such questions are not being examined carefully with the aim of reaching some solution based on rational examination of alternatives. Instead, the typical pattern is that of a constant tussle between sectional interests for more or less regulation in the furtherance of their own objectives.

A Rapidly Developing Economy?

Turning to the first major myth about the Australian economy—that it is a "rapidly developing economy"—we find that in the decade of the 'fifties, the rate of growth of the Australian economy was relatively modest. The following statistics give estimates of the average annual rate of growth in the 'fifties of gross domestic product in real terms.[4]

TABLE 1

Rates of Economic Growth in the 1950s

	%
Japan	9·1
Germany	7·5
Austria	5·7
Italy	5·7
Netherlands	4·6
Australia	4·3
Finland	4·2
France	4·0
Canada	3·9
Norway	3·4
United States	3·3
Sweden	3·3
New Zealand	3·1
Belgium	2·7
Denmark	2·7
United Kingdom	2·5

Australia's performance has been somewhat better than that of the United States and Canada, but not markedly better; it has been considerably better than that of the United Kingdom but markedly worse than that of Italy, Japan and Germany. When it is remembered, however, that over this period Australia enjoyed an above average rate of increase of population—some 2½% per annum—it is clear that the annual rate of increase of productivity in Australia has been fairly low, when compared with other advanced countries.

How much the population factor affected Australia's apparent rate of growth emerges from the following table, which shows the average annual rate of growth of real national product per man-year, between 1950 and 1959.[5]

[4] Figures derived from United Nations *World Economic Survey*, 1961, and *Australian National Accounts*, Commonwealth Statistician, Canberra, 1963.
[5] National Institute of Economic and Social Research, *Economic Review*, July 1961.

233

Over this period the average annual rate of increase of real gross national product per head of the population (which is not quite the same as per man) in Australia was between 1½% and 2%. Thus, while Australia's real product rose at a rate which was at least mediocre, compared with that of other advanced countries, the rise in her *efficiency* was very low by world standards.

TABLE 2

Rates of Growth per Man-Year

	%
Japan	6·1
Italy	4·7
Germany	4·5
France	3·6
Netherlands	3·4
Norway	3·1
Sweden	2·8
United States	2·2
Canada	2·0
Denmark	1·8
United Kingdom ..	1·7

The most interesting conclusion from these figures is that Australia's economic performance during the 'fifties was not particularly striking. It was certainly nothing like sufficient to justify any popular belief that Australia's growth over this decade was "immense" or "remarkable". It was, rather, average in total and well below average in terms of increasing efficiency.

Another well-known feature of Australia's growth over the decade of the 'fifties was its uneven character. The following table shows the annual increases in real gross national product in recent years.[6]

TABLE 3

Annual Increase in Gross National Product

	%
1949–50	+7·4
1950–51	+5·3
1951–52	+2·9
1952–53	−1·1
1953–54	+6·4
1954–55	+5·9
1955–56	+5·3
1956–57	+1·8
1957–58	+1·8
1958–59	+7·1
1959–60	+4·0
1960–61	+4·5
1961–62	−0·6

These figures are even more striking when shown graphically.

[6] Figures derived from *Australian National Accounts*.

TABLE 4

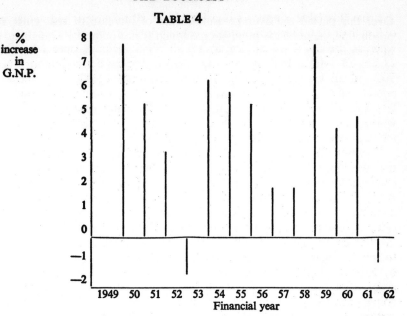

This unevenness is merely a reflection of the "stop-go" style of economic progress which was a feature of the 'fifties and has probably been an important contributor to the unspectacular total increase in output achieved over this time.

Economic Equality

There is a widespread myth that Australia is an egalitarian country, and that this is reflected in a more equitable distribution of income than exists in other advanced countries. An analysis of incomes as given in published taxation statistics gives little support to this view. The following table is based on the 41st annual report of the Commonwealth Taxation Commissioner, which gives figures for the financial year 1960-61.

TABLE 5

Income Distribution in Australia

Grade of Actual Income (£)	Number of Taxpayers	% of Taxpayers	Actual Income (£m)	% of Actual Income
105–499	772,000	17·7	237	5·0
500–999	1,410,000	32·4	1,052	22·2
1,000–1,999	1,850,000	42·5	2,453	51·6
2,000–4,999	284,000	6·5	740	15·6
5,000–9,999	29,000	0·7	185	3·9
10,000–19,999	4,300	0·1	58	1·2
20,000–49,999	640	—	19	0·4
50,000 and over	60	—	5	0·1
	4,350,000	100·0	4,750	100·0

235

From this table it appears that 92.6% of all taxpayers had actual incomes of less than £2,000 a year, but they earned only 78.7% of total actual income, whereas the 7.4% of all taxpayers who had incomes over £2,000 earned 21.3% of total actual income. Or, to put the matter differently, just over 50% of all taxpayers had incomes of less than £1,000, and these people earned only 27.1% of total actual income. If we exclude the group earning less than £1,000, which undoubtedly includes many young people, part-time workers and the like, we find that 30% of all income accruing to people with incomes over £1,000 was earned by the 14.7% with incomes over £2,000.

Taxation figures, of course, tell only part of the story, and the practice of tax avoidance—*i.e.* legal measures to reduce the liability—means that the extent of income inequality is almost certainly greater than shown in Table 5. As H. P. Brown has written, tax avoidance is mainly worth while for higher incomes and the degree to which it is worth while is directly related to tax rates. Consequently, apparent reductions of income inequality through high taxation are probably fictitious, and little if any significance should be attached to trends towards greater income equality. It has also been pointed out, *e.g.* by Kuznets, that income inequality shows a tendency to become greater in a period of rapid economic development, such as Australia has been undergoing since the second world war, and it is obvious that many large private fortunes have been made during this period. It is true that, compared with Britain, the United States and Western Europe, the size of the differentials in income is smaller in Australia, but the proportional distribution of large and small incomes is much the same.

Finally, there is no evidence that the strength of the Labour movement, or the working of the arbitration system, has enabled trade unions to secure a greater share of the national income during this century. There is no convincing statistical evidence of any radical change in "labour's share of the national income" over half a century. Since 1946 the ratio of wages and salaries to non-farm national income has remained remarkably stable, varying between 64% and 67% at the extremes.[7]

The Myth of "Free Enterprise"

What meaning is to be found in the myth, accepted by many sections of the community, that Australia has a "preponderantly free enterprise" economy? Here we enter a very tangled and difficult area of discussion. It is true that in some important respects private business in Australia operates under less restraint, and under fewer obligations to account to the community for its actions, than in other advanced economies. Thus, there is no effective anti-trust legislation in Australia. There is, accordingly, little information about the extent of restrictive practices and manipulation of markets by business itself, although ordinary observation and the large volume of evidence presented to the Tariff Board indicate clearly that there is a mass of restrictive trade practices at work in Australia. Nor is there any Securities and Exchange Commission in Australia to supervise the markets in securities. Supervision

[7] For discussion of these points see Karmel and Brunt, *op. cit.*, pp. 42-7; H. P. Brown, "The Composition of Personal Income", *Economic Record*, June 1949; Simon Kuznets, "Economic Growth and Income Inequality", *American Economic Review*, vol. 45, no. 1, 1955; H. P. Brown, "Estimation of Income Distribution in Australia", in *Income and Wealth* series 6, 1957, and other papers in the same volume; R. M. Titmuss, *Income Distribution and Social Change;* Gabriel Kolko, *Wealth and Power in America.*

of standards in this sphere is left to the Stock Exchanges themselves, often with unfortunate results for investors. In so far as business is not obliged by law to account for its actions, there is no doubt that the environment is unusually favourable for private enterprise.

However, in this environment, it is clear that the operation of "normal competitive market forces" has been considerably muted by the actions of business itself. This has followed from the high degree of concentration in Australian industry and from the freedom for the development of restrictive practices. Some examples of the degree of concentration in Australian industry are given below where the firms mentioned under each industry heading control more than half the output in the industry concerned.[8]

TABLE 6

Concentration in Manufacturing Industry

Iron and Steel	B.H.P. Co. Ltd.
Flat Steel Products	John Lysaght (Aust.) Ltd.
Steel Tubes	Tubemakers Ltd. (majority interest held by Stewarts & Lloyds of the U.K. and minority interest by B.H.P.)
Nitrogenous Fertilizers	I.C.I.A.N.Z. and Australian Fertilizers, in joint venture at Botany, N.S.W. E.Z. Industries Ltd. B.H.P. Co. Ltd. Australian Gas Light Co. (marginal producer) A.C.I. Ltd.
Can Manufacture	Containers Ltd. (which has close links with Metal Box Co. of U.K.) J. Gadsden Ltd. Queensland Can Ltd. (in which Containers Ltd. and Metal Box Co. of U.K. are minority shareholders).
Sugar Refining	C.S.R. Ltd.
Plastics—rigid and flexible containers	I.C.I.A.N.Z. Moulded Products Ltd. A.C.I. Ltd.
Soap and detergents	Unilever (Aust.) Pty. Ltd. Colgate-Palmolive (Aust.) Pty. Ltd.
Motor Cars	General Motors-Holdens Pty. Ltd. Ford Motor Co. of Australia. British Motor Corporation. Volkswagen. Chrysler. (together accounting for more than 85% of the market).
Rubber	Dunlop Rubber (Australia) Ltd. Olympic Industries Ltd. Goodyear Tyre and Rubber Co. (Aust.) Ltd. H. C. Sleigh (through subsidiary, Hardie Rubber Co. Pty. Ltd.) S.A. Rubber (accounting together for more than 80% of the market).

[8] For discussions of industrial concentration see Karmel and Brunt, *op. cit.*, ch. 3; E. L. Wheelwright, *Ownership and Control of Australian Companies;* A. R. Hall, *Australian Company Finance 1946-55;* Alex Hunter, "Restrictive Practices and Monopolies in Australia", *Economic Record,* March 1961; and the periodic reviews of industry published by the Industries Division, Commonwealth Department of Trade and Industry.

Beer	Carlton and United Breweries group. South Australian Brewing Co. Ltd. Swan Brewery Ltd. Tooth and Co. Castlemaine Perkins Ltd. (together accounting for more than 80% of the market).
Copper—primary production and extraction	Mt. Isa Mines Ltd. Mt. Lyell Mining Co. Mount Morgan Ltd.
Lead and Zinc smelting	E.Z. Industries. Sulphide Corporation. Broken Hill Associated Smelters.
Aluminium—primary production and extraction	Comalco Industries Pty. Ltd. Alcoa of Australia Pty. Ltd.
Telephone equipment	Standard Telephones & Cables Pty. Ltd. Telephone & Electrical Equipment. Ericsson Telephones Ltd.
Tobacco	Rothmans British Tobacco Godfrey Phillips Philip Morris (together accounting for more than 90% of the market).
Photographic Film	Kodak (A/asia) Pty. Ltd. Ilford (Aust.) Pty. Ltd. (together accounting for more than 70% of the market).
Railway Rolling Stock	Clyde Industries Ltd. A. G. Healing-Goodwin Group. Comeng Holdings (together accounting for more than 70% of the market).
Pulp, Paper and Board	Australian Paper Manufacturers. Associated Pulp & Paper Mills. Bowater-Scott. Cellulose Australia Ltd. (together accounting for more than 75% of the market).
Newspapers, Magazines, Television	Consolidated Press. John Fairfax & Sons Ltd. Herald & Weekly Times Ltd. News Ltd.

These are merely examples of a situation which applies in much of Australian industry. There is nothing original in the discovery that there is a large degree of concentration. According to Karmel and Brunt, one-third of Australian manufacturing industry is *highly* concentrated, *i.e.* the largest four firms in the industry account for 50% of employment, and one-half is at least *fairly* concentrated, *i.e.* the largest eight firms account for 50% of employment.[9] By comparison with the United States, monopolistic and highly oligopolistic markets are "overwhelmingly more important"; by comparison with the United Kingdom and Canada, they are "significantly more important".[10]

Nor is there anything original in the discovery that restrictive trade practices are very widespread in Australia. But at least this can be said. The existence of a high degree of concentration in industry and the existence of widespread restrictive practices mean that the responsiveness of industry to

[9] *Op. cit.*, pp. 78-9.
[10] *Ibid.*, p. 87.

238

demand can be very much slower than if a more freely competitive environment prevailed. The absence of anti-trust legislation makes it particularly difficult, in the Australian environment, to decide to what extent the administration of restrictive practices and the use of the power concentrated in a few hands in major industries are being deployed in the public interest. It is no answer to such doubt that "competition will make things right", because competition is not a particularly strong force working in the Australian economy.

Methods of Regulation

It follows from what has already been said that the operation of the market mechanism in Australia is prevented by two major features of the economic system: the concentration of ownership on the one side, which places great power in the hands of a small number of individuals, and the pervasiveness of government intervention and regulation on the other. In the long run, of course, no industrial economy can fail to respond to the play of market forces. In everyday life, however, these two factors are of the greatest importance; they permeate the institutional structure of the economic system, their effects are felt throughout the social framework, and they provide foci of interest and attention which influence the wider patterns of thought and behaviour throughout Australian society.

Perhaps the outstanding instance of government intervention, and one with a history going back a century, is the tariff system. The tariff has its most direct influence on those industries whose products compete with imported goods. Since this category represents the bulk of secondary industry, the impact is far-reaching indeed. Between 55 and 60% of the 1.2 million people engaged in secondary industry in Australia work in industries whose economic viability depends in varying degrees on tariffs. Almost 70% of this proportion is accounted for by industries producing machinery, motor vehicles, light to medium engineering products, paper, textiles, electrical apparatus and chemicals. The precise extent to which individual industries depend on tariffs hinges not only on their effective level of protective duties, but also on their interdependence with other industries producing import-competing products. As it is not normal practice to indicate the *ad valorem* equivalents of specific or composite duties, it is extremely difficult to appraise the exact level of protection enjoyed by import-competing industry.

But, to judge from recent estimates by Dr W. M. Corden, the average tariff for those goods which the tariff protects is as high as 30% *ad valorem*.[11] For some industries—notably sections of the textile industry—the effective tariff wall may be as high as 100%. It is therefore quite clear that the tariff is a major factor affecting the level of output of major areas of industry, levels of profitability and of investment.

As is well known, the last few years, since the abolition of most quantitative import controls, have seen considerable increases in tariff levels for major industries and the introduction of the system of temporary or emergency tariff protection which has added a further complicating factor. What has also emerged over these years is a developing confusion about the principles which should guide the Tariff Board in the administration of the tariff.

[11] W. M. Corden, "The Tariff", in Alex Hunter (ed.), *The Economics of Australian Industry*, p. 193.

Eventually, of course, all tariff decisions are decisions which have to be taken by the Commonwealth government, which means there is a great and growing field for government intervention in the direction of resources and the manipulation of investment and profitability of individual industries. It is remarkable, bearing in mind the importance of the tariff for the future disposition of resources in the community, that there is so little concern with tariff matters outside the circles of directly interested parties. This also goes for the Federal parliament, where great issues of tariff protection, involving the future viability of industries as important as the paper industry, the chemical industry, the textile industry and the motor industry, are rarely discussed except on the most banal level.

Much has been made in the past of the "independence" of the Tariff Board. In fact, it is up to the Minister for Trade and Industry to decide whether a matter will be referred to the Tariff Board in the first place. This means that the Minister—and his Department—need to be convinced that there is a *prima facie* case for a tariff to help an industry. After the Tariff Board has investigated the matter, it is up to the Minister to decide whether he will accept the recommendation. There is thus enormous scope for ministerial direction of the tariff, and accordingly the direction of use of resources in the community. There is also a powerful incentive for the development of industry pressure groups to excite the interest of the Minister in the problems of the industry.

Thus, inevitably, there has developed an intricate pattern of political and industrial relationships whose result has been a great extension of the degree of regulation of economic activity in Australia. A distinguishing feature of much of this regulation has been its unsystematic and chaotic nature. A tariff, once granted, is only rarely re-examined at some fixed future date to see whether the same degree of protection is still required. Applications for tariff protection often arise from particularly difficult temporary situations which may soon change—but there is little provision for going back to earlier tariff decisions to see whether they are still appropriate. The Tariff Board itself has relatively scanty resources for investigating and analysing the problems brought before it—despite its crucial importance for the very survival of many large industry groups. The Tariff Board is continually having to go back again and again to provide for the survival of some industries—chemicals and textiles are good examples—but there is no provision, under the present machinery or principles, for the Tariff Board to outline some more permanent solution for particular industry problems.

There is a strong case, for example, for the preparation of a "Beeching Report" on the textile industry providing for definite proposals about re-allocation of industry, retrenchment and modernization.

On the political level, the effect of regulation through the tariff has been largely to by-pass parliament as an effective forum for the discussion of these economic issues. In part, this is a reflection of the general failure of parliament as a body for supervising the public interest in the regulation of the economy. In addition, a sort of subterranean political system has developed where industry pressure groups maintain steady liaison with Commonwealth officials and ministers in furthering their own interests. The result is that great decisions are being taken, affecting the direction of the whole economy and the profitability of individual companies, spasmodically and to a large extent beyond the knowledge of the mass of the people and beyond the reach of public criticism. When it is also recognized that many tariff decisions have the effect of bolstering domestic restrictive practices against the main form of competition that is left—competition from abroad—it can be seen that there is room for enormous improvement in the administration of the tariff and in the institutions and means by which the public interest is served and can be seen to be served in the decisions that are made.

It seems reasonably certain that the Tariff Board is carrying out a function analogous to that of a national planning body in making recommendations about the direction of resources in the community. Yet it is essentially a rather amateurish body, ill-equipped with secretariat and research staff, and confused about its objectives. The Federal Government, through its responsibilities for the tariff, is also deeply committed to a form of economic planning. But the Liberal government, which has been in power since 1949, is not willing to face this issue squarely. It wants to maintain the myth that "competitive private enterprise" is the dominant force in the economic life of the nation and to treat tariff matters as aberrations from the norm which can be treated in an *ad hoc,* random fashion. The community at large knows that economic planning is taking place but has no way of being confident that its interests are being looked to.

But regulation of industry—and *de facto* economic planning—goes much farther in Australia today than the mere ramifications of the tariff. Concentration of industry, restrictive trade practices, economic planning and direction of resources through the tariff—these are only part of the pattern of regulation in Australia. In several key areas, other forms of economic regulation exert a dominating force on the level of output, prices, investment and profits. One such area is that of money and credit. In the field of banking, some of the more important aspects of regulation include the control of trading bank advances and the trading banks' free liquidity through the instrument of statutory reserve deposits; control over trading banks' and savings banks' interest rates; and control over the disposition of trading bank and savings bank assets.

The present system of central bank control dates from the emergency measures adopted in 1941 under the wartime powers of the Commonwealth government. These included various controls over bank liquidity, qualitative control of bank credit, power to give directions on bank advance policy, and power over trading bank purchases of government securities. Under the Commonwealth Bank Act and the Banking Act of 1945, the Commonwealth Bank retained most of these powers, although the exercise of some of them was later abandoned. Under legislation passed by the Liberal government in 1953, minor changes were made under pressure from the private banks which had no material effect on the powers of the central bank. Following renewed pressure from the private banks, further legislation was passed in 1959. The "special account" system to which the private banks had objected so strenuously was replaced by a system of statutory "reserve deposits", which was little more than a change of name, and that little may actually have strengthened the powers of the central bank. In addition, the central bank was renamed the Reserve Bank of Australia, and its trading and savings bank

241

functions were placed under a new body, the Commonwealth Banking Corporation.[12]

Some of the most important controls now exercised by the Reserve Bank are the so-called 70/30 rule, under which savings banks must invest a minimum of 70% of assets in government securities; the conventional agreement by which trading banks hold 18% of deposits in the form of government securities, cash and other liquid assets; the Term Lending fund, which may consist of 4% of trading banks' deposits; and controls over the amount of their deposits which trading banks may invest in the short term money market. The effect of these controls has been, in recent years, to encourage a decline in the importance of the banks as a source of credit, as the controls discriminated against banks compared with other financial institutions. A major liberalization of controls over banks was made in April 1962 and since that time there has been a recovery in the profitability of banks and in their importance as sources of credit.

This merely underlines the importance of regulation as a factor in the development of banks, and a feature of regulation in the last decade has been that it has operated in such a way as materially to inhibit the progress of banks as compared with other sources of credit in the community—but the regulation has not been based on any recognizable, consistent policy or doctrine. On the contrary, the development of official policy towards banking has comprised a series of expedients aimed at meeting some particular exigency. This policy of expediency has usually operated within a basic framework of reluctance on the part of the Liberal government to pursue a leading role in the field of interest rates, where official policy, acting principally through changes in the long term Commonwealth bond rate, has been consistently laggardly, attempting to meet situations only as they arose.

While there is much to criticize in the formulation and execution of banking policy in the last decade, the policy cannot be adequately explained by reference to what is generally supposed to be the overriding political dogma of the Liberal and Country Parties, namely a concern for the interests of "private enterprise". It is perhaps best explained as the rather stumbling process of learning how to administer controls over the total volume of credit in the community, against the background of an imperfect understanding of the trends in the market for credit as a whole and of the importance of interest rate changes.

Outside the field of banking, these are some of the more important aspects of regulation of money and credit:

(a) Short term money market dealers operate within individual borrowing quotas set for them by the Reserve Bank;

(b) Life insurance companies and superannuation funds now operate under a very complicated set of official quotas obliging them to meet certain targets—under pain of substantial tax penalties—for their holdings of government securities of different kinds;

(c) Tax advantages accruing to holders of government securities—both individuals and institutions—have largely distorted the pattern of

---

[12] For a full discussion of central banking, see H. W. Arndt, *The Australian Trading Banks,* ch. 8, and H. C. Coombs, *Conditions of Monetary Policy in Australia,* the R. C. Mills Memorial Lecture, 1958.

interest rates in the community. One such important tax advantage is the 2/- in the pound rebate of tax on Commonwealth loan interest, introduced to solve a particular problem upon the establishment of uniform taxation in 1942, which now has a deeply distorting effect on interest rates. A feature of this non-banking regulation—as of the regulation of the banks—is that much of it has evolved haphazardly, partly as a result of the efforts of those responsible for regulation to avoid paying a higher market price for the product they are trying to sell—namely, government bonds.

As in the field of tariff policy, so in the regulation of the money market, real power has lain with the officials in the government bodies concerned. In the case of tariff administration, the locus of power is in the Department of Trade and Industry; in the case of the money market, with the Treasury and the Reserve Bank. *Ad hoc* administrative methods have been evolved, instruments for carrying them out have been devised. Broad political considerations of "socialism" or "liberalism" are hardly relevant. Not only has much of the dogma gone out of the arguments, but the real issues of policy, being matters essentially of administration, rarely become the subject of effective public discussion, partly because of a relatively unsophisticated public opinion, and partly because the level of understanding in parliament of the issues at stake has always been low. As a result, ministers and public servants are largely free from detailed, knowledgeable interrogation about their administration.

Another area which is the subject of detailed and powerful regulation is that of primary industry. Some of the more important aspects of regulation in this field are:

(a) the discriminatory tax advantages accruing to primary producers, including the power to average income over five years; the right to depreciate buildings; freedom from sales tax over a large range of items; freedom to deduct practically all capital expenditure made for the purpose of increasing productive capacity.

(b) outright embargoes on competitive imports—as of dairy products, sugar, fruit, rice.

(c) control over the production of competitive margarine.

(d) administered "home price" schemes which provide for high domestic prices and dumping of export surpluses—as in the cases of butter, cheese, sugar, wheat, canned and dried fruits.

(e) "customs drawback" schemes, such as that operating for tobacco, where manufacturers are obliged to take up certain arbitrary proportions of domestic leaf in order to qualify for customs duty concessions on imported leaf.

(f) outright subsidies, as in the cases of butter and wheat.

As in the case of financial regulation and of tariff regulation, a notable feature of state intervention in primary produce marketing is that it has followed no uniform pattern. Some products do not qualify for special advantages (outside the general taxation concessions which advantage primary production as a whole) and among these are wool and meat. For wheat, a formula has been evolved under which the "cost of production" of wheat is established, and this price is paid under the present scheme (now due to be altered) for all wheat consumed domestically and for up to 150 million bushels of export wheat. A key item in the calculation is the average yield of wheat per acre, taken as the basis for calculating the "cost of production". This figure is determined by a process of departmental and political haggling, with the outcome based on the assessment by the government of the balance of political forces between country and city interests rather than by any objective and predetermined procedure.

There is no need to go into great detail to describe the pattern of regulation of primary industry (I have not begun to describe the further pattern of regulation at state level), but it is perhaps the most erratic form of regulation in existence. Some products qualify for outright subsidy; others do not. Some qualify for "home consumption price" schemes, others do not. Some qualify for "price stabilization" schemes based on publicly available "formulae" (wheat); others qualify for "price stabilization" schemes but the methods used for determining the "cost of production" are shrouded in mystery. This is the case with sugar, which is surely one of the most outrageous schemes of all. The "home consumption" price of sugar is determined jointly by consultation between the Commonwealth and Queensland governments—but there is no public information available to tell how the "cost of production" is determined. The Colonial Sugar Refining Co. Ltd. represents a virtually complete monopoly whose position is, in effect, guaranteed by government action, and the relations between C.S.R. and the two governments concerned are impenetrable. The report of a committee of inquiry into the sugar industry, presented to the Commonwealth government in 1962, was suppressed by the Minister for Primary Industry.

Confusion in the regulation of primary product markets is not peculiar to Australia. In all advanced countries, and for that matter in many economically backward ones, farm interests have succeeded in manipulating political processes to achieve special advantages for themselves. The United States, France, and Britain are outstanding instances. In Australia the position of farmers is strengthened by some circumstances peculiar to this country. The political strength of rural interests has been fortified in State politics by the gerrymandering of electorates, as in South Australia and until recently in Victoria, and in Federal politics by the disproportionate weight given to rural votes in the distribution of seats. The ability of the Country Party, with the aid of the preferential voting system, to hold the balance of power in both State and Federal parliaments, has meant that farmers' representatives are frequently able to hold ministerial portfolios which enable them to advance rural interests directly. The report of an inquiry into the dairy industry in 1961, presented to a Country Party minister for Primary Industry, was quietly slipped under the mat because the solutions it recommended for major problems of the industry were unpalatable to the dairy farmers. The influence of the Country Party has also been important in establishing the practice by which most decisions affecting rural industries are in effect taken by the producers themselves, either through a vote or by the operation of marketing boards which consist almost entirely of producer representatives. A recent example of a vote was the proposal for a reserve price scheme for wool. The abdication of responsibility by governments in the case of wool has serious long-term implications. As a recent symposium on the wool industry observes, "much more economic research on wool marketing problems has been done by the U.S. Department of Agriculture than in Australia". The same writer adds that the most serious indictment of the wool marketing system is that it "operates on a day-to-day basis with little attempt to improve or adapt itself to changing conditions".[13] Another contributor, after outlining the case for a central marketing authority, concludes gloomily that the political problems of establishing one are "considerable".[14]

The great political interest attaching to the regulation of primary production is, therefore, that the development of sectional pressure group activity has been carried to greater lengths, and has evolved into more formal machinery, than is the case for other community pressure groups. This development is facilitated by the great limitations placed on the Commonwealth government by the federal constitution. It is also aided by the fact that urban manufacturing interests, which might be expected to oppose the use of political power by rural groups, have usually found it expedient to unite politically with the Country Party to prevent the Labour Party from gaining power. Also, manufacturing interests have been just as anxious as the farmers to use political power to gain useful concessions for themselves. They are consequently unable to argue against farmers' activities in principle, and are left only with the much weaker contention that farmers have been making too much of a good thing. Farmers, in their turn, contend that if Australia wants "national development", and if this means forced industrialization, it is not fair to expect rural interests, selling on open world markets, to absorb the higher costs entailed in forced industrialization without some compensations. The result is a kind of merry-go-round, with farmers demanding more subsidies because of high costs, and manufacturing interests demanding more protection and other advantages in the name of "national development".

Thus, inefficient or costly producers of all kinds have a mutual interest in devices to bolster their position, whether they are industrial monopolists or small primary producers. The loser, in general, is the community at large in its role of consumer, and in the regulated economy the consumer is likely to go on being the loser.

The Transport Chaos

Transport is another highly regulated area where the picture is one of erratic and conflicting forms of regulation. In the field of road transport, interstate road traffic is largely free of controls, while intra-state road operations are subject to a very complex system of restrictions, which differ in their incidence from state to state. State governments have acted to inhibit intra-state road transport in order to protect their railway systems. One effect of the resulting pattern of regulation has been to cause traffic on comparatively short hauls, best suited to road transport, to go by rail and long hauls, best suited to rail, to go by road. This already bad situation was aggravated as a result of the 1954 Privy Council decision in the Hughes and Vale case.[15]

Present rail freight charges are still conditioned by the original rate structure, which was conceived against the background of a monopoly in inland

[13] F. H. Gruen, in Alan Barnard (ed.), *The Simple Fleece*, p. 506.
[14] R. Boyer, in *ibid.*, p. 541.
[15] (1954) 93 C.L.R.1 (P.C.); *ibid.*, 127; *ibid.*, 247.

transport, on an *ad valorem* basis, or what the traffic would bear. Before their monopoly was seriously challenged by road transport, the railways were able with this pricing policy to maximize the volume of business they lifted by subsidizing freight loads, which were highly sensitive to price changes, from traffic which could be safely charged relatively high rates. Growing road competition had undermined the railways' traditional tariff structure. But because railway fare and rate structures have been, and still are, used as instruments of state government policies they have yet to reflect the vastly changed conditions of the last few decades. Thus, costs per ton-mile in railway operations will be comparatively low in those operations where the railways can run trains loaded to full or near-full capacity on dense traffic lines. On branch lines or low-density lines railway costs rise sharply. As railway freight rates tend to be highly inflexible, reflecting for the most part what are seen to be state political exigencies, railways are often unable to compete effectively on main trunk routes with road transport, while unduly low rates on low-density lines cause the railway to undercut the road at just the point where railway operations are the most uneconomic.

Clearly, a major overhaul of railway rating patterns, involving major political decisions, is needed for the achievement of a more economical distribution of the national transport effort between road and rail.

In addition, there is a chaotic pattern of regulation of road transport between the various states. Whereas in N.S.W. and Queensland, for example, the regulatory authorities restrict road transport by applying a ton-mile tax on road haulage, in other states a permit system operates. Again, whereas in Western Australia vehicles operating within 20 miles of the G.P.O., Perth, or within a 20-mile radius of the owner's place of business are exempt from licensing, in N.S.W. the matter is at the discretion of the Commissioner of Motor Transport. In Tasmania the whole licensing and permit system is geared to protect rail services at almost any cost, while Queensland applies relatively mild restrictions on road competition with rail. And so it goes on.

In theory, regulated competition in inland transport is supposed to eliminate "wasteful competition", but in practice it has evolved into a method of protecting the states' railway systems—with the open door of unregulated interstate road transport in the background.

In the field of air transport, the Commonwealth government has most of the power, subject to its lack of constitutional control over intra-state air transport. The Commonwealth has effective control over the rates, schedules, investment plans and, to a considerable degree, profits, of the two main trunk operators, Ansett-ANA and Trans-Australia Airlines. It has been able in recent years to control the types of aircraft purchased and to manipulate the division of traffic routes between the two main operators to bring about a finely balanced equilibrium of strength between Ansett-ANA and TAA. A feature of the regulation of domestic air transport in recent years is the intensely political atmosphere in which it has been conducted, and the lengths to which the Liberal government has gone to protect Ansett-ANA, the key part of its "two airline" policy. Indeed, the intense lobbying and pressure exerted during the administration of this policy in recent times provide a striking example of the problems and issues which arise in the regulated economy. Parliament has discussed the issues at great length, but the debates are more notable for the heat than the light they have generated. In the event, the Cabinet has been deeply and frequently involved in regulation down to the most detailed level.

In the field of transport regulation, the problems arising from the federal political structure emerge in some of their most difficult manifestations. The Commonwealth has major authority over sea and air transport, the state governments control road and rail. It is almost impossible to arrive at sensible alternative investment policies as between different forms of transport, and even if constitutional problems were absent, there are deep-seated political problems to be solved before any order can be drawn out of the chaotic administration of intra-state traffic on road and rail. The whole area is clouded by intense political pressure, and there is enormous scope for administrative action which is rarely challenged in public debate.

Here is another area where economic planning is taking place all the time but where the criteria governing the planning are confused, where reliable information is grossly deficient (particularly as to relative real costs of different forms of transport) and where the long-term role of transport in the economy as a whole is rarely considered.

Special Interests and the General Interest

One could go on to continue the catalogue of regulation of economic life, of which this chapter merely gives the briefest of outlines. Summing up, it is clear that economic planning and the manipulation of markets is the order of the day in Australian economic life. There is regulation by business itself—through the use of concentrated economic power and restrictive practices. There is regulation by governments—through the tariff, through regulation of transport, through regulation of money markets, through regulation of primary industry. There is interaction between governments and industries, between governments and individual firms, where the interests of government administrators and of sectional pressure groups are resolved. It is here that the real substance of political activity is to be found.

This is not political activity in the traditional sense, involving arguments about principle. In the regulated economy, most arguments are about money, and are concerned with the thousand issues of detailed administration which have such a major bearing—in many situations *the* major bearing—on profits, investment, output and prices. In this process, issues of principle hardly arise—except where they can be exploited for sectional gain. Regulation of economic life in Australia has evolved to such a point of complexity, and the web of regulation is so tangled, that the larger interests of the community appear to have been lost sight of; indeed, there are some students of politics who deny the existence of a general interest, or the possibility of identifying it if it does exist. Such a viewpoint is understandable in the face of a tangled network of decision-making where questions of policy are settled not as the result of public debate but through negotiation between the administration and interested parties. Yet the undesirable consequences of this situation can only be remedied, even if only partially, if some opportunity exists for identifying and pursuing the general interest as a counter to the claims of multifarious special interest groups.

For this, at least three major reforms seem to be required. The first is a recognition in the community that the Australian economy is in most important respects a regulated economy. It is not, to quote the 1962 Economic Survey again, "a preponderantly free enterprise economy, in which the great bulk of goods and services are provided in response to demand, local or foreign"—not at least in the traditional sense of such an economy, one in which "normal market forces" determine the direction of resources. It is riddled with controls and interventions, quotas and fixed prices, subsidies and barriers to competition. Above all, it is in many respects, possibly in most important respects, a planned economy—although it may not seem so because the "planning" which takes place is chaotic.

This lack of realism about the nature of the Australian economy is widespread in popular thinking and is undoubtedly fostered by those groups benefiting from the regulation which takes place. An understanding of what is actually going on is not lacking among Australian economists, nor among public servants responsible for administering our regulated economy at the official level; yet for political reasons, an official document like the Economic Survey gives support to myths about the nature of the economy. The currency of such myths helps to give us many of the vices of a regulated economy without the virtues which could flow from more rational and co-ordinated regulation. Of course, the federal structure of government is a major barrier to co-ordination, but even in a field where the Commonwealth has practically the sole power—as with money and banking—regulation still remains sporadic.

The second major reform which seems to be required is the evolution of new institutions responsible for drawing some order out of the web of planning which exists. In other words, there is a need for a great improvement in the quality of economic planning. The Tariff Board is lamentably ill-equipped for the tasks it has to assume. The administration of regulation of primary industry needs to be greatly improved, to bring order and consistency into the prevailing disorder and inconsistencies of planning in this area. Reform is needed in the present divided state-federal control over transport.

Finally, there is a great need for new institutions to allow the community at large an effective voice in the critical examination of the regulatory apparatus, at least on the federal level. In particular, the role of parliament needs to be strengthened as against the executive, perhaps through the development of the committee system which would enable parliamentarians to examine the details of administration and to focus more public attention on the workings of the system.

The Role of Overseas Ownership

Earlier in this chapter, reference was made to another strand of popular thought about the Australian economy, i.e. the general pride in the "development of Australian industry". It was pointed out that it is only dimly understood how Australian manufacturing industry is steadily falling under the control of foreign enterprises. The list which follows shows industries in which foreign companies are dominant and industries heavily infiltrated by foreign companies.

Naked nationalism is a comforting emotion at times, but it would be wrong to treat growing foreign control over Australian industry as undesirable merely because it is foreign. In many respects, the invasion of the Australian economy by foreign companies in recent years has had a salutary effect, by helping to break down local restrictive trade practices and by bringing in a new range of improved management and technology. But Australians would be foolish to close their eyes to the growing foreign control of the Australian economy, or to fail to recognize that this may eventually prove a very costly exercise for this country, which will have to find the resources to service the heavy debts now being incurred.

TABLE 7
Foreign Ownership of Industry
1. Industries Dominated by Foreign Companies

Agricultural Machinery—
Tractors

Massey-Ferguson (Aust.) Ltd.
International Harvester Co.
Ford Motor Co.

Motor Cars

General Motors-Holdens.
Ford Motor Co.
Volkswagen.
British Motor Corporation.
Chrysler.
Rootes.

Motor Trucks

General Motors-Holdens.
International Harvester Co.
Ford Motor Co.
British Motor Corporation.
Rootes.
Chrysler.
Leyland Motors.

Heavy Chemicals—
Petrochemicals

A.P.C. Ltd. (owned by two U.S. Standard groups, Socony Mobil and Standard Oil of New Jersey).
B.F. Goodrich-C.S.R. Chemicals (60% owned by B.F. Goodrich).
Australian Synthetic Rubber (70% owned by U.S. Standard Oil group).
Shell Chemicals (Aust.) Pty. Ltd.
I.C.I.A.N.Z. (53-54% owned by I.C.I.)
Australian Petrochemicals (50% owned by Monsanto Chemicals).

Other heavy chemicals

Union Carbide.
Monsanto Chemicals.
C.S.R. Chemicals (in which Distillers Ltd. of U.K. has a 40% stake).
Albright & Wilson (Aust.) Pty. Ltd. (in which U.K. parent has majority control).
Laporte Industries Pty. Ltd. (wholly owned subsidiary of Laporte, U.K.)
Australian Titan Products Pty. Ltd. (owned by U.K. parent).

Light Chemicals, such as
fluorocarbons

Australian Fluorine Chemicals Pty. Ltd. (jointly owned by Monsanto Chemicals and C.R.A. Ltd., which in turn has more than 90% of stock owned by U.K. parent).
Pacific Chemical Industries Pty. Ltd. (a joint venture of Ugine Chemical Co. of France and Stauffer Chemical Co. Pty. Ltd., which in turn is effectively controlled by U.S. parent).

Paints and Industrial
paints

B.A.L.M. Paints Ltd. (70% owned by I.C.I.A.N.Z.; remainder by consortium of U.K. companies).
Lewis Berger & Sons Pty. Ltd. (wholly owned subsidiary of U.K. parent company).
Taubmans Industries Ltd. (54% owned by Courtaulds, U.K.)
British Paints Pty. Ltd. (wholly owned by U.K. parent).
International Paints Pty. Ltd. (wholly owned by International Paints (Holdings) Pty. Ltd., a British company).

249

Aluminium—primary production and extraction	Comalco Industries (jointly owned by C.R.A. Ltd. and Kaiser Aluminium).
	Alcoa of Australia Pty. Ltd. (51% by Alcoa of U.S., remainder by Western Mining, B.H. South and North Broken Hill).
Aluminium fabrication	Comalco Products Pty. Ltd. (C.R.A. and Kaiser).
	Australuco (wholly owned subsidiary of Alcan).
	G. E. Crane & Sons Ltd. (substantial minority interest by Comalco Industries.)
Oil Refining	Caltex Oil.
	Amoco Australia.
	Socony Mobil.
	Australian Lubricating Oil Refinery (in which Caltex owns 50%, Ampol 25%, H. C. Sleigh 25%).
	H. C. Sleigh (in which California Texas Oil Corporation has substantial minority interest).
	B.O.R.A.L. (in which California Texas Oil Corporation has about a 23% equity).
	B.P. Kwinana Pty. Ltd.
Matches	Bryant & May Pty. Ltd.
	Federal Match Co. Pty. Ltd.
	W.A. Match Co. Pty. Ltd.
	(all three effectively controlled by Bryant & May Ltd., U.K.)
Soap and detergents	Unilever Australia Pty. Ltd. (U.K.-Dutch parent).
	Colgate-Palmolive Pty. Ltd. (U.S. group), and still in the background Procter & Gamble (associated with local Marrickville group).
Telephone equipment	T.E.I. (owned by British Plessey group and General Electric).
	L. M. Ericsson (Sweden; local company Ericsson Telephones Ltd.)
	Standard Telephones & Cables (U.S.).
Cables	Cable Makers Australia Pty. Ltd. (U.K. parent—British Insulated Callenders Cables Ltd.)
	Insulated Wires Australia Pty. Ltd. (U.K. parent—British Insulated Callenders Cables Ltd.)
	Pyrotenax Australia Pty. Ltd.; Pyrotenax Cables Pty. Ltd.; Pyrotenax (N.S.W.) Pty. Ltd.—all controlled by Pyrotenax Ltd., U.K.
Pharmaceuticals—ethicals	Abbott Laboratories (U.S.)
	Burroughs Wellcome (U.K.)
	Ciba (Swiss).
	Glaxo-Allenburys (U.K.)
	Lederle (subsidiary of U.S. Cyanamid).
	Eli Lilly (U.S.)
	Parke Davis (U.S.)
	Merck, Sharp and Dohme (U.S.)
	Pfizer Corporation (U.S.)
	Schering companies (one U.S. controlled and the other West German controlled).
	Squibb (U.S.)
	Smith Kline & French (U.S.)

2. *Industries Heavily Infiltrated by Foreign Companies*

Food	Nestlé Company, which also owns Crosse & Blackwell interests (Swiss subsidiary).
	Unilever (U.K.-Dutch subsidiary).
	Kraft Foods (effectively controlled by U.S. National Dairy Foods Corporation).
	H. J. Heinz (U.S.)
	General Foods of U.S. (through takeover of Parsons).

Campbell's Soups (U.S.)

Geo. Weston (U.K. group with big interests in bread, flour and biscuits).

Nabisco (U.S.), through takeover of Purina cereal interests.

Pillsbury Corporation of U.S. (through joint flour interests with Gillespie in "White Wings").

Rubber

Goodyear Tyre & Rubber Co. (in which Goodyear Tyre & Rubber of Akron, U.S., has an overwhelming interest).

B. F. Goodrich (75% owned by U.S. parent).

S.A. Rubber Mills (in which U.S. Rubber Co. has a 25% interest).

Soft Drinks

Pepsi Cola Co. of Aust. Pty. Ltd. (effectively controlled by U.S. parent).

Coca-Cola Export Corporation.

General agricultural equipment

Massey-Ferguson.

International Harvester Co.

New Holland Pty. Ltd. (wholly owned subsidiary of Sperry Rand Corporation of U.S.)

Cement

Cockburn Cement Pty. Ltd. (a wholly owned subsidiary of Rugby Portland Cement Ltd. of U.K.)

Victorian Portland Cement Co. Pty. Ltd., Metropolitan Cement and Commonwealth Portland Cement—all three controlled by U.K. Associated Portland Cement Manufacturers (the so-called U.K. Blue Circle group).

Non-ferrous metals other than aluminium

Mt. Isa Mines Ltd. (effectively controlled by American Smelting & Refining Co.)

Sulphide Corporation (owned by C.R.A. Ltd.)

Broken Hill Associated Smelters (50% owned by C.R.A. Ltd.; remainder by B. H. South and North Broken Hill).

Pharmaceuticals— proprietary lines

Beechams (U.K.)

Geigy (Swiss).

Johnson & Johnson (U.S.)

Sterling Pharmaceuticals (U.S.)

Decorative paints

Taubmans.

B.A.L.M.

British Paints.

Lewis Berger.

Domestic Electrical Appliances

A.E.I. (which in 1963 became a wholly owned subsidiary of Associated Electrical Industries Ltd. of U.K.)

General Electric (Aust.) Pty. Ltd. (U.S. parent).

Kenwood Manufacturing (Aust.) Pty. Ltd. (U.K. parent).

Philips Electrical Industries Pty. Ltd. (parent Philips Gloeilampenfabrieken N.V., Holland).

Thorn Electrical Industries (U.K. parent).

General Motors-Holdens, through its Frigidaire division.

Hoover (U.K. parent company).

Sunbeam Corporation (U.S. parent).

Automotive Parts

British Automotive Industries Pty. Ltd. (wholly owned subsidiary of Automotive Products Associated Ltd. of U.K.)

Bendix-Tecnico (financial links with Solex Ltd. and Zenith Carburettor Co. Ltd. of U.K.)

Joseph Lucas (subsidiary of U.K. parent).

Birmid Auto Castings Pty. Ltd. (subsidiary of Birmid Industries Ltd. of U.K.)

Robert Bosch (West German parent).

Armstrong York Engineering Pty. Ltd. (subsidiary of Armstrong Shock Absorbers Ltd., U.K.)

General Motors-Holdens.

Wool Yarn

Patons & Baldwins.

Nylon Yarn

Fibremakers Ltd. (50% owned by I.C.I.A.N.Z. and 50% by British Nylon Spinners).

251

The implications of this extension of foreign ownership and control have been receiving increased attention in recent years. Wheelwright, in a detailed study, points out that a large proportion of direct foreign investment can have unsettling effects on the balance of payments. It is liable to strengthen the tendencies towards concentration of ownership which were described above. There is a loss of revenue from taxation because of the concessions made to attract the overseas investor—a topic which attracts press comment annually when the profits of enterprises such as General Motors-Holden's are published. Overseas investment means more reliance on imported technology and "know-how", and a consequent reduction of the incentive to carry out research and development work in Australia. Wheelwright concludes that "the case for continued and virtually indiscriminate reliance on overseas capital which is put forward in official quarters, at both Commonwealth and state level, is not nearly so clear cut as it is made out to be".[16]

There have been suggestions for ways in which Australia may succeed in gaining the benefits of overseas investment—in superior management, techniques and products—without being obliged to surrender control and ownership of large tracts of the economy. Among these have been legislation to ensure local equity partnership with overseas enterprise in the development of local industry; overhaul of double-tax agreements to diminish favourable treatment for foreign investment; the use of "management contracts" whereby use can be obtained of superior foreign techniques at less cost to Australia in the long term; much stronger efforts to increase the skill of our own management and workers; particular encouragement, through taxation incentives, of indigenous research. These reforms need to be examined with much greater energy than has been the case in the past.

However, it should also be said that there are some dangers of over-compensating in efforts to reduce possible long-term dangers in the current extension of foreign ownership and control. Among these are the possibility that control over foreign investment could be used by local industrial and commercial interests to consolidate current monopoly power, threatened by the incursion of more efficient overseas entrants. There is also the danger that the entry of foreigners, which at present may be making some contribution to the breaking down of local restrictive trade practices, will be frustrated by well-intentioned efforts to mitigate the dangers of foreign investment on the recent scale. Foreign participation does provide at least the potentiality of increasing competition in a regulated economy where the danger of cosy little arrangements, benefiting small groups of producers at the expense of the community at large, is an ever-present problem.

[16] E. L. Wheelwright, in Hunter (ed.) *The Economics of Australian Industry*, p. 159.

F. H. GRUEN

16   Rural Australia*

Two attitudes appear to affect those who write about rural Australia. The most common is the "heroic pioneer" syndrome, whose sentimental out-pourings serve to drown any useful observations. The second group—smaller but also vocal—believes in the "idiocy of rural life", a phrase coined by Karl Marx, though implicitly accepted by many who would shudder at the con-nection.

To confine such emotive waffling to a minimum, I have turned, in the first place, to the statistical evidence available on rural Australia. This is followed by a discussion of attitudes of farmers and farm workers, backed wherever possible by public opinion polls and other surveys of attitudes and opinions. Although there are many widely divergent communities in the Australian countryside, farm owners and farm labourers—despite class differences—show important similarities of outlook. That is, their "country" way of life has a strong influence upon their attitudes. This is one justification for a social discussion of "Rural Australia" as an entity. Because of lack of data, I have confined the discussion of "rural" Australia mainly to "farm or station" Aus-tralia. The final section of the chapter discusses some of the different groups found in the Australian countryside. Here evidence is scarcer and speculation often takes its place.

What the Statistics Tell Us

At the time of Federation, one in every two Australians lived in a rural area. Since then, there has been a steady decline in this proportion until, according to the 1961 Census, less than one in every five Australians now lives in a rural area.[1] In terms of absolute numbers, Australia's rural popula-tion has been constant at round 1.8 million since the 1954 Census, having reached a peak of 2.4 million during the depression (1933 Census).

The periodic censuses can be used to provide us with other demographic and social information about rural Australians. Since the rural population is

---

* This paper has been considerably improved by the helpful comments I have received from Dr L. Hume and Mr R. Boyer and from members of the seminar where a first draft of this paper was presented. I am also indebted to Mrs A. M. Coutts for general research assistance and the compilation of the tables.
[1] There have been many changes in boundaries and some changes in definitions which make an exact comparison difficult, but the substantial decline in the proportion of the population living in rural areas is beyond question.

a declining proportion of the total, it is not surprising that it contains relatively fewer migrants than the urban population.[2] This has not always been the case with individual nationalities. For instance, the majority of Italian migrants, up to the end of the last war, settled in rural areas.

The religious affiliations of rural Australians do not differ greatly from the population as a whole. Catholics and Anglicans are slightly under-represented in rural areas; Presbyterians and Methodists slightly over-represented. In Australia, as in most other countries, the rural population has a considerably higher birthrate. Rural Australia contains relatively more children and adolescents and fewer aged people, especially women. Rural Australia might be regarded as a "man's country"; in 1954 the masculinity ratio was 121:100 for rural areas compared with 102:100 for Australia as a whole. Proportionately fewer divorced people live in rural areas—either because they have fewer divorces, remarry less quickly or because they move to urban areas when they have divorces.

Three out of every five rural Australians work in the traditional rural occupations of farming, grazing, forestry, trapping, etc. Other important occupations are road and rail construction, transport services generally, and sawmilling. Probably the most significant difference between rural and urban occupations is the contrast in the occupational status of the two groups. Less than 15% of urban males are either employers or self-employed, compared with over 40% of rural males. There is some slight evidence suggesting that the proportion of employers and self-employed in the total work force on farms is increasing.

RURAL VOTING PATTERNS AND ATTITUDES

The relative importance of employers and self-employed in the rural popu-lation is partly responsible for the prevalence of political conservatism among country people—a feature of Australian rural society which has been stressed by other observers.[3] By the prevalence of political conservatism I mean a widespread disinclination to change the basic political and economic in-stitutions which exist in Australia.

Some dissections of Australian public opinion polls are available by occupational groups, which enable us to examine the differences in attitudes of farm residents and others in more detail. A cross-classification of voting intentions and occupations by Australian Public Opinion Polls (the Australian Gallup organization) for the 1961 Federal election is given in Table 1.

Less than one-fifth of the farmers interviewed intended to vote for the Labour Party, and almost half the farm labourers intended to vote against Labour. The farm "anti-Labour bias" appears significantly greater than the similar bias among what might be regarded as the corresponding urban occupational group. Thus while only 15% of farm owners intended to vote Labour, 40% of small business owners intended to do so; again, 47% of farm labourers intended to vote for the A.L.P. compared with 66% of semi-

---

[2] Foreign born population as a percentage of total (1954 Census) was: urban population 15.2%; rural population 10.3%.

[3] *E.g.* O. A. Oeser and F. E. Emery, *Social Structure and Personality in a Rural Com-munity;* Jean I. Craig, *Some Aspects of Life in Selected Areas of Rural N.S.W.* (un-published M.A. thesis, University of Sydney, 1945).

254

skilled urban workers. (These differences are statistically significant at the 1% level.)

TABLE 1

Voting Intentions—1961 Election

Occupational Group	Labour	Liberal/ Country Party	DLP/ QLP	Undecided	Number in Sample
	%	%	%	%	
Professionals, executives and owners of large businesses*	18·0	73·9	1·8	5·9	272
Farm owners	15·0	73·8	4·6	6·6	259
Clerks, shop assistants ..	36·9	48·9	8·7	5·5	507
Small business owners ..	39·6	49·1	1·9	9·4	106
Farm employees	46·4	47·7	1·2	4·7	86
Skilled workers*	54·5	32·5	4·9	7·3	532
Semi-skilled workers	66·0	23·4	4·1	6·5	415
Unskilled workers	74·1	17·1	4·4	4·4	158
Not specified*	27·7	56·9	3·1	9·2	65
TOTAL ..	44·0	44·5	4·8	6·4	2,400

* (For these groups the total percentages fall short of 100% because of intended voting for independents and minor parties).

A classification of occupational groups by voting intention for the 1951 Federal election shows the same relationships.

It may be felt that the emphasis being laid here on the political attitudes of rural people is too strong. As Oeser and Emery point out in their study of Mallee Town, "Politics are seen (by country people) as mainly concerned with national or State issues, not local, and as mainly an activity for parliamentarians or would-be-parliamentarians (except for the three-yearly intervention of the electors)".[4] Politicians and political issues seem far away in most country settings and more tangible local issues such as droughts, floods, harvests, pests, stock and produce markets tend to monopolize male attention and conversation.

There is little doubt that rural political attitudes are more implicit than overt, but the things people take for granted are as important and probably more basic than the things they discuss. An inquiry into the reasons for their basic political attitudes will be used here to make a fairly wide examination of the differences between rural and urban groups.

There are, broadly speaking, three reasons why farm residents might be expected to vote, in proportion, more conservatively than comparable urban occupational groups.

(i) *The Existence of the Country Party*

There is, firstly, the possibility that the Country Party—by virtue of its specific sectional appeal—obtains a significant proportion of farm votes which might go to Labour in a straight-out Labour/Liberal electoral contest. D. A. Aitkin's unpublished thesis on the N.S.W. Country Party, which showed that

[4] Oeser and Emery, *op. cit.,* p. 32

Country Party support was particularly strong at small polling booths—*i.e.* with less than 300 voters—might be regarded as providing some evidence supporting such a view.[5]

Nor is it difficult to find indications of strong rural support for many regional, country and anti-city causes. Thus, in elections in rural areas identification with country interests and opposition to city influence is usually claimed as a matter of course by all candidates.[6]

An illustration of an extreme form of anti-city sentiment is provided by the following quotation from an editorial in a country paper: "It is a shameful thing that a predominantly agricultural country such as ours should have overcrowded cities while rural areas are being denuded of population. . . . Wars are bred in overcrowded cities, the enfeeblement and extinction of nations begins there."[7]

The trend towards a smaller relative—and even absolute—number of people engaged in the farming industries is often deplored and has given rise to movements to make Australia's development more closely in tune with farmers' ideas of proper priorities—such as greater emphasis on general basic developmental expenditure and the provision of more adequate transport facilities in country districts. A corollary is condemnation of expenditure on more "frivolous" matters such as the Sydney Opera House and the Canberra Lakes Scheme.

In a rapidly changing world where developments in the rest of the economy threaten to overshadow the farmer's economic role, it is not surprising that farm residents feel a special need for a party to represent them and them alone. The feeling of numerical weakness and of physical isolation from the urban centres where political and economic power is concentrated, provides the *raison d'être* for the continuing support of the one party which has no other loyalties.

Whilst these considerations may be used to explain the existence and persistence of the Country Party, they do not answer the question posed earlier —namely, whether the Country Party obtains a significant proportion of farm votes which might go to Labour in a straight-out Labour/Liberal contest. This of course is a hypothetical question and it is impossible to be certain of the answer. But some suggestive evidence can be obtained from the distribution of second preferences of defeated Country Party candidates. As the Country Party allows multiple endorsement, we can compare the voting behaviour of normal Country Party voters under different electoral situations. In particular, we can compare the *second* preferences of Country Party voters when their remaining choice is Country Party or Labour with the situation where their remaining choice is Liberal (or previously Nationalist-U.A.P.) or Labour.

If people vote Country Party primarily because of its rural appeal and not because of its general political stance, we would expect that their second preferences would be more evenly divided between Liberals and Labour where this is the only remaining choice, than the division between Country Party and

[5] D. A. Aitkin, *The United Country Party in New South Wales; 1932-41, a study of electoral support.* (M.A. thesis, University of New England, 1960.)

[6] *E.g.* D. W. Rawson and Susan M. Holtzinger, *Politics in Eden-Monaro,* pp. 121-4; Henry Mayer and Joan Rydon, *The Gwydir By-Election 1953,* pp. 175-8.

[7] Cited by Oeser and Emery, p. 33.

Labour where *this* is the remaining choice. An examination of election data does not bear this out. A study was made in N.S.W. elections from 1930 to 1941 and all State and Federal elections from 1940 to 1962.

The electorates used in this comparison were as follows:

N.S.W. 1930-1941

1930—Ashburnham, Murray, Yass, Casino (four candidates)
1932—Albury, Goulburn, Maitland, Orange, Young
1938—Lachlan (two candidates), Temora
1941—Namoi, Murrumbidgee (two candidates), Raleigh

All Elections 1940-1962
Federal

1940—Bendigo (V.), New England (N.S.W.)
1946—Wannon (V.)
1949—New England, Paterson (N.S.W.), Wimmera (V.), Indi (V.)
1954—Indi (V.)
1955—Scullin (V.)

N.S.W.

1944—Byron
1947—Ashburnham, Barwon
1950—Murray
1953—Casino, Lismore
1956—Young
1959—Dubbo, Mudgee, Raleigh
1962—Gloucester, Oxley

Victoria

1940—Bulla and Dalhousie, Gippsland N., Hampden
1943—Benalla, Mildura, Walhalla
1945—Allendale, Borung, Evelyn, Grant, Mernda, Mildura, Rodney, St. Kilda, Swan Hill, Toorak
1947—Allendale, Grant, Portland
1950—Allendale, Gippsland N., Mildura, Murray Valley, Shepparton, Wonthaggi
1952—Gippsland W., Murray Valley, Shepparton
1955—Ballarat N., Benalla
1961—Benalla, Moorabin

Western Australia

1943—Mt Marshall, Wagin
1947—Bunbury, Forrest, Middle Swan, Wagin
1950—Bunbury, Canning, Harvey
1956—Albany, Narrogin, South Perth
1959—Toodyay
1962—Canning, Darling Range

Queensland

1941—Cunningham

The average percentage of second preference Country Party votes going to Liberal (U.A.P.-Nationalist) candidates was 85.37 and to other Country

Party candidates 85.18. Voting patterns in those country electorates held by Liberal M's.P. show as high a rural non-Labour vote as those held by Country Party members. In other words, the loyalty shown by "normal" Country Party voters to their party is no greater than their willingness to vote for the other conservative party when this is the only alternative to voting Labour. We must look elsewhere to explain the consistently larger conservative vote of farm residents.

(ii) Opposition to Labour Party Policy

One obvious reason for rural conservatism is the opposition of farm residents to basic planks of Labour Party policy. Two important areas of political opinion where farmers side strongly with non-Labour views generally are their attitude to trade unions and their preference for private rather than state ownership of industries.

Farmers are generally more hostile to the power of trade union officials than are other occupational groups (with the exception of professionals and executives of large businesses). According to Australian Public Opinion Polls, proportionately more farmers were in favour of Arbitration Court controlled union elections (1948) and in favour of freezing union funds during the 1949 coal strike. In 1948 Australian Public Opinion Polls asked whether the Arbitration Court should consider the claims of men on strike or defer consideration until the men go back to work. Answers according to occupational groups are given in Table 2.

TABLE 2

Should the Arbitration Court consider men's claims while they are on strike?

Occupational Group	Work First	On Strike	Undecided
	%	%	%
Professionals and executives	83	13	4
Farmers	79	17	4
Shopkeepers	67	23	10
"White collar"	65	29	6
Farm workers	63	26	11
Skilled and semi-skilled	50	43	7
Unskilled	43	48	9
TOTAL	61	32	7

Source: Australian Public Opinion Polls, February/March 1948.

In public opinion polls on the desirability of the nationalization of specific industries such as coal mines, banks and shipping, farm owners favoured private enterprise more strongly than all other occupational groups listed by the polling organization except owners and executives of large businesses.[8]

On the other hand Australian farmers have often objected to the operation of unrestricted private enterprise in those industries with which they have a close and direct economic contact—such as the handling and processing of

[8] *Cf.* Australian Public Opinion Polls: September/December 1946 (coal mines); July/August 1947 (shipping); September 1947 (banks).

the different primary products.[9] For many products including wheat, butter, cheese, sugar, dried fruits and eggs, marketing is undertaken either by boards set up under government auspices with substantial producer control, by co-operatives, or by private firms under government supervision. The major areas of producer dissatisfaction are in those fields where relative *laissez-faire* prevails (*e.g.* wool, meat, fruit and vegetables). There are two separate but related sources of dissatisfaction with unregulated private enterprise marketing. Such a marketing system implies fluctuations in the prices paid to producers. Large price fluctuations are widely felt to be arbitrary and, however much they may be dictated by impersonal market forces, as basically unjust. The existence of price fluctuations enables a profit to be made from astute buying and selling. While farmers may sometimes successfully make such points (*e.g.* in livestock markets), they generally believe that, compared with professional merchants, dealers and speculators, their lack of information and of prompt access to all marketing channels places them at a disadvantage in such dealings. This belief has, no doubt, some justification. The feeling of suspicion and distrust of farmers for middlemen is similar to that of the labourer or factory worker for those who have the "cushy" jobs in the office or on the road. In both cases hard work is identified with physical effort and the importance of other types of work belittled. Since the economic contribution which transport, organization and management make is, in many respects, more nebulous than the physical production of goods, the wide prevalence of such attitudes is perhaps not surprising.

Distrust of middlemen has not made Australian farmers into Labour voters—even though the Labour Party is probably basically more opposed to private merchants, dealers and speculators than the other two parties. The sponsorship of "organized marketing" (*i.e.* Board or government control of marketing, generally associated with higher local prices than those ruling overseas) by the Country Party, and perhaps more reluctantly by rural interests in the Liberal Party, has satisfied farmers' requirements and enabled them to retain their broader political attitudes without sacrificing their opposition to *laissez-faire* in the marketing of primary products.

(iii) *Satisfaction with present conditions*

Lipset and other political scientists have suggested that leftist voting is an expression of dissatisfaction, an indication that needs are not being met. In particular the following needs have been regarded as central:

1. The need for security of income. This is quite closely related to the desire for higher income as such; however, the effect of periodic unemployment or a collapse of produce prices, for example, seems to be important in itself.

2. The need for satisfying work—work which provides the opportunity for self-control and self-expression and which is free from arbitrary authority.

[9] Farmers have also favoured the establishment of government banks to provide an alternative to (but not a substitute for) private banking services. The establishment of the Commonwealth Development Bank in 1959 is believed to have been at least partly the result of pressure from rural interests within the ruling Liberal-Country Party coalition. The influence of rural pressure groups is also discussed in chapter 15.

3. The need for status, for social recognition of one's personal value, and freedom from degrading discrimination in social relations.[10]

A discussion of the needs and aspirations of Australian farmers in these terms seems to provide a rationale for the relatively small Labour vote. Whilst farm incomes have always fluctuated more than urban incomes, farm product prices and seasonal conditions were generally satisfactory in the post-war decade—the period for which we have opinion poll information—and Australian farm incomes compared favourably with incomes in the rest of the economy. In February 1958, Australian Public Opinion Polls asked a sample of Australians whether their standard of living was improving, getting worse or remaining about the same. The replies, grouped by occupations, are given below:

TABLE 3

Changes in Living Standards

Occupational Group	Improving	Getting worse	No difference	No. in sample
	%	%	%	
Professionals and executives	45	16	39	152
Farmers	36	15	49	198
"White collar"	35	19	46	499
Small business	32	18	60	182
Semi-skilled workers	27	24	49	325
Skilled workers	25	27	48	370
Unskilled workers	21	34	45	159
Farm labourers..	13	31	56	45
Not specified	17	31	52	84
TOTAL ..	30	23	47	2,014

Source: Australian Public Opinion Polls, February/April 1958.

In recent years the incomes of woolgrowers and other farmers, who are largely dependent on external prices, have fallen substantially from the levels reached in the early 'fifties. This has led to much soul searching and to demands for reforms of the marketing system, but there is no evidence to suggest that such dissatisfaction has changed the basic political attitudes of those affected by the drop in wool, sheep-meat and other external prices. If this dissatisfaction increases it could give rise to more radical movements among woolgrowers and other farmers. If such movements become important, they are more likely to be radical right-wing movements than to rely on existing parties of protest of the left.

There is limited evidence of a significantly higher degree of job satisfaction among farmers and farm labourers than among persons in urban occupations. Spearritt and Oddie asked a group of Victorian National Service trainees in 1952/53 how much they liked their civilian jobs. The responses of trainees in selected occupations are given in Table 4. "Trainees were asked to write '3' on their test form if they liked their civilian job very much, '2' if they

[10] S. M. Lipset, *Political Man: The Social Bases of Politics*, p. 232.

thought it was 'all right', and '1' if they did not like it at all."[11] (To ensure that test results would be affected to a negligible degree by attitudes and experiences of trainees which were attributable to service conditions, an attempt was made to keep the period between the entry of trainees to camp and the date of testing to a minimum.)

TABLE 4

Percentage of members of selected occupations indicating various levels of job satisfaction

Occupation	No. of cases	Job Satisfaction Levels			Not given
		"3"	"2"	"1"	
		%	%	%	
Salesmen	79	62	34	3	1
Clerks	142	63½	30	6½	—
Bank clerks	58	67	33	—	—
Carpenters	65	69	29	2	—
Fitters and turners	32	69	28	3	—
Farm labourers	61	79	19½	1½	—
Farmers	143	92	7	½	½

(The difference in the relative frequency of "3" level of satisfaction between farm residents and all others is statistically significant at the 1% level. The difference between farm labourers and urban employees is statistically significant at the 3% level.)

Some confirmation of the greater satisfaction of farm dwellers with their present mode of living is provided by a 1948 opinion poll when the following question was asked: "Where do you prefer to live—in a big city, a medium sized town or on a farm?" Only 16% of farm residents wanted to move (to either a city or town) compared with 26% of town dwellers (*i.e.* to a farm or a city) and over 50% of city dwellers.[12]

We have little information on the social status of farm residents in Australia. One study by Ronald Taft, based on rankings of different occupations by 277 Western Australian high school students and adults put farm owners sixth out of twenty occupations and farm labourers second last.[13] A more detailed and comprehensive study of occupational status by Congalton, published in 1963, shows a similar ranking, with farm owners generally in the upper-middle brackets of occupational status and farm labourers near the bottom.[14]

The picture of farmers' attitudes which emerges from these comparisons is one of a high level of satisfaction with their occupation, their way of life, and

[11] D. Spearritt and N. M. Oddie, Some activities of Australian Adolescents, Vol. III. Some Occupational Characteristics of Victorian Male Adolescents, Australian Council for Educational Research, June 1959, p. 52. (Cf. A.C.E.R. Information Bulletin No. 31, *Preparation of Test Norms based on Victorian National Service Programme, 1952/53.* August 1954, p. 2.)

[12] Australian Public Opinion Polls, January 1948. See also W. J. Campbell, *Growing Up in Karribee*, p. 102.

[13] R. Taft, "The Social Grading of Occupations in Australia", *British Journal of Sociology*, vol. 4, no. 2, 1953.

[14] Athol A. Congalton, *Occupational Status in Australia.*

their economic progress in the post-war decade, coupled with reasonably high social standing of farming as an occupation. Evidence of farm labourers' dissatisfaction with their economic progress is scanty—based on a total sample of 45—but the low status of farm labouring might have been expected to produce a proportionately higher Labour protest vote. The level of job satisfaction, the isolation of permanent farm workers, their opposition to strike action (cf. Table 2) and identification of Labour as an "urban" party have probably been the main counterweights.

Other Attitudes

Probably the most important difference between urban and rural modes of living is the relative isolation of the farm resident. Isolation reduces the opportunities for social intercourse and throws a man back on his own resources; he necessarily becomes more self-reliant and less dependent on the outside world. On the other hand he is more likely to help his neighbour (or a fellow motorist) in difficulties. Another less obvious effect of isolation is an awareness of what might be called the crushing superiority of natural forces. Where men live close together they can, to a large extent, control and mould their environment; in isolation man cannot control, he must adapt. An extreme illustration of this is provided by natural calamities—such as fires. In the city sufficient resources can usually be mobilized to control a fire. In the country man adapts as often as he controls. He adapts by driving his livestock into ploughed paddocks where they are likely to be safe, or by burning counterbreaks; often he may be forced to take shelter in sheds, huts, trucks or homesteads while a grass fire rages outside—then he will try, after it has passed, to put out any fires on his shelter.

But isolation is becoming less important with the improvement in communications. Roads are being improved rapidly; cars are better and faster and more people have them. These changes lead to a greater access to professional, technical and shopping facilities for an increasing proportion of rural inhabitants. They have also led to the growth of larger country towns at the expense of smaller ones.

Again, technological improvements have somewhat mitigated drought, water shortage, flood and fire dangers and have greatly strengthened farmers' associations with urban-based experts and suppliers. Improved technology has reduced the arduous traditional nature of many farm chores. To take one example, automatic loaders and bulk handling have virtually eliminated the manual lifting of millions of wheat bags during the course of the harvest; similar heavy manual labour and drudgery in many other forms of farming have been greatly reduced. In the farm home, environmental forces are being softened. Electricity grids in, say, New South Wales, now serve all but a minor proportion of the farm population and, of the remainder, many have private power units. As a result, urban consumer amenities such as washing machines are becoming common; less frequent but also growing rapidly are the possession of television, pressurized home water supplies, and, in the hotter areas, air conditioning. Thus the differences in modes of living between urban and rural Australians have been greatly reduced during the last twenty years. The increasing contact with urban life and the gradual spread of urban amenities in country districts may make the outlook and attitudes of country people less distinctive in the future.

While rural attitudes are changing in some fields of opinion, they are probably still more "traditional" than urban attitudes. One such traditional attitude is to regard "experience" more highly than "learning". Twenty years ago, fewer farm owners wanted the school leaving age raised than any other occupational group.[15] Again, judging from a 1961 opinion poll, rural inhabitants have had considerably less education than country town or city dwellers. But there is some evidence to suggest that country attitudes to education are changing. Thus, according to Campbell's Karribee study—undertaken during 1957/59—more than half the parents in this dairying and vegetable producing district wanted their children to go to a teachers' college or a university.[16] This is confirmed by some unpublished survey work of Dr Joan Tully in the Rochester and Warragul districts of Victoria. On the other hand, Dr Tully found the traditional lack of interest in education in a third survey—of 58 farm families in a community some 30 miles north of Brisbane. The levels of income, housing and amenities in this group were considerably lower than in the two Victorian districts studied.

The emotional attachment to the "Mother Country" which has been regarded as an important component of rural attitudes in the past is probably also changing. There has probably been a decline in the long-standing practice by leading farmers and graziers of sending their children to England for their secondary or university education.

In 1962 an opinion poll was taken on the desirability of an Englishman, as opposed to an Australian, for Governor-General.

TABLE 5

Should our next Governor-General, after Lord de L'Isle, be an Englishman, Australian or someone else?

	Englishman	Australian	Other and No opinion	Total no. in sample
	%	%	%	
City	19·2	66·7	14·1	1,691
Country (including country towns)	22·2	68·8	9·0	882
Occupational Group				
Professionals, executives and owners				
of large businesses	37·4	44·3	18·3	273
Farm owners	28·9	63·2	7·9	253
Clerks and shop assistants ..	25·1	60·6	14·3	602
Small business owners ..	20·6	68·3	11·1	126
Skilled workers	14·3	75·2	10·5	581
Farm labourers	11·0	75·0	14·0	100
Semi and unskilled workers ..	9·7	78·5	11·8	535
Others	21·4	68·9	9·7	103
TOTAL ..	20·2	67·4	12·4	2,573

Source: Australian Public Opinion Polls, June 1962.

[15] According to a 1943 opinion poll, 52% of farm owners wanted a school leaving age of 16 years or higher, compared with 55% of semi-skilled or unskilled workers, 61% of skilled workers, 68% of clerks and 72% of professionals and executives. (A.P.O.P., October 1943.)

[16] W. J. Campbell, *op. cit.*, p. 38.

Table 5 reveals little difference between attitudes in the city and country (including country towns); a larger proportion of city residents were indifferent to the nationality of the Governor-General; if we exclude these, differences between the two groups were not statistically significant (at the 10% level). While proportionately more farmers than small business owners wanted an English Governor-General (statistically significant at the 10% level), a sizeable majority of farm owners preferred an Australian for the position.

An interesting contrast in rural and urban attitudes is provided by opinions about the desirability of capital punishment. Table 6, taken from a 1962 poll, gives the cross-classification according to occupation and city/country break-up. It will be noticed that farm owners and farm labourers have identical views on this subject, with the highest proportions in favour of the death penalty of any occupational group, and less doubt about their views, *i.e.* a smaller proportion with "no opinion". (It may be of interest to note that this was one question where the views of "professionals" differed markedly from "owners and executives of large businesses".)

TABLE 6

If someone is convicted of murder, what should be the penalty?

Occupational Group	Death	Life Im- prisonment	No Opinion	No. in sample
	%	%	%	
Professionals	36	53	11	47
Owners and executives ..	52	34	14	176
Owners small businesses ..	48	42	10	152
Clerks	48	43	9	575
Skilled workers	55	36	9	555
Semi-skilled workers	62	30	8	307
Unskilled workers	55	35	10	157
Farm owners	63	29	8	261
Farm labourers	63	29	8	62
Not specified	46	44	10	78
TOTAL ..	54	37	9	2,370
Metropolitan	51	39	10	1,559
Country town	56	34	10	493
Rural	63	28	9	318

Source: Australian Public Opinion Polls, April 1962.

(The difference in attitude between farm residents and all others is statistically significant at the 1% level. The difference in attitude between metropolitan, country town and rural areas is statistically significant at the 3% level.)

This difference could be the result of factors other than "tradition". Death is a much more common occurrence on farms. Farmers kill stock for their own meat supply; diseases and drought take their toll; injured animals are killed, so is a savage and dangerous bull. The attitude to the murderer is perhaps akin to that adopted towards the bull.

Norman MacKenzie, in his study of *Women in Australia,* points out that one women's organization in Australia stands out because of its size and level of activity. This is the Country Women's Association which had, in 1960, over 117,000 members and 2,700 branches. It aims to make country life easier and to improve the welfare and conditions of women and children in the country. To this end it has provided 500 rest rooms in country towns, 270 baby health clinics, 92 holiday homes and 40 hostels for expectant mothers. MacKenzie pays tribute to the success of the organization in the following terms:

> There can be no doubt about the effectiveness of the C.W.A. as an organization: the loyalty and enthusiasm of its members is matched by great competence on the part of its senior officials. There is equally no doubt that this effectiveness stems from the fact that it has quite definite aims that relate directly to the interests and capacities of its members. A good deal of trouble is taken, in fact, to ensure that its activities are kept within these limits. Where a view is expressed on wider issues, it must still be linked to "the welfare and conditions of women and children in the country".[17]

Why has the most successful women's organization in Australia become established in country areas? MacKenzie argues that the reason the C.W.A. functions smoothly and is widely accepted as a desirable and socially useful organization is that "its role is one that fits into the traditional division of interests between the sexes".[18] I think an additional reason is that life in the country is much more burdensome for women. As Oeser and Emery have pointed out:

> The farm wife has considerably more duties in the area of home maintenance if only because she has more extensive household economic duties than the town wife. In addition she has more duties in the area of child raising because she has more children to raise.[19]

And, one might add, no kindergarten facilities at her disposal. She also has much more difficulty getting help in cases of sickness and childbirth. The C.W.A. helps here and, last but not least, meets the need of countrywomen for some female company. Needs of this type have probably been largely responsible for the unique success of the Country Women's Association.

Little information is available regarding the strength of family ties in country areas as compared with cities. As mentioned earlier, fewer country residents are divorced, although as Dr. Day shows elsewhere in this book, the social significance of this fact is somewhat doubtful. Oeser and Emery found significantly less tension and more solidarity among the farm families they studied in their Mallee Town sample than among the country town families.[20]

SOME DIFFERENCES AND CONTRASTS

So far the Australian "rural community" has been discussed as a single entity; stressing differences between urban and rural Australians exaggerates the uniformity of our subject. The contrast between the community of men

[17] Norman MacKenzie, *Women in Australia*, p. 309.
[18] *Ibid.*, p. 310.
[19] Oeser and Emery, *op. cit.*, p. 134.
[20] *Ibid.*, p. 137.

running the vast cattle and sheep stations of the outback and, say, a group of poultry farmers just beyond the suburban fringes of the major cities is every bit as great as that between wheatgrowers and suburban commuters.[21]

The "Outback"

Being the most peculiarly Australian variety of rural life, the "outback" has received a disproportionate amount of attention from writers and students of Australian life generally. Whatever may be a useful boundary between the outback and more settled areas, it is as well to remember that most Australian farm residents live on properties where they are within five miles of their neighbours on other farms.

Extreme isolation is one of the major characteristics of the outback, extreme seasonal variability is another. Extreme seasonal variability has its main effects on the organization of productive units in the outback. The periodic decimation of livestock numbers by drought, with its consequent income and capital losses calls for individuals or companies with large capital resources; the small man will usually not survive economically under these conditions. It has been argued that the boom-or-bust conditions of the inland discourage rational economic calculation and foster a happy-go-lucky, gambling attitude to the environment—but there is little evidence on which to base such views.

In some respects the isolation of the outback preserves those features which were characteristic of all Australian rural life—and rural life in other countries —a century ago. In the more densely settled areas the need for economic self-sufficiency has declined dramatically; improvements in transport and communications have led to the growth of specialist producers of wool, meat, wheat and milk, often as dependent on specialist contractors and outside technical services as many city enterprises. But in the outback, reliance on outside help is both chancy and costly.

This combination of the extremes of seasonal variability and isolation has led to the emergence of relatively large stations—*i.e.* large in terms of labour force as well as area. Outback stations vary in size; most of them have between two and five resident white families, with additional single station hands, stockmen, etc. The homestead is the social and economic centre of the station. Within the homestead compound most of the labour force is huddled together—in protection against the hostility of nature rather than of man. The communities of families and single men and women not only carry on their normal grazing pursuits, but also make their own electricity, often construct their own housing, maintain their transport, roads, fences and telephones and plumbing (if any); not to mention educating their own children through correspondence schools (usually until the age of 10 or so when they are sent to boarding schools or hostels in more densely settled areas).

While it is not surprising that the manifold skills of the bushman have evoked the admiration of outsiders, the romantic picture sometimes painted of life in the outback as a classless companionship among mates and "characters" does not often correspond to the facts. However much masters and men

---

[21] No comment has been made here about one part of "Rural Australia", namely "Country Town Australia". Little has been written on this subject since the McIntyres' pioneering social survey *Country Towns in Victoria*, 1944. While it is outdated, it contains a wealth of information not found anywhere else on the service towns which are an important part of the life of "farm or station Australia".

may help each other in those periods of stress and crisis which occur so much more frequently under conditions of extreme isolation, in their normal lives there is a fairly strict social hierarchy.[22] Managers and overseers have their meals at the homestead (or in their own cottages); station hands and stockmen eat "outside"—*i.e.* in separate quarters. Similar distinctions can be seen at picnic races or local tennis parties. Again, in many parts of the outback, the stock work is done by aborigines who are not usually included in the mateship group of the whites.

The Grazing "Élite"

Returning to the more densely settled areas, one distinction within the traditional rural occupations is between graziers and other farmers. Prominent graziers are often the descendants of the large squatters of the nineteenth century; their holdings have become much smaller—both in area and sheep numbers—but are still usually above average in size. The main distinction is not so much property size or wealth; it is to be found more in their mode of living and leisure activities. As Jean Martin put it when discussing the "old families" of country origin:

> . . . they spent their money in characteristic ways: in sending their children to the highest status non-government schools; in travelling to visit friends and relatives scattered throughout their State and beyond, and to take part in the picnic races, the country shows, the city weddings and other events through which their identity as a group is maintained; they also spend their money on maintaining large establishments, sometimes in both country and city, and in observing the ritual and formality they regard as appropriate to a gracious life. Although these families do not form a leisured class—the men usually running their own properties or businesses—they are expected to take a leading part in occupational organizations like the Graziers' Association, and in service groups like the Red Cross and the Victoria League.[23]

Martin's further suggestion that "they act as leaders only in their own communities or in promoting the interests of particular groups such as the primary producers; they seldom take office in local government or in parliament" is questionable. One might point to men like Fairbairn, J. M. Fraser, Mackinnon, Downer and C. R. Kelly in the recent Commonwealth parliaments; similar groups can be found in most state parliaments.[24]

The differences in upbringing and outlook between leading graziers and other prominent farmers are exemplified by their educational background.

[22] In this respect the Northern Territory (excepting three or four very large stations) is generally more egalitarian and less given to social stratification than say western New South Wales or Queensland. In the Northern Territory social and economic class distinctions tend to be drowned in drinking mateship; authority, especially "Canberra" authority, is resented. The Territorian is bent on maintaining the Australian frontier masculinity myth and on showing no sentiment for women or "abos" (although it is often there). Many are proud of their self-inflicted stoicism and live under conditions of considerable hardship, often unwilling rather than unable to spend money on better living conditions because they are hell-bent on making a fortune and getting out.

[23] Jean I. Martin, "Marriage, the Family and Class" in *Marriage and the Family in Australia* (ed. A. P. Elkin), pp. 36-7.

[24] The role of pastoral families in politics is discussed by B. D. Graham, "Graziers in Politics 1917-29", *Historical Studies*, no. 32, 1959, and by Katharine West, *Power in the Liberal Party*.

For this purpose all elected presidents, vice-presidents, past presidents of producers' organizations in all states (or regions, such as Riverina for graziers) and producer members of the Commonwealth Boards and Bureaus were classified as "leaders". The replies to a mail questionnaire sent by Encel to the leaders of these organizations in 1958 enables us to compare leaders in the associations affiliated with what was then called the Graziers' Federal Council with other primary producers' organizations. The comparison is given in Table 7.

TABLE 7
Education of Leaders of Farm Organizations

	Total number	Number with secondary education	Number with private secary education	Number with university education
Graziers' associations	25	24	24	4
Other farmers' organizations ..	38	19	8	0

Source: Replies to Encel's mail questionnaire.

Practically all leaders of Graziers' Associations had received some secondary education—and at private schools; a significant minority had been to a university. On the other hand, only half the leaders of the other farm organizations had received any secondary education and less than a quarter had attended private schools. This contrast relates, of course, only to the leaders in these organizations. At the ordinary membership level there is considerable overlap between the Graziers' Associations and the wheat and wool growers' associations affiliated with the rival federal organization, the Australian Wool and Meat Producers' Federation, but the different organizations do have distinct "personalities" and attitudes towards society and towards governments. Thus, Graziers' Associations have been traditionally in favour of a minimum of government activity, whilst the other wheat and woolgrowers' organizations have tended to look to governments to protect their economic position.

Rural Wage-earners

The total Australian farm work force amounts to slightly less than half a million men and women. Of this number, approximately 100,000 work as permanent farm and station employees; a further 100-120,000 work as casual, temporary or seasonal workers. About 90% of the employees are men. The largest single group work for the pastoral industry, amounting to perhaps 65,000-70,000. According to Gollan 30,000 of these were members of the Australian Workers' Union in 1960. "12,000 were shearers and an equal number were other workers involved in shearing, workers such as shed-hands, cooks, wool pressers and so on. The remainder were station hands."[25]

Although employees make up two-fifths of the farm work force, comparatively little is known about their present-day lives, attitudes or aspirations.

[25] R. Gollan, "Industrial Relations in the Pastoral Industry", in Alan Barnard (ed.), *The Simple Fleece*, pp. 602-3.

This is strange, considering the articulate expression of the bushmen's ethic in *The Bulletin* at the turn of the century and the turbulent industrial relations in the grazing industry in the eighteen nineties. While there was a shearers' strike in 1956, the Australian Workers' Union has for many years now been firmly wedded to arbitration in industrial relations and is generally a conservative influence in the Labour Party.

This is probably also true of the rank-and-file A.W.U. member. In this connection one should distinguish between permanent and temporary farm employees. Many permanent employees work on farms which employ only one or two men; the men work with the owner and probably regard him as a colleague as well as a boss. On bigger properties, especially in the drier inland areas, larger properties with absentee landlords are more common. In such districts a more impersonal relationship exists, with concomitant lack of sympathy on both sides.

This lack of sympathy, understanding and above all lack of community of interest is also marked in the relations between farmers and temporary employees. The most obvious example is the shearing shed. The nature of shearing is probably largely responsible. Owners do not want to spend much money on accommodation which is used one month in twelve; on the other hand, shearers do not see why they should have to spend most of their working lives in poor and makeshift quarters. Owners look after their sheep twelve months of the year, and resent the lack of care shown by shearers. Shearing is a hard, back-breaking job and the shearer's interest is to get through as many sheep as possible in a day, for he is paid per 100 sheep shorn. If some sheep get roughly handled and cut in the process that is the grazier's worry, and the shearer is not too concerned. The result is that, over the years, arbitration tribunals have laid down extremely detailed conditions regulating every facet of the work and employment of shearers; any ambiguity is likely to lead to friction between the two parties in the performance of the annual shearing.

Mechanization of many farm chores has reduced the demand for unskilled and semi-skilled labour in the country. Reference was made earlier to the virtual disappearance of bagging wheat during the harvest, with the concurrent decline in demand for bag sewers and wheat lumpers. Similarly the milking machine has reduced the amount of labour needed for milking; cane-cutting is likely to suffer a similar fate in the not too distant future. Other rural occupations which have declined in importance as a result of technological change are droving, which is being displaced by motor transport even in outback areas, and rabbiting, which has been greatly reduced—at least for the time being—by the phenomenal success of myxomatosis. Oeser and Emery, in their study of Mallee Town, speculated that with the growth of mechanization higher levels of skills will be demanded of farm labourers. "The type of labourer now demanded has to be not only skilled in the use and maintenance of mechanical equipment, but also capable of making decisions directly affecting productive activities. It appears likely that in the future development of the community this trend will continue, and there will emerge a group of farm labourers with technical qualifications whose status will, if anything, be higher than that of the marginal farmers."[26]

[26] Oeser and Emery, *op. cit.*, pp. 22-3.

There is little evidence either to support or refute this view. There has, it is true, been a decline in the demand for unskilled farm labour. This is particularly marked for unskilled temporary or seasonal labour, and the Commonwealth Statistician's estimate of the number of temporary male farm employees engaged on March 30th every year (*i.e.* when the annual agricultural statistics are collected) shows a substantial decline over the last ten years. But it is doubtful whether there has been any corresponding growth in the demand for skilled *hired* labour. Instead, farmers have let out more work on contract—*e.g.* fencing, dam sinking, fertilizer spreading, etc. This changes the contractual relationship, and makes for the emergence of a class of rural non-farm entrepreneurs. Sometimes these are themselves farmers who do contracting on nearby properties, or they may be farm labourers who have saved enough to buy equipment.

In the opinion of some, the social gap between farmer and farm labourer has widened; most enterprising farm labourers now seem to try to leave the industry—either by going to the cities, becoming share-farmers or engaging in one or other of the many types of contracting.

Soldier Settlers

Since 1860 governments in all states of Australia have sought to "unlock the land", *i.e.* break up the big pastoral holdings which deny "too many people the right to hold land in their own interest". During the nineteenth century little was accomplished towards this goal. Thus in 1891, 1,245 large graziers (running flocks of 10,000 sheep or more) owned three-quarters of all sheep in New South Wales. Since then there has been a drastic decline in this proportion; in 1956 less than 10% of the N.S.W. sheep population was concentrated in flocks of 10,000 or more.[27] Changes in rural production, progressive death duties and land taxes, have contributed to this trend. One of the most direct causes, though probably not the most important, has been the resumption of big estates after the two world wars and their distribution to returned soldiers. After the first world war, over 37,000 ex-servicemen were settled on the land by the various state governments. The effects were disastrous; within eight years, one in every three settlers had walked off their blocks and the accumulated losses incurred by governments over the next twenty years amounted to about £45 million—or £1,200 for each original settler. In a report to the Federal government in 1929, Mr Justice Pike found that the main reasons for the debacle were: inadequate farm size, unsuitable settlers, and unprofitable farm prices in the years after settlement.

After the second world war, soldier settlement was not undertaken with the same carefree abandon. Less than 10,000 men were settled on the land, although originally over 37,000 applicants were classified as "suitable". With Commonwealth prodding, much more generous areas were allotted to each settler; with the help of the better prices ruling since the war, most settlers have been able to meet their commitments and the amount that has had to be written off so far by governments has been very small—less than 1%. But the cost of settling each man has been great—of the order of £20,000 per holding.

[27] The number of N.S.W. flocks with 10,000 sheep or more increased from 322 in 1956 to 475 in 1960, but the number of sheep carried on these large holdings in 1960 is not available.

270

While the total number of settlers is not large—in comparison with the rural or farm population—in some districts soldier settlers comprise a large fraction of the total. This is especially true of the irrigation areas along the Murray and Murrumbidgee Rivers. Although settlers are established on land which has been compulsorily acquired—sometimes at low valuations—from the existing landholders, there is no sign of any major friction between settlers and other landholders. Business interests in country towns usually favour such settlement on the grounds that small men are less likely to by-pass local shopping facilities than larger landholders. However, the major organization favouring it is the Returned Servicemen's League, which regards soldier settlement as one tangible form of rehabilitation of ex-servicemen.

Italian Immigrants in Rural Areas[28]

About 10% of the farm work force consists of foreign-born (*i.e.* not born in Australia or the United Kingdom). Of these the largest group are the Italians, amounting to about one-third of the foreign-born. Immigrants have concentrated in certain rural districts where they account for much larger fractions of the total population and work force. Among these districts are the more densely settled rural areas surrounding the capital cities, the major irrigation districts and the sugar cane fields of Northern Queensland.

Italian settlement in the northern canefields goes back to the eighteen nineties. According to Easterby, by 1916, 45% of cane farmers in the Innisfail area (*i.e.* Johnstone River District) and almost 80% of cane cutters were non-British (mainly Italian).[29] Italian immigration became much more marked after the first world war, it declined during the depression and rose again after the second.

Typically, Italian male immigrants have been unskilled labourers; in Queensland a large proportion began as cane cutters—in fact, they were often brought out for this specific purpose because an insufficient number of local men were willing to do it. Cane cutting is hard work for physically fit men, and about one-third of newcomers usually leave the canefields before the end of the season. Italian cane cutters have often managed to live very cheaply, and save a large proportion of their wages; savings of £500 out of an annual income of £700 were not uncommon. The purpose of saving is to become independent by purchasing a farm or becoming a share farmer, as quickly as possible. How successful have the immigrants been in achieving this goal? According to Hempel, over 50% of sugar cane growers in 1958 in the Northern district (*i.e.* north of Townsville) had Italian names; for Queensland as a whole the proportion was 28%. This is an understatement, as it does not allow for those who have anglicized their names. Growers with Italian names also supplied about half the number of Queensland tobacco growers. This does not, however, give us any idea how many failed to reach their goal of farm ownership and independence. A mail survey undertaken by Bertei does add some further information on the point. The survey was undertaken

---

[28] This section relies heavily on three sources: J. A. Hempel, *Italians in Queensland*, 1959 (duplicated); J. M. Bertei, *Innisfail*, B.A. thesis, University of Queensland, 1959; Joan Tully, "Leadership and Integration", *Australian Journal of Social Issues*, vol. I, no. 2, 1962. Unfortunately Dr Charles Price's valuable survey of *Southern Europeans in Australia* (1963) was published after this chapter was written.

[29] H. T. Easterby, *The Queensland Sugar Industry*, quoted by Bertei, p. 20.

in the Innisfail area; unfortunately the response was slightly less than 50%. But the figures—reproduced in Table 8—do show a remarkable progression towards business and farm ownership with increasing length of residence in Australia—of at least this group willing to provide the information.

TABLE 8

First and Present Job of Italian Immigrants
(Innisfail area)

	Years of residence in Australia									
Type of job	*9 years or less*		*10–19 years*		*20–29 years*		*30 years or more*		*TOTAL*	
	1st Job	*Pres. Job*	*1st Job*	*Pres. Job*	*1st Job*	*Pres. Job*	*1st Job*	*Pres. Job*	*1st Job*	*Pres. Job*
Labourer	78	77	9	0	15	3	51	10	153	90
Tradesman ..	7	1	4	4	3	3	—	—	14	8
Professional ..	—	—	—	—	—	—	2	3	2	3
Cane farmer ..	1	4	—	6	3	9	1	32	5	51
Own business ..	—	4	1	4	—	6	—	9	1	23
	86	86	14	14	21	21	54	54	175	175

Source: J. M. Bertei, *Innisfail*, p. 49.

It seems, then, that many Italian immigrants in the northern canefields have been able to achieve their economic goals. In the course of achieving their ambitions, they have provided economic competition for both Australian landowners and unionists, which has caused considerable antagonism. This is not to say that economic competition has been the only factor responsible for antagonism; there were important cultural differences in values, beliefs, habits, and customs. Tully has pointed to some of the differences: "marriages were still arranged occasionally, daughters were chaperoned and courting customs differed. . . . Italians sometimes used knives in fights, they drank wine instead of beer, and so on. Most of the Italian community were Roman Catholic and the majority of the Australian community Protestant."[30]

Nor were the differences restricted to modes of everyday life. In the 'thirties the Black Hand Gang, an Italian criminal society, extorted money from Italians in North Queensland and bombed cars and houses. One go-between for the gang, Giovanni Iacona, had both ears cut off by one, Nicola Mammone; in retaliation, Iacona killed Mammone in the main street of Innisfail.[31] Nor did the establishment of branches of the Fascist Party in the 'thirties make assimilation any smoother.

At the same period a British Preference League became active in North Queensland, whose principal aim was the replacement of Italian cane growers and cane cutters by Britishers. Similar movements sprang up in the irrigation

[30] Tully, *op. cit.*, p. 13.
[31] These incidents may be compared with disturbances in the Italian community in Melbourne in 1963-4, involving murder and extortion practised against vegetable growers and stallholders in the Victoria Market.

districts in southern Australia. During the early 'thirties a British quota of 75% for cane cutters was enforced. During the second world war many Italians were interned, and representations were made by the R.S.L. that all foreigners be ousted from some of the Northern cane districts after the war in favour of ex-servicemen.

Union officials have also been opposed to the practices of Italian workers. Thus the Queensland Branch Secretary of the A.W.U.: "They are breaking down our conditions. I can go back to 1921. There were Finns, Italians and Yugoslavs. They wanted to work as long as they could, break down every union rule, and yet get every penny they could by using the award. . . . They have broken their contract and scabbed on Saturdays and Sundays. *Union officials have to work at week-ends to see they observe the award.* It is time they learnt our way." At the same A.W.U. convention one district secretary said of migrant cane cutters: "They are very cunning people. They know all the short cuts and ways to defeat the rules of the Union. One gang of Sunday canecutters worked from the centre out in a two acre field so they would not be observed. All they had to do on Monday morning was to knock down the outside ring."[32] On the other hand Italians do not seem to be opposed to the unions. In Bertei's sample, 83% believed that unions were "necessary" and 26% felt that unions had helped them personally.

In the post-war years there has been much less antagonism between Australians and Italians. The prosperity of farming, the widespread acceptance of a large-scale immigration policy and the conscious attempts by press and governments to facilitate the adjustment problems of migrants have probably been the major factors responsible. In one district, the Murrumbidgee Irrigation Area, the broad initiative of the local extension service has been responsible for a much wider acceptance of Italians by the Australian farming community. Some Italians are now leading members of farming organizations in the Irrigation Area, are on the boards of local producer and consumer co-operatives and belong to clubs such as Rotary. In Bertei's Innisfail group, however, there is little evidence of Italians taking any prominent part in the affairs of their community.

CONCLUSION

The picture presented here stresses the differences between rural and urban Australians; one should also point out that both social and cultural differences between town and country are probably smaller in Australia than in most western countries. Rural-urban income differentials are much smaller than overseas; historically Australian farmers have always produced largely for the market rather than for their own consumption. Technical change in the farming industries has been rapid—at least since the end of the second world war.

Yet the differences which do exist are those which are to be found in other countries. They include: higher birth rates in rural areas; more conservative voting patterns; intrinsic satisfaction with farming as a "way of life"; somewhat less stress on intellectual and educational attainments and somewhat more on the practical skills of man; and a traditional division of interests between the sexes.

[32] Hempel, *op. cit.*, pp. 165-6.

L. R. HIATT

17   Aborigines in the Australian Community

THE recorded observations of missionaries, government officials, pastoralists, and, in recent years, anthropologists form a large body of information about the effects of European settlement on the Australian aborigines. Yet the task of ordering and analysing the data has hardly begun.[1] In this chapter I shall offer a typology of mixed communities (that is, communities which include European and aborigines) and distinguish in each type a characteristic attitude among European members towards the aborigines. Many people, I suppose, will find my generalizations too broad, but I shall be happy if the analysis stimulates discussion and investigation that lead to greater accuracy. I shall begin by briefly describing the traditional life of the aborigines and how it disintegrated, and to conclude I shall indicate some current trends in aboriginal-European relationships. I shall try throughout to avoid value judgments and "loaded" statements.[2] I have feelings about the treatment of aborigines, but to convey them here would only throw the theoretical object of the paper out of focus.

TRIBAL DISINTEGRATION

Aborigines have lived in Australia for at least 13,000 years. At the time of the first white settlement in 1788 they were distributed over the whole continent and numbered about 300,000; one hundred and seventy years later the indigenous population had fallen to about 58,000 and, with 48,000 part-aborigines, composed an under-privileged minority in the new society.

The 300,000 aborigines were divided into some 500 tribes whose membership ranged from about 100 to 1,500. Population density varied from as high as one person to the square mile in rich coastal areas to one person to 35 square miles in desert regions. Each tribe spoke a different language and occupied a continuous tract of land. Members of small tribes often lived as

---

[1] See A. P. Elkin, "Reaction and Interaction: A Food Gathering People and European Settlement in Australia", *American Anthropologist,* vol. 53, 1951; J. W. Bleakley, *The Aborigines of Australia.*

[2] Unfortunately people often use a word to refer to a certain state of affairs and, at the same time, to convey approval or disapproval. But here, when I say that some Europeans have exploited aborigines, I am to be understood merely as describing a certain type of relationship. The question how I feel about exploitation is irrelevant.

single communities and moved about together over the tribal territory in search of food. Large tribes usually comprised several subdivisions.

Communities numbered about 100 to 400 people, who belonged to one or other of several patrilineal clans. Boundaries separated the territory of one community from that of another, but friendly communities often visited each other, especially for the purpose of performing ceremonies. Most adults spoke or understood several languages besides their own.[3]

The Australian environment contained no animals or plants suitable for domestication. The people lived by hunting and gathering, and they shifted camp from time to time as food became scarce in one place or plentiful in another. There was little economic specialization apart from a sexual division of labour in which men provided flesh and women plant foods. Groups occasionally undertook co-operative ventures, such as the construction of a fish trap across a creek or an animal drive, but production depended mainly on individual effort. Each family (a man, his wife or wives, and his children) slept and ate together around its own fire.

To a large extent people pursued their interests and behaved towards each other in accordance with rules stated in the idiom of kinship. Although old men, because of greater knowledge of dogma and ritual, held positions of esteem in the sphere of totemic religion, evidence now available casts doubt on the view of earlier observers that they executed administrative and judicial functions in the everyday life of the community.[4] The nomadic subsistence economy offered little scope for leadership, and public opinion against non-conformity, together with considerations of mutual advantage, to a large extent maintained orderly social relationships. When disputes arose (mostly over the acquisition of wives and alleged adultery), opponents were supported by some of their immediate kin; but other people, closely related to members of both sides and hence torn by conflicting loyalties, worked to bring the fights under control.[5]

Aborigines saw no virtue in suppressing their emotions. They laughed and cried easily, expressed affection and sexual interest without embarrassment, and indulged in violent outbursts of anger. Life proceeded at a leisurely pace and offered the simple pleasures of eating, copulating, raising families, performing ceremonies, gossiping, and sleeping. Generosity was a dominant value, and successful hunters willingly shared their catch with others. In at least one tribe, where the word "good" was synonymous with "generous", some men even ignored their wives' extra-marital sexual affairs in order to establish a reputation for magnanimity.[6] There was little scope in aboriginal communities for acquisitiveness, social climbing, or authoritarianism.[7]

The same cannot be said of the white society that spread over the continent after 1788. Tribe after tribe disappeared within a few generations as

---

[3] The nature of land ownership and residential associations is still a subject for dispute. See L. R. Hiatt, "Local Organization among the Australian Aborigines", *Oceania,* vol. 32, no. 4, 1962.

[4] See M. J. Meggitt, "Indigenous Forms of Government among the Australian Aborigines", *Bijdragen,* Part 120, no. 1.

[5] See L. R. Hiatt, "Conflict in Northern Arnhem Land", unpublished Ph.D. thesis, Australian National University, 1962.

[6] *Ibid.,* ch. 6. See also R. and C. Berndt, *Sexual Behaviour in Western Arnhem Land.*

[7] In some tribes men sought to acquire numerous wives as a mark of prestige. See C. W. M. Hart and A. R. Pilling, *The Tiwi of North Australia.*

settlers appropriated land for agriculture and stock-raising, subdued the original owners with guns and poisoned flour, and brought diseases against which the aborigines had little resistance. In 1846 Westgarth described rugged country in south-western Victoria that:

> served as a retreat or hiding place for the numerous Aborigines who occupied that part of the country on the first approach of depasturing colonists. The sheep and cattle of the settlers were repeatedly attacked and carried off to these inaccessible wilds, where the blacks were occasionally descried by those in pursuit, luxuriating in all the wastes of savage and uncontrolled appetite, with their mangled and half-roasted prey. The provocation of such annoying and revolting scenes, the privacy and solitude, the absence of all witnesses, were too much for the infirmity of human nature. The blacks were in their turn followed and attacked and repeatedly shot with very little ceremony.[8]

The writer estimated that whites in the area had killed at least 200 natives in the course of two years and remarked that "the diminution of his number and the final extinction of savage man, as he makes room for the civilized occupant of his territory, is a feature of which Australia furnishes neither the first nor the only example".[9]

Table 1, which follows, gives some idea of the decline in the indigenous population since the coming of the European to Australia and of recent increases in the part-aboriginal population. The 1788 figures were estimated by Radcliffe-Brown on the basis of somewhat questionable assumptions; they should be regarded as minimum figures. The 1927 figures were also arrived at by Radcliffe-Brown, who published his calculations in the Commonwealth Year Book, no. 23, 1930. The 1961 figures are drawn from the census of that year and published in the Commonwealth Year Book, nos. 49-50 (1963 and 1964). The bracketed figures are the independent findings of Dr D. Barwick.

It is impossible to determine the effects of introduced diseases and malnutrition on aborigines in all parts of Australia. Governor Phillip, in a letter to Lord Sydney in 1790, estimated that about half the native population of the Sydney area died from smallpox,[10] and other reports indicate that measles, whooping cough, and tuberculosis have also taken heavy tolls. Disease and white attacks seem sufficient to account for the population decline in Table 1, but a persistent view is that numbers dwindled largely because aborigines lost the will to live.[11] There is no more evidence for this[12] than for the theory, advanced by Strzelecki in 1845, that an aboriginal woman loses the power of

---

[8] William Westgarth, *Report on the Condition, Capabilities and Prospects of the Australian Aborigines*, p. 8.

[9] *Ibid.*, p. 5. Aborigines from time to time attacked and killed whites but paid dearly for their temerity. See *Australian Encyclopaedia* (1958), pp. 99-103; and I. A. H. Turner, "From Phillip to Hasluck", *Outlook*, vol. 6, no. 4, 1962.

[10] *Historical Records of New South Wales*, Vol. I, Pt. 2, p. 299, quoted in J.H.L. Cumpston, *The History of Small-Pox in Australia, 1788-1908*.

[11] See, for example, N. B. Tindale, *Australian Encyclopaedia* (1958), p. 87 ("However, the primary cause of the decline was undoubtedly a mental and spiritual one . . . belief in the future and the will to survive were weakened. . . . ")

[12] See H. I. Hogbin, *Experiments in Civilization*, pp. 132-6.

TABLE 1

The Aboriginal Population

State or Territory	1788	1927		1961	
		Fullblood	*Part-aborigine*	*Fullblood*	*Part-aborigine*
New South Wales	40,000	965	5,830	1,488	13,228
Victoria	11,500	55	505	253	1,543
				(10)	(2,979)
Queensland	100,000	13,500	4,210	8,686	11,010
				(11,445)	
South Australia	10,000	2,150	1,550	2,147	2,737
Western Australia	52,000	23,000	2,590	10,121	8,155
Tasmania	2,500	nil	nil	nil	38
Northern Territory	35,000	20,250	780	17,386	2,318
				(18,760)	(2,500)
TOTAL	251,000	59,920	15,465	40,081	39,172

conception with men of her own race after sexual intercourse with a European.[13]

To say that expropriation of land and depopulation caused tribal disintegration gives only one side of the picture. Many aborigines were eager to acquire European goods, and often left their territories voluntarily to live in the vicinity of white settlements. Some years ago a group of natives from northern Arnhem Land migrated some 200 miles on foot to Darwin and returned only when the Administration established an outpost in their homeland where they could obtain desired commodities.[14] Stanner has stressed a point that the sentimentalists regularly ignore:

> The blacks have grasped eagerly at any possibility of a regular and dependable food supply for a lesser effort than is involved in nomadic hunting and foraging. There is a sound calculus of cost and gain in preferring a belly regularly if only partly filled for an output of work which can be steadily scaled down. Hence the two most common characteristics of aboriginal adaptation to settlement by Europeans: a persistent and positive effort to make themselves dependent, and a squeeze-play to obtain a constant or increasing supply of food for a dwindling physical effort.[15]

TYPES OF MIXED COMMUNITY

A few hundred aborigines in arid areas of central Australia remain unaffected by European influences. The rest, including part-aborigines, live in three main types of residential association with white Australians: on farms

---

[13] P. E. de Strzelecki, *Physical Description of New South Wales and Van Diemen's Land*, pp. 346-7.

[14] Hiatt, unpublished Ph.D. thesis, pp. 12-15.

[15] W. E. H. Stanner, "Dumurgam, a Nangiomeri", in J. B. Casagrande (ed.) *In the Company of Man*, p. 70. Elkin writes: "The Aborigines have always shown an irresistible urge to migrate to the nearest white stations. ... " (*The Australian Aborigines*, p. 326).

and cattle stations, on government settlements and missions, or in non-institutional urban settings. I shall classify the associations as rural, settlement, and urban; and I shall argue that the characteristic aim of whites in the first type has been to exploit aborigines, in the second to reform them, and in the third to avoid them.

I am using "rural" in a narrow sense to refer solely to people who live out of towns and cities but not on government settlements or missions; and "urban" to refer to people who reside in towns or cities, again excepting those who live in state or church institutions. I recognize that the division does not rest on a uniform set of criteria, and I am also aware that particular cases do not fit neatly into any of the categories. For example, some aborigines have permanent homes on the outskirts of towns or cities but leave for varying lengths of time to work as itinerant farm labourers. Again, dark people placed in houses by Welfare Boards in Adelaide, Sydney, and various country towns may be subject to as much reformist pressure as some folk living on missions or government settlements. But at this stage I am less concerned with detailed pigeon-holing than with indicating general tendencies.

Rural

Aborigines along the frontiers of settlement, to obtain the commodities they desired, sooner or later began to work for the new landholders. Though labour was scarce, native employees were rarely paid as much as white workers. In some instances a group lived more or less permanently on one property, but many people moved about seeking work. There were few white women, and native women profited (though never handsomely) from prostitution and concubinage.

Beckett's history of race relations in western New South Wales describes a common pattern of events.[16] The first settlers arrived about the middle of the last century and soon clashed with local inhabitants over the killing of stock. The natives in some areas suffered heavy losses[17] but within a generation or so were working as shepherds and stockmen. By the turn of the century the people had forsaken hunting and gathering as a means of livelihood and were dependent upon the pastoral industry and government rations.

The aborigines' closest associates were not the owners and managers but the workers. Many white bushmen at this time, especially drovers and shearers, were itinerants moving from one job to another. Known sometimes as the "nomad tribe", they were mostly unmarried, rarely owned more than a horse and swag, and at the end of a period of work spent their earnings in the nearest bar in a spirit of revelry and mateship.[18]

Aborigines found this mode of living more congenial than the middle-class values of thrift, diligence, cleanliness, sobriety and settled domesticity pressed upon them in later years. As indicated by the following account of Wilcannia in the 'nineties, even the towns lacked respectability:

[16] J. R. Beckett, "A Study of a Mixed-Blood Aborigine Minority in the Pastoral West of New South Wales", M.A. thesis, Australian National University, 1958.

[17] "It did not matter who was shot. Every blackfellow that was shot was considered a pest. . . . The law at this time could hang a man for killing a blackfellow. But there was nobody to enforce the law. . . . " C. E. W. Bean, quoted in Beckett, *op. cit.*

[18] See, for example, Russel Ward, *The Australian Legend.*

The appearance of the town is spoilt by means of a large number of very inferior, small and temporary structures called cottages by courtesy, but in reality mere iron shells or huts. . . . I think the history of the town might be read in the heaps of beer and spirit bottles which lie half buried in the sand all around the town . . . no householder dreams of any other custom than pitching their surplus tins and bottles as far as they can throw them from their own back doors.[19]

Beckett remarks that the description calls to mind nothing so much as an aboriginal humpy settlement of the present day.

The average white worker admired aborigines for their expert knowledge of the bush and skill as stockmen; and he was often prepared to eat, work, and play with them. Yet he never completely accepted them. Europeans at all levels of society regarded the blackfellow as socially inferior, and, although station managers and workers alike commonly used aboriginal women for sexual purposes, they rarely married them. Already by 1913 the half-castes in western New South Wales, who were usually named after their white fathers but reared by their mothers, outnumbered the full-bloods.

The Aborigines Protection Board of New South Wales, for about twenty years after its formation in 1882, did little more in western districts than to arrange the distribution of rations to indigents by station owners and police. Later it established several native settlements under the control of white managers, whose main duty was to protect aborigines from the harmful influences of white contact. Aged, infirm, and unemployed began to take up residence after the Board introduced a regulation displacing pastoralists as distributors of rations, and requiring indigents to collect from settlement managers or police. After the first world war, the state government divided many large landholdings into blocks too small to support a blacks' camp. By the end of the economic depression in the 'thirties, most aborigines of the area were living on settlements, but many left to live independently as economic conditions improved.

In 1956 Bell described the economic life of part-aborigines along the south coast of New South Wales, where the tradition of itinerant rural work has persisted for many years.[20] During the summer people worked as crop-pickers, sometimes earning as much as £30 a week. The gravitation of large numbers (including folk from Victoria and other parts of N.S.W.) to farms where employment was available generated an air of excitement, and large sums of money changed hands in card games and two-up.

Although New South Wales state law compels employers to pay aborigines the same as white workers doing similar work, Bell found that the accommodation provided for coloured farm labourers was inferior. During the winter aborigines took up casual unskilled occupations, such as road maintenance, fencing, and gardening, but often found work difficult to obtain. White employers criticized them as unreliable, lazy, and dirty, and white labourers saw them as competitors for jobs. Aborigines when out of work drew unemployment benefits or received rations on settlements.

[19] *Adelaide Post*, quoted in Beckett, *op. cit.*, p. 41.

[20] J. H. Bell, "The Economic Life of Mixed-Blood Aborigines on the South Coast of New South Wales", *Oceania*, vol. 26, no. 3, 1956.

279

Part-aborigines on the south coast, like aborigines elsewhere, rarely acquired much durable property and spent freely on liquor, tobacco, taxis, and cinema. They shared readily with each other, honoured kinship obligations of mutual aid in times of need, and seldom formed close associations with whites, most of whom regarded them as social inferiors.

Itinerant aboriginal workers on the north coast of N.S.W. find employment as cane-cutters, drovers, fencers, ring-barkers, and crop-pickers. Calley[21] reports that in 1954 wages in certain districts for coloured rural workers were about half those paid to whites doing the same jobs At the time the sale of liquor to aborigines was illegal, but farmers frequently persuaded employees to take cheap wine as payment instead of money. The employers justified economic discrimination by arguing that the mixed-blood is lazy and unpunctual and therefore not worth as much as a white man. Some said that the aborigine has lower standards than the European and wastes anything beyond a subsistence wage on drink and gambling. Aborigines replied that until they were paid at the same rates as white employees they would not work as hard. As a result of an inquiry conducted in 1955 by the Department of Labour and Industry, pastoralists in N.S.W. are now required to pay coloured workers the full award.[22]

Cattle stations in the sparsely-populated areas of northern Australia could not have survived but for the availability of cheap native labour. Groups of aborigines lived on the properties and constituted a pool from which stockmen and domestic servants were recruited as required. In return they received food, clothing, and sometimes low wages. In 1935 M. and E. Durack wrote of the black community on Argyle Station (Kimberleys, W.A.):

> Our darkies have none of the docile inferiority complex which makes such excellent servants of their brothers of other lands. They never bow and scrape to the white man. . . . They work for us because we give them "tucker" and whatever else they need. We give them what they want because we need them to work for us—just a matter of convenience from both points of view.[23]

Pastoralists in the north rarely interfered with native custom as long as it did not conflict with work on the station. Some treated the people with kindness and tried to encourage a sense of loyalty and belonging, partly for humanitarian reasons and partly to avoid losing workers to neighbouring stations.[24] Others, especially managers working for companies, used less gentle methods.[25]

Not all white settlers in the north had comfortable homesteads where native women waited on the tables and worked the punkah. Stanner[26] describes

---

21 M. J. Calley, "Economic Life of Mixed-Blood Communities in Northern New South Wales", Oceania, vol. 26, no. 3, 1956.

22 On the other hand, pastoralists in the Northern Territory have been able to water down the minimum wage provisions, and Queensland pastoralists have maintained a long battle to prevent an increase in the wages laid down by law in 1939.

23 M. and E. Durack, "All-About". The Story of a Black Community on Argyle Station, Kimberley, p. 25.

24 See, for example, K. S. Prichard, Coonardoo; H. E. Thonemann, Tell the White Man.

25 R. M. and C. H. Berndt, "A Northern Territory Problem: Aboriginal Labour in a Pastoral Area" (unpublished MS, 1948), pp. 57-66.

26 Stanner, op. cit., p. 73.

peanut farmers of the Daly River region in the 1930s as rough uneducated bushmen, living in shanties with earthen floors and eating the same food (mainly wallaby stew) with which they paid their aboriginal workers. Hard on the natives, sometimes brutally so, they believed their livelihood depended on maintaining physical dominance. Yet despite the harsh conditions and meagre rewards aborigines sought jobs eagerly. Unemployed relatives battened on workers or women having sexual relationships with the owners, and each farm was "in fact or in aboriginal prospect the locus of a group of natives who made, or wanted to make it, the centre of their lives". Nevertheless, individuals were likely to wander away at whim after a period of employment.

It is apparent that in many parts of Australia the aborigines' earliest contacts were with men interested in them as sources of cheap labour and sexual services and that, in general, the natives fulfilled the demands in order to obtain European commodities. Many attached themselves in small groups to particular properties, which they came to regard as their homes; others, especially where large holdings were divided, found employment as seasonal workers. Although some pastoralists adopted a paternalistic attitude towards their natives, the aborigines' closest associations in country areas were with workers or small farmers who had neither refinement themselves nor the urge to foster it in others.

Settlement

Governments and churches in Australia have played a protective and reforming role in race relations. Both institutions have justified their policies as promoting what is best for aborigines in particular and society in general, and have been supported with various degrees of enthusiasm by limited sections of the white community. Other sections, and often the aborigines themselves, have been reluctant to co-operate.

Instructions from the British government to colonial governors stated that "the natives should be protected in the enjoyment of their possessions, preserved from violence and injustice, and that measures should be taken for their conversion to Christianity and their advancement in civilization".[27] The words were seldom translated into action. Governors, no matter how strong their humanitarian sentiments, also wished to see the colony expand and realized that, in relation to aborigines, the aims of the home government and of land-hungry settlers were irreconcilable. Expropriation and "pacification" proceeded along a wide frontier, unimpeded by official action.

In 1838 the British Government appointed five Protectors to educate natives and develop agriculture on five large reserves (four in the newly-settled Port Phillip district), but settler opposition and high running costs forced abandonment of the scheme by 1848. Land Commissioners were subsequently empowered to set aside smaller areas and to issue rations of food and clothing.

Official attitudes for the next 80 years were coloured by the belief that the rapidly-declining aboriginal population was doomed to extinction. To "smooth the pillow of a dying race", state governments made laws and formed Protection Boards to "ameliorate the condition of the blacks and to exercise a

---

[27] Bleakley, *op. cit.*, p. 78.

general guardianship over them".[28] The Protectors were primarily concerned with moral aspects of the problem. In particular, they enforced laws prohibiting the supply of alcohol and sexual relations between white men and native women. They tried to force employers of aboriginal labour to pay better wages but also discouraged improvidence among the recipients.[29] And they attempted to impose on the people higher standards of cleanliness and hygiene.

Aborigines did not respond enthusiastically to attempts at changing their morals; nor did certain white men appreciate measures taken to prevent economic and sexual exploitation.[30] But changing social conditions enabled officials to implement the policy of protecting aborigines (from themselves as well as whites) in ways previously not realizable. Although humanitarian influences were gaining strength in the cities, the crucial factors were a decreasing demand for native labour in closely-settled rural areas and a growing demand among townsfolk for segregation. In these circumstances police and Protection Board representatives in some states began persuading the impoverished and unlovely groups of aborigines gravitating to country towns that it was in their best interests to live out of sight on isolated reserves.

From about the turn of the century, Protection Acts and amendments in New South Wales gave officials increasing control over aborigines. Authorities could apply pressure on coloured people to stay on reserves, where in some cases they lived under the supervision of a resident manager, and to prosecute Europeans who entered protectorates without permission.[31] Although settlement managers made attempts to ˙develop horticulture and agriculture on a small scale, to educate children, and to inculcate the habits, manners, and attitudes of middle-class whites, the institutions depended largely on state aid and, by insulating their members, did little to facilitate their entry into intolerant communities outside. Many aborigines, especially in areas where lack of staff and finance prevented the authorities from exercising effective control, continued to live independently in camps on the outskirts of towns or as pastoral workers.

The situation in Victoria differed in some respects. A law forbidding part-aborigines to live on reserves was introduced in 1886 in an effort to "merge into the general population all half-castes capable of earning their living".[32] The Protection Board in Victoria had no power to compel any aborigine to live on a reserve, and it had no jurisdiction over dark folk living independently, except that Europeans could be fined for exploiting their services or

---

[28] J. H. Bell, "Official Policies towards the Aborigines of New South Wales", *Mankind*, vol. 5, no. 8, 1959.

[29] In Queensland employers were required to register with the Chief Protector before employing aborigines and to pay about 60% of each employee's earnings into a trust account. Aborigines could not draw on their compulsory savings without official permission. (Bleakley, *op. cit.*, p. 167.)

[30] Bleakley, Chief Protector of Aborigines in Queensland from 1914 to 1942, writes: "Checking the illicit employment, drink and drug traffic and moral abuse looked easy on paper, but was a stony road to travel. Perhaps the greatest obstacle was the opposition of the natives themselves, for whose protection these measures were instituted. They did not want to be deprived of these new-found joys, even though obtained at the price of their own degradation." (*Op. cit.*, p. 127.)

[31] Bell, *loc. cit.*, 1959.

[32] Quoted in Diane E. Barwick, "A Little More than Kin", unpublished Ph.D. thesis, Australian National University, 1963, p. 86.

supplying liquor to them. From 1863 to 1954 the reserves never contained more than 70% of the aboriginal population at any one time.

Even in New South Wales attempts were made to force aborigines into the general community. Regulations passed in 1909 forbade managers to supply rations to able-bodied individuals without permission from the Protection Board and stated that aborigines must be "made to understand that they must support themselves and their families".[33] But it was not until the early 1930s that charitable and humanitarian organizations began urging governments to give up the policy of protection and segregation altogether and to work whole-heartedly for the eventual assimilation of remaining dark people into white society. The leading figure in the movement was Professor A. P. Elkin of Sydney University, who argued that aborigines need not die out or remain an underprivileged minority. Settlements, in particular, should be converted into training bases from which aborigines should go forth equipped to accommodate themselves successfully to modern conditions.[34] The acceptance of these arguments by the New South Wales government led to new legislation in 1939 and to the establishment of the Aborigines Welfare Board in place of the Aborigines Protection Board. After the war the new approach spread to other governments and was stimulated by international criticism of racial discrimination. In 1961 a conference of federal and state authorities said that in the view of all Australian governments,

> aborigines and part-aborigines are expected eventually to attain the same manner of living as other Australians and to live as members of a single Australian community enjoying the same rights and privileges, accepting the same responsibilities, observing the same customs and influenced by the same beliefs, hopes and loyalties as other Australians.[35]

In N.S.W. the change in policy relieved pressure on aborigines to stay on reserves. But Fink, writing in 1955 of the settlement nine miles from Brewarrina, explains why those in residence (143 in 1954) chose to stay.[36] The government provided free houses, education, and health services, and free rations for the indigent; and, as the settlement had been in existence for over half a century, many members of the community were related to one another. They felt a sentimental attachment to the place, regarded it as their home, and were reluctant to begin a new life in less friendly surroundings.

This is not to say they were completely happy. The main objection was to the settlement staff's constant supervision and interference. A Welfare Board regulation states that "every aborigine, whilst within a station or reserve, shall obey all reasonable instructions and commands of the manager or other responsible officers of the Board", and, although officials at Brewarrina differed in the degree of their authoritarianism, all acted towards those in their charge in ways that white people would regard as infringements of personal liberty if subject to the same treatment. Officers entered and inspected

---

[33] *Ibid.*, p. 164.
[34] A. P. Elkin, "Anthropology and the Future of the Australian Aborigines", *Oceania*, vol. 5, 1934; "Aboriginal Policy 1930-1950. Some Personal Associations", *Quadrant*, vol. I, no. 4, 1957; "Australian Aboriginal and White Relations. A Personal Record", *Journal of the Royal Australian Historical Society*, vol. 48, part 3, 1962.
[35] Quoted in "The Dark People", *Current Affairs Bulletin*, vol. 29, no. 4, 1961.
[36] Ruth A. Fink, "Social Stratification: A Sequel to the Assimilation Process in a Part-aboriginal Community", unpublished M.A. thesis, University of Sydney, 1955.

aborigines' houses unannounced and uninvited, interfered in domestic quarrels, and suppressed behaviour not in keeping with European standards.[37] The people sometimes referred to the old Protection Board as the "Persecution Board".[38]

Beckett[39] describes similar mixed feelings among aborigines at Murrin Bridge Settlement, established in 1948 ten miles from Euabalong (N.S.W.). About 250 were in residence in 1957, some with outside jobs, others working or receiving free rations on the settlement. Although the people resented official interference, they stayed because institutional life offered material and social security. The manager's main sanction was threat of expulsion, but he might also call the police. Nevertheless, many of those under his charge continued to drink, gamble, and fornicate, hoping they would not be found out. Settlement officers rarely admitted aborigines to their homes, expected to be addressed as "mister" or "boss", rode in the cabin of the truck with aborigines in the back, and on visits to town mixed with the local *élite*. Coloured men who had become accustomed to white workers addressing them by Christian name or as "mate" resented this attitude of superiority and on occasions came close to questioning it. But most people had grown up in the regime and regarded the manager's authority as unchallengeable. Beckett reports an occasion on which two lads from the settlement were astonished to find that some white fishermen they met were "as dirty as us", used bad language, and made no attempt to preserve social distance.[40]

The Aboriginals' Preservation and Protection Acts (1939-46) in Queensland require aborigines on settlements to obey all lawful orders given by the superintendent. Regulations empower a superintendent to prohibit any game (whether played with cards or not), dancing or other native practices after midnight, and any behaviour likely to cause a disturbance of harmony, good order, or discipline. He has the right to direct natives to work for 32 hours a week, to inspect letters written to or by an inmate, and to refuse permission to leave the reserve.[41]

The Queensland Acts allow establishment of settlement courts and gaols for trying alleged breaches of regulations and confining those convicted. Superintendents act as judges and usually conduct proceedings in private. Recently, Tatz drew attention to marked differences between the powers and procedures of these courts and those in white communities. He reported that of 177 natives charged on one settlement in 1956 all were found guilty. I give four examples of cases quoted by Tatz from official records.

(a) 1961. Breach of Settlement Rules in that on 19th February, 1961, you allowed your home to be used for the purpose of gambling. Plea: guilty. Convicted and sentenced to 21 days.

[37] A settlement manager told Fink (*op. cit.*, p. 27): "If anybody wailed at a funeral while I was there, I would have them thrown out of the cemetery."
[38] People at La Perouse refer to the Welfare Board as "the Unfair Board", "the Farewell Board", "the Destruction Board". J. H. Bell, "The La Perouse Aborigines: A Study of their Group Life and Assimilation into Modern Australian Society", unpublished Ph.D. thesis, Sydney University, 1959, p. 392.
[39] Beckett, *op. cit.*, pp. 83-101.
[40] *ibid.*, p. 92.
[41] C. M. Tatz, "Queensland's Aborigines", *Australian Quarterly*, vol. 35, no. 3, 1963

(b) 1962. Conduct prejudicial to the good order and discipline of the Settlement, viz. Immoral behaviour with H.S. Plea: guilty. During an argument with his wife, E.W. admitted having intercourse with H.S. H.S. said that E.W. came to her home and she had intercourse with him several times. Convicted and sentenced to 14 days lockup.

(c) 1962. Conduct prejudicial to the good order and discipline of the Settlement, viz. Evading Work, being Found Asleep at W.P.I.'s house. Plea: guilty. Convicted and sentenced to 10 days' imprisonment.

(d) 1952. Committing an act subversive to the good order and discipline of the settlement, viz., being found under the influence of liquor under the steps of the Recreation Hall whilst a dance was in progress. Plea: guilty. Convicted and sentenced to 21 days imprisonment.[42]

Aborigines regularly plead guilty and rarely oppose authority openly. They think that resistance would make matters worse. Beckett reports that at Murrin Bridge Settlement (N.S.W.) two aborigines individually on different occasions tried to organize protests against certain forms of official action. The people resented the treatment to which they were subjected, but when the spokesmen confronted the staff no one else came forward to voice disapproval[43]

Several factors besides a common sense of subjection tend to keep aboriginal members of settlement communities at the same social level. One is the constant sharing of earnings with relatives and friends in conformity with a prevailing ethic of generosity. An aboriginal lay preacher at Brewarrina, speaking to Fink about the aboriginal settlement, said: "The people always share everything they own, and this stops anyone from having any incentive to learn or to do better."[44] Another factor is resentment within the community towards any member who tries to rise above his fellows, especially by assuming delegated authority. In 1960 I observed several natives on a settlement in Arnhem Land temporarily alienating themselves from their own people by acting on behalf of white officials. The community in its nomadic state, forsaken only a few years previously, lacked an administrative hierarchy, and the incipient leaders, on becoming aware of their growing unpopularity, sank down to their former level.[45] Beckett describes how part-aborigines at Wilcannia ostracized a mixed-blood who accepted the position of manager of the reserve.[46] From time to time people report misdemeanours to white officials to protect their own interests (a wife may complain about her husband's infidelity or drunkenness) but public feeling is strongly against carrying tales.

Clergymen conduct services on most settlements, and in several instances conversion of some members has produced cleavages in the aboriginal communities. At Brewarrina settlement, external religious influences gained a momentum of their own during the early 1950s when the few existing Christians began baptizing converts in the river and holding services regularly in

[42] *Ibid.*

[43] Beckett, *op. cit.*, pp. 99-100.

[44] Fink, *op. cit.*, p. 39.

[45] Hiatt, unpublished Ph.D. thesis, pp. 15-20.

[46] Beckett, *op. cit.*, pp. 110-2.

private homes. Members of the congregation condemned drinking, gambling, swearing, and dancing, and they regarded all, including whites, who carried on such activities, as non-Christians. Doctrinally they stressed personal salvation from the Devil and an afterworld free of racial discrimination.[47]

Calley[48] in 1955 described a Pentecostal cult among aborigines living on settlements on the north coast of New South Wales. This was a form of revivalism[49] characterized by public conversion, adult baptism, and manifestations of the Holy Ghost in particular individuals ("the Gift of Tongues"). Membership, which was exclusively aboriginal, entailed abstention from smoking, drinking, sport, gambling, and swearing. Non-members included the old people, who retained some attachment to traditional religious beliefs, and many young folk, who showed little interest in any form of religion and regarded Pentecostalist prohibitions as ridiculous.

The cult, in Calley's view, was the result partly of the rejection of the aborigines by the whites. Clergymen of several denominations travelled from neighbouring towns to conduct services on settlements but rarely encouraged aborigines to worship with white congregations. In particular, Church of England parsons wished to forestall objections to administering the "common cup" to white and coloured communicants. The origins of the cult are uncertain, but it appears to have started about 30 years ago (possibly a travelling white evangelist made contact with the people). At the time of Calley's visit members held meetings in private homes and organized conventions attended by adherents from different settlements. They had no ties with other Christian denominations, nor even with white Pentecostal groups, and were regarded with disapproval by local clergymen.

From time to time, religious bodies of various denominations have received grants of land from governments for the purpose of establishing a mission. During the first hundred years of settlement, the demands of pastoralists for native labour (and even for the reserved areas), combined with the aborigines' lack of interest in a secluded Christian life, regularly led to failure. Missionaries realized that their best prospects lay in regions lacking economic potential, and most missions still in existence are located on or beyond the frontiers of settlement. This has meant that, whereas until the 1940s government settlements have dealt mainly with detribalized and mixed-blood aborigines, missions have been the principal agencies of reform among people living according to native custom.

Aborigines in remote areas have quickly attached themselves to missions in order to obtain European goods. The missionary, in so far as he controls the distribution of supplies, exercises power similar to that of the manager of a government settlement. The primary aim of missions had been to replace indigenous religious beliefs and ritual with Christian counterparts and to eliminate such practices as polygyny, extra-marital sexual intercourse, and arranged marriages (especially where girls are given to old men). They have also raised living standards, in many cases by supplementing supplies from outside with food produced on the mission.

[47] Fink, op. cit., pp. 31-3.
[48] M. J. C. Calley, "Aboriginal Pentecostalism: A Study of Changes in Religion, North Coast, N.S.W.", M.A. thesis, University of Sydney, 1955, Part I, pp. 3-4; Part III, pp. 7-24; Part IV, p. 2.
[49] H. Davies, Christian Deviations: The Challenge of the Sects, ch. 6.

Worsley has described techniques used by missionaries on Groote Eylandt (Gulf of Carpentaria).[50] Despite opposition from parents, they placed boys and girls from the age of ten in separate dormitories and insulated them as far as possible from tribal influences. Their main sanctions against polygyny and fornication among adults were withdrawal of rations and expulsion, and by the time of Worsley's visit in 1954 many people were conforming to the missionaries' demands.[51] Nevertheless in 1958 a number of married men took additional wives. In the words of a representative of the Church Missionary Society, this led to an upset, "and the offenders knew they would have to relinquish the second wife. Most of these men were Christians. When challenged on Christian principles, they admitted their wrong and returned their second wife to the dormitory. Only three remained defiant and, with the assistance of the Welfare Branch and the Police Department they were removed from the island in 1959. Since then the mission has gone ahead smoothly."[52]

Some missionaries have shown patience and subtlety. The Roman Catholic priest who founded a mission on Bathurst Island in 1911 also regarded polygyny and infant bestowal as sinful. Instead of trying to stamp them out within a generation, he persuaded increasing numbers of men to give him, in return for a quantity of goods, bestowal rights to their daughters. The girls lived in the convent until aged about eighteen. The priest then asked them to choose one of the young bachelors as a husband and permitted the union if the man promised never to take another wife.[53]

People brought up in the traditional religion, with its relevance to the social and physical environment and its emphasis on ritual rather than dogma and morals, found little to attract them in Christianity. If missions accepted the compromise (as many did), they attended church services but continued to perform their own ceremonies in the bush. Yet within a few generations, young folk reared on the mission were sceptical of the beliefs of their ancestors and saw little to be gained by following tribal custom. Youths in particular were glad to escape the rigours of painful initiation practices. Rising generations, even if they did not fully understand the new religion, were prepared to go through the prescribed motions. In return they enjoyed the goodwill of the missionaries in a regime that offered many advantages, including marriage by mutual consent and higher status for women. Having no experience of independence, they did not yearn for it. And they paid no attention to the few old people mourning the death of a culture.[54]

Settlements, whether run by government officials or missionaries, are places located away from white communities where aborigines modify their behaviour in response to reformative pressures and for less effort enjoy a higher standard of living than they could obtain elsewhere. The values imposed are characteristic of, though not peculiar to, respectable middle-class whites. So far

[50] P. M. Worsley, "The Changing Social Structure of the Wanindiljaugwa", unpublished Ph.D. thesis, Australian National University, 1954.
[51] "At the Mission, food is issued to those who attend services, a practice described (with no hint of sarcasm) by one aborigine as 'No pray, no tucker' ", *ibid.*, p. 290.
[52] *Northern Territory News,* 24 January 1961.
[53] See Hart and Pilling, *op. cit.,* pp. 107-9; and F. X. Gsell, *The Bishop with 150 Wives,* pp. 96-106.
[54] L. R. Hiatt, unpublished report for Australian Institute of Aboriginal Studies on fieldwork in the Kimberley region of Western Australia, 1963.

neither government nor churches have indicated whether they think the latter are likely to assimilate the products of their institutions.

Urban

Governments in Australia have never attempted to enforce a rigorous policy of segregation. The actual separation of aborigines from whites is mostly due to the wish of white townsfolk to have as little to do with coloured people as possible. Many aborigines have lived neither on reserves nor in settlements, but in or near white urban areas. Here they have found various forms of exclusion, such as being barred from hotels and swimming pools, being relegated to separate sections of cinemas and hospitals, and being discouraged from building in white residential areas. They have reacted to the prejudice against them in a number of different ways.

In 1946 Harvey described the mixed-blood population of Alice Springs (N.T.), which numbered about 300 and mostly lived together in a quarter known as "Rainbow Town".[55] Except for purposes of employment, they rarely entered other parts and were never invited to white dance halls or private homes. One cinema excluded aborigines and certain cafés discouraged them. Several Europeans legally married to half-caste women had been ostracized by respectable whites. Government officials were the most intolerant members of the community and avoided aborigines outside the course of duty.

Harvey reported that continuous exposure to white prejudice had aroused among Alice Springs part-aborigines a strong sense of group loyalty and a mounting resentment of Europeans. They believed that marriage with their own kind was in the best interests of the group. Most had abandoned any hope of social acceptance and even ridiculed part-aboriginal visitors from other towns who represented themselves as Maoris or Malays. But they also began to challenge the white assumption of racial superiority and to strive for a community of their own with full civic rights. In 1963 a young man, Charles Perkins, reared in this environment, enrolled as a matriculated student in the Faculty of Arts at Sydney University. Although European in appearance, he readily acknowledges his aboriginal ancestry and hopes by his example to further his people's cause.

In other towns differences in place of origin, skin colour, or degree of acculturation have combined with the desire for white acceptance to produce marked divisions in the coloured population. R. and C. Berndt, writing in 1951, distinguished three social ranks among the aborigines of Oodnadatta (S.A.).[56] The largest comprised full-bloods who spoke little English and lived in a squalid camp a mile or so from the outskirts. They still followed some of their tribal customs and were discouraged by local whites from entering the town except for work. The smallest group consisted largely of part-aboriginal women reluctantly accepted as members of the European community because of their relationships through marriage to white men of some standing or practical importance. (For example, one woman was married to the town baker, another to a butcher.) They spoke English with

[55] Alison Harvey, "Ethnic and Sociological Study of an Australian Mixed-Blood Group in Alice Springs, Northern Territory, with Reference to Ethnic Assimilation and Interaction of Groups", unpublished thesis, Sydney University, 1946.
[56] R. M. and C. H. Berndt, *From Black to White in South Australia*, pp. 145-8.

hardly a trace of accent, lived in comfortable homes, dressed neatly, and avoided other aborigines. They mixed with whites on social occasions but were sensitive to slights. Although respectable townsfolk treated them with formal politeness, they found it difficult to conceal an appearance of condescending.

The third group consisted mainly of women related by marriage to white men of low social status. They lived in shacks, but dressed neatly and kept themselves clean. Although they regarded themselves as superior to aborigines in the camp, they were not generally accepted by whites or by the few coloured people who were. They participated neither in social functions in the town nor corroborees at the blacks' camp. They spoke English in the presence of whites, who ranked them above the camp aborigines, but used native dialects when by themselves.

Reay and Sitlington in 1948[57] and Fink in 1955[58] described similar divisions at Moree (N.S.W.) and Brewarrina (N.S.W.) respectively. Although whites in both places were prejudiced against anyone known to be of aboriginal ancestry, some coloured people conformed to European standards in an attempt to gain acceptance. Economically they were on the same level as white labourers, but their behaviour and outlook in some ways reflected the values of middle-class Europeans, for whom many of the women had worked as domestics. Industrious, thrifty, and moral, they lived in proper houses and looked down on aborigines whose habits and living conditions white people found offensive. In general, the lighter a person's skin, the better was his chance of assimilation. At Brewarrina, better-class aborigines were extremely sensitive to discrimination but exhibited strong colour prejudice themselves, avoiding contacts with disreputable sections of the mixed-blood community to the extent of snubbing relatives. At Moree they regarded the blacks' camp near the rubbish dump not only as a disgrace to the town (a view that echoed the sentiments of respectable whites) but as an insult to themselves.

R. & C. Berndt in 1951[59] and Inglis in 1961[60] described the conditions of part-aborigines in Adelaide. Most had migrated from country areas during and after the second world war and found employment as industrial workers. Although all regarded themselves as assimilated members of white society, some associated regularly with each other and also retained links with their places of origin, returning occasionally for holidays and extending hospitality to coloured friends and relatives on visits to the city. Others had severed connections with dark people, including close relatives, concealed their mixed ancestry where possible, and rigorously avoided dealings with officers of the Aborigines Department. They regarded themselves as socially and morally superior to other part-aborigines but, as dispersed and anonymous residents of a metropolis, lacked the opportunities of their small-town counterparts to make the attitude visible. At most they could refuse hospitality to a visitor or snub someone accidentally encountered in the street.

[57] Marie Reay and Grace Sitlington, "Class and Status in a Mixed-blood Community (Moree, N.S.W.)", *Oceania*, vol. 18, no. 3, 1948.

[58] Fink, *op. cit.*, pp. 57-67; also "The Caste Barrier", *Oceania*, vol. 27, no. 2, 1957.

[59] R. M. and C. H. Berndt, *op. cit.*, pp. 234-268.

[60] Judy Inglis, "Aborigines in Adelaide", *Journal of the Polynesian Society*, vol. 70, no. 2, 1961.

People of both categories lived in various working-class suburbs and were generally on friendly terms with white neighbours. Their homes and standards of living were indistinguishable from those of Europeans on the same economic level. But in the early years of migration some whites had urged that aborigines be kept out of the city, and isolated instances of prejudice and discrimination continued. Dark people who acknowledged their ancestry and associated with their own kind were cautious in their relations with Europeans and aware in particular of white opposition to mixed marriages. They usually criticized attempts to break out of the group and deeply resented the implication of racial inferiority when people of aboriginal ancestry gave fictitious explanations of their dark skin. Few accepted slighting remarks meekly. One girl told of a white man who leaned over and said to her during a film of an Arnhem Land corroboree: "They relations of yours?" She replied: "They may be primitive, but they're not as ignorant as you."[61]

A recent survey indicates that the part-aboriginal population of Sydney is widely dispersed and numbers from 5-6,000.[62] Some 550 live on or near a long-established reserve at La Perouse (an outer suburb) under the supervision of a resident manager and belong to the type of community described in the previous section on settlements. Many of these folk hail from the south coast and return regularly as itinerant rural workers. Some earn a living by making artifacts for tourists, but hardly anyone seeks employment in the metropolis.[63]

Little is known of other aborigines in Sydney, but they probably fall into the two categories found in Adelaide. Part-aboriginal industrial workers in the inner working-class suburb of Redfern, for example, live in the same locality, associate regularly with each other, and show signs of inter-dependence and group loyalty.[64] Others are severing ties for the sake of white acceptance. During a recent study, Bell[65] interviewed a few of the small number of aborigines from La Perouse who had married Europeans and moved to another area. The husbands of several wanted them to live like white women and refused to let them visit or entertain coloured relatives. One part-aborigine, under similar pressure from his white wife, had not seen his relatives for eight years and on one occasion ignored a letter asking him to help pay a fine imposed on his brother, who subsequently went to gaol.

It must be apparent by now that although all white Australians in contact with aborigines have in some degree regarded them as social inferiors, differences in class affiliations within the European community have constituted an important factor in determining the nature of associations. As yet we have little precise information on the subject. But, using broad terms in common usage, I suggest that middle-class whites in their dealings with aborigines have rarely gone beyond establishing formal relationships for the purposes of exploiting (as with outback pastoralists) or reform (as with settlement managers

[61] Inglis, op. cit.

[62] W. R. Geddes in the Sydney Morning Herald, 12 November 1963.

[63] Bell, Mankind, 1959, loc. cit.

[64] A highly-developed group life has been observed among aborigines in Melbourne. See Diane Barwick, "Economic Absorption without Assimilation?: The Case of some Melbourne Part-aboriginal Families", Oceania, vol. 32, no. 1, 1962.

[65] Bell, unpublished Ph.D. thesis, 1959.

and missionaries). When they have had neither of these aims (as with most respectable townsfolk), they have preferred to avoid contact.

The attitude of the working class has been more complex and less uniform. Trade unions have regularly opposed the use of cheap native labour but have done little to encourage aboriginal membership, and for a long time coloured workers were restricted to poorly-paid occupations for which there was little white competition. This meant that, although aborigines entered the new productive system as labourers, they did not, in either a political or economic sense, become members of the Australian working class. Except for a handful of *lumpen* proletariat, lower-class whites have never been eager to accept aborigines as social equals and have mostly been less refined than the middle class in expressions of superiority. But in some circumstances, especially those of isolation, occupational associations between white and coloured workers have led to familiarity, tolerance, and even friendship. And as differences in skin colour, habits, and standards of living have decreased, residents in working-class areas, especially in cities, have begun to accept aborigines as neighbours. Mixed marriages have regularly entailed either a loss of status for the white spouse or a struggle to retain it by removing the coloured spouse from associations formed in the past.

Aboriginal responses to white attitudes of superiority have differed according to the type of association. Black communities on cattle stations and bands of itinerant rural workers have maintained a largely independent group life untroubled by class aspirations, and have had little ambition in relation to whites beyond making the most of economic opportunities they offered. On missions and settlements aborigines have accepted their subordinate status in an authoritarian regime and have regularly preferred its social and material security to an independent life outside. Some dark people living in non-institutional urban settings have subsisted apathetically as paupers on the outskirts of the white community and have made no effort to improve their conditions; others have gained a footing in the white economy but, in the face of continued colour prejudice, have developed a sense of inter-dependence and group loyalty that has sometimes become the foundation for militancy; and, finally, there have been those who have sought to overcome or evade prejudice by severing ties with their own kind and living exclusively with whites.

CURRENT TRENDS

Although white aims remain in accordance with the classification proposed in the previous section, official policies since the second world war have significantly influenced the character of race relations. Australia's sensitivity to charges of colour discrimination in a new era of international politics, and the ability of the Commonwealth government, at least, to afford expensive welfare programmes, have been important factors in determining the direction and increased intensity of government efforts. The goal is to create the conditions in which aborigines and Europeans will live together in a culturally homogeneous society free from all forms of special treatment based on differences in skin colour; and success depends on modifying the attitudes and interests not only of dark people but of whites who are to accept them on equal terms. Government aims, once subordinate in practice to the interests of exploiters and avoiders, have now acquired an independent reformist character and are (or are rapidly becoming) the dominant force in race relations in Australia. The change is merely part of a general trend in which governments are gaining control in more and more areas of social life. I shall illustrate the point with several examples.

As indicated earlier, governments in recent years have increased pressure on employers of aboriginal labour to raise rates of pay and working conditions. In 1961 a Darwin newspaper reported a statement in which the Director of Welfare warned pastoralists that their attitude would leave the government no alternative but to introduce legislation prescribing a margin for skill among native stockmen.[66] The prescribed rate is £2 per week plus keep. The worker is responsible for the keep of his wife and one child; all other dependants are maintained by the pastoralist, who receives a subsidy for the purpose. The secretary of the Cattlemen's Association of North Australia opposed an increase on grounds of the aborigines' laziness and inefficiency.[67] But it is evident that the period of exploitation of native labour in the pastoral industry is drawing to a close. In an editorial supporting the Director, the newspaper told cattlemen that the social conscience of Australia has been awakened and that they "will just have to play their part in the gigantic, heart-breaking task of bringing independence and dignity to a people stripped of these qualities by the white pioneers who, in their fight for survival, could do little else at the time".[68]

Pastoralists in both the Northern Territory and Queensland complain that they can no longer obtain good, cheap coloured labour because many aborigines nowadays prefer to live on settlements and missions, which pay the same wages as pastoralists and give free hand-outs as well. The work of a stockman is arduous, and it is no longer true that aborigines in the north eagerly seek jobs in the cattle industry (except perhaps in some parts of Queensland as an alternative to life under an authoritarian settlement regime).

The courts have become increasingly severe in dealing with white men found guilty of intercourse with aboriginal women, and it is apparent that the phase of sexual exploitation is also coming to an end. At the Darwin Police Court in 1961 a man admitted offering a bottle of beer to a native woman in the early hours of the morning and saying: "I want to see someone. I got six bottles of beer. I want a woman." The woman, who had been asleep with her husband, refused to co-operate and said it would be hard to find a lubra at so late an hour. The magistrate sentenced the offender to nine months' gaol for trying to buy a native woman with liquor.[69]

Official policy is a source of frustration even to citizens who merely wish to keep aborigines at a distance. Recently, a dozen white residents of a country town in Western Australia signed a petition protesting against a government plan to build cottages for aborigines in the town area, but the Minister for Native Affairs said his department intended to go ahead.[70] Several years ago, white residents of a Darwin suburb complained about liquor orgies and obscene language among coloured neighbours. Under the

[66] *The Northern Territory News,* 14 March 1961.
[67] *Ibid.,* 18 April 1961.
[68] *Ibid.,* 16 March 1961.
[69] *Ibid.,* 4 May 1961.
[70] *Sydney Morning Herald,* 28 December 1963

present Welfare Ordinance police cannot prevent aborigines from entering the town whenever they wish, whereas a previous regulation had forbidden natives to be in the town area between sunset and sunrise unless in proper accommodation provided by their employers. Some citizens in Alice Springs have been putting pressure on the authorities to ban natives from the town after dark,[71] but official policy is opposed to segregation, and it seems clear that the avoiders, like the exploiters, are fighting a losing battle.

This is not to say that all white citizens in outback areas are in favour of separation. Prejudice in Alice Springs is milder now than it was twenty years ago (when Harvey made her study). Part-aborigines are no longer classified officially as "aborigines", and a number of white men, well-respected in Alice Springs, have dark wives. Darwin is an outstanding example of racial tolerance: in 1963, for example, the death of a full-blood aboriginal footballer named Stanislaus was the occasion for widespread public mourning.

Although the adoption of assimilation as an official goal has been hailed as a landmark, the new policy in fact retained many features of the previous one. Aborigines were still "protected" in matters such as marriage, liquor, movement in and out of reserves, and sexual relations with Europeans. But substantial changes have been effected: in particular, the Federal government recently gave aborigines the right to vote, and some state governments have revoked discriminatory liquor laws. Although the pace of legislative reform is not uniform throughout the continent,[72] there is little doubt that within a short time the political and legal status of aborigines will be the same as that of Europeans. (Laws protecting native women from white men will probably be the last to go.) Moves in this direction will be supported by a growing section of the white community, mainly in southern cities, with liberal opinion but no personal dealings with coloured folk. A recent letter in the *Sydney Morning Herald* stated: "I feel sure that there are many people like myself who simply feel that aborigines are a different race springing from a totally different civilization from our own, but the question of social inferiority never even enters our minds."[73]

How long aborigines will go on living together in separate groups (either within or away from white communities) is another matter. Many modern reformers see group loyalty among dark people as a form of conservatism that impedes the process of assimilation, and, where possible, they encourage alienation and dispersion. The techniques used include separating children from parents, allocating houses in different parts of a town, and discouraging those who (like Albert Namatjira) rise in status from associating with backward friends and relatives. Such pressures regularly cause conflicting feelings in those subject to them: folk wish to please their white benefactors and yet to remain in the social network that offers emotional security and a sense of belonging. In recent years a number of white people, notably anthropologists, have argued that the authorities should adopt a programme of community development and, instead of steering promising individuals into urban isolation, allow them to remain as exemplars and leaders in the groups in which

[71] *Northern Territory News,* 15 April 1961.
[72] Western Australia did not revise its legislation until 1960, South Australia not until 1962. Queensland, in 1964, still had its protection laws of 1939.
[73] *Sydney Morning Herald,* 19 December 1963.

they have grown up. These critics of enforced assimilation use the term "integration" to designate an alternative policy; they prefer cultural diversity to homogeneity and support the right of ethnic groups (Chinese and European immigrants as well as aborigines) to live together and in whatever manner they please as long as they do not break the law.[74]

Probably in the long run hard realities more than criticism will force governments to adjust their present aims. Acts of parliament that raise the legal status of dark people do not eliminate snubs, condescension, and opposition to mixed marriages, and while colour prejudice persists among Europeans most will steadily become like working-class whites; and with award wages and improved employment opportunities creating a sense of growing economic independence, they will become increasingly intolerant of reformers. From time to time light-skinned individuals will leave the groups and disappear into the white community. Current trends suggest strongly that most town and country aborigines will seek integration but for a long time resist assimilation.

Official predictions that settlement communities will dissolve of their own accord and mingle happily with whites are expressions of hope with even poorer chances of fulfilment. A recent editorial article in *Australian Territories* (published by the Department of Territories) forecasts that aborigines in the Northern Territory will pass through three phases. The first

> will encompass the whole period of residence at a settlement or mission. During this time the aborigines, most of whom have led nomadic tribal lives, will be introduced to the various special facilities on the settlement and will become familiar with their use and function in the larger pattern of society.[75]

The second phase begins when the trainee leaves the settlement or mission and enters

> a less circumscribed environment. . . . Instances of trainees in this phase will be found at town hostels accommodating young people from outlying settlements or missions or among apprentices, or among persons attending courses such as are conducted periodically by the Welfare Branch at Darwin or Alice Springs for teaching assistants, nursing aides, and hygiene assistants.[76]

Aborigines in this phase "may even occupy an accepted place within a somewhat restricted non-aboriginal community".[77]

At the end of the second phase the aborigine "will be ready to go out into the community proper as a worker following a chosen vocation".[78] In the third phase he will be

> employed side by side with other Australian workmates to whom he is now a true competitor for all benefits offered within the wider society. . . . If the initial training given during the preceding phases has been adequate,

---

[74] See, for example, W. R. Geddes, "Maori and Aborigines: A Comparison of Attitudes and Policies", Presidential Address, Section F, A.N.Z.A.A.S., 1962; C. D. Rowley, "Aborigines and other Australians", *Oceania*, vol. 32, no. 4, 1962.

[75] "The Tools of Assimilation", *Australian Territories*, vol. 2, no. 1, p. 30.

[76] *Ibid.*

[77] *Ibid.*

[78] *Ibid.*, p. 31.

the need to seek assistance from Welfare Officers (still keeping him under observation) should decline significantly. In the ideal case it will cease almost entirely, for the task will have been taken over by fellow citizens within the settled community prepared to offer encouragement and give assistance whenever such is required.[79]

Two questions seem relevant. First, where in the sparsely-settled north are white communities capable of absorbing large numbers of aborigines? In 1962 the European population of the Northern Territory was 27,000 compared with 19,000 aborigines and 2,000 part-aborigines, and recent studies have indicated that the dark population is increasing at an unprecedented rate.[80] More than half the whites live in Darwin and Alice Springs, whereas 97% of the full-blood aboriginal population live away from towns. Jobs are scarce. The process of assimilation has barely begun, and unless large-scale economic developments take place in the north it is difficult to see how it can go much further. Indeed, the policy of training large numbers of natives for occupations in an external economy that may be incapable of providing the expected openings seems bound to create trouble.

Second, what incentives will encourage aborigines to leave settlements? The former Minister for Territories recently told missionaries in the Northern Territory that they, along with managers of government settlements, must aim to work themselves out of a job within 60 years.[81] But, at the moment, settlements and missions provide aborigines with most of their material needs in a familiar social and physical environment. Many natives will feel that the advantages of settlement life outweigh the uncertain rewards of an independent life in a town and will remain on the settlements unless forced out.[82]

Despite government policy, welfare officers and missionaries in many areas have been and are establishing industries of various kinds on settlements and missions. It seems likely that community development will eventually be given official recognition as an acceptable way of dealing with the problem, although there is little evidence to show that either the missions or the administration have any clear idea of the complexities entailed in mounting and operating community development programmes. Moreover, it implies some form of local self-government, which so far has not been contemplated in official policy. Governments will continue to do things for aborigines (no doubt on an increasingly lavish scale); and the aborigines will become increasingly accustomed to charity and to white people running their lives. One may safely forecast that neither aboriginal communities nor European management of native affairs will have shown signs of withering away by the turn of the century.

---

[79] *Ibid.*

[80] See F. L. Jones, "A Demographic Survey of the Aboriginal Population of the Northern Territory, with special reference to Bathurst Island Mission", *Occasional Papers in Aboriginal Studies,* no. 1, A.I.A.S., 1963.

[81] P. M. Hasluck, "The Future of the Missions", *Australian Territories,* vol. I, no. 5, 1961.

[82] Another aspect is that missions are puritanical enclaves whose products already find much of the behaviour of townspeople out of keeping with the teaching and conduct of missionaries. The *Northern Territory News* recently published an item headed "Drinking, Gambling Disgust Natives" in which an employee of the Groote Eylandt Mission said that mission natives on visits to Darwin were appalled by the immorality they found there and were glad to return to the mission at the first opportunity.

18   Urban Communities

The Pattern of Urbanization in Australia

Australia covers a vast area, being roughly the same size as the United States minus Alaska, and the country is thinly populated, since the total population is only around 11 million compared with the U.S.A.'s 200 million. The continent as a whole is thinly populated because large parts of it are empty. Australia has an overall density of about three persons to the square mile, compared with 50 persons in the U.S.A. and 246 in India. The parts which are settled are very densely settled. If concentration of population rather than overall density is what affects the conditions of living for most people, then the immediate environment of most Australians is as urbanized as that of any people in the world. What constitutes urbanization varies according to different authorities, but all definitions contain some idea of concentration of population and the standards of services and division of labour which this concentration makes possible.

Degree of Urbanization

If we take the simplest though rather crude definition of the degree of urbanization in a country, *i.e.* the proportion of the total population living in areas classified as "urban" for census purposes, then Australia is more urbanized (with approx. 68.8%) than the U.S.A. (with 63.7%) or Belgium (62.7%); roughly four times as urbanized as India (17.3%); and indeed only preceded by the U.K., Israel, Netherlands, West Germany and Hawaii out of a list of 66 urbanized countries in the world.[1]

But any measure of the degree of urbanization of a population clearly should mean something different, depending upon whether the population is living in one large city or the same population is distributed among several lesser cities or even among hundreds of small towns, each of which would qualify as "urban". Davis, to take account of the degree of concentration, constructed an index which assigns greater weight to large cities than to smaller ones.[2]

---

[1] W. E. Cole, *Urban Society*, table 5, p. 32 (adapted from U.N. Demographic Year Book, 1952).

[2] K. Davis and A. Casis, "Urbanization in Latin America", quoted in . Broom and Selznick, *Sociology*, p. 416.

(Briefly, Davis's index is calculated by taking the percentage of total population in cities over 5,000

plus the % in cities over   10,000
plus the % in cities over   25,000
plus the % in cities over   100,000
—divided by 4.)

On this basis the index of urbanization for Australia is 68 compared with, among the examples already mentioned, 65.9 for Great Britain, 42.3 for U.S.A. and 8.8 for India. On this fairly sensible criterion of concentration of population, Australia is probably the most urbanized country in the world and on any other measure which is likely to be adopted it would at least be among the top few.

The description of the pattern of this urbanization and the search for the distinctive features of Australian urban life, until very recently a neglected area of study, have in the past four or five years aroused a good deal of interest and study in Australian universities. These studies are now beginning to show up some of the interesting features of Australian urbanization.[3]

Dominance of the Capital Cities

The first outstanding feature of the pattern of urbanization is the dominance of the capital cities of the five mainland states in their own states and in the country as a whole.

Dealing with the separate states first, Brisbane is relatively less important in its own state of Queensland than are the other capital cities, but even here it contains 41% of the state's population. The corresponding figures for the other states are N.S.W. 56.2%, Victoria 65.4%, South Australia 61.5%, Western Australia 57.4%, living in the capital city. In the country as a whole the capital cities which are also the five largest centres of population contained, in 1961, 56.12% of the total population. Outside the capital cities other urban areas, on which more will be said later, account for another 25.82% of the total population, leaving all the rural areas of the country with only 17.82% of the total population among them.

The dominant position of the capitals is thus clear. Even among the "other urban areas" there are no very large towns to challenge the dominance of the capital cities. The distribution of towns by size calculated from the 1961 census shows that there are in Australia only six medium-sized towns between 50,000 and 100,000.[4] Indeed, there are only ten towns altogether in the whole size range from 50,000 to 500,000 and if we exclude Perth, Hobart and Canberra, there are only seven towns in the whole continent which might earn the title of large or medium-size cities. There is a big gap before the rest of Australia's 246 towns appears.

Not only are there few large towns outside the capitals, but even sizeable provincial towns seem to be missing. As Robinson points out, even Western Australia, with more of its labour force in rural occupations than any other state, and therefore the state in which one would expect to find sizeable country towns, "can support only one provincial town of more than 15,000

[3] See, particularly, *Readings on Urban Growth*, Sydney University Geography Department in conjunction with the Geographical Society of N.S.W.

[4] K. W. Robinson, "Processes and Patterns of Urbanization in Australia and New Zealand", *New Zealand Geographer*, vol. 18, no. 1, 1962.

persons—and that is a mining town". Queensland, on the other hand, does have seven of these "sizeable" towns in the 15,000-50,000 range and in other ways too, shows a degree of nucleation outside the capital which is not found elsewhere.

Historical Influences

This concentration of population has not come about by a drift from the countryside to the cities, which was so much a feature of urbanization in other countries. Close settlement has always been a feature of Australia since the establishment of colonial outposts. In 1900 the cities of Brisbane, Sydney and Melbourne contained 60% of the whole population and even a hundred years ago contained as much as 45%.[5]

Why this was so can fairly easily be seen. The Australian colonies depended on connections with Britain, and the capital-ports provided this contact. These capital-port cities, having become well established, strengthened their positions first as administrative and financial centres and later as the foci of state-controlled railway and road systems. The long history of "state socialism" in Australia, and the centralized control of resources resulting from this, rather than the efforts of resourceful entrepreneurs, set the pattern of its development. Deliberate political planning to protect the area of influence of the capital cities (*e.g.* the change in railway gauges at state boundaries) and the necessity for making use of expensive installations, too costly to duplicate elsewhere, operated in the same direction. By the time rapid expansion of population was taking place, improved automobile transport was making it possible for the population to live spread out over the hinterland of the large cities, and thus militated against the nucleation of population in the countryside from which towns might grow as they had in other parts of the world. Transport made it possible for people to get into the distant countryside, but at the same time made it unnecessary for them to develop self-contained and independent communities there.

Then, too, immigration has been a big factor in the growth of Australian population even after the period of initial settlement. Since 1947, net immigration has accounted for around 1,250,000. In 1906 "it was found that immigrants to Australia linger longer in their port of debarkation, and they seldom care to leave it while employment is procurable",[6] a tradition which they continue today.

In 1954 the foreign-born population in Australia amounted to about 15% of the total. More than 80% of the foreign-born population lived in urban areas and slightly more than 64% in the metropolitan areas. The immigrant population which constituted a substantial proportion of the total has thus maintained and reinforced the pattern of concentration in urban areas.

Had Australian industry grown largely by the exploitation of natural resources, rather than by the expansion of secondary industries behind a tariff wall, both native and immigrant population might have been spread more widely to work these resources. The accepted policy of the development of secondary industries tied to a local market, however, which Australia has followed at least since the depression of the 1930s, is a process which pro-

[5] Asa Briggs, "Historians and the Study of Cities", George Judah Cohen Memorial Lecture, University of Sydney, 1960, p. 4.
[6] *A Guide for Immigrants and Settlers,* Intelligence Department of N.S.W., 1906.

duces its own momentum. The markets became manufacturing centres which in turn became bigger markets; and so on. Therefore any new industrial enterprise, unless rigidly tied to the site of some natural resources, had no alternative location to the cities. The cities not only held their position but increased faster than the rest of the population, which influence continues today. Every state capital has a bigger share of its state's population in 1961 than it had in 1911, as follows:

	1911	1961
Sydney	42·08	55·69
Melbourne	45·09	65·25
Brisbane	23·02	39·09
Adelaide	45·01	60·66
Perth	37·96	57·03

Urban Decentralization

During the last decade the capital cities of Australia have been undergoing a change in their growth patterns, called urban decentralization. New suburban centres have been formed, similar in many respects to the principal centres. A single central area is adequate as long as the journey to work of those who are employed there remains within reasonable limits. It is adequate also if people can reach it conveniently in their business pursuits and in acquiring their material needs. Inadequacy in these respects generally leads to decentralization. Any central area activity is likely to decentralize through unsatisfactory conditions, but the commonest are industrial and retail.

In Sydney the trend has been very marked and widely distributed. Secondary industry was the first to move. It was probably precipitated by the labour shortage which occurred a few years after the second world war. Moving out to the suburbs placed industry in a stronger competitive position for labour by shortening the journey to work. Measured in employment, central area industry declined by about 10 per cent. between 1954 and 1962. Retail decentralization became pronounced about 1958, probably being precipitated by the introduction of the so-called regional shopping centre in the United States. However, instead of taking this form it tended to exploit established well-located suburban centres such as Parramatta and Bankstown.

Melbourne's growth has followed similar trends, although the distribution is not as wide as in Sydney. A large industrial area was opened up more than ten years ago about 14 miles to the south-east of Melbourne, while more recently there has been extensive development in the outer suburbs to the north. In retailing the move began with Chadstone, an entirely new centre which is probably the largest of its kind in Australia and the closest approach to the American example.

Adelaide and Perth are notable for the form their decentralization has taken. It has been deliberately planned, and instead of occurring within the present urban limits has reached beyond to form entirely new communities. Elizabeth has developed as a separate town seventeen miles north of the centre of Adelaide, and Kwinana is about the same distance south-west of Perth.[7]

The possibility of providing ample car parking facilities at these centres has, for retail shopping at least, reversed some of the traffic flow towards the centre. To call these new nuclei "satellite towns" is to overstate what is hap-

[7] We are indebted for the above paragraphs to Mr R. D. L. Fraser, lately Chief Planning Officer, Cumberland County Council, Sydney.

pening, because although it is becoming increasingly possible for their populations to meet most material requirements locally and without recourse to the city, for the most part the absence of any break between these suburban centres and the city makes them just that—suburban centres rather than satellite towns.

Some of the other effects of this very high concentration are not so easy to describe, but may be more important. They might be very roughly described by the statement that since the urban culture dominates the lives of such a large proportion of the country's population it has become the normal way of life to which the rest aspire. Access to tertiary education, for example, is one of the accompanying features of modern urbanization, with the pressure for places and the demand for the output of the universities both rising. Each capital city has its own university. Melbourne and Adelaide have each recently opened their second university, while Sydney is planning its third. In 1964 Australia had 75,000 university students out of a total population of approximately 11 million. Great Britain, for example, had only about twice as many from a population nearly five times as big. Discussions about the relative quality of the work done in the two sets of institutions are important for university education, but are irrelevant here. Australia has proportionally many more of its (admittedly younger) population in the universities than Britain has, and it is almost certain that part of the explanation is in its population settlement pattern. Another part of the explanation is also likely to be found in the development of secondary and tertiary industries which demand a higher proportion of trained workers than primary industries.

The demand for university expansion is, at the same time, a demand for university places from a population which expects to have access to the educational facilities which it sees on its doorstep, and partly a demand for the products of university training by industry and general population alike. People sometimes move into or stay in a city to be able to send their children to the university there, but it is just as likely that other people first think of a university education when they live in a city where it can be obtained. Then, too, a large industrial city produces its own demand for types of skill which did not exist before—some aspects of government and police work, traffic control, town planning, public health, specialists in packaging, selling and market research; even parking meter manufacturers and attendants; all the specialized and linked industrial services which are only necessary and can only exist in large centres of varied activity. What is going on in these two kinds of process might be summarized as a massive division of labour and growth of specialization, the economics resulting from doing things on a large scale which this specialization makes possible, and the pressure of population to gain access to the products of these economics.[8] It is uncontrolled working of the forces behind these processes which accounts for the continued growth of our largest centres.

Public Control of Urban Development

In some areas of activity the pattern of Australian development has been subject to strong public control, for example, the founding of the colonies

[8] The relation between the growth of the professions and the demand for higher education is further discussed in chapter 3.

themselves, the state-owned rail and road systems. In other areas, a great deal has been left to private individuals and to voluntary agencies which in other societies would be the responsibility of government. For example, in the health field there is no compulsory health insurance and essential services like chest X-rays and blood banks are carried out by voluntary agencies (the Anti-TB Association and the Red Cross respectively). Similarly, the control of urban development has been left largely to private decision, and government authorities have been slow to control, either by public spending or by planning and guiding the activities of private citizens and businesses.

In New South Wales the Local Government Act empowers a city, municipal or shire council to prepare a planning scheme. A scheme may include zoning for the use of land, the reservation of land for public purposes such as schools, parks and roads and provision for its acquisition, the preservation of places and objects of historical or scientific interest or natural beauty, and in general any provision of local government significance necessary for improvement or embellishment of urban or rural communities.

The Act also provides for planning on a regional scale, as a result of which the Cumberland and Northumberland County Councils and the Illawarra Planning Authority were established. These bodies had the responsibility of preparing and administering planning schemes for the areas which contain Sydney, Newcastle and Wollongong respectively.

The Planning Scheme for the County of Cumberland was the first in New South Wales to receive statutory approval. It took the form of an ordinance which divided the responsibility for administering the scheme between the County Council for the whole County and the local governing body for its particular area. In an amendment to this ordinance in 1962 the local councils were given almost the entire responsibility for administration, with provision that the concurrence of the County Council had to be obtained in matters of overall metropolitan significance. This amendment expedited the consideration of applications to carry out development as the applicant was required to deal with only one of the two authorities concerned. At the same time, the Local Government Act was also amended with the object of expediting the procedure for the submission and examination of planning schemes.

Late in 1962 the Minister for Local Government proposed the establishment of a State Planning Authority to take over the responsibilities of the County planning authorities and exercise general supervision of planning by local governing bodies.[9] The Authority was constituted in 1964.

The exception to the rule of uncontrolled growth of the capital cities comes from South Australia—the new town of Elizabeth which is discussed later. Only here have the needs for expansion of the capital been directed into anything which could compare with the "New Towns" programme of Britain and elsewhere. Elizabeth, a new town planned for a population of 50-60,000, is about 17 miles to the north of Adelaide, separated from it by a green belt and planned as an independent town with its own employment and services.

Elizabeth is interesting in its own right, but it is interesting also because it draws attention to other features of Australian urbanization. The first

[9] We are again indebted to Mr R. D. L. Fraser for the above account of town planning powers in N.S.W.

feature is the place of public housing. The development authority for Elizabeth is the South Australian Housing Trust—a statutory authority charged with providing medium priced housing for rental and for sale. Public housing is much less important in Australia than in the United Kingdom, for example, where over one-third of all houses are built and owned by local authorities. In Australia, even in recent years, when government house building has been functioning well above the traditional level, the number of government-built houses completed each year has been around 12,000 out of a total of 70-80 thousand.

Up until 1957 there was a scheme in operation whereby the Federal Government subsidized rent rebates through the State Housing Commissions. Since that date the states have been helped through preferential lending rates and are empowered to give rent rebates on their own responsibility. So far, neither state nor Federal governments have clearly accepted the responsibility for housing the country's population. The pressure for additional housing arising from the immigration programme and the example of the War Service Homes scheme plus, perhaps, a growing attitude that house-building should be used as a public works programme in time of unemployment, together represent a growing opinion that the states should accept this responsibility as governments have elsewhere.[10]

Partly on account of their low level of activity in Australia, and partly because nobody else has taken planning seriously, Housing Commissions have been traditionally less concerned with planning the maximum number of houses from the funds fully available. Elizabeth as a fully planned new town is a welcome departure from this policy, but the fact that it is so unusual emphasizes a further feature of Australian cities—not only is there relatively little public housing but there are relatively few big developments of any kind. The typical developer, at least until recently, has been the individual houseowner or the small speculative builder working on two or three houses at a time from the sale of which he finances the next batch.

A final point of interest suggested by the introduction of Elizabeth as one of the rare examples of comprehensive planning is that Elizabeth is in a very loose sense a "company town". That is, although it is a public housing commission and not a private enterprise project its viability to a large extent rests on the pay packets from one employer—in this case, the Weapons Research Establishment operating in connection with the Woomera Rocket Range. It is not, of course, intended to continue this close dependence on one source of employment and already other industries are being established there.

There have been other examples of company towns in Australia which were in fact developed by industrial operators. Examples are Kwinana, in Western Australia, built in connection with an oil project; Rum Jungle, to house workers attracted to the uranium mines; and Mount Isa, as a mining centre. There are also a few highly specialized towns, like Wollongong, depending on a particular small range of industries. But these, together with the "company towns" just mentioned, underline the general lesson that, except in the

[10] Cf. Ruth Atkins, "Local Government", in R. N. Spann (ed.), *Public Administration in Australia*.

cases where there are large fixed resources to be exploited Australia has not developed planned towns away from the capital cities.

Part of the explanation of the uncontrolled development of Australian cities is to be found in the structure of their government. In spite, or maybe because of, their dominance in their own states, none of the Australian capital cities except Brisbane is governed by a unitary metropolitan authority. Instead, each metropolitan area is governed and serviced by "a bewildering array of local elected councils, *ad hoc* authorities, and State Departments".[11] In Sydney, for example, 66 different government agencies concern themselves with railways, roads, road transport, and the general supervision of many safety and health controls. Several county councils (*e.g.* Sydney County Council) provide electricity. A Water, Sewerage and Drainage Board provides these essential services. Forty separate local elected councils (including the City of Sydney, the City of Parramatta, and suburban municipalities and shires) separately are concerned with raising and allocating funds for streets, some roads, street lighting, cleaning, garbage disposal, some local planning and building controls, provision of many welfare, cultural and recreational services (to mention only some of their possible tasks). A separate state authority deals with port facilities, another with housing, another with fire prevention. "The list is enormous."[12]

The argument that the metropolitan areas ought to have their own area authority, which could be also an all-purpose authority, has been canvassed and campaigned for in each state in turn. The reason why, except in Brisbane, it has not succeeded seems to be that it is politically impossible for the state authorities to hand over to a new authority such a large proportion of their powers and be content with the remainder. The Labour-dominated city government in Brisbane succeeded, however, in achieving unitary powers and independence of the state authorities.

Inside the Cities

What special features, if any, do Australian cities show in their internal organization? First of all, Australian cities are relatively new and could therefore not be expected to show some of the features shown by cities with a longer history. For example, no Australian city is based on a walled-for-defence town, a guild town, or a medieval cathedral town. All were established as ports and all grew during a period of rapidly developing transport. The resulting internal pattern is one of low density development—large house blocks and single-family one-storey houses going on for miles (the continuously developed area of Sydney covers 600 square miles). The features resulting from this low density development are both economic and social. On the economic side there is the fantastically high volume of traffic produced in the course of employment, servicing and recreation of such a dispersed population, which has been estimated to absorb about one-third of the national income. Parallel with this high cost of distribution is the high cost of providing services like roads, sewers and water with the result that the high level of services which might be expected by an urban population with a high standard of living is in many cases lacking.

[11] Ruth Atkins, "The Metropolitan Muddle", *Australian Journal of Social Issues*, vol. 1, no. 1, 1961.
[12] *Ibid.*

The high proportion of income spent communally—the spending in the so-called "public sector"—is one of the features normally associated with urbanization, and in many countries urban status is only given to an area's population when the public purse can pay for the services thought to be appropriate to urban living.

Very large areas of Australian cities are unsewered (in 1960, 376,000 people in the outer suburbs and probably 500,000 in the whole metropolitan area of Sydney were without mains sewerage), including some only two or three miles from the city centre and developed more than fifty years ago. These badly serviced areas are not slum areas in the sense of being made up of sub-standard buildings occupied by low-income families. Some of them are near the city centres and fetch quite high prices. Here individual house-holders have themselves installed quite costly substitutes for the missing com-munal services—chemical closets and septic tanks instead of sewers; exten-sions from house lighting instead of publicly lighted footpaths and so on.

But most of such areas are on the city fringe, and include housing ranging from the poorest asbestos-cement shack to well-designed, large and costly houses. The fringe areas contain properties over the whole range of quality, though not often mixed in the same immediate vicinity, and large numbers of them are only provided with the absolute minimum of services—partly-made roads and electric light and power lines. For the rest, from catching their water in rain tanks to disposing of all except the simplest household refuse, each householder makes his own arrangements. Understandably, many residents of these areas spend large sections of their non-work time in activi-ties which would seem to be more in keeping with rural living than with life in a modern city—clearing street and road gutters; tending incinerators or carting rubbish; disinfecting, maintaining or repairing inefficient lavatories in addition to the normal jobs of maintaining their own house property.

A study of a Melbourne housing estate in 1962 showed that by far the greatest slice of non-work time was spent doing jobs around the house, which together with shopping and 1 to 1½ hours daily travel to work for the main earner left little time for other leisure pursuits. There was certainly no evidence of any problem of finding a use for the unlimited leisure which various prophets have forecast as likely to result from technological change. Almost everybody who did not own their own house would wish to do so. Improvements on the house, or a move to a better house, were the most frequent way in which people said they would use additional income or in which they would invest a windfall. The same study found that for the most part people had a controlled and limited contact with neighbours, limited to specific activities, and for the rest were busy travelling to work and running their suburban homes.[13] For the residents of such areas it is difficult to see what exactly is the city-like quality in their style of living except the access to a variety of employment opportunities; perhaps the main reason why the large cities will continue to hold population.

It would be wrong, however, to regard the city as an amorphous mass.

Brief mention of the special character of the fringe has been made. This special character is consistent with their relatively low land costs; people who cannot afford to build nearer the city centre have to go out to the fringes.

[13] D. Scott and R. U'ren, *Leisure*.

304

Here they not only are poorly serviced but can themselves only afford to rent or buy a cheaper though newer kind of property. Some people have suggested that it is on the fringes rather than in the decaying inner rings that Australian slums are developing.

In the city centres the same process is taking place as in cities elsewhere. Occupation of the central business districts is becoming more dense, buildings are becoming higher, residents are being crowded out in favour of offices and stores. Getting a larger and larger daytime population in and out of the centre is already a major concern of planners and transport authorities.

Outside the city centres particular areas, many of them new, are settling down to show a special character, i.e. there are areas which are clearly areas of "good quality", "high reputation", etc. A recent survey of Sydney showed that the areas of high or low reputation tend to be together and also that for most areas the same judgment of their ranking tends to be fairly widely held through different sections of the city's population.[14]

On a more objective basis and using the quality of housing (size, site-value, etc.) as the criterion, it is possible to rank districts according to whether they contain more or less than their quota of "A" class houses compared with their quota of all dwellings. In Sydney the four "best" local authority areas out of a total of 35 contain 57% of "A" class houses but only 10% of all dwellings. In Melbourne the comparable figures show that the six "best" local authority areas out of a total of 40 contain 62% of "A" class houses but only 22% of all houses. Though the proportions of the two cities which contain the majority of "A" class dwellings are very roughly the same, the concentration of "A" class dwellings in particular areas seems to be greater in Sydney whose four "best" areas have roughly six times their quota of "A" class houses (57% of "A" class dwellings out of 10% of all dwellings), compared with three times their quota for Melbourne's "best" areas. Among Sydney's four "best" areas are two (Ku-ring-gai and Woollahra) which have respectively nine times and five times their quota, whereas none of Melbourne's "best" areas has much more than three times its quota. In both cities there is clear geographical segregation of population by social standing—a segregation which is more obvious in Sydney than in Melbourne.[15]

A study of differentiation between areas was carried out for Melbourne in 1949.[16] The 29 municipalities in the Melbourne metropolitan area were divided into six groups, each group being fairly homogeneous with regard to physical characteristics and date of development. For example, Group III was made up of the municipalities of Brighton, Camberwell, Caulfield, Hawthorn and Kew; all areas of slow and steady development, distant from industrial areas and with residential property of high quality. Another grouping (Group V) of quite different character comprised Collingwood, Fitzroy, Richmond, South Melbourne, Port Melbourne and Melbourne, all older areas of poorer property with factories, shops and housing mixed together. Similarly, with the other four groupings, an examination of data on occupation and incomes showed that each grouping had not only a definite physical character

---

[14] A. A. Congalton, *Status Ranking of Sydney Suburbs*.

[15] This is probably the result of topography. Sydney's harbour gives it the North Shore and the harbour-side Eastern Suburbs, which have no counterpart in Melbourne.

[16] G. R. Bruns, "Some Neglected Aspects of Melbourne's Demography", unpublished M.A. thesis, University of Melbourne, 1949.

but a definite socio-economic character too. When the socio-economic status of each group of municipalities is represented on a map it shows the metropolitan area to be divided into distinct tracts, the general shape and meaning of which are indicated by the diagram below. The heavier hatchings show the groupings of municipalities of low socio-economic status.

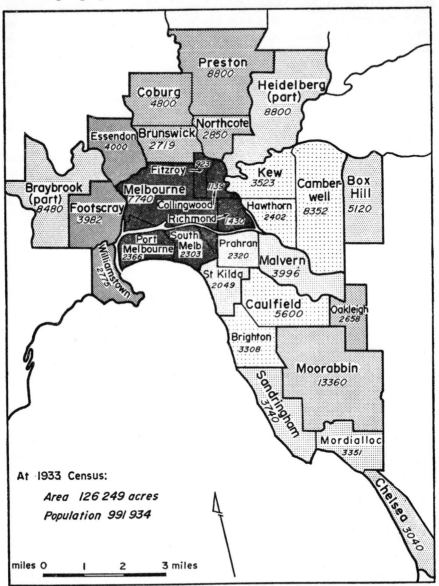

Preston
8800

Coburg
4800

Heidelberg
(part)
8800

Northcote
2850

Essendon
4000

Brunswick
2719

Fitzroy
923

Kew
3523

Camber-
well
8352

Box
Hill
5120

Braybrook
(part)
8480

Melbourne
7740

1139

Footscray
3982

Collingwood

Hawthorn
2402

Richmond
1430

Port
Melbourne
2366

South
Melb
2303

Prahran
2320

Malvern
3996

Williamstown
2775

St Kilda
2049

Caulfield
5600

Oakleigh
2658

Brighton
3308

Moorabbin
13360

Sandringham
3740

Mordialloc
3351

Chelsea
3040

At 1933 Census:

Area   126 249 acres

Population 991 934

miles 0   1   2   3 miles

As in the case of many other cities, the areas of lowest economic status are concentrated in a ring around the city centre, and these poorer areas quickly give way to a solid block of "good" areas on the east-and-waterfront side of the city. This may be compared with Sydney's inner areas and the obvious differences between its eastern and western suburbs.

As in other cities, socio-economic status is not only a question of occupation and income. The religious composition of the areas varies too. In both 1931 and 1933, for example, Bruns reports that the proportion of Catholics to non-Catholics was highest in the areas of low economic status, and that the ranking of areas according to the proportion of Catholics went in inverse order to the ranking on socio-economic status.

The group of municipalities with the heaviest hatching in the diagram (Fitzroy, Collingwood, Melbourne, Richmond, South Melbourne, Melbourne and Port Melbourne) had a death rate 10% higher than the Australian death rate corrected for age distribution, while the "superior" areas of Kew, Brighton, etc., had a rate 10% less than average. Infant mortality rates varied even more widely. In 1915 the mortality rates of the two extreme groups of municipalities had been 120 per 1,000 and 60 per 1,000 respectively, though by 1947 both rates had been drastically reduced and the difference cut considerably (30 per 1,000 and 24 per 1,000 respectively).

The Melbourne study referred to also showed that in other important aspects of life: ethnic origin of population, reliance on public hospitals and even the proportion of the population divorced, great contrasts existed between the inner and the outer city areas. For example, in Melbourne all Labour-held seats are north and west of the Yarra (roughly the two most heavily-hatched tracts in our diagram) and none to the south or east.[17]

How Different are Australian Towns and Cities?

Some of Australia's towns are highly specialized. The best known examples are, as might be imagined from what has gone before, those based on the exploitation of natural resources—Kwinana, Mount Isa and Broken Hill. In a different category, but just as highly specialized, are the towns devoted to catering for holiday makers. By far the best known example of this kind of specialization is Surfers' Paradise, a holiday town on the Queensland coast south of Brisbane. Surfers' Paradise has developed extremely rapidly in the past ten years from almost nothing to a settlement with a permanent population of over 20,000 and an "in season" population of many times that number.

How different are the capital cities? On account of their size and dominant positions in their respective states, each of the capital cities has to provide a wide range of products and services for its population—or to express the same idea in a more useful way, it has to be capable of performing most of the steps in converting primary resources into finished goods and services. In a paper which classifies industries on the basis of inputs, whether raw materials or materials already processed in the chain of production, Bunker divides the occupied population into ten categories and calculates the industrial profile of each of the five cities and of Australia.[18] This material is then used, with the device of the Location Quotient, to show how different and in what respects the industrial profile of each city is from that of Australia and in what respects they differ from each other. An area has an L.Q. of 1 for a particular industrial group when it engages the same proportion of its occupied

[17] James Jupp, *Victoria Votes* (A.P.S.A. monograph).

[18] Raymond Bunker, "The Metropolis in Australia", *Readings on Urban Growth,* pp. 18-37.

population in that group as are engaged in the whole country. An L.Q. above 1, therefore, represents some degree of specialization. Whether the degree of specialization is important depends upon the size of the industrial group and the proportion of the local occupied population working in the specialized activity. The variance between employment distribution in the capital cities and total Australian employment is then summarized into an index of dissimilarity for each city. The indices are (approximately) Sydney 20, Melbourne 19, Brisbane 14, Adelaide 17 and Perth 16, which means that Sydney has 20% of its labour force employed differently from the Australian pattern (*i.e.* Australia minus Sydney), some industrial groups being over-represented and some under-represented. In the same way, for Melbourne's industrial structure to correspond to that of the rest of Australia, 19% of its labour force would have to shift between groups—for Brisbane 14% and so on for the others. The analysis goes on to discuss the significance of the difference between Sydney's 20, Melbourne's 19, Brisbane's 14, and so on. One point which is neglected in Bunker's paper is that by far the major part of the dissimilarity of each capital's industrial structure from that of Australia rests on one fact. This is that whereas Australia as a whole employs 14.98% of its work force in industries classified as primary resource extractors, only one of the capitals so employs more than 2.4%, *i.e.* Brisbane. Sydney and Melbourne proportions in this group are 1.3 and 1.5 respectively. Thus, if one asks the question, "Apart from the working of primary resources, how do the industrial structures of the Australian capital cities differ from that of the whole country?" the answer is, "By very little".

Leaving aside the primary resource extraction industries, there is no industrial group in any of the capital cities having an L.Q. greater than 1.54 (Class 4 Industries in Adelaide, accounted for by the location of the motor body works of General Motors-Holden). If one therefore asks the additional question, "How much do the capital cities differ in this respect from each other?" the answer is, "By very little indeed".

On a finer classification of industries by products rather than by stages of manufacture there is, of course, more differentiation of activity between cities. Melbourne specializes in textiles, chemicals and motor car manufacturing. Within manufacturing industry Sydney has some specialization in industrial chemicals, wireless and metal founding, Brisbane and Perth have some specialization in food processing, as might be expected from the great agricultural bias of their areas. The same cities specialized most in what Bunker calls "central place" functions, *i.e.* tertiary industries serving more than the local population. If a still finer classification were used the differences would naturally be more numerous, but would not hide the main fact that by and large the state capitals appear as complete and independent structures.

What of the Future?

One might speculate on the possibilities that the concentrated urban pattern described might change in the future. Cheap sources of power would make the inland areas of Australia habitable. Discoveries of new minerals for which search is daily being carried out would make it profitable as well as possible for people to live there. But at present it is difficult to imagine anything very different from the opening up of one or two centres in each state with new concentrations growing up around them.

There are no examples in the modern world of large populations moving away from cities. As far as we can see the urban way of life, industrialization and mechanization are inextricably linked to each other and to the higher standards of living which populations everywhere demand when they get within striking distance of it. It is in the cities too, and particularly in the new cities, that populations make contact with global networks—of industrial structure, of standardized equipment and tastes. City firms often have direct worldwide dealings with customers and suppliers; things like building materials, telephones, and a host of appliances associated with urban living change on a world scale; a popular song starting in the city of one country may be heard within weeks in similar cities all over the world. In some respects, therefore, the city dweller lives in a worldwide community. One can scarcely imagine a population raised in this climate being willing to reverse the process, and if the undeveloped areas of Australia are populated it seems likely this will only be done by a spread of urbanization, not by de-urbanization. Australia might have more cities, but it is unlikely that it will ever have any villages or more small towns.

If, for any reason, Australia operated a vast new immigration programme attracting large numbers of people from Asia for example, who did not demand accommodation in the existing centres of population, the story might be quite different. But without such a vast and deliberately managed programme Australia will probably continue to present a picture of what is probably the truly urban society.

19   A Note on the Urban Consumer

URBAN life, with its specialization of functions and roles, has thrown up the notion of the individual as a "consumer", and as a consequence stimulated large-scale advertising, and market research directed to "consumer incitement" (J. K. Galbraith). Frequently dubious in motive and method, market research has nevertheless been long enough in train to tell us something about change in those social activities directly concerned with the acquisition of material goods, and with consumption in its original limited sense—the intake of food and drink.

Carried out almost entirely in cities, market surveys are "descriptive" research, emphasizing the what, when, where and how of behaviour without exploring the why. Questions about why consumers behave in particular ways involve a good deal of conjecture, and, to reduce guesswork, steps have been taken towards "psychological", "dynamic", or "motivational" research. Each is open to criticism and has been the subject of polemic, but whatever the term, the specific aim is to collect consumer testimony on why they do certain things, and to evaluate this in the light of some psychological or other theoretical orientation. People, however, are seldom aware of all the reasons for their behaviour, and they are not as concerned to discover their motives as manufacturers may wish. "Because I like it" is as far as most consumers will go with self-analysis. However, given the opportunity, they display a wealth of conjecture on why *others,* if not themselves, would act in a particular way.

In studies of the consumption of sweets in Australia and Britain, consumers stress the sharing of the chocolate they buy. In fact, this is difficult to do with certain very popular lines, especially the individually wrapped chocolate-coated bar which, though new, is now (at least in the U.K.) outselling blocks or filled bars equivalently priced. Their point, indeed, is that they are designed for one-person consumption. Is their growing popularity, then, to be attributed to the fact that one does not really want to share one's chocolate?

Consumers' propensity to proffer the socially accepted reason for their behaviour is even more poignantly demonstrated in baby feeding. Despite the baby health centres' stress on breast feeding, consumer surveys in Australia indicate that more than 50% of babies are breast fed for less than three months. Mothers justify this—a much shorter time than was normal ten or more years ago—by claiming that they "did not have enough milk". Typically, convenience has determined the preference for bottle feeding as a method that ties them down less. Yet, true to conventional expectations, most mothers will claim that breast feeding is best for the child. (British mothers use this rationalization too, though it seems to be more common in Australia.)

Market research makes certain sociological assumptions about the consumer universe. The following are among the most important:

1. That the housewife is the person who does the buying and cooking for the household, and is therefore the most reliable source of information on these topics.

2. That there is a division between male and female spheres of responsibility and interest.

3. That different consumer behaviour patterns are to be expected between groups. Breakdowns by age, sex, socio-economic group and geographical area are standard in market research surveys.

4. That all consumers interpret the question asked in exactly the same way.

5. That in Australian society material possessions are the main index of social standing.

6. That consumption habits are changing, particularly in food and drink, *e.g.* the rising popularity of coffee compared with tea, of prepared soup mixes, of cake mixes and quick-frozen vegetables. The obvious influences for change are immigration; the mass production facilities introduced by overseas companies; and new methods of merchandising, especially self-service stores.

Market research, then, generally confirms the importance of the kinds of social differentiation and social change which are discussed elsewhere in this book. To the market researcher, for instance, the steady increase in the number of very young children and of teenagers—the fastest-growing segment of the consumer population—is of particular interest. The number of children under four—1.0m. in 1960—is expected to rise to 1.4m. in 1970. Adolescents aged between 15 and 19 years—.7m. in 1960—will become 1.0m in 1970.

Personal income has also risen significantly from £3,544m. in 1953 to £5,197m. in 1960. Table 1 shows the increase in "real" disposable income, *i.e.* allowing for price rises.

TABLE 1

Disposable Income 1953-60

Year ending June 30th	Consumer Price Index	"Real" Disposable Income Total (million £s)	"Real" Disposable Income per head £s
1953	100·0	3,129	358
1957	113·1	3,598	377
1960	118·9	3,957	389

Table 2 shows the amounts of disposable income spent per head on the various categories of expenditure from 1953 to 1960. Rent payments absorbed 8.4% in 1960, compared with 5.9% in 1953; expenditure on food rose by 29%, *i.e.* the same proportion as total income; hardware, electrical goods and furniture (which includes TV sets) rose by 54% and made up 10% of disposable income in 1960.

311

TABLE 2

Allocation of Disposable Income per Head (£s)

Item of expenditure	Year ended 30th June		
	1953	1957	1960
Rent	21·3	30·7	38·7
Food	79·9	97·0	103·7
Clothing, footwear	40·8	46·4	50·0
Hardware, electrical goods, furniture	30·1	37·1	46·4
Tobacco, cigarettes, beer	32·3	41·7	44·0
Fares	8·9	10·2	9·9
Gas and electricity	6·1	8·1	9·4
All other consumer expenditure	71·4	95·5	116·1
Overseas remits	2·4	2·8	2·5
Savings-assurance funds	5·0	6·0	6·9
Other personal savings	60·0	51·1	34·8
Total disposable income	358·2	426·6	462·4

The spectacular rise of expenditure on motor vehicles is shown separately, in Table 3. The figures relate both to individuals and to private corporations.

TABLE 3

Expenditure on Motor Vehicles 1953-60 (£ millions)

	Year ended 30th June		
	1953	1957	1960
Trucks and utilities	58	77	91
Cars, station wagons, and motor cycles	109	180	269

Food Consumption Patterns

Every culture prescribes for its members the meaning of food substances, methods of preparation, tastes, preferences, time and style of consumption. Consumer research may be used to observe certain aspects of this social behaviour. Most countries carry out government-sponsored surveys of food habits, Australia does not. No major study has been done since 1944. The Commonwealth Statistician issues consumption figures per head for some food items, but this tells us nothing about eating habits as such.

In recent years in most Western countries the processing of foods has been radically modified; preparation has shifted more and more to the manufacturer. It is less that new foods are coming in, than that old foods are being newly presented with particular emphasis on features that will save time and effort to ensure success. A dramatic instance is instant coffee, whose growing popularity is instructive. Australians have never been coffee-drinkers, as Table 4 shows.

TABLE 4

Consumption of Coffee (lb. per head)

Year			Australia	U.K.	U.S.A.	France	Holland	Germany
1939	..	..	0·6	0·7	14·8	9·8	9·8	5·0
1945	..	..	1·2	1·2	16·8	2·5	1·3	n.a.
1949	..	..	0·9	1·8	18·5	4·6	5·3	1·0
1953	..	..	0·7	1·3	16·7	8·4	5·9	3·1
1957	..	..	1·6	1·9	15·7	8·9	6·3	4·5
1958	..	..	1·5	2·0	15·9	n.a.	7·0	5·3
1959	..	..	2·0	2·0	n.a.	n.a.	n.a.	5·3

Since 1959 consumption has risen well above 2 lb. per head, but in international terms this hardly makes us a coffee-drinking community. Comparative figures for tea-drinking underline the point.

TABLE 5

Tea Consumption in Australia

Year					lb. tea per head
1939	..	..	..	..	7·1
1945	..	..	..	..	5·8
1949	..	..	..	..	6·3
1953	..	..	..	..	6·5
1957	..	..	..	..	6·2
1958	..	..	..	..	6·0
1959	..	..	..	..	5·8

Non-British immigrants have certainly been the largest single factor in increasing coffee consumption, especially as British and Australian trends are very similar. But not the only factor, as the *rate* of increase is greater than this could account for. Market surveys confirm that more "old" Australians—and particularly women—are drinking coffee. Though Australians are slowly giving up some cups of tea in preference to cups of coffee, the style of coffee consumption is still consistent with, rather than violently opposed to, their tea habits. For example, 80% of those who drink coffee claim that they always have it with milk rather than black. A few claim they always have it black; the rest sometimes with, sometimes without.

A continuous survey of 2,625 housewives in the mainland capital cities, conducted in 1959 and again in 1960, found that in 57% of homes some form of coffee was served "yesterday". Instant coffee accounted for 75% of these cases. Results also suggested some connection between the propensity to drink ground coffee and higher economic status. Ground coffee drinkers, for instance, were more likely to own telephones: in 1959, 59% as against the average 47%; in 1960, 58% as against 49%. Coffee essence drinkers were the poorest by the same criterion: in 1959, only 35% had telephones. Age mattered too: in both surveys, the essence drinkers were appreciably older than the others.

A parallel survey of 2,484 persons in Britain in 1960 produced similar results. Women drink more coffee than men—it is popular as a mid-morning beverage, easier to prepare. "Motivational" researchers would have us believe women have a greater psychological need for coffee as a stimulant and release from nervous tension or boredom.

From the statistical and survey material we may infer that the increase in coffee-drinking in Australia is not due to any radical change in food habits. The largest single factor seems to be the introduction of instant coffee—intensively advertised, especially since the advent of television.

So far, in fact, Australian food habits confirm the suspicion that this is one area of social life which is extremely resistant to change. This conclusion emerges very strongly from the results of a survey carried out in 1,552 households in Sydney in 1962 by the Nestlé Company of Australia—the only important investigation of food consumption since the Commonwealth government survey of 1944. Housewives were questioned about the menu for the "main" meal on the previous day.[1] Answers emphasized the force of tradition. Over 90% of meals consisted of meat as the main dish: lamb and beef accounted for 69%, with lamb slightly more popular. The traditional meat was cooked in the traditional manner: roasted or grilled in 58% of cases. Two meals in three included dessert, of which a good half were puddings, pies, tarts or jelly, mostly home-made. A cup of tea ended three meals out of four. Bottled sauces were very popular. Foods particularly affected by changed methods of production or marketing were not strongly represented. Chicken and other poultry figured in only 4% of menus, ready-made desserts of any kind in only 7%. The moral is that although advertising, high-pressure merchandising and other forms of consumer incitement may give the impression of a rapidly changing profile of consumer habits, the changes are relatively superficial.

Calculated pressure on the consumer has provoked in retaliation the organized consumer. The Australian Consumers' Association, modelled on American and British bodies, was set up in 1959. By 1964 it claimed a membership of more than 50,000, and its monthly journal *Choice* was regularly quoted in the daily press and in radio news broadcasts. In some cases, its exposure of misleading claims, faulty or dangerous products has brought rapid reactions from manufacturers—*e.g.* anomalies in the pricing of chocolate. Its influence was detectable in the report of a Victorian inquiry into packaging produced in 1964. Local consumers' groups have sprung up; Canberra has had an active one since 1962.

Market research may, just occasionally, transcend its function by revealing something about wider patterns of social behaviour. Questions about a respondent's occupation often produce an answer which implies a higher occupational status than is actually the case, and women upgrade the occupations of their husbands in Australia as elsewhere.

But on the more personal question of age, Australian women are likely to be uniquely truthful. The relevance of this curious observation to other aspects of relations between the sexes, such as those discussed elsewhere in this book, may provide a minor field of interest for sociologists and psychologists. As far as market research is concerned, it confirms that consumers are capricious, and that their caprices may be persistent.

[1] The evening meal was generally the "main" meal.

Bibliography

1. BOOKS AND PAMPHLETS

Adorno, T.W. *et al., The Authoritarian Personality*. New York, 1950.

Aitken, H.G.J. (ed.), *The State and Economic Growth*. New York, 1959.

Alford, Robert R., *Party and Society: the Anglo-American Democracies*. Chicago, 1963

Almond, G. and Verba, S., *The Civic Culture*. Princeton, 1963.

Anchen, J.O., *Frank Tate and his Work for Education*. Melbourne, 1956.

Arndt, H.W., *The Australian Trading Banks*. Melbourne, 1960 (2nd ed.)

Australian Council of Salaried and Professional Associations, *The Australian National Income and its Distribution*. Sydney, 1959.

Australian Labor Party Federal Platform, Constitution and Rules. Canberra, 1964.

Bain, F.W., *A Digit of the Moon*. 1905.

Ball, W.M. (ed.), *Press, Radio and World Affairs: Australia's Outlook*. Melbourne, 1938.

Bantock, G.H., *Education in an Industrial Society*. London, 1963.

Barnard, J.A., (ed.), *The Simple Fleece: Studies in the Australian Wool Industry*. Melbourne, 1962.

Bean, C.E.W., *On the Wool Track*. Sydney, 1963 (reprinted).

————, *The Story of Anzac*. In *Official History of Australia in the War*, vols. 1-2. 1921-4.

Bell, Daniel (ed.), *The Radical Right: the new American right: expanded and updated*. New York, 1963.

Bendix, Reinhard, *Max Weber: An Intellectual Portrait*. New York, 1960.

Berdie, R.F., *Manpower and the Schools*. Melbourne, 1956.

Berger, P.L., *The Noise of Solemn Assemblies*. New York, 1961.

Berndt, R.M. and C.H., *From Black to White in South Australia*. Melbourne, 1951.

————, *Sexual Behaviour in Western Arnhem Land*. New York, 1951.

Bleakley, J.W., *The Aborigines of Australia: their history—their habits—their assimilation*. Brisbane, 1961.

Blishen, Bernard R., Jones, Frank E., Naegele, Kaspar D., and Porter, John, *Canadian Society: sociological perspectives*. New York, 1961.

Booth, Charles, *Life and Labour of the People in London* (1891-1903). London, 1902.

Borrie, W.D., *Australia*. In U.N.E.S.C.O. series, *The Positive Contribution by Immigrants*. 1955.

————, *Italians and Germans in Australia—a study of assimilation*. Melbourne, 1954.

————, *Population Trends and Policies: a study in Australian and world demography*. Sydney, 1948.

———— and Dedman, R.M., *University Enrolments in Australia, 1955-70: a projection*. Canberra, 1957.

Boulard, F., *An Introduction to Religious Sociology*. London, 1960.

Boyd, Robin, *The Australian Ugliness*. Melbourne, 1960.

Broom, Leonard and Selznick, Philip, *Sociology*. New York, 1958.

Bryce, James, *Modern Democracies*. 2nd ed., London, 1929.

Burns, Creighton, *Parties and People: a survey based on the La Trobe electorate*. Melbourne, 1961.

————, *The Tait Case*. Melbourne, 1962.

Burns, Eveline, *Social Security and Public Policy*. New York, 1956.

Burton, W.W., *The State of Religion and Education in New South Wales*. London, 1840.

Caiger, G. (ed.), *The Australian Way of Life*. London, 1953.

Calwell, A.A., *How Many Australians Tomorrow?* Melbourne, 1945.

Cambridge History of the British Empire, vol. 7, pt. 1. Cambridge, 1933.

Campbell, Ian and Loveday, Peter, *Groups in Theory and Practice*. Melbourne, 1962.

Campbell, W.J., *Growing up in Karribee*. Melbourne, 1963.

————, *Television and the Australian Adolescent: a Sydney survey*. Sydney, 1962.

Caplow, Theodore, *The Sociology of Work*. Minnesota, 1962.

Casagrande, J.B. (ed.), *In the Company of Man: twenty portraits by anthropologists*. New York, 1960.

Centers, Richard, *The Psychology of Social Classes: a study of class consciousness*. Princeton, 1949.

The Challenge to Australian Education. Addresses to the Australian College of Education. Melbourne, 1961.

Childe, V.G., *How Labour Governs: a study of workers' representation in Australia*. London, 1923.

Chisholm, A.H. (ed.), *The Australian Encyclopaedia* (10 vols.), Sydney, 1958.

Clark, C.M.H., *Select Documents in Australian History 1851-1900*. Sydney, 1955.

————, *Sources of Australian History*. London, 1957.

Cole, W.E., *Urban Society*. Massachusetts, 1958.

Coleman, P. (ed.), *Australian Civilization: a symposium*. Melbourne, 1962.

The Collected Letters of D.H. Lawrence (ed. Harry T. Moore). New York, 1962.

Condorcet, Marquis de, *Outline of the Progress of the Human Mind*. 1794.

Congalton, A.A., *Occupational Status in Australia*. Sydney, 1963.

————, *Social Standing of Occupations in Sydney*. Sydney, 1962.

————, *Status Ranking of Sydney Suburbs*. Sydney, 1961.

Connell, W.F. et al., *Growing up in an Australian City: a study of adolescents in Sydney*. Melbourne, 1957.

Crane, A.R. and Walker, W.G., *Peter Board: his contribution to the development of education in New South Wales*. Melbourne, 1957.

Crawford, R.M., *An Australian Perspective*. Melbourne, 1960.

Crisp, L.F., *The Australian Federal Labour Party 1901-51*. London, 1955.

————, *Ben Chifley: a biography*. Melbourne, 1961.

Crowley, F.K., *State Election: the fall of the Hawke government*. Perth, 1959.

Cumpston, J.H.L., *The History of Small-Pox in Australia, 1788-1908*. Melbourne, 1914.

The Dark People. Current Affairs Bulletin, vol. 29, no. 4, Sydney, 1961.

Darling, J.R. et al., *Educational Values in a Democracy*. Melbourne, 1956.

Davies, A.F., *Australian Democracy: an introduction to the political system*. 2nd ed. Melbourne, 1964.

————, *Private Politics: a study of five political outlooks*. Melbourne, 1962.

———— and Serle, Geoffrey, *Policies for Progress: essays in Australian politics*. Melbourne, 1954.

Davies, H., *Christian Deviations: the challenge of the sects*. London, 1954.

Dax, E. Cunningham, *Asylum to Community: the development of the mental hygiene service in Victoria, Australia*. Melbourne, 1961.

Day, Lincoln and Day, Alice Taylor, *Too Many Americans*. Boston, 1964.

Don't Marry a Catholic. Australian Catholic Truth Society, 1958.

Deane, R.P., *The Establishment of the Department of Trade: a case-study in administrative reorganization*. Canberra, 1963.

Durack, M. and E., *"All-About"*. *The story of a black community on Argyle Station, Kimberley*. Sydney, 1935.

Economic Security in Old Age: addresses by speakers at a conference held in Melbourne by Old People's Welfare Council of Victoria. Melbourne, 1961.

Education in Australia—Students' Report. Melbourne, 1963.

Eggleston, F.W., *State Socialism in Victoria*, London, 1932.

Elkin, A.P., *The Australian Aborigines: how to understand them*. 3rd ed., Sydney, 1954.
————, (ed.) *Marriage and the Family in Australia*. Sydney, 1957.
Emerging Techniques in Population Research. New York, 1963.
Encel, S., *Cabinet Government in Australia*. Melbourne, 1962.
Esson, Louis, *The Southern Cross and other plays* (with an introduction by Hilda Esson). Melbourne, 1946.
Etzioni, Amitai, *A Comparative Analysis of Complex Organizations: on power, involvement and their correlates*. New York, 1961.
Family Welfare: a guide to developing local services. Melbourne, 1963.
Fichter, J.H. (S.J.), *Southern Parish*. New York, 1951.
————, *Social Relations in the Urban Parish*. Chicago, 1954.
Financing of Voluntary Welfare Agencies in Victoria. Melbourne, 1961.
Fitzpatrick, B., *The Australian Commonwealth*. Melbourne, 1956.
Fletcher, J.H., *The Second Century of Australian History*. Melbourne, 1888.
Frankenberg, R., *Village on the Border: a social study of Religion, Politics and Football in North Wales*. London, 1957.
Freedman, R., Whelpton, P.K., and Campbell, A.A., *Family Planning, Sterility and Population Growth*. New York, 1959.
Friedmann, W. (ed.), *The Public Corporation*. Toronto, 1954.
Freud, S., *The Future of an Illusion*. London, 1949.
Gerth, H.H. and Mills, C. Wright, (eds.) *From Max Weber: essays in sociology*. New York, 1953.
Glick, I.O. and Levy, S.J., *Living with T.V.* Chicago, 1962.
Gollan, R.A., *Radical and Working Class Politics: a study of Eastern Australia 1850-1910*. Melbourne, 1960.
Gorer, G., *Exploring English Character*. London, 1955.
Grattan, C. Hartley (ed.), *Australia*. Berkeley, 1947.
————, *Introducing Australia*. Sydney, 1944.
Gravell, K., *A Report on Professional Incomes in Victoria*. Melbourne, 1957.
Gsell, F.X., *The Bishop with 150 Wives: fifty years as a missionary*. Sydney, 1956.
Guthrie, Tyrone, *A Life in the Theatre*. London, 1960.
Hall, A.R., *Australian Company Finance: sources and uses of funds of public companies—1946-55*. Canberra, 1956.
Halsey, A.H., Floud, Jean and Anderson, C. Arnold, *Education, Economy and Society*. New York, 1961.
Hancock, W.K., *Australia*. Sydney, 1944.
Hart, C.W.M. and Pilling, A.R., *The Tiwi of North Australia*. New York, 1960.
Herberg, W., *Protestant-Catholic-Jew*. New York, 1955.
Hofstadter, Richard, *The Age of Reform—from Bryan to F.D.R.* New York, 1955.
Hogbin, H.I., *Experiments in Civilization: the effects of European culture on a native community of the Solomon Islands*. London, 1939.
Hoggart, Richard, *The Uses of Literacy: aspects of working-class life with special reference to publications and entertainments*. London, 1957.
Holden, W.S., *Australia Goes to Press*. Michigan, 1961.
Hunt, Hugh, *The Making of Australian Theatre*. Melbourne, 1960.
Hunter, Alex (ed.), *The Economics of Australian Industry: studies in environment and structure*. Melbourne, 1963.
Income and Wealth Series 6. Papers by Carl F. Christ and others. London, 1957.
Inglis, K.S., *Churches and the Working Classes in Victorian England*. London, 1963.
————, *Hospital and Community: a history of the Royal Melbourne Hospital*. Melbourne, 1958.
————, *The Stuart Case*. Melbourne, 1961.
Jacobson, Paul H. and Pauline F., *American Marriage and Divorce*. New York, 1959.
Jennings, H.S., *The Biological Basis of Human Nature*. 1930.
Jesuit Year Book. 1962.

Jones, A.W., *Life, Liberty and Property: a story of conflict and a measurement of conflicting rights*. London, 1941.

Jones, Ernest, *Sigmund Freud: Life and Work*. London, 1953-7.

Jose, A. W., & Carter, H. J. (eds.), *The Australian Encyclopedia* (2 vols.) Sydney, 1927.

Jupp, James, *Australian Party Politics*. Melbourne, 1964.

Kardiner, A., *The Individual and his Society*. New York, 1939.

Karmel, P.H., *Some Economic Aspects of Education*. Melbourne, 1962.

——— and Brunt, Maureen, *The Structure of the Australian Economy*. Melbourne, 1962.

Keller, Suzanne, *Beyond the Ruling Class: strategic elites in modern society*. New York, 1963.

Kiddle, Margaret, *Caroline Chisholm*. Melbourne, 1950.

Kiser, C.V. (ed.), *Research in Family Planning*. Princeton, 1962.

Kolarz, W., *Religion in the Soviet Union*. London, 1961.

Kolko, Gabriel, *Wealth and Power in America: an analysis of social class and income distribution*. New York, 1962.

Labour's Policy for Security in Old Age. London, 1957.

Lenski, G., *The Religious Factor*. New York, 1961.

Linton, R., *The Study of Man*. New York, 1936.

Lipset, S.M., *Political Man: the Social Bases of Politics*. New York, 1960.

——— and Bendix, Reinhard, *Social Mobility in Industrial Society*. London, 1959.

Lloyd, B.E. and Wilkin, W.J., *The Education of Professional Engineers in Australia*. 2nd ed., Melbourne, 1962.

Lockwood, D., *The Blackcoated Worker: a study in class consciousness*. London, 1958.

Long, Gavin, *To Benghazi*. Canberra, 1952.

McGregor, O.R., *Divorce in England: a centenary study*. London, 1957.

McIntyre, A.J., *Sunraysia: a Social Survey of a Dried Fruits Area*. Melbourne, 1948.

——— and J.J., *Country Towns in Victoria: a social survey*. Melbourne, 1944.

Mackay, I.K., *Broadcasting in Australia*. Melbourne, 1957.

MacKenzie, Jeanne, *Australian Paradox*. Melbourne, 1961.

MacKenzie, Norman, *Women in Australia*. Melbourne, 1962.

McLeod, A.L. (ed.), *The Pattern of Australian Culture*. Melbourne, 1963.

Marx, Karl, *Capital*. Trans. by E. and C. Paul for Everyman's Library. vol. 1. London, 1930.

Matthews, D.R., *Social Background of Political Decision-Makers*. New York, 1954.

Mayer, H. (ed.), *Catholics and the Free Society*. Melbourne, 1961.

———, *The Press in Australia*. Sydney, 1964.

——— and Rydon, Joan, *The Gwydir By-Election 1953: a study in political conflict*. Canberra, 1954.

Melbourne Studies in Education 1957/8. Melbourne, 1958.

Métin, Albert, *Le socialisme sans doctrines*. Paris, 1901.

Mills, C. Wright, *The Power Elite*. New York, 1956.

———, *White Collar: the American middle classes*. New York, 1951.

Nicoll, J.R. Allardyce, *British drama: an historical survey from the beginnings to the present time*. London, 1925.

Niebuhr, H.R., *Christ and Culture*. London, 1952.

———, *The Social Sources of Denominationalism*. New York, 1929.

Northcott, C.H., *Australian Social Development*. New York, 1918.

Oeser, O.A. and Emery, F.E., *Social Structure and Personality in a Rural Community*. London, 1954.

——— and Hammond, S.B., *Social Structure and Personality in a City*. London, 1954.

Official Handbook of the Cremation Society of Australia, 1924.

Page, Sir Earle, *What Price Medical Care?: a preventive prescription for private medicine.* Philadelphia, 1960.

Palmer, Vance, *The Legend of the Nineties.* Melbourne, 1954.

Phillips, A.A. (ed.), *The Australian tradition: studies in a colonial culture.* Melbourne, 1958.

Pope, L., *Millhands and Preachers.* Yale, 1942.

Presthus, Robert V., *The Organizational Society: an analysis and a theory.* New York, 1962.

Price, C.A., *Southern Europeans in Australia.* Melbourne, 1963.

——————, *Jewish Settlers in Australia.* Canberra, 1964.

Prichard, K.S., *Coonardoo.* Sydney, 1929.

Pringle, J.D., *Australian Accent.* London, 1958.

Proceedings of Conference on Multi-Problem Families. Melbourne, 1959.

Queens, S.A., Habenstein, R.W. and Adams, J.B., *The Family in Various Cultures.* New York, 1961.

Rawson, D.W., *Australia Votes: the 1958 Federal Election.* Melbourne, 1961.

—————— and Holtzinger, Susan, *Politics in Eden-Monaro.* London, 1958.

Readings on Urban Growth: selected papers from the Sydney conference of ANZAAS, 1962. Sydney, 1963.

Rees, Leslie, *Towards an Australian Drama.* Sydney, 1953.

Reiss, Albert J., *Occupations and Social Status.* New York, 1961.

Reissman, Leonard, *Class in American Society.* London, 1960.

Rentoul, J.L., *The Church's Word to Australia in a 'Century of Unrest'.* Melbourne, 1912.

Riis, Jacob, *How the Other Half Lives.* New York, 1890.

Rivers, W.H.R., *The Todas.* London, 1906.

Rogoff, Natalie, *Recent Trends in Occupational Mobility.* Illinois, 1953.

Roscoe, J., *The Baganda.* London, 1911.

Rose, A.M. (ed.), *The Institutions of Advanced Societies.* Minnesota, 1958.

Runciman, W.G., *Social Science and Political Theory.* Cambridge, 1963.

Saunders, Carr -, A.M. and Wilson, P.A., *The Professions.* Oxford, 1933.

Scarrow, H.A., *The Higher Public Service of the Commonwealth of Australia.* North Carolina, 1957.

Schonell, F.J., Roe, E., and Meddleton, I.G., *Promise and Performance: a study of student progress at university level.* Brisbane, 1962.

Schumpeter, J.A., *Capitalism, Socialism and Democracy.* New York, 1942.

Scott, D. and U'Ren, R., *Leisure: a Social Enquiry into Leisure Activities and Needs in an Australian Housing Estate.* Melbourne, 1962.

Selznick, Philip, *Leadership in Administration.* Illinois, 1957.

Siegfried, A., *America at Mid-Century.* London, 1955.

Smith, J.W. and Jamison, A.L. (eds.) *Religion in American Life.* Princeton, 1961.

Spann, R.N. (ed.), *Public Administration in Australia.* Sydney, 1959.

Spiro, M.E., *Kibbutz: Venture in Utopia.* Cambridge, 1956.

St. John Stevas, N., *Life, Death and the Law.* London, 1961.

Strachey, John, *The Coming Struggle for Power.* London, 1932.

Strzelecki, P.E. de, *Physical Description of New South Wales and Van Diemen's Land.* London, 1845.

Swan, Jean Aitken -, *Widows in Australia.* Sydney, 1962.

Tawney, R.H., *Equality.* London, 1931.

Ten Years of Personal Earning and Spending in Australia, published by *Herald* Research. Melbourne, 1963.

Tench, Watkin, *Complete Account of the Settlement at Port Jackson in New South Wales.* London, 1793.

Thompson, E.P., *The Making of the English Working Class.* London, 1963.

319

Thonemann, H.E., *Tell the White Man: the life story of an aboriginal lubra.* Sydney, 1949.

Three Australian Plays. Introduction by H.G. Kippax. Melbourne, 1963.

Tierney, Leonard, *Children Who Need Help: a study of child welfare policy and administration in Victoria.* Melbourne, 1963.

Titmuss, R.M., *Essays on the Welfare State.* London, 1958.

————, *Income Distribution and Social Change: a study in criticism.* London, 1962.

Transactions of the Third World Congress of Sociology. London, 1956.

Trenaman, J. and McQuail, D., *Television and the Political Image: a study of the impact of television on the 1959 general election.* London, 1961.

Truman, T.C., *Catholic Action and Politics.* Melbourne, 1959.

Underwood, K., *Protestant and Catholic.* Boston, 1957.

Walker, A., *Coaltown: a Social Survey of Cessnock.* Melbourne, 1945.

Walker, K.F., *Industrial Relations in Australia.* Massachusetts, 1956.

Ward, Russel, *The Australian Legend.* Melbourne, 1958.

Webb, L.C., *Communism and Democracy in Australia: a survey of the 1951 referendum.* Melbourne, 1954.

West, Katharine, *Power in the Liberal Party.* Melbourne, 1965.

Westgarth, William, *Report on the Condition, Capabilities and Prospects of the Australian Aborigines.* Melbourne, 1846.

Westoff, C.F. *et al., Family Growth in Metropolitan America.* Princeton, 1961.

Wheelwright, E.L., *Ownership and Control of Australian Companies: a study of 102 of the largest public companies incorporated in Australia.* Sydney, 1957.

Wickham, E.R., *Church and People in an Industrial City.* London, 1957.

Wilkes, J. (ed.), *Australia's Defence and Foreign Policy.* Sydney, 1964.

Wilson, B.R., *Sects and Society.* London, 1961.

Zweig, F., *The Worker in an Affluent Society: family life and industry.* London, 1962.

2. Monographs, Papers, Etc.

Australian Council for Educational Research, Information Bulletin no. 31— *Preparation of Test Norms based on Victorian National Service Programme 1952/3.* Melbourne, 1954.

The Australian Economy, 1962. Treasury Report to Commonwealth Parliament.

Australian Immigration Quarterly Statistical Bulletin, vol. 2, no. 4, 1962.

Briggs, Asa, *Historians and the Study of Cities,* Sydney, 1960.

Brown, L.M., An enquiry into the teaching of the history of Britain and empire in N.S.W. secondary schools. *Educational Research being undertaken in Australia.* Commonwealth Office of Education, 1955.

Campbell, Ian, *State Ballot: the New South Wales general election of March 1962.* Sydney, 1963.

Carruthers, J.E., *Addresses, etc.* Mitchell Library, Sydney.

Church Congress Report. Brisbane, 1913.

Clark, J.F. and Olley, A.K., *Pre-Television Social Survey.* Sydney, 1958.

Coombs, H.C., *Conditions of Monetary Policy in Australia.* R.C. Mills Memorial Lecture, 1958.

Dependent Children. Interstate Congress of Workers. Adelaide, 1909.

Easterby, H.T., *The Queensland Sugar Industry.* Brisbane, 193–.

Edwards, A.E., *A Socio-Economic Grouping of the Gainful Employed Workers of the U.S., 1930.* Government Printing Office, Washington, D.C., 1938

Encel, S., *Is There an Australian Power Elite?* Chifley Memorial Lecture. Melbourne, 1961.

Families. Chapter 18 of Statistician's Report, vol. 8, Census of the Commonwealth of Australia, 1954. Canberra, 1962.

Facts and Figures about the Church of England. London, 1962.

Fitzgerald, T.M., *The Role of the Finance Editor.* A.N. Smith Memorial Lecture, 1962.

"Government and Semi-Government Pensions and Superannuation Schemes" in *Finance 1952-3*, Bulletin no. 44, Commonwealth Bureau of Census and Statistics. Canberra, 1955.

A Guide for Immigrants and Settlers. Intelligence Department of New South Wales, 1906.

Hempel, J.A., *Italians in Queensland: some aspects of post-war settlement of Italian immigrants*. Brisbane, 1959.

Jones, F.L., *A Demographic Survey of the Aboriginal Population of the Northern Territory, with special reference to Bathurst Island Mission*. Australian Institute of Aboriginal Studies. Canberra, 1963.

Jupp, James, *Victoria Votes: the state election of 15 July 1961*. Melbourne, 1961.

McNair Survey of Radio and Press Audiences. Sydney, 1963.

McNair Survey of "Reader's Digest" and Competitive Magazines. Sydney, 1958.

McNair Survey of Television Audiences. Melbourne, 1963.

Neild, J.C., *Report on old age pensions, charitable relief, and state insurance in England and on the continent of Europe*. 1898.

Olley, A.K., *Post-Television Social Survey*. Sydney, 1962.

Primary Education Today. Papers by H.P. Schoenheimer *et al.* for Victorian Institute for Educational Research. Melbourne, 1960.

Reports of Australian Broadcasting Control Board.

Report of the Committee appointed to Survey Secondary Education in New South Wales, 1956.

Report of Committee on State Education in Victoria, 1960.

Report on Contraception, New South Wales Humanist Society, 1963.

Report of the Royal Commission on Charitable Institutions. Victoria, 1891.

Report of the Royal Commission on Child Endowment or Family Allowances. Parliamentary Paper 20. Canberra, 1929.

Report of the Royal Commission on Municipalities and Charitable Institutions, 1862-3, Parliamentary Paper 52, Melbourne, 1863.

Report of the Royal Commission on National Insurance, 1925-27. Parliamentary Papers 12, 78, 79, and 120. Canberra, 1927.

Report of the Royal Commission on Old Age Pensions. Parliamentary Paper 28, Victoria, 1898.

Report of the Royal Commission on Population. London, 1949.

Research and Guidance Branch, Queensland Department of Education, Bulletins no. 13 (1957) and 24 (1962).

Schaffer, B.B., & Knight, K.W., *Top Public Servants in Two States*, Brisbane, 1963.

A Statement of Some Needs of Australian Education. Australian Education Council, 1963.

Stoller, A., *Report on mental health facilities and needs of Australia*. Canberra, 1955.

Survey of Private Pension and Retiring Allowance Schemes 1955-6. Commonwealth Bureau of Census and Statistics. Canberra, 1957.

United Nations *World Economic Survey*, 1961.

Wilson, I.F., *The 1958 Federal Election in Yarra*. Melbourne, 1959.

Wyeth, E.R., *Interim Report on Wastage of Talent in Victoria*. Melbourne, 1957.

Index

(A separate list of "Surveys" appears at end of index)

322